THE WALL STREET DICTIONARY

THE WALL STREET DICTIONARY

R. J. SHOOK
and
ROBERT L. SHOOK

New York Institute of Finance

New York London Toronto Sydney Tokyo Singapore

Library of Congress Cataloging-in-Publication Data

Shook, R. J. (Robert James)
     The Wall Street dictionary / R. J. Shook, R. L. Shook.
          p.   cm.
     ISBN 0-13-950189-4
          1. Finance—Dictionaries.   2. Investments—Dictionaries.
     I. Shook, Robert L., 1938– .   II. Title.
     HG151.S424   1990
     332'.03—dc20   90-37567
                                                                        CIP

This publication is designed to provide accurate and authoritative information in regard to the subject matter covered. It is sold with the understanding that the publisher is not engaged in rendering legal, accounting, or other professional service. If legal advice or other expert assistance is required, the services of a competent professional person should be sought.

From a Declaration of Principles
Jointly Adopted by
a Committee of the American Bar Association
and a Committee of Publishers and Associations

Printed in the United States of America
10 9 8 7 6 5 4 3 2

NEW YORK INSTITUTE OF FINANCE
2 Broadway
New York, New York 10004-2207

A division of Simon & Schuster
A Paramount Communications Company

Dedication

This book is for Bobbie, our beloved mother and wife.

R. J. S.
R. L. S.

Acknowledgements

Several people contributed to the publication of *The Wall Street Dictionary*, all of whom we are very grateful. Our agent, Jeff Herman, was inspirational throughout the entire preparation of the manuscript, and we are thankful to him for having selected a fine and prestigious firm, New York Institute of Finance, to publish this dictionary. It has also been a pleasure to work with such professionals as associate publisher, Philip Ruppel and managing editor—production, Sheck Cho.

Tom Risher has been a terrific educator, role model, and great friend to whom we are deeply indebted. Mary Liff did an extraordinary job in typing the 800-page manuscript. Marty Rainbow's research contributions and support are greatly appreciated. Diane Niermeyer has always given us wonderful encouragement. Oliver Chamberlain has been an ideal source of information. And Carrie Shook and Mike Shook also provided a great deal of assistance. We thank these wonderful people for their assistance and inspiration; without them, it is doubtful that *The Wall Street Dictionary* would have been possible.

Preface

As the twentieth century comes to an end, the prospect of peace among the world's powers looks more promising than ever. This, coupled with the European Common Market, has moved the subject of business into the limelight on the evening news, and on to the front pages of newspapers everywhere. Advanced technology has made globalization a reality, and along with a shrinking world, change is becoming more rapid than was ever imagined. Our world has also become more vastly complex.

As a consequence, *The Wall Street Dictionary* has been written to provide the most complete collection of economic, financial, and investment terms ever available. More than 5,000 terms are included, making this dictionary an essential addition to the library of today's serious investor and astute businessperson. Its contents range from the most basic terms to little-known words and phrases used by the professionals on Wall Street. Included are buzz words and new terminology that did not exist as recently as the late 1980s. You are advised to keep this lexicon in a convenient place and be sure to refer to it often. There is no shame in being unfamiliar with a particular investment term and having to look it up in *The Wall Street Dictionary*; it is a shame, however, to be negligent in obtaining its definition. Such negligence can result in a misunderstanding that could have devastating economic consequences. Being well-informed is not an option any longer, it has become a necessity.

ABC AGREEMENT. A contract explaining a brokerage firm's rights when it purchases a New York Stock Exchange (NYSE) membership for one of its employees. After the purchase, the individual can retain membership and buy another seat for someone else the firm designates, sell the seat and give the proceeds to the firm, or transfer the seat to another of the firm's employees. Only individuals may own seats on the NYSE. The individual may work primarily for one major brokerage firm, but a firm may not have a seat titled in its own name.

ABOVE PAR. A stock or bond whose market price is higher than its face value.

ABOVE THE MARKET. A sell order identified as being higher in price than the market's current price for that security.

ABSOLUTE ADVANTAGE. The power of one producer to make or sell a product below the price of any other producer, sometimes through national subsidies.

ABSOLUTE PRIORITY RULE. During bankruptcy or a corporate reorganization, the superseding of the owner's right to equity by creditors' rights and their financial claims.

ABSORPTION POINT. The point at which the market no longer can accept securities without making price concessions.

ABSTINENCE THEORY. The purchaser of goods or services may receive a rebate when these goods or services are not utilized as such or as quickly as specified in the contract. For example, the owner of a leased automobile that is driven only 12,000 miles per year on a contract allowing 15,000 miles per year may be entitled to a refund. When goods or services are not used right away, some of their cost should be reimbursed through interest or other payments.

ACCELERATED AMORTIZATION. Writing off a cost before it normally would be written off, which then reduces taxes. Also, moving up the payment date on a debt by special agreement (*see* Accelerated Depreciation).

ACCELERATED COST RECOVERY SYSTEM (ACRS). This method allows for quicker depreciation of assets than was permitted before 1980. ACRS allows costs to be recovered before an asset's estimated economically useful lifespan is due. Conversely, in straight-line depreciation, equal charges are made each year throughout the asset's estimated useful life.

ACCELERATED DEPRECIATION. The writing off of the costs of fixed assets faster than through straight-line depreciation. A company's cash flow is aided by the tax benefits of this practice. The higher cost of maintenance and repair during the later years of an asset's useful life are offset by the tax advantages of the early years, thus providing a more steady stream of earnings from the asset. Accelerated depreciation promotes capital spending and modernization.

ACCELERATION CLAUSE. A provision that the unpaid balance of a mortgage or other contract will become due if the debtor fails to meet interest, principal, or sinking fund payments, if the debtor becomes insolvent, or fails to pay taxes on mortgaged property.

ACCELERATION THEORY. A change in the consumption rate will cause even greater changes in the amount of purchases and production levels. This action is considered to be the impetus for one form of inflation.

ACCEPTANCE. Agreement to buy or sell a particular security by a specific date for a specific price.

ACCEPTANCE CREDIT. Substituting the credit of a bank for that of an individual or a firm (*see* Banker's Acceptance).

ACCEPTANCE HOUSE. An agency that lends money using bills of exchange as security, or offers its name to endorse a bill drawn on someone else.

ACCEPTANCE LIABILITY. A bank's liability when it accepts a negotiable instrument drawn on the bank by one of its customers.

ACCEPTANCE SUPRA PROTEST. A company or individual other than the debtor who agrees to pay off a debt.

ACCOMMODATION ENDORSEMENT. One person endorses a note so a bank will lend money to another person with a poor or inadequate credit history.

ACCOMMODATION PAPER. A note or other obligation guaranteed by someone other than the person who will benefit (*see* Letter of Credit).

ACCOUNT. Any bookkeeping record of a client's transactions, including credit or debit balances, either in cash or securities. Also, an investment syndicate's books that indicate contractual relationships, securities currently or previously owned, and the financial balance between a syndicate participant and the syndicate.

ACCOUNTANT'S OPINION. A statement signed by an independent public accountant describing an audit of a company's financial records. The opinion can be unqualified or qualified, the latter warranting further investigation.

ACCOUNT BALANCE. The difference between debits and credits in an account. If debits are higher than credits, the account has a negative balance.

ACCOUNT DAY. The day stock or commodity exchanges must be settled between exchange members.

ACCOUNT EXECUTIVE. An employee of a broker-dealer who is registered with the National Association of Securities Dealers or one of the exchanges. Account executives are allowed to solicit buy and sell orders for securities, and may handle client accounts. (*see* Broker, Registered Representative, or Customer's Man.)

ACCOUNT STATEMENT. A periodic report giving the status of a client's transactions, debits and credits.

ACCOUNTING CYCLE. Accounting activities that occur during a specific period of time. The period starts and ends with the account balance, all its credits, debits, and any other transactions recorded during the cycle.

ACCOUNTING PERIOD. A time span for keeping taxpayers' records. Most businesses operate on the calendar year. A fiscal year is established if the accounting period does not end in December.

ACCOUNTING PROCESSES. The classification of accounting procedures and controls through which changes in financial status and condition are recorded.

ACCOUNTING RATE OF RETURN. Any income during a specific period of time divided by the amount of money invested during that period.

ACCOUNTS RECEIVABLE. Money owed, but not yet collected, for goods or services.

ACCOUNTS RECEIVABLE FINANCING. Short-term financing in which accounts receivable are used as collateral for advances (*see* Factoring).

ACCOUNTS RECEIVABLE TURNOVER. The ratio of total credit sales divided by the accounts receivable for any given accounting period. Business efficiency and profitability is increased by cutting this ratio. Divide the total credit sales by the accounts receivable; the answer will indicate the number of times the receivables portfolio has been collected during the accounting period.

ACCREDITED INVESTOR. An individual with sufficient assets and/or income who is permitted, according to the Securities Act of 1933, to be excluded from the 35 investors in a private limited partnership. To be accredited, the investor must have a net worth of at least $1 million, an annual income of at least $200,000, or must put at least $150,000 into the deal, which cannot account for more than 20 percent of his or her net worth. Private limited partnerships use accredited investors to raise more money than would be possible with 35 less affluent people.

ACCRETION. The carrying value of a bond bought at an original discount is adjusted upwards over time approaching the bond's face value. The Internal Revenue Service clearly and precisely defines its provisions for this upward adjustment.

ACCRETION ACCOUNT. A record of the increase between the price of a bond purchased at discount and the bond's face value.

ACCRUAL BASIS. An accounting system through which revenues are recorded when they are earned and expenditures are recorded when they result in liabilities for benefits received. This differs from cash accounting under which an entry is made only when cash is paid or received.

ACCRUED INCOME. Income which is earned, but not received.

ACCRUED INTEREST. The amount of interest accumulated between interest payments. Accrued interest on bonds must be added to their purchase price.

ACCRUED LIABILITIES. Liabilities which arise from expenses incurred, but not yet paid.

ACCUMULATED DISTRIBUTION. Money put into a trust to be distributed later. The money is taxed when it is put into the trust, but not when the trust funds are distributed.

ACCUMULATED DIVIDEND. Dividend owed to stockholders of cumulative preferred stock.

ACCUMULATED EARNINGS TAX. A tax corporations must pay if they accrue earnings without distributing dividends to stockholders. Some companies would rather pay this tax than distribute dividends because the dividends would place the individual stockholders in higher tax brackets.

ACCUMULATED SURPLUS. A company's excess profits that are not held or reinvested.

ACCUMULATION. Absorbing an excess supply of stock, thereby increasing the demand for it. Accumulation generally occurs after a stock's price drops and stabilizes, thus increasing demand. Accumulating shares of a security over a stretch of time avoids attracting attention.

ACCUMULATION AREA. Price range in which investors buy stock.

ACCUMULATION PLAN. A method through which an investor regularly can buy mutual fund shares in varying amounts, with dividend income and capital gains distributions reinvested in additional shares.

ACID TEST RATIO. Cash and cash equivalents divided by current liabilities (*see* Current Ratio and Quick-Asset Ratio).

ACQUIRED SURPLUS. Working capital received when a company is purchased.

ACQUISITION. Controlling interest over an asset, usually referring to one company buying out another.

ACQUISITION COST. The sales charge a client must pay to invest in a specific mutual fund, or the costs of acquiring property. (*see* Closing Costs, and Sales Charge.)

ACQUISITION DATE. The day someone commits to buying an asset.

ACROSS THE BOARD. Widespread, overall action.

ACRS. *See* Accelerated Cost Recovery System.

ACTING IN CONCERT. Two or more people working together to buy up stock or take over a company. When 5% of the outstanding shares of a stock are acquired, a report must be filed with the Securities and Exchange Commission stating the acquirer's intentions.

ACTIVE ASSETS. Physical assets a corporation uses for its daily operations.

ACTIVE BOND CROWD. New York Stock Exchange bond department members responsible for the heaviest amount of bond trading.

ACTIVE BOX. The place where collateral for securing a broker's loan or a customer's margin position is held, or where securities are held for safekeeping either for a dealer or a dealer's customer.

ACTIVITY. The trading volume of a stock, or a group of stocks, on a particular exchange.

ACTUAL. A physical commodity, as opposed to a futures contract, that is present and ready for delivery or storage. It is sold on a cash market. Delivery is rarely taken. Rather, the customer pays a fee to store the commodity (*see* Commodity Futures Contract).

ACTUAL CASH VALUE. The theoretical value of a contract when it is redeemed, as opposed to its market value.

ACTUALLY OUTSTANDING. Stocks and bonds that a corporation has issued, but not reacquired.

ACTUARY. An insurance company mathematician who calculates, among other figures, premiums, dividends, and annuity rates using risk factors from experience tables, which are based on the company's history of claims and other data.

ADD-ON INTEREST. A procedure through which a certain percentage of the principal is used to calculate the interest cost. The interest cost then is added to the principal to determine the amount the borrower must repay.

AD HOC. A specific action taken to solve a particular problem.

ADJUSTABLE RATE CONVERTIBLE NOTE. A debt security issued at a higher price than its value will be when it matures. The note, however, can be traded for shares of common stock that are worth the original price of the note.

ADJUSTABLE RATE MORTGAGE. A mortgage agreement that establishes interest rate adjustments to be made at regular intervals. The adjustments are based on an index that cannot be controlled by the lending institution, such as the interest rate on U.S. Treasury bills, the cost of funds rate, or the average national mortgage rate. Because the borrower takes some of the risk of rising interest rates, he or she receives a lower initial rate than he or she would get on a fixed-rate mortgage.

ADJUSTED BASIS. Base price from which to calculate capital gains or losses when a stock or bond is sold. The price is adjusted to compensate for stock splits and transactions costs that have occurred since the stock's original purchase.

ADJUSTED DEBT BALANCE. Formula used to determine the position of a margin account which is calculated by netting the balance owed to the broker with any unused portion of the margin account and any paper profits on short accounts.

ADJUSTED EXERCISE PRICE. Process the Options Clearing Corporation uses to adjust an option contract because of stock splits or stock dividends. Adjusting is done to maintain, as much as possible, the original amount of the contract.

ADJUSTED GROSS INCOME. Income figure an individual or couple uses to compute federal income tax. To reach the adjusted gross income, a person subtracts unreimbursed business expenses and other deductions from his or her gross income.

ADJUSTMENT BOND. Bondholders exchange a bond for a new security in a company facing bankruptcy. The new security would pay interest or dividends only to the extent that the corporation meets certain financial goals.

ADJUSTMENT PREFERRED SECURITIES. Following any restructuring these preferred securities would have a priority claim over a company's assets.

ADJUSTMENT RATE PREFERRED STOCK. A senior issue of corporate stock that is usually purchased by another corporation because of tax advantages (85% of preferred stock dividends are tax-exempt to another corporation). The dividend, normally paid quarterly, is pegged to a short-term index such as the 3-month Treasury Bill rate or a Commercial Paper Composite (*see* Preferred Stock).

ADMISSION BY INVESTMENT. By investing cash in a partnership and increasing that firm's assets, an individual can become a part owner.

ADMITTED TO DEALINGS. Securities approved by the Securities and Exchange Commission for listing and trading on a stock exchange.

ADRS. *See* American Depository Receipts.

AD REFERENDUM. A signed contract with provisions and issues not yet resolved.

AD VALOREM TAX. Tax based on a property's assessed value.

ADVANCE COMMITMENT. Agreement by an individual buyer to purchase a bond issue on a specific, future date.

ADVANCE-DECLINE. Ratio of stocks that have gone up versus those that have dropped during a given time period. If more stocks advance, analysts consider the market bullish. If more drop, the market is considered bearish.

ADVANCE REFUNDING. The exchanging of fixed-income securities before they are due for another issue. This allows the issuer to issue the new bonds at lower rates.

ADVANCING MARKET. Widespread increase in market prices, with indications that the market will remain on the upswing.

ADVISORY FUNDS. Money a client deposits with his or her bank which the institution then invests at its own discretion.

ADVISORY SERVICE. An agency investors use to obtain market information and investment advice.

AFFIDAVIT. Sworn, notarized statement concerning a financial or other transaction.

AFFIDAVIT OF DOMICILE. Document provided by the executor of an estate verifying the decedent's place of residence at the time of death. The affidavit is necessary before any securities can be transferred from the estate because the securities have to be checked for possible liens in the decedent's home state.

AFFILIATE. Relationship between at least two companies when one owns less than a majority of the other's voting stock, or when both are subsidiaries of a third company.

AFFILIATED PERSON. Person in a position to directly influence a corporation's actions, such as the director or someone who owns more than 10 percent of the stock. Anyone who can directly influence one of these people, such as a family member or close friend, is also considered an affiliated person.

AFTER-ACQUIRED CLAUSE. Provision in a mortgage whereby a second mortgageable property can be used as additional security on a prior loan.

AFTER-ACQUIRED PROPERTY. Asset or real property purchased after a corporation has executed a mortgage or after a person has drawn up his or her will. Such asset or property is not subject to the prior mortgage or will.

AFTER-MARKET. Market created after a company goes public with its stock.

AFTER TAX. Corporate or individual profits or losses after state and federal taxes are considered.

AFTER TAX REAL RATE OF RETURN. Comparison of the after tax total return of a taxable investment with the total return of a tax-exempt investment after the amounts are adjusted for inflation.

AGAINST THE BOX. Sale of borrowed shares of stock in which an investor's position is long. Sellers may sell "against the box" in order to avoid ownership, disclosure, or to benefit from tax considerations.

AGED FAIL. Contract between two brokers that is not settled by the agreed upon date. The opening balance no longer can be considered an asset, and the buying broker must adjust his or her capital accordingly.

AGENCY FOR INTERNATIONAL DEVELOPMENT. U.S. government program that helps developing nations finance basic projects such as low-cost housing. The bonds associated with the agency are exempt from registration, but are taxable to U.S. investors as a foreign-source income.

AGENCY SECURITY. A U.S. government-issued security that was not issued by the Treasury Department and may be backed by the full faith and credit of the United States depending upon the issuing agency.

AGENT BANK. Bank that acts as an intermediary between customer and broker.

AGE OF MAJORITY. Age at which a person can legally sign a contract; typically 18 or 21 in most states.

AGGREGATE EXERCISE POLICY. Number of shares in a put or call contract multiplied by the exercise price.

AGGREGATE INDEBTEDNESS. Total amount of money or shares a broker or dealer owes to customers.

AGGREGATE SUPPLY. Total amount of goods and services supplied to the market at different price levels during a specific time period; also called total output. The amount corresponds with the number of goods and services demanded by different income levels during the same time period.

AGGRESSIVE GROWTH. Stressing riskiness and profit potential over quality and security. This approach is a philosophy that may be applied to the direction of an individual company or an investment outlook.

AGGRESSIVE PORTFOLIO. Collection of securities purchased for short-term profit potential rather than defensive quality and income.

AGGRIEVED PARTY. One who files a complaint or requests arbitration claiming to be the victim of an exchange member's unfair practices.

AGING SCHEDULE. Schedule of monthly receivables shown by maturity and classified as current or delinquent. This classification of accounts helps a company analyze the quality of its receivables investments.

AGREEMENT AMONG UNDERWRITERS. A contract among members of an investment banking syndicate which covers a number of points: appointing the syndicate manager, agent, and additional managers if necessary; defining members' liability; agreeing to pay each member's share on a settlement date; authorizing the manager to distribute units to a selling group; and, defining the life of the syndicate.

AGRIBUSINESS. Any large-scale farming or agricultural enterprise. Giant corporations are replacing individual family farms.

AIR POCKET STOCK. When stock prices take a dramatic nose dive and shareholders rush to sell. The action is compared to a plunging aircraft that has hit an air pocket.

ALIENATION. Transferring interest or property to someone else.

ALIENATION CLAUSE. Provision in a contract whereby a note must be paid in full when the mortgage title is transferred.

ALIEN CORPORATION. A company, originally incorporated under the laws of another country, that now operates in the U.S. or another country outside its home nation (*see* Foreign Corporation).

ALLIED MEMBER. Partner or stockholder in a New York Stock Exchange firm who is not a member of the exchange. Since a firm doesn't need more than one partner or stockholder as a member, even a board chairman may be only an allied member, who cannot do business on the trading floor.

ALLOCATION. Exchange members issue stock option exercise notices by a random drawing to ensure fair trading through random selection.

ALL OR ANY PART. Brokers may execute any part or all of an order in a discretionary account within a client's price limit.

ALL OR NONE OFFERING. A new security that is offered publicly with the requirement that the entire issue must be sold by a certain date or all offers will be canceled.

ALL OR NONE ORDER. A request to buy or sell a security in which all of the security must be involved in the transaction, or all of it will be canceled. For example, an investor may place an order with a broker to purchase 1,000 shares of XYZ stock at $50 per share. If only 500 shares are available at that price the order will not be completed.

ALLOWABLE DEPRECIATION. An amount that could have been deducted as depreciation, but instead is added to the value of the asset.

ALLOWANCE. Money reserved to compensate for bad debts or for depreciation.

ALPHA. The premium an investment portfolio earns above a certain benchmark (such as the Standard and Poor's 500). A positive alpha indicates the investor earned a premium over that index.

ALTERNATE ACCOUNT. An account held by at least two people, with any of those named allowed to draw from the account.

ALTERNATE DEPOSITORS. Two or more people who hold a joint account.

ALTERNATIVE MINIMUM TAX. Requires taxpayers with substantial taxable incomes to pay a minimum tax, even if their income normally would not be taxable.

ALTERNATIVE MORTGAGE INSTRUMENTS. Various mortgage choices a person may pick to avoid taking out a fixed-rate mortgage (*see* Graduated Payment Mortgage, Reverse Annuity Mortgage, Adjustable-Rate Mortgage, and Variable-Rate Mortgage).

ALTERNATIVE ORDER. A buy or sell order that allows several alternatives to be used to fill the order. When part of the order is executed, the unused alternatives will be canceled. For example, an investor may be willing to purchase 20,000 shares of stock at $26 1/2, but he or she may only post an initial bid of 5,000 shares at $26 1/4. The broker may be given some discretion in this matter.

AMALGAMATION. The union of two or more companies when such a union financially benefits all businesses involved.

AMBAC. *See* American Municipal Bond Assurance Corporation.

AMERICAN BOARD OF TRADE. Provides spot and deferred markets, and offers investors stock market information.

AMERICAN DEPOSITORY RECEIPTS (ADRS). Certificates issued by a U.S.

bank and traded in this country as domestic shares. The certificates represent the number of foreign securities the U.S. bank holds in that security's country of origin. ADRs make trading foreign securities in the U.S. easier by eliminating currency exchange, legal obstacles, foreign ownership transfers and the need to trade on a foreign exchange.

AMERICAN MUNICIPAL BOND ASSURANCE CORPORATION (AMBAC). Insures the payment of principal and interest on new municipal bonds. AMBAC-insured bonds carry the highest bond rating.

AMERICAN OPTION. Any option an investor can exercise before its maturity.

AMERICAN PARITY. U.S. funds equal to the foreign price of securities abroad.

AMERICAN STOCK EXCHANGE (AMEX). The second-largest stock exchange in the United States. Otherwise known as Amex, the exchange is located at 86 Trinity Place in downtown Manhattan. The Amex tends to specialize in securities of slightly smaller capitalization.

AMERICAN STOCK EXCHANGE MARKET VALUE INDEX. The average value of all common shares, rights, and warrants listed on the American Stock Exchange.

AMERICUS TRUST. A five-year investment trust fund in which American Telephone & Telegraph stockholders deposit their shares.

AMEX. *See* American Stock Exchange.

AMEX OPTIONS SWITCHING SYSTEM. A computer that transmits incoming orders for options to the proper trading posts. The computer also notifies the exchange member who made the order if the option has been executed.

AMICUS CURIAE. Usually referring to a friend-of-the-court, it is a brief filed by a company or other party interested in the outcome of a specific court case, though not an actual litigant. The brief states reasons why the court should decide on one litigant's behalf, and why a ruling that went the other way could be detrimental to the overall business climate.

AMORTIZATION. Method of accounting whereby the cost of an asset is spread over its useful life. Can be applied to such items as patents, copyrights, and goodwill.

AMORTIZATION OF PREMIUM. Any premium paid for a bond above its par value or call price is amortized over the life of the bond.

AMORTIZED LOSSES. Losses may occur when interest-bearing instruments are sold prior to maturity during a time when interest rates are fluctuating.

AMORITZED MORTGAGE LOAN. A loan that must be repaid within a specific period through regular payments that reduce the loan's principal and cover interest as it falls due.

AMOUNT AT INTEREST. The amount of principal deposited to earn interest.

AN ACTUAL. A security that underlies an option or the security that satisfies a contract when it is delivered.

ANALYST. An investment firm professional who makes estimates upon the investment value of individual companies, industries, and the economy as a whole.

AND INTEREST. The buyer of an outstanding bond must pay the seller any interest that has built up between the last interest payment and the settlement date.

ANNOUNCEMENT DATE. The specific day a company announces that its stocks will be paying dividends. The company also will announce the amount of the dividends on this date.

ANNUAL EARNINGS. All income, minus expenses, received in a year, i.e., annual profits.

ANNUAL FINANCIAL STATEMENT. A document that gives a company's financial status, stating profits and losses, for the year. The document is released on the last day of the company's fiscal year.

ANNUALIZED LINKED-MEDIAN RETURN. Annualization of the compounded yearly median returns. Companies that do not have calendar year ending dates have comparison returns.

ANNUALIZED PERCENT. Translating a partial year's figures into an annual rate.

ANNUALIZED RETURN. Based upon interest, dividends, and unrealized appreciation, this is the value that an investment has achieved over a 12-month period.

ANNUAL MEETING. A yearly meeting in which stockholders elect a board of directors and vote on other company concerns.

ANNUAL REPORT. A comprehensive financial statement that corporations issue yearly to shareholders. The report defines the company's financial condition, announces new products or services, explains past performances, and projects future prospects. Copies usually can be obtained upon request.

ANNUAL YIELD. The amount of money an investment earns in interest or dividends each year.

ANNUITANT. One who receives an annuity.

ANNUITY. Periodic payments, usually in equal amounts, made over a specified period of time, such as interest payments on bonds.

ANNUITY BOND. A security with no date of maturity that pays interest for an indefinite length of time.

ANNUITY METHOD OF DEPRECIATION. Subtract the salvage value from a capital asset's original cost, and the straight-line portion of the difference is charged to each period.

ANNUITY PLAN. A retirement fund from which a person receives income after paying into the fund for a specific number of years.

ANNUITY UNIT. Accumulation units converted to units upon which annuity payments can be made.

ANNUNCIATOR BOARDS. A paging device on the stock exchange wall formerly used to direct a floor broker to the firm's booth for orders and executions. Electronic paging boards are used now in the stock exchanges.

ANTECEDENTS. The determination of whether a corporation has had the same owner for a long time, or if the firm has frequent ownership changes.

ANTICIPATED HOLDING PERIOD. The length of time a limited partnership expects to remain in operation before business is terminated.

ANTICIPATION. An account payment made before it is due.

ANTICIPATION NOTE. A short-term municipal debt instrument issued to secure funds backed by current revenues.

ANTITRUST. A court action restricting companies that try to monopolize a particular industry or trade.

ANY-QUANTITY RATE. A set rate charged to transport any quantity of a commodity.

APPLICATION OF FUNDS STATEMENT. A report taken from balance sheets during two different periods which then provides an overview of changes that occurred during the periods.

APPLIED PROCEEDS SWAP. When one block of bonds is sold to buy another block of bonds.

APPRAISAL. Evaluation of an asset to determine its value.

APPRAISAL RIGHTS OF MINORITY STOCKHOLDERS. A statutory right of dissenting stockholders when a company is consolidated or merged with another firm.

APPRAISAL SURPLUS. The difference between an asset's appraised value over its book value.

APPRECIATION. The increase in value of an asset over time.

APPRECIATION POTENTIAL. The expected increase in market value.

APPROPRIATE SURPLUS. A portion of a company's surplus that the board of directors has set aside for a particular purpose, and should not be considered a liability.

APPROPRIATION. An amount of money set aside for a specific purpose.

APPROVED DEPOSITORY. A bank or trust company approved by the exchange in which the members of that exchange deposit cash and securities.

APPROVED LIST. A list of approved investments that a fiduciary may buy for a client.

ARBITRAGE. The buying and selling of stocks, foreign exchange, precious metals, bonds or other commodities from one market to be sold at a profit to a separate but related market. An arbitrage opportunity arises when two companies plan to merge or when one security is convertible into another.

ARBITRAGE BONDS. Municipal bonds issued with the intention of refunding higher rate bonds in advance of their call date. In order to gain an interest rate advantage, the proceeds from the new issue will be invested in treasuries until the call date of the issue being refunded.

ARBITRATION. An industry-operated, binding method of eliminating or reducing conflicts between stock exchange members or between members and nonmembers. Arbitration is sought after parties cannot resolve a conflict on their own, and mutually request arbitration and agree to adhere to whatever decision the arbitration panel may reach.

ARIEL. Automated Real-time Investments Exchange is a computer network that handles transactions involving large blocks of stock.

ARITHMETIC INVESTING. A method of investing that reduces the investor's risk by estimating rates of return during a specific period.

ARM'S LENGTH SYSTEM. A method of calculating corporate state income taxes whereby only profits earned in a particular state are taxed by that state. Earnings from elsewhere are not taxed by that state, buy may be taxable elsewhere unless they were earned by a parent company abroad.

ARM'S LENGTH TRANSACTION. A contract in which the parties act as though they are independent of each other.

AROUND. The number of points on either side of par. For example, when quoting a premium or discount, a three-three around would mean three points on either side of par.

ARREARAGE. Cumulative preferred shares' unpaid dividends (*see* Preferred Stock).

ARREARS. Any past due amount.

ARTICLES OF ASSOCIATION. Similar to a corporate certificate. This document usually is associated with nonstock companies, such as charities.

ARTICLES OF INCORPORATION. A document that establishes a corporation and, after certification, becomes the corporation's charter.

ASCENDING TOPS. A chart that shows that each peak is higher than the previous peak (*see* Descending Tops).

ASIAN DEVELOPMENT BANK. An international bank with its headquarters in the Philippines that promotes both social and economic growth in Asia by making loans to underdeveloped countries.

ASK. The specific price accompanying an offer to sell.

ASKED PRICE. The lowest price at which a dealer will sell a security.

ASPIRIN COUNT THEORY. A lighthearted market indicator that says the market will fall a year after aspirin production increases, and will rise a year later if aspirin production goes down.

AS PRINCIPAL. A brokerage firm which is buying or selling securities for or from its own account. In such cases, commissions are not charged.

ASSAY. Examination of a metal's content, composition, and purity.

ASSAY OFFICE BAR. A bar of nearly pure gold or silver from the U.S. mint that has been tested by an assay office.

ASSEMBLAGE. Bringing together two or more people or items to form an aggregate; the cost of bringing two or more items into a single ownership.

ASSENTED SECURITIES. Owners of a particular corporate security agree to change the security's status because of corporate restructuring, bankruptcy, or some other change.

ASSESSABLE STOCK. A company that goes through a reorganization is subject to an assessment of its stock.

ASSESSED VALUATION. The amount of money a government attaches to an asset and upon which it bases taxes.

ASSESSMENT. Any charge made against an asset and upon which taxes are based.

ASSESSMENT BOND. A municipal bond issued to pay for improvements to government-owned property, such as streets or sewers.

ASSESSMENT RATIO. The difference between the assessed property value and the fair market value.

ASSESSMENT ROLL. A list of all legal information with a description of each piece of property and its assessed value.

ASSESSOR. A government official responsible for evaluating the value of a piece of property.

ASSET. Everything owned by a corporation or individual, from buildings and equipment to intangible assets such as patents and reputation.

ASSET ALLOCATION DECISION. Investments are made with a proper mix of assets to achieve certain goals such as risk level, income, and appreciation potential.

ASSET AND LIABILITY STATEMENT. A balance sheet.

ASSET COVERAGE. The ratio of assets to obligations. The indicator measures a corporation's ability to meet debt service payments.

ASSET DEPRECIATION RANGE SYSTEM. The Internal Revenue Service's guideline in defining and allowing depreciable lives for specific depreciable assets.

ASSET FINANCING. The conversion of assets into cash in exchange for security interest in the assets (*see* Accounts Receivable Financing).

ASSET LIABILITY MANAGEMENT. Matching items on opposite sides of the balance sheet. A corporation that wishes to acquire an asset must decide whether to A) pay cash, thereby reducing an asset, or B) take out a loan, thereby increasing a liability.

ASSET MANAGEMENT ACCOUNT. A bank or other financial institution that combines regular banking services, such as checking and savings accounts, with brokerage house services.

ASSET PLAY. An attractive security with a current price that does not reflect the worth of the firm's assets.

ASSIGNMENT. Transfer of ownership from one party to another.

ASSIGNMENT OF LEASES. Securities that sometimes are assumed in association with commercial property mortgages.

ASSIGNMENT OF MORTGAGE. A document that transfers a loan obligation from one owner to another.

ASSIMILATION. Syndicate members' and issue underwriters' public distribution of a security's new shares.

ASSOCIATED PERSON. Anyone connected with a broker-dealer, including (but not limited to) directors, officers, and branch managers.

ASSOCIATE MEMBER. A person with limited membership rights at the American Stock Exchange.

ASSOCIATE SPECIALIST. An exchange member who assists the market specialist.

ASSOCIATION OF INTERNATIONAL BOND DEALERS. A Switzerland-based organization made up of banks and brokers involved in international debt securities.

ASSUMABLE MORTGAGE. The buyer takes over the previous owner's mortgage, which usually provides the buyer with a lower interest rate than he or she could have received by taking out a new mortgage.

ASSUMED LIABILITY. One person takes over loan payments or other obligations from someone else.

ASSUMPTION OF DEBT. One person takes over another person's debts.

AT A DISCOUNT. A security that sells for a price that is below its par value.

AT A PREMIUM. A security that sells for a price that is above its par value.

AT BEST. A customer order to buy a security at the best rate possible.

AT MARKET. A customer order to buy or sell securities immediately at the best price available.

AT OR BETTER. A customer order to buy a security at or below a specified price, or to sell a security at or above a specified price.

AT PAR. A security that sells at its par value.

AT RISK. Possibility of a loss. Investors in limited partnership can receive tax deductions if their investments are not guaranteed a rate of return.

AT SIGHT. A securities payment that is due immediately upon presentation or demand.

AT THE BANK'S RISK. The bank, and not the customer, assumes most of the risk of losing money in this type of an investment. In return, the customer relinquishes some of the profit potential.

AT THE CLOSE. A customer order that is to be completed at the best price possible when the market closes for the day.

AT THE MONEY. A put or call option with an exercise price equal to the underlying security's current market value.

AT THE OPENING. A customer order that is to be completed at the best price possible when the trading for the security opens. The order is canceled if not executed immediately.

ATTORNEY-IN-FACT. Written permission to represent another person outside of court, such as a broker with the authority to transfer securities. Also known as "power of attorney."

AT YOUR RISK. The bank customer, and not the bank, assumes most of the risk of losing money in this type of an investment.

AUCTION MARKET. Trading securities through exchange brokers with buyers and sellers competing against one another to get the best prices. The New York Stock Exchange is the prime example.

AUDIT. An evaluation of a company's financial records to verify that stated assets and liabilities match the actual assets and liabilities.

AUDIT TRAIL. The printed and tangible records of a company's financial transactions.

AUSTRIAN SCHOOL OF ECONOMICS. A school of thought that follows a line of human action and is skeptical of government intervention in economic affairs. People who hold to this philosophy emphasize the actions of individuals in economics.

AUTEX SYSTEM. A computer network that relates which brokers want to buy or sell large blocks of stock.

AUTHENTICATED COPY. A security certified by an appropriate official.

AUTHENTICATION. A trustee signs a bond certificate to validate it and to verify it was issued under a particular indenture.

AUTHORITY BOND. Municipal bond issued by a governmental body for a public services project such as building a new hospital wing or installing new roads. The bonds are repaid from revenues generated by the project.

AUTHORIZED STOCK. The maximum amount of stock a corporation may issue. The fixed amount is stated in the company's certificate of incorporation.

AUTOMATED BOND SYSTEM. A New York Stock Exchange computer network that lists all orders for nonconvertible bonds.

AUTOMATED CLEARINGHOUSE. A firm set up with computers and used by member financial institutions to combine, sort, and distribute payment orders.

AUTOMATED CUSTOMER ACCOUNT TRANSFER SERVICE. Members of

the National Securities Clearing Corporation can transfer customer accounts through a computer.

AUTOMATED PRICING AND REPORTING SYSTEM. The New York Stock Exchange computer network used to process and assign prices to certain odd-lot orders.

AUTOMATIC ORDER EXECUTION SYSTEM. An American Stock Exchange system in which market and limit orders for active option series (up to 10 contracts at a single price) are instantly executed.

AUTOMATIC REINVESTMENT. A system that enables investors to buy new shares with income dividends or other money earned from the stock market.

AUTOMATIC TRANSFER SERVICE ACCOUNT. A savings account with funds that can be transferred immediately by computer to cover checks written against a checking account.

AUTOMATIC WITHDRAWAL. A system that entitles mutual fund shareholders to receive regular payments. Shares are liquidated if the payments cannot be met through dividend income.

AUTONOMOUS INVESTMENT. A new investment created by unrelated interest rate changes or changes in the national income level.

AVAIL. The balance after discounts and expenses are deducted.

AVAILABLE ASSET. Asset not mortgaged or pledged that can be readily sold.

AVERAGE. Buying or selling of securities in order to obtain a better overall price.

AVERAGE DOWN. Buying shares at a lower price in order to reduce a stock's average price.

AVERAGE EQUITY. A trading account's average daily balance. It is used to ensure that margin requirements are met.

AVERAGE LIFE. The length of time it is expected to take to retire half of a debt through amortizing payments, or through serial maturity or sinking fund.

AVERAGES. A single value given to a specific set of market information and used to reflect the market's current strengths or weaknesses. The most widely followed is the Dow Jones Industrial Average.

AVERAGE UP. Buying additional shares of a stock at a price higher than the original cost to lower the stock's average cost basis. The stock is perceived as a good investment even at higher prices.

AVERAGING. *See* Dollar Cost Averaging.

AWARD. A borrower accepts a competitive bid for a security by notifying the high bidder.

AWAY FROM ME. A market-maker's quote. The best bid or offer price is someone else's.

AWAY FROM THE BLUE. A dealer offers municipal securities that he or she has not advertised in the Blue List Book.

AWAY FROM THE MARKET. A limit-order bid is lower or the offer price is higher than the stock's current market price.

AXE TO GRIND. Securities traders solicit business without telling the salespeople whether they want to buy or sell, which gives them an idea of the market's interest before they commit to a deal.

_B_

BABY BOND. A convertible or straight-debt bond with a face value of less than $1,000. Baby bonds bring the market within reach of small investors, but they also cost more to administrate, distribute, and process, and they are not part of the active market that guarantees liquidity. For this reason they are almost extinct.

BACK-DATING. Putting a date on a check or other document that is earlier than the actual date drawn. Also, an investor who holds mutual funds and who didn't originally sign a letter of intent can sign one within 90 days as long as the original date is entered.

BACK DOOR. A nickname for the U.S. Department of Treasury.

BACK DOOR FINANCING. A government agency borrows money from the U.S. Treasury rather than waiting for Congress to appropriate more funds.

BACK DOOR LISTING. One company that has not qualified for listing on the stock exchange buys another company that is listed, thereby enabling it to qualify for listing.

BACK-END LOAD. Investment products that do not have initial sales charges sometimes have a redemption fee. Such charges often are lowered over time. For example, 5% in the first year, 4% in the second year, etc.

BACK-END RIGHTS. Rights which protect shareholders' financial interests. This tactic is used by management when the corporation is threatened with a takeover. Stockholders are able to exchange rights and shares for cash, preferred stock, or debt securities in case those attempting the takeover get a certain percentage of the outstanding stock, but do not complete the takeover at a value equal to management's offer.

BACKING AWAY. A market maker in a specific security fails to honor a firm bid for the minimum quantity. Backing away is considered unethical under the National Association of Securities Dealers guidelines.

BACK OFFICE. The operational department of a bank or brokerage house. The department is not directly involved in selling or trading, but is responsible for accounting, compliance with government regulations, and interbranch communications.

BACKSPREAD. An investment strategy that involves the purchase of one option and the sale of two others with either higher or lower strike prices.

BACK UP. The reversal of a stock market trend. The change may be up or down.

BACKUP LINE. A commercial paper issuer would take out this credit line to cover maturity notes in case new notes could not be found to replace them after they reached maturity. The credit line always should have the same value as the outstanding commercial paper.

BACKUP SYSTEM. A settlement system established by the Options Clearing Corporation to ensure that its members honor their obligations of exercised options contracts.

BACKWARDIZATION. This occurs in commodities and foreign-exchange trading when deliveries made sooner have a higher price than those made later.

BAD DEBT. An account or loan balance that a company is unable to collect and subsequently writes off.

BAD DEBT EXPENSE. The amount of money a company spends on accounts it has been unable to collect.

BAD DELIVERY. A securities certificate that is delivered in less than acceptable form as a result of damage or improper signature.

BAD FAITH. An intentionally misleading or deceptive practice.

BAG. The unit of trading used in silver coin investing. One bag holds coins with face values that total: 1,000 silver dollars, 2,000 half dollars, 4,000 quarters, or 10,000 dimes.

BAIL OUT. Selling securities arbitrarily while in a panic without first considering the potential loss. The term also applies to a financially strong company coming to the rescue of a weaker company.

BAIT AND SWITCH. The practice of advertising an item at a low price, but pressuring a potential buyer to purchase a higher-priced substitute. A common practice is to tell the customer the lower priced item is no longer available, and the more expensive item would be more beneficial to the customer anyway. Such tactics are illegal, and many companies have been prosecuted for employing them.

BALANCE. Subtraction of debits from credits in a given account.

BALANCED BUDGET. When expected revenues equal expected expenses for a specific time period.

BALANCED MUTUAL FUND. A fund that buys both growth and income securities in an effort to get the highest returns with the least amount of risk.

BALANCE OF PAYMENTS. Method in which all of a nation's financial transactions with the rest of the world are recorded in double-entry bookkeeping. The system precludes surpluses and deficits by maintaining a balance of payments in the current account (which covers imports and exports), the capital account (which covers investment movements), and the gold account (which covers movement in the gold market). Surpluses and deficits show up in the different accounts.

BALANCE OF TRADE. The difference between the value of a country's imports and exports. It is considered a favorable trade balance when exports exceed imports.

BALANCE SHEET. Financial accounting of a company's assets, liabilities, equity, and net worth as of a specific date.

BALANCE SHEET EQUATION. Liabilities added to stockholders' equity equals a company's total assets.

BALLOON. The final payment on a loan or mortgage that is much larger than previous payments, sometimes because interest rates increased during the life of the loan.

BALLOONING. Manipulating stock prices so they increase far beyond the stocks' real values.

BANK. A financial business, chartered by the state or federal government. Banks borrow money at one rate from individuals and organizations that have excess cash. They then lend the money at higher rates to entities that are in need of cash. In recent years service charges have joined interest rate spreads as a major source of bank revenue.

BANK ACCOMMODATION. A bank loans a customer money on the customer's own note or on a note someone else owes to the customer. Such loans allow the customer to avoid transaction costs.

BANK CHECK. A check a bank draws upon itself. A bank check is considered beneficial, especially in the securities industry, because payment is assured.

BANKED COST. A dealer who previously charged less than regulations permitted can add those undercharges to current margins to make up for the loss of commissions.

BANK-ELIGIBLE ISSUES. Commercial banks can buy U.S. Treasury-issued obligations (usually those that are due within 10 years).

BANKER'S ACCEPTANCE. Banks issue this short-term financial instrument to finance international trade. A banker's acceptance produces a high rate of return for the investor with little risk involved.

BANKER'S SHARES. Stocks issued to an investment banker that have features allowing the banker to control the firm. The stocks, for example, may have voting features, while other shares do not, giving the banker an advantage over other stockholders.

BANK FOR COOPERATIVES. A government-sponsored corporation that loans money to agricultural cooperative associations. The Farm Credit Administration supervises the bank.

BANK GUARANTEE LETTER. A document issued by a bank and approved by the New York Stock Exchange, verifying that a customer has sufficient funds to cover the writing of a put option or enough shares to take care of a call option.

BANK-GUARANTEED BOND FUNDS. A major bank stands behind a portfolio of bonds against default because the bank has agreed to buy the portfolio's underlying securities at agreed upon prices with only six days notice.

BANK HOLDING COMPANY. A corporation which controls several companies and whose principle business is a commercial bank. A corporation may form a holding company to establish subsidiaries not governed by state banking laws.

BANKING AND SECURITIES INDUSTRY COMMITTEE. An organization responsible for establishing securities guidelines and certificate handling procedures.

BANKING SYNDICATE. A group of banks that have banded together to under-write and sell a specific issue of securities.

BANK INSURANCE FUND (BIF). Formerly the Federal Deposit Insurance Corporation. This fund insures commercial and savings bank deposits up to $100,000. These monies cannot be commingled with the Savings Association Insurance Fund.

BANK LINE. A lending establishment's implied commitment to loan a client up to a specific amount of money during a particular time period. This is not a contractual commitment.

BANKNOTE. A bank-issued promissory note that can be used as cash. It is payable on demand and is considered legal tender.

BANK QUALITY. Any bond with a top investment grade rating of AAA, AA, A, or BBB, with AAA being the highest quality rating. Bonds with these ratings are suitable for purchase by institutions such as bank trust departments. Also known as investment grade.

BANK RUN. Depositors begin to doubt the solvency of their bank, and they start withdrawing their money. Because most of a bank's assets are not kept on hand in cash, such runs can cause serious damage to a financial institution.

BANKRUPTCY. An individual's or organization's inability to pay debts. Whether the insolvent debtor petitions for such action or the debtor's creditors make the petition, the objective is the same: an equitable distribution of assets to eliminate as many of the debts as possible.

BANK SECURITIES. Capital debentures, preferred stock, or common stock issued by a commercial bank.

BANK TERM LOAN. A loan issued instead of a long-term bond in times of high interest rates, which expires no sooner than one year.

BANK TRUST DEPARTMENT. An area of a bank responsible for settling estates, administering trusts, acting as trustees for corporate bonds, and administering pension and profit-sharing plans.

BANK WIRE. A computer system that transmits information about credit transfers, loan participants, securities transactions, credit histories, and other material that may require a prompt response from one participating bank to another.

BAR CHART. A market chart that illustrates stocks' highs, lows, closing information, and other index and volume changes that occurred during a specific time period.

BARE ASS. Used to refer to the Boeing Company because the company's stock symbol is BA.

BARGAIN. A security that represents good relative value when the underlying company's assets and earning power are considered.

BAROMETER. A compilation of market information that simulates overall market trends.

BAROMETER STOCK. A widely followed issue that is used as a yardstick to predict future market conditions.

BARREL OF OIL. Equal to 42 American gallons of oil at 60 degrees Fahrenheit. A barrel is the standard measure of crude oil volume in international trading.

BARREN MONEY. Any money that does not earn interest or bring the holder any other additional profit.

BARRON'S CONFIDENCE INDEX. Comparison between yields on high-grade bonds and low-grade bonds. As this spread drops, the index reflects investors' building confidence in the economy.

BARTER. Trading goods or services for other goods or services without using legal currency.

BASE. A stock pattern that indicates a long-term, tight price range that usually follows a market decline.

BASEBUILDING. A long-term, lateral price trend, which sometimes is considered necessary after a long decline in the stock market before prices can start going up again.

BASE MARKET VALUE. The average price of a group of securities over a specific period.

BASE PERIOD. A specific period used for measuring economic data. The data is compared to information from previous periods.

BASE-YEAR ANALYSIS. A company's financial statements for several years are compared to a common base year to analyze the company's performance.

BASIC BALANCE. The current balance of payments added to the company's expected long-term capital movements.

BASIC YIELD. The annual rate of return on a no-risk investment.

BASIS. The original cost plus transaction costs and adjustments for splits, in the case of equity. The Internal Revenue Service requires that this figure be used to calculate capital gains and losses.

BASIS BOOK. A reference manual of the Financial Publishing Company of Boston that contains such information as coupon interest rates and the time remaining until maturity of many bond issues. The book enables investors to calculate the dollar prices and yields of various securities.

BASIS GRADE. An exchange establishes quality standards for a commodity before it is considered acceptable for delivery on a futures contract.

BASIS POINT. One one-hundredth of one percent. For example, an addition of 40 basis points to a yield of 7.50% would increase the yield to 7.90%. Basis points normally are used when quoting yields on bonds or notes.

BASIS PRICE. The figure upon which a stockholder calculates all capital gains or losses when selling his or her securities.

BASIS QUOTE. The difference between the cash price and the futures price of a commodity.

BASIS TRADING. Large investors establish underlying stock and index futures positions. If index futures look cheap, these investors buy futures and sell their stock. When stocks look cheap, the opposite takes place.

BASIS VALUE. A security's value as an investment, and a bond's value at maturity.

BASKET TRADING. Buying or selling a group of assets at one time in an effort to duplicate the performance of a specific market index or average instead of trying to outperform the market (*see* Index Fund).

BD FORM. A document containing names of principals, capital compliance, and financial information about a broker-dealer firm. All broker-dealers are required to file this form with the Securities and Exchange Commission.

BEAR. A person who expects the stock market to fall or the economy to slow down.

BEAR ACCOUNT. A short account in which a person has sold stock or a futures contract with the expectation of buying it back later at a cheaper price if the stock market falls.

BEAR CAMPAIGN. The selling of securities short in an effort to force prices downwards, then buying the securities back at a profit.

BEAR CLIQUE. A group that sells a specific stock short in an effort to drive the price down. Forming such a group is illegal.

BEAR COVERING. The act of repurchasing borrowed securities that had previously been sold short.

BEARDING. A large order for securities is split into several smaller orders that will be executed by several brokers. Bearding keeps private the intentions of the large investor so he or she will not drive up the price of the securities before the buy program is complete.

BEARER. Any person who holds a negotiable instrument.

BEARER BOND. A bond issued and payable to anyone with physical possession, as opposed to a bond issued and registered in the owner's name.

BEARER FORM. A security the issuing company hasn't registered on its books that, therefore, is payable to whomever holds it.

BEAR HUG. A takeover offer. Corporate officers are caught in a bear hug when a takeover offer is good enough to entice some shareholders, but not attractive enough to make everybody happy. No matter which way they decide, they will be in trouble with at least some of the stockholders.

BEAR MARKET. A long-term decline in security prices.

BEAR PANIC. A wave of bearish liquidations may create a selling climate. Afterwards, bargain hunters may enter the market, driving prices up and panicking bears, particularly those who sold short.

BEAR RAID. A group of investors manipulate the price of a stock by selling large quantities of it short. The sale of so many shares causes the price to drop dramatically. The investors then buy the stock back, pocketing the difference. Collusion makes the act illegal.

BEAR SPREAD. When an investor simultaneously buys one type of option and sells another type on the same security. The spread becomes profitable when the price of the underlying security declines (*see* Option).

BEAR SQUEEZE. Institutions sometimes know bears have sold securities short before prices go up, resulting in a bear panic. High bid prices force the bears to cover their shorts and take losses.

BEAR STRADDLE. The writing of an uncovered call and a covered put are invested in the same underlying stock with identical striking prices and expiration dates. The writer profits if the underlying security does not vary much in price over the life of the straddle.

BEAR TRAP. A stock price that drops, after which many people sell, but then surges back up again.

BEATING THE GUN. Accepting orders for a new stock before the security's registration becomes effective. The Securities and Exchange Commission prohibits this practice.

BED AND BREAKFAST TRANSACTION. A British term for selling a security at a profit at the close of the trading day, then buying it back in the morning after the price has dropped.

BEDBUG LETTER. A letter the Securities and Exchange Commission sends to a company after the company files a preliminary registration statement for permission to sell stocks. The term got its name from the Securities and Exchange Commission's desire to get the bugs out of the registration statement before the company can begin to issue securities.

BELL. A ringing or buzzing that signals the opening and closing of major stock exchanges each day.

BELLS AND WHISTLES. Special features, such as subscription warrants, that a company may add to a security to attract potential investors' attention.

BELLWETHER. A specific stock, such as Xerox or IBM, that serves as a general indicator of the direction of the overall market (*see* Benchmark).

BELLY UP. Describes a company facing bankruptcy.

BELOW PAR. Selling for a price that is less than the security's face value.

BELOW THE LINE. An unusual revenue or expense that doesn't normally appear on a company's balance sheet and therefore requires a separate classification.

BELOW THE MARKET. A bid that is lower than the highest bid for a specific security.

BENCHMARK. A quantitative gauge in the securities market (*see* Bellwether).

BENEFICIAL INTEREST. Held by someone who owns something of value, such as stock in a company or placement in a trust.

BENEFICIAL OWNER. A person who benefits from owning a security, even though the security's title actually is in the name of a bank or broker. The classic example is stock held in "street name" by a broker for a client.

BERNE UNION. An organization, represented by members from 26 countries, that works toward the acceptance of "sound principles of export credit and investment insurance."

BEST EFFORTS. Used by underwriters in selling an entire new security issue by a certain date. Instead of buying and reselling the issue, the underwriter leaves the risk with the issuer.

BEST'S RATING. Service measuring the quality of insurance companies.

BETA. A measure of risk; the higher the beta, the higher the risk. Beta represents the average percentage change in the price of a stock compared to the percentage change of the market index.

BID AHEAD. Limit orders of equal price are processed on a first-come, first-served basis.

BID AND ASKED. The highest price an investor will pay for a security (bid), or the lowest price someone will sell a security (asked).

BID-ASK SPREAD. The difference between the best buying price and the best selling price for any given security.

BIDDING UP. The bid price for a security moves higher and higher as demand for the security increases.

BID IN COMPETITION. An investor with a block of securities to sell approaches several dealers, then sells the securities to the one dealer with the highest bid. The dealer may inventory the stock in an effort to attract future business from the investor.

BID PRICE. The highest price an investor will pay for a given security.

BID WANTED. An investor, through a broker, announces that he or she wants to sell a security and is ready to accept bids.

BID WILL IMPROVE. Traders tell a seller who requests a market picture that the trader can pay more than the bid represents, but first the seller must offer a counter-proposal. Often the buyer and seller will split the bid-ask spread.

BIF. *See* Bank Insurance Fund.

BIG BOARD. The nickname for the New York Stock Exchange, the oldest and largest stock exchange in the United States. Historically, the companies listed on the Big Board are bigger and more established than those listed on the American Stock Exchange.

BIG MAC. A nickname for New York City's Municipal Assistance Corporation.

BIGGER FOOL THEORY. Investors buy a security because they believe they can sell it at a later date to someone less knowledgeable.

BIG SIX. The six largest accounting firms in the United States, listed alphabetically, they are: Arthur Andersen & Co., Coopers and Lybrand, Deloitte Haskins & Sells, Ernst & Whinney, KPMG Peat, Marwick Mitchell, and Price Waterhouse & Co.

BILATERAL CLEARING. All payments from countries with scarce foreign exchange make payments through a central bank instead of through foreign trade banks in an effort to economize, with the requirement that the countries maintain a balanced mutual trade every year. Examples of countries with scarce foreign exchange include Guyana and Bulgaria, which produce few products with any demand on the foreign market. Each country has its own currency, but no other nations want the currency because there's nothing in Bulgaria or Guyana they want to buy with the currency.

BILL DISCOUNTED. Interest is deducted from the face amount at the time of purchase and the face amount is paid at maturity. The classic example is the U.S. Treasury Bill.

BILLING CYCLE. The period, usually one month, between customer billings.

BILL OF EXCHANGE A short-term debt, the collateral for which is either a commodity or another product in the midst of transit.

BILL STRIP. The U.S. Treasury Department auctions Treasury bills of different maturities at the same average price.

BINDER. A written document describing a contract's terms and conditions and serving as a temporary contract until the final agreement can be submitted. Binders are most commonly used in the insurance industry.

BITSY. A nickname for Brokers Transaction Services Incorporated.

BLACK BOX. A computerized portfolio selection model that incorporates any number of economic and company variables. Proponents of such models claim that the value lies in the fact that they are completely objective.

BLACK FRIDAY. A quick, dramatic drop in the market. The first Black Friday was September 24, 1869. A group of investors tried to corner the gold market, which prompted such a panic in the business community that a depression ensued.

BLACK KNIGHT. A person or company that makes a takeover offer that would be hostile to the existing management of the target company.

BLACK MARKET. Any illegal securities trading.

BLACK MARKET BOND. Dealers who are not part of the investment syndicate trade in a bond registered with the Securities and Exchange Commission between the bond's effective date and the date the account members lift the pricing restrictions. Such bonds can seriously damage the investment syndicate's efforts to distribute the bonds itself.

BLACK-SCHOLES OPTION PRICING MODEL. Fischer Black and Myron Scholes developed a model to estimate the fair market value of option contracts. The model uses, among other data, interest rate levels and the price volatility of the underlying security to gauge the contracts.

BLACK TUESDAY. Tuesday, October 29, 1929, the day the stock market crashed, marking the onset of the Great Depression.

BLANK CHECK PREFERRED STOCK. Stockholders allow the company's management to issue preferred stock that includes voting rights to approved parties in an effort to avoid hostile bids.

BLANK ENDORSEMENT. A person or firm signs a financial instrument to make it negotiable without restriction.

BLANKET CERTIFICATION FORM. Foreign brokers and dealers provide this document when they buy newly issued securities. The document says the foreign broker or dealer understands and will obey the regulations of the National Association of Securities Dealers (NASD Form FR-1).

BLANKET FIDELITY BOND. The brokerage insurance that protects firms from incidents of fraudulent trading, forgery, and loss of securities. Dealers are required to maintain this coverage by the Securities and Exchange Commission's regulations.

BLANKET MORTGAGE. A single debt, or mortgage, that covers all of a company's property.

BLANKET RECOMMENDATION. Investors are advised by their broker that they should buy or sell specific securities despite their portfolio size or their investment goals.

BLANK STOCK. A company doesn't set the terms of a stock in the articles of incorporation, but establishes them later when the stocks are issued.

BLENDED CREDIT. Credit issued with more than one funding source.

BLIND AD. An advertisement that does not name the advertiser, such as some job listings that do not name the prospective employers. Such ads solicit written replies and eliminate phone calls and personal visits.

BLIND BROKERING. One person acts as an intermediary between a borrower and lender; sometimes one of the parties remains anonymous.

BLIND ENTRY. An incomplete bookkeeping entry with only account credits and debits listed without any further financial information.

BLIND POOL. Money from several people is collected, put into a fund and invested for their profit. The investors receive periodic reports on their money, but they cannot manage the money themselves.

BLIND TRUST. A trust fund established to protect a person from any conflict of interest charges. The person's finances are handled by a designated fiduciary.

BLOCK AUTOMATION SYSTEM. A communications computer at the New York Stock Exchange used when institutional investors trade large blocks of securities. The computer allows investors to identify buyers and sellers quickly.

BLOCKED. A trader is told that his or her blocks cannot be crossed at the trader's price either because the spread is too tight or because another dealer is offering a deal as good or better.

BLOCK HOUSE. A brokerage firm that specializes in trading blocks of stocks.

BLOCK OF STOCK. A trading unit of stock—10,000 shares or more.

BLOCK ORDER. An order to buy or sell $1 million or more worth of bonds or 10,000 or more shares.

BLOCK POSITIONER. A dealer who takes a position in the securities market so his or her client can profit from increased market prices. A block positioner, who must be registered with the Securities and Exchange Commission as well as with the New York Stock Exchange, takes the market position while representing a client who wants to sell a block of stock. Block positioners' clients are usually large, well-capitalized firms.

BLOOD BATH. Occurs when the stock market plummets and investors lose tremendous amounts of money—at least on paper.

BLOTTER. A written manuscript of broker or dealer activity for any given day, including purchases, sales, and other transactions.

BLOWING OFF. The peaking of stock prices after a lengthy advance and heavy trading. A buying climax.

BLOWOUT. All shares of a new securities offering are quickly sold, which brings the corporation higher stock prices, but limits the number of shares a buyer may be able to purchase.

BLUE CHIP. Nationally known common stock with a lengthy history of profit, growth, and quality management. IBM and Du Pont are examples of blue chip stocks.

BLUE LIST BOOK. A financial list published daily that reports which bonds are for sale, their prices, and their yields. The list includes bonds for sale by more than 700 dealers.

BLUE SKY LAW. Securities must be registered according to the laws of each particular state before they can be sold in that state. Those stocks which do not follow a particular state's registration laws become restricted. The nickname came from a judge who once said a certain stock had as much value as a patch of blue sky.

BOARD BROKER. A Chicago Board Options Exchange member who acts as an agent for other brokers and who performs the duties of a principal when trading for his or her own account.

BOARD OF ARBITRATION. A committee of three to five people who decide the outcome of disputes between stock exchange members as well as nonmember brokerage firms. An arbitration board may also be used to work out disagreements between clients and brokers. Those involved in the dispute first must agree to settle their fight with the board. The board's decision is binding.

BOARD OF DIRECTORS. A committee elected by the company's stockholders at their annual meeting. The board's duties include appointing corporate officers, issuing shares of stock, and declaring dividends.

BOARD OF GOVERNORS OF THE FEDERAL RESERVE SYSTEM. A committee of seven people who set banking regulation policy for the country. The committee members are heads of the regional federal reserve banks.

BOARD ROOM. Brokerage houses have a room where customers can watch the consolidated tape of stock transactions. To some extent the "tape" has been replaced by individual quotation machines provided for the customer's use.

BOBTAIL POOL. A group of investors involved in a speculative venture who have a common goal, but who act independently of each other.

BOILER ROOM. A room jammed with telephones where salespeople call long lists of prospective investors and try to sell them speculative or fraudulent securities.

BOND. A long-term debt security, issued by a corporation or government, with a stated interest rate and fixed due dates when interest and principal must be paid. Specific features are written into each bond's indenture, including whether the interest and principal will be paid to the person in whose name the security is registered, or if it will be payable to anyone presenting it, in which case it is considered a bearer bond.

BOND ANTICIPATION NOTE. A government-issued, short-term debt instrument that will be paid off by the proceeds from another bond sale soon to be issued.

THE BOND BUYER. A newspaper published daily that lists indexes and statistics from fixed-income markets.

BOND BUYER'S INDEX. Published in *The Bond Buyer*, this index contains gauges to judge the yields from municipal bonds and to help predict future trends.

BOND DISCOUNT. The negative difference between a bond's market or purchase price and its par value.

BOND DIVIDEND. A stockholder who is owed a dividend receives payment in the form of a bond instead of cash or additional shares of stock.

BOND FUND. Mutual fund invested in fixed-income instruments.

BOND HOLDER. Anyone who owns a bond, whether it is in registered or bearer form.

BOND HOUSE. A firm that deals in securities, but concentrates its business on bonds.

BOND INVESTORS GUARANTY INSURANCE COMPANY. Insures the timely payment of interest and principal to municipal securities investors. Municipalities pay for this coverage but it often results in lower interest costs.

BOND POWER. A certificate that accompanies a bond when it is transferred from one owner to another. The certificate appoints an attorney-in-fact, the seller's broker, who will complete the ownership transfer in the corporation's records.

BOND PREMIUM. The positive difference between a bond's market or purchase price and its par value.

BOND QUOTATION. While corporate bonds carry face values in dollar amounts, they are quoted in points based on the dollar amounts. One point represents $10, with minimum variations of one-eighth of a point. U.S. Treasury Bonds are quoted in 32nds of a point.

BOND RATING. A rank of quality ranging from AAA to D (default) given to a bond based on its value as a sound investment. The rating is based on such things as the issuer's reputation and its record in paying interest.

BOND RATIO. Divide the total number of bonds outstanding by the same number plus the company's equity. This ratio determines a company's level of leverage. A number higher than 33 percent is considered a high measure of leverage, but this guideline varies with each industry.

BOND SWAP. Selling one bond issue and buying another at the same time in order to create some advantage for the investor. Some benefits of swapping may include tax-deductible losses, increased yields, and an improved quality portfolio.

BOND WASHING. Some British bonds trade ex-interest instead of on an accrued interest basis; so to avoid paying taxes, an investor would sell the bond to a nontaxable holder before the ex-date, after which the investor buys the bond back at its original price plus interest. By doing this, the interest has become a capital consideration instead of being taxable.

BONUS FUTURES. If executives believe their companies' year-end bonuses will be low, they can hedge their bets by selling futures to a colleague. **The buyer guarantees the seller a certain percentage of the seller's annual salary, and if the bonus is more than that percentage, the buyer gets the difference. If the bonus is less, the buyer must make up the difference.**

BOOK. A written record either of anticipated interest for a proposed underwriting, or the activities of underwriting account members.

BOOK CREDIT. Financial commitments that are not backed by any securities, but show up in ledger accounts.

BOOK ENTRY SECURITIES. Securities, such stocks held in "street name," that are recorded in a customer's account, but are not accompanied by a certificate. The trend is toward a certificate-less society.

BOOKKEEPING EQUATION. A one-line balance sheet summary, expressed as assets minus liabilities equals shareholders' equity.

BOOKSHARES. A procedure of recording stock shares in investment companies. This process eliminates the need for mutual fund share certificates and records fractional share holdings.

BOOK VALUE. The original cost of an asset minus depreciation. In corporate terms, book value equals the net asset value.

BOOK VALUE PER SHARE. From total assets subtract all liabilities and the par value of stock and divide by the number of outstanding shares of common stock. This figure represents the break-up value per share if a company were liquidated.

BOOM. A fast and strong upswing in the economy proceeded by an increase in the stock market.

BOOT. Nickname for branch operations and orientation training, which new brokerage firm employees must go through before they can work in the firm's operations departments.

BOOTSTRAP ACQUISITION. A friendly corporate takeover. In a bootstrap acquisition, the target company gives some of its assets to dissident stockholders in exchange for their shares. The acquiree then sells 100 percent of the shares to the acquirer. In the process, the new owner gets 100 percent of the company at a lower price because the purchased company, in essence, helped to finance its own takeover.

BORROWED RESERVES. A bank borrows money at the Fed funds rate from another member bank to maintain the reserve ratio mandated by the Federal Reserve Bank.

BORROWED STOCK. A broker borrows shares of a security to complete a client's short sale.

BORROWING POWER OF SECURITIES. The amount of money an investor can borrow from his or her broker to buy securities based on the value of assets in their account. The brokerage firm lists each customer's borrowing power on his or her monthly statement.

BORROWING SHORT, LENDING LONG. A bank makes long-term loans using cash it owes to depositors in the short term. Since long-term rates are generally higher than short-term rates, banks earn revenue from the spread.

BOSTON INTEREST. Interest is based on a 30-day month, no matter how many days a particular month has in actuality. For example, interest in February would be the same as in June and in December, even though the actual numbers of days in the three months vary.

BOSTON STOCK EXCHANGE. Located at One Boston Place, this regional stock exchange handles securities not only from the New England area, but some from the exchange listings in New York City as well.

BOTTOM. The price level at which a security is not expected to drop below before it starts to go up again.

BOTTOM FISHER. An investor who concentrates his or her efforts on looking for securities that have bottomed out, or those expected to soon bottom out, such as the stocks of companies facing bankruptcy. The investor can buy the stocks at a reasonable rate and expect them not to drop any lower before they start increasing in value.

BOTTOM OUT. The point at which a stock price has dropped so far that demand exceeds supply and the price begins to rise again.

BOTTOM-UP APPROACH TO INVESTING. An investor who concentrates on individual stocks that are performing well without considering possible changes in economic trends. For example, an investor may put money into a computer software company that he or she has carefully researched, even if prospects for the overall economy are not good.

BOUGHT DEAL. A commitment to buy the entire issue of a security from the issuing company.

BOUTIQUE. A small brokerage firm that specializes in a limited number of securities with a select number of customers.

BRACKET. The manner in which investment bankers in an underwriting are classified in relation to financial responsibility—the higher the bracket, the higher the financial responsibility and the higher the bank's name appears in the "tombstone" ad.

BRACKET CREEP. As a person's income rises because of inflation, he or she inches into a higher tax bracket. The Tax Reform Act of 1986 lowered the number of tax brackets and thus limited the effect of bracket creep.

BRASSAGE. A government orders bullion to be minted into coins.

BREADTH OF THE MARKET. The number of stocks involved in a market move compared to the total number listed. If two-thirds of all stocks rose in price on a given day, investors say the breadth was good for an advancing day.

BREAK. An abrupt, unexpected reversal in market prices.

BREAKAWAY GAP. Price movements with highs and lows that do not overlap the previous day's movement and begin a new trend. For example, a positive trend may be forthcoming if today's low price is higher than yesterday's high price.

BREAKING THE SYNDICATE. Dissolving the investment organization that was formed to underwrite an issue of securities by eliminating the agreement among underwriters. The members then can sell their holdings without restriction.

BREAKOUT. The price of a security increases above its previous high point, or falls below its previous low point. In a breakout, the security is expected to continue in the same direction for some time.

BREAKPOINT. In buying certain mutual funds, increments in the level of dollars invested will allow the commission percentage to be reduced.

BREAKPOINT SALES. Occurs when a broker sells mutual funds in dollar amounts slightly below that needed to reduce the commission percentage. The practice is considered unethical.

BREAK-UP VALUE. The separate worth of a company's various components, as if they all existed independent of the company. Equal to the company's book value.

BRIDGE LOAN. A borrower arranges short-term financing while awaiting the approval of a long-term loan.

BRING OUT. One or more underwriters offers a new security issue for sale publicly.

BROAD MARKET. When securities trading is unusually heavy.

BROAD TAPE. Wire service stock reports that provide a wider range of information than the ticker tape which merely shows prices and sizes of trades.

BROKEN CONVERTIBLE. A convertible bond with a yield that has risen to the level of yields from similar, nonconvertible securities.

BROKEN LOT. Fewer than 100 shares of a specific stock. Also referred to as an odd lot.

BROKEN PERIOD. A foreign exchange arrangement with a future settlement date and without a standard maturity period.

BROKER. The intermediary between a buyer and a seller of securities. The broker, who usually charges a commission, must be registered with the exchange in which he or she is trading.

BROKERAGE ACCOUNT. A broker will keep records of all transactions in which his or her clients ever have been involved. The customer will receive statements disclosing monthly transactions, current positions, and cash balances.

BROKERAGE HOUSE. A firm that buys and sells securities for customers.

BROKER-DEALER. A firm that not only handles transactions for customers, but also buys securities for its own account and then sells those securities to customers for a profit.

BROKER LOAN RATE. The interest rate brokers pay when they borrow money to pay for their customers' positions in the securities market.

BROKER'S FREE CREDIT BALANCE. The New York Stock Exchange provides a monthly report of the amount of money each firm has sitting idle in its brokerage account.

BROKER'S MARKET. Describes heavy trading by brokers in their own accounts, but little interest by individual investors.

BROKER'S TICKET. A record of a broker's executed buy and sell orders, including all information pertinent to the orders, such as names, dates and prices.

BROKER'S TRANSACTION SERVICES INCORPORATED. Sells trade processing and reporting services to brokers.

BUBBLE. A speculative venture that has little chance of making a profit. When this fact becomes evident, the bubble bursts and prices fall.

BUBBLE COMPANY. A company that never planned to do any legitimate business, created to defraud potential investors.

BUCKETING. A broker who executes a customer's order in his or her own account rather than on the open market because the broker believes he or she will profit from a balancing transaction later. The Securities and Exchange Commission prohibits bucketing.

BUCKET SHOP. A brokerage house will confirm a customer's order at a specific price without executing the order on an exchange in hopes of obtaining a better price. The firm would then pocket the difference between the two prices. Such practices are prohibited by the Securities and Exchange Commission.

BUCKING THE TREND. Doing the opposite of the rest of the market. For example, buying long when the market is going down, or selling short when the market is on an upswing.

BUDGET. The total amount of money needed to complete a project, or the amount of money needed to operate an organization during a one-year period.

BUILDING AND LOAN ASSOCIATION. A firm that saves and lends money, specializing in financing construction projects. Deposits often are represented by shares in the name of the depositor. Somewhat antiquated, these institutions have largely been replaced by savings and loan associations.

BULGE. A short, quick price rise in an entire market or an individual stock.

BULK SEGREGATION. Securities owned by individuals, but not registered in their names and kept separate from securities owned by the broker-dealer.

BULL. Someone who expects the securities price, or economy in general, to improve.

BULLDOG SECURITIES. Foreign securities traded in England with face values and interest payments quoted in pounds sterling.

BULLET. Borrowed money or a borrowed security that must be repaid in one lump sum at the end of its term, instead of having smaller payments that are due regularly.

BULLETPROOF. Any contract, agreement or other document that contains absolutely no loopholes.

BULLION. A refined precious metal, such as gold or silver, that has been melted and shaped into bars, rounds, or another form.

BULLION COIN. A coin with a value close to its bullion content, as opposed to a rare coin with a value higher than its gold content because of its rarity, or collector interest.

BULL MARKET. A long-term rise in security prices.

BULL POOL. Investors organize with the purpose of manipulating stock prices upwards. Members are not permitted to make any individual transactions. Bull pools are illegal.

BULL SPREAD. A strategy using option contracts that increase in value with the price of the underlying security. An investor buys a call option while simultaneously selling a put option. The option sold will have a higher exercise price than the one purchased.

BULL STRADDLE WRITING. An uncovered put option and a covered call option are written on the same underlying option.

BUNCHING. Putting together a lot of small orders to be executed at the same time, instead of spending time on them individually.

BUOYANT. Securities that are rising in price.

BURNOUT. An investor begins to take taxable profits from his or her investment after all available tax shelters have been exhausted.

BUSINESS CONDUCT COMMITTEE. Determines the facts and enters a judgment in complaints of improper trade practices. Committees are established in all of the 13 districts of the National Association of Securities Dealers, and are organized under the association's rules and regulations.

BUSINESS CYCLE. The time period from the top of a Gross National Product rise to the bottom of a fall and back to the base line.

BUSINESS DAY. Any day the brokerage community and stock exchanges are open for trading. There are several days during the year where banks are closed but stock trading continues.

BUSINESS SEGMENT REPORTING. A company divides its income, sales, assets, and other data into separate accounting categories according to the subsidiary or division where they originate so management can compare and analyze strengths and weaknesses from the different branches.

BUSINESS SOLVENCY. When a business has more assets than liabilities.

BUSTED CONVERTIBLE. One stock that could once have been exchanged for another—conversion is no longer appealing because the underlying equity's price has fallen too low.

BUST-UP PROXY PROPOSAL. One group of company stockholders asks the other shareholders to approve the company's liquidation or sale in an attempt to get rid of the existing management.

BUTTERFLY SPREAD. Selling two calls and buying two calls with several different expiration dates and exercise prices. The investor will profit from premium income if the market value of the underlying security does not move dramatically by the expiration dates.

BUY A PUT. An investor pays extra for the right to sell 100 shares of a specific stock at a preset price within a specific time frame. If market conditions are such that proceeding with the sale at the preset price would cause the investor to lose money (if the current market price is higher than the original put price), he or she is under no obligation to sell.

BUY AND HOLD. The accumulation of a security for long-term appreciation and/or income rather than short-term profits.

BUY AND WRITE. An investor buys securities, then sells or writes covered call options on the same securities so that he or she can profit from the stock dividends as well as from the call option premiums. The investor sacrifices some appreciation potential in return for the premium.

BUY AT BEST. In the purchase of a large block of over-the-counter securities, the dealer-broker is instructed to buy at the best price available, but all securities need not be purchased at the same price.

BUYBACK. A customer purchases the same type of stock he or she just sold short in an effort to satisfy a contract or to cover a short position in the market. In the corporate sense, a company may utilize excess cash to repurchase shares of their own stock.

BUYERS' MARKET. Supply exceeds demand, so prices are attractive.

BUYER'S MONOPOLY. A market with one buyer and several sellers.

BUY IN. A selling broker fails to deliver on time, so the buying broker must obtain the securities from someone else.

BUYING BASIS. The difference between a cash commodity's price and a future that was sold to hedge that price.

BUYING CLIMAX. A quick surge in the price of a security or the overall market, which prompts investors to purchase more. Soon, there is no one to whom they can sell the higher priced stock, which creates a vacuum and a sudden drop in the stock's price.

BUYING HEDGE. A long position in the futures market which equals the cash commodity that eventually is needed.

BUYING ON A SHOESTRING. Purchasing securities on the minimum margin.

BUYING ON BALANCE. A broker's buy orders exceed his or her sell orders.

BUYING ON MARGIN. An investor can buy securities by borrowing money from his or her broker. The amount a customer can borrow is dependent upon the securities and cash in his or her account.

BUYING ON SCALE. A broker is instructed to buy certain securities at specific intervals while the security's price is dropping. By buying on scale, the investor's price per share drops with each consecutive purchase.

BUYING OUTRIGHT. The opposite of buying on margin—buying a security by paying 100 percent cash.

BUYING POWER. The amount of money a person has available to spend on securities; this hinges on the level of assets the person has in his or her brokerage account and how much is on margin.

BUYING RANGE. If market prices are dropping, an advisor determines the point at which he or she believes prices may start to increase again. Based on that information, the advisor recommends when an investor should start buying stock.

BUYING SIGNAL. A series of prices on a stock chart that does not fall into the normal pattern and, therefore, is used to gauge an attractive price level for purchase.

BUYING THE INTERMARKET SPREAD. An investor hedges his or her position in the market by buying and selling two different securities at the same time. An example might be the purchase of a bond and the short sale of a utility stock.

BUY-IN PROCEDURE. If a broker or dealer does not deliver a promised security to a purchaser, the purchaser can notify the agent, and within two days can buy the security on the open market and charge the delinquent agent with any losses incurred.

BUY MINUS. An order to buy stock at a price lower than the current market value. Normally, an investor will try to make such a deal when the stock's price is dropping.

BUY ON BID. An investor buys a listed stock from an odd-lot trader who is selling at bid price, instead of waiting to buy from the odd-lot trader after a round-lot sale.

BUY ON THE OFFER. An investor buys an odd-lot stock at the lowest asking price plus the odd-lot differential so that he or she does not have to wait for a round-lot sale to determine the odd-lot price.

BUY ORDER. A client orders his or her broker to buy a specific amount of stock at a particular price.

BUYOUT. Buying a percentage of stock large enough for the purchaser to own the biggest share of a corporation, which permits him or her to take control of a company's management and assets.

BUY SIGNAL. A chart indicator that, because of market movements, shows a buyer that it's a good time to purchase stock or other securities.

BUY STOP ORDER. A client orders his or her broker to buy a security that is increasing in value after it has hit a certain price, then to buy at the best price available.

BUY THE BOOK. A client orders his or her broker to buy all shares of a specific security that are available at the offer price.

BUY TICKET. An investment department document that tells the order department to buy a specific security. The ticket states the date, time, size, and price of the security purchased.

BYLAWS. Self-imposed rules by which an organization or company must abide. Bylaws include such regulations as to how directors are to be named and how stock shares are to be transferred.

BYPASS TRUST. A contract with which parents transfer their assets to their children while reducing the amount of money the children will have to pay in estate taxes. Once initiated, the terms of the trust cannot be changed, but the parents can receive income from the trust during their lifetimes and, in some cases, use some of the principal.

C

CABINET BID. A deal that is not made on the exchange floor and that closes an out-of-the-money option contract for one cent.

CABLE. The spot exchange rate between the dollar and sterling.

CALCULATED RISK. The estimated probability that a business venture will succeed, based on any unknowns associated with such an investment.

CALENDAR. A list of securities that will be offered publicly for sale. Separate calendars are issued for new stock issues, corporate bonds, and municipal bonds.

CALENDAR SPREADING. Buying and selling options within the same class—all puts or all calls—but with different expiration dates.

CALLABLE CAPITAL. Investors have made commitments to contribute capital to a company. Under prescribed conditions, corporate directors can demand that this capital be paid.

CALLABLE PREFERRED STOCK. Any preferred stock a corporation can redeem for payment at a preset price.

CALL AWAY. The exercise of an option contract forces the option writer to relinquish the stock. The security is said to be "called away."

CALL CONTRACT. A *call option* equivalent to 100 shares.

CALL DATE. A bond issuer specifies a date that the bond can be redeemed before maturity.

CALL FEATURE. A clause in a senior security that permits the issuing company to buy the security back at a predetermined price as long as the purchase is made before the security matures.

CALL LOAN. A loan with the provision that the lender can demand payment in full at any time. Also, a broker deposits collateral with a bank and is loaned money. The broker then loans the money to customers to finance margin activities.

CALL LOAN RATE. The rate banks charge brokers on call loans; this rate forms the basis for minimum margin interest charges.

CALL MONEY. Money that banks have lent to brokers that must be repaid upon demand.

CALL MONEY MARKET. Used by brokers and dealers with call funds secured by stock exchange collateral and government securities to cover their customers' margin accounts as well as the brokers' and dealers' own securities inventory.

CALL OPTION. The right to purchase 100 shares of a specific stock at a specific price within a given time in exchange for a premium. The buyer will profit if the stock's market value rises above the sum of the striking price and the amount paid for the call at the time of expiration. Options are traded on several exchanges. The premium can provide extra income for the seller (writer) of the option.

CALL OPTION BUY-SELL RATIO. Divide call option buying by call option selling. If the ratio is higher during a drop in the market, the ratio is considered bearish. If the ratio is lower when the market is moving up, the ratio is considered bullish. This evaluation is based upon the opinion that option buyers are not successful in the long run.

CALL PRICE. The price at which a corporation or other obligor is permitted to redeem a bond or preferred stock which contains a *call provision* or *call feature*.

CALL PRIVILEGE. A bond issuer can repay the bond at any time before its maturity. Differs from a call feature which has more limitations.

CALL PROTECTION BONDS. Prevents the issuing corporation from redeeming the bond for a certain number of years. Investors who bought bonds with high yields are protected in case interest rates drop, after which the corporation probably would want to refinance the bond. If the bond is redeemed, investors usually receive a premium over the face value of the bond.

CALL PROVISION. Defines the circumstances under which the issuer can redeem a bond before its maturity (*see* Call Features).

CALL PURCHASE. A person selling commodities holds some pricing options that can be exercised later, as long as the pricing options fall within a specific range of the existing price. The purchase hedges against a swift price rise.

CALL SALE. An investor agrees to sell a security with the buyer setting the price at a later date. A call sale is the opposite of a call purchase.

CALL SPREAD. A position formed when an investor buys one call and sells one call on the same security, the options having different expiration dates and different exercises. The investor believes that the underlying security will make a quick, but limited move. The proceeds from the sale help to offset the cost of the purchase, but upside potential is limited.

CAMBISM. Selling foreign currencies.

CAMBISTRY. The study of foreign currencies.

CANADIAN INSTITUTE OF CHARTERED ACCOUNTANTS. An organization of Canadian public accountants that reports changes in corporate accounting practices ordered by the Canadian government. To be admitted into the organization, an accountant must be a college graduate and must pass a battery of tests.

CAP. The highest interest rate a securities issuer will pay on a bond issue, or the highest price at which a securities underwriter will sell a new stock. Also, an upper limit to the interest rate payable on a variable rate bond or mortgage.

CAPITAL. A company's net assets, including all retained earnings.

CAPITAL ACCOUNT. A businessowner's account that indicates his or her equity.

CAPITAL APPRECIATION BOND. A zero-coupon municipal bond.

CAPITAL APPRECIATION AND PROTECTION INSURANCE. A type of variable life insurance policy that allows the owner to change investment premiums between investments, including mutual funds or zero-coupon bonds. Profits from the investments remain in a tax shelter as long as they are not distributed.

CAPITAL ASSET. All fixed assets, such as property, buildings and equipment, that are used in the normal course of doing business.

CAPITAL ASSET PRICING MODEL. The relationship between a company's expected risk and anticipated return. According to the model, an asset's or stock's return equals risk-free return plus risk premium. The higher the risk, the higher the premium.

CAPITAL BUDGET. A program used to finance long-term projects such as advertising, plant expansion, and research and development.

CAPITAL CHARGES. Capital needed to satisfy interest and to amortize money invested in a company.

CAPITAL CONSUMPTION. A company's investments earmarked for production.

CAPITAL CONSUMPTION ALLOWANCE. The amount of depreciation—usually about 11 percent—that economists subtract from the gross national product. After depreciation is subtracted, the figure is called the net national product. Economists, however, continue to quote the GNP because NNP figures are not always available or reliable.

CAPITAL EXPENDITURE. The amount of money a company spends to buy capital assets or upgrade its existing capital assets (*see* Capital Spending).

CAPITAL FLIGHT. An investor moves large sums of money from one nation to another in an effort to seek a safe haven. To preserve capital, for example, an investor will move money out of countries suffering from political or economic turmoil.

CAPITAL FORMATION. A company weighs the cost of expanding its capital base. The alternatives are: equity or debt offerings, short-term loans, or internal financing.

CAPITAL GAIN. In capital assets, the difference between the sale price and the cost less depreciation. In financial assets, the difference between the sale price and the purchase price adjusted for splits and transaction costs.

CAPITAL GAINS DISTRIBUTION. Paying investment company stockholders out of long-term capital gains that came from selling portfolio securities. Investment companies are not taxed on such gains if they are passed on to shareholders.

CAPITAL GAINS TAX. Tax on an asset that has been held for a certain period (usually six months or one year) and then sold for a profit. When the capital gains receive favorable tax treatment, it is advantageous to hold the asset for at least the minimum period.

CAPITAL GOODS. Assets used to produce other goods. For example, a machine used to produce bolts would be a capital good.

CAPITAL INTENSIVE. The cost of capital assets exceeds the cost of labor in the manufacturing of a product.

CAPITALISM. An economic system based on the theory that profit provides motivation to achieve. In a capitalistic society, property is privately owned, and profits from a company remain with that company's owners instead of reverting to the government for control and distribution.

CAPITAL ISSUES. Permanent and fixed securities, such as common and preferred stock.

CAPITAL LEASE. A lease in which the lessee gets all of the economic benefits, as well as the risks, of the property. A company is required to show such a lease on its balance sheet as an asset *and* a liability.

CAPITAL MARKETS. A market in which capital funds, such as equity and debt, are traded.

CAPITAL REQUIREMENTS. The amount of money needed to finance business operations for the foreseeable future.

CAPITAL RISK. A person may not be able to recover all of his or her original investment when the investment is liquidated. This is in direct contrast to insured investments, such as certificates of deposit, wherein principal is guaranteed.

CAPITAL STOCK. The source of a corporation's equity capital, indicating stocks that represent ownership. Capital stock usually refers to common, not preferred, stock.

CAPITAL STRUCTURE. A basis for comparing a company's debt-to-equity ratio. It is the structure or condition of a company's long-term debts, preferred stock, and net worth.

CAPITAL SURPLUS. The amount by which a security's balance sheet value exceeds its par value.

CAPITAL TURNOVER. A company's annual sales divided by the average shareholder's net worth, this figure indicates whether the company can continue to grow and expand without further investments.

CAPITALIZATION. Permanent funds, such as stocks and bonds, used to finance a business venture.

CAPITALIZATION RATE. An interest rate economists use to convert a group of future payments into one present value. An internal discount rate.

CAPITALIZATION RATIOS. The percentage of bonds and other long-term debts, preferred and common stock, retained income, capital surplus, and capital stock premiums, that are capitalized.

CAPITALIZE. To categorize a specific cost as a long-term investment instead of charging it to current operations.

CAP ORDER. A large buy or sell order giving the exchange specialist permission to use his or her own discretion in executing the deal. While this practice is formally prohibited by the exchanges, it still is used in some instances for expediency.

CAPPING. A person or group of people try to keep an underlying security's market price below the exercise price of a particular stock option contract because of a personal interest in the security. This practice normally takes place near an expiration date. Depending on how capping is done, the practice often is illegal.

CAPTIVE. A company owns production capabilities which the company uses solely instead of selling them publicly. For example, a television manufacturer may own a lumber mill so it can use the mill's products to build cabinets for its products.

CAPTIVE FINANCE FIRM. A subsidiary formed to finance customer purchases from the subsidiary's parent corporation. For example, an automobile manufacturer may establish an acceptance corporation, which makes car loans to people who want to buy cars from the main company.

CARAT. A unit to measure the weight of some gems; equal to 200 milligrams.

CARRY. The act of holding stocks for a customer.

CARRY INCOME OR LOSS. The difference between the interest income and the financing cost of an investment portfolio purchased on margin.

CARRYING BROKER. The broker or dealer who holds a customer's account.

CARRYING CHARGE. The amount of money a broker charges to carry securities for a client on credit. It also refers to the amount of money a person must spend to carry, store, and insure commodities.

CARRYING MARKET. When distant positions hold a premium over nearby positions, with the premium high enough to pay for carrying charges.

CARRYING VALUE. A fixed asset's value after deducting its accumulated depreciation reserve from the original depreciable cost.

CARRYOVER. United States tax laws allow an individual who had a net capital loss of more than the maximum annual deduction of $3,000 to carry over the remainder to ensuing tax years until the amount is offset against either capital gains or income.

CARTEL. A group organized to manipulate prices by regulating the production and marketing of a specific product, such as silver. The organization of petroleum exporting countries (OPEC) is the world's most famous cartel. Cartels are illegal in the United States.

CARTER BONDS. A medium-term debt instrument denominated in a foreign currency that the United States issued during President Carter's Administration in an effort to solve foreign currency imbalances.

CASH. Any negotiable currency in spendable form.

CASH ACCOUNT. A brokerage firm account in which all transactions are completed in cash.

CASH BASIS. Money is credited to a person's account only as it is received. The alternative is a method whereby money is credited to an account when it is accrued.

CASH BASIS ACCOUNTING. An accounting technique in which the basis for recording transactions is the receipt and payment of cash. It is the date on which cash changes hands, not the date on which goods and services are rendered.

CASH BOARD. The part of a commodity exchange's chalkboard designated for the listing of cash commodity contract sales.

CASHBOOK. An accounting record with both cash receipts and cash disbursements. The cashbook's balance should correspond with the cash balance on the general ledger.

CASH BUDGET. The amount of cash a company expects to receive and disburse over a given period of not more than one year.

CASH BUYING. Buying securities and commodities to be delivered immediately.

CASH COMMODITY. A commodity accepted on delivery after the transaction contract is completed. It is the reciprocal of a futures commodity, which is not completed until a future date.

CASH CONVERSION CYCLE. The time between when cash for raw materials is paid and when finished goods are sold. The shorter the cycle, the more money a company can generate and the less money it has to borrow.

CASH COW. A business that generates a high level of cash flow.

CASH DELIVERY. Securities are traded and delivered in the same day.

CASH DIVIDEND. A cash distribution from earnings or accumulated profits to company stockholders.

CASH EARNINGS. The amount of cash taken in minus cash paid out, excluding noncash expenses.

CASH EQUIVALENTS. Investments with a high level of liquidity.

CASH FLOW. A company adds the annual depreciation charge for fixed assets to its earnings after interest, taxes, and preferred dividends.

CASH FLOW BOND. A fully amortizing debt instrument with a fixed coupon rate and a fixed payment schedule, having an average life equal to or less than its securing collateral.

CASH FORWARD SALE. A commodity is sold with the actual delivery taking place at a later date.

CASH ITEMS. A company's bank deposits, government bonds, etc., that are listed on its financial statement as cash equivalents.

CASH MANAGEMENT ACCOUNT. A joint venture of banks and brokerage houses whereby wealthy clients can use a credit card to draw from their investment balances.

CASH MANAGEMENT BILL. A short-term money market instrument the U.S. Treasury issues to pay for its short-term financial obligations.

CASH MARKET. The ownership of a security or commodity is transferred and payment is made when the security or commodity is delivered.

CASH POSITION. The percentage of a company's total net assets that is available in cash.

CASH PRICE. The amount it would cost to buy a specific quantity of a commodity to be delivered immediately.

CASH RATIO. Comparing a company's cash and marketable securities to its current liabilities. The ratio is a gauge of the company's liquidity.

CASH RESERVES. Investment funds being held in short-term assets while awaiting more permanent investment opportunities.

CASH SUBSTITUTE. A liquid investment with a dollar value that remains relatively constant. The investment is held in place of cash.

CASH SURRENDER VALUE. The amount an insurer will return upon cancelation of the policy to a policyholder. The cash surrender value of life insurance (CSVLI) can be used as collateral against loans.

CASH TRADE. A security transaction in which settlement with payment and delivery on the security occur on the same day as the trade date.

CASH VALUE LIFE INSURANCE. A type of life insurance in which part of the premium is used to provide death benefits and the remainder to earn interest, this being a protection plan and a savings plan.

CASH WITH FISCAL AGENT. The amount of money a person has deposited with a commercial bank or other fiscal agent that will be used to pay for matured bonds and interest.

CASINO SOCIETY. Investors who put their money into undervalued corporate assets, volatile futures contracts or other speculative ventures in an effort to make fast money.

CASUALTY INSURANCE. Insurance that protects a business or homeowner against loss, damage, and related liability.

CATCHER. A trading ring employee responsible for recording transactions.

CATS. *See* Certificate of Accrual on Treasury Securities.

CATS AND DOGS. Speculative stocks with brief histories of sales, earnings, and dividend payment.

CAVEAT EMPTOR. Let the buyer beware.

CAVEAT VENDITOR. Let the seller beware.

CBOE. *See* Chicago Board Options Exchange.

CBOT. *See* Chicago Board of Trade.

CD. *See* Certificate of Deposit.

CEASE AND DESIST ORDER. Used by the Securities and Exchange Commission to stop people it believes are violating federal trading laws.

CEDEL. A Luxembourg firm that banks and broker-dealers use as a clearing house for Eurobond transactions.

CEILING PRICES. Maximum prices under a system of price controls.

CELLER-KEFAUVER ANTIMERGER ACT. A law that restricts anticompetitive mergers resulting from the acquisition of assets.

CENTRAL ASSETS ACCOUNT. An account that provides both banking and investment services for the person in whose name the account is carried.

CENTRAL BANK. A bank established for the government and through which the government issues currency, administers monetary policy including open market operations, holds deposits representing the reserves of other banks, and engages in transactions to facilitate the conduct of business and protect the public interest. The central bank, in this country, is a function of the Federal Reserve System.

CENTRAL CERTIFICATE SERVICE. To reduce the physical movement of stock certificates, subscribers of this service can deliver securities to each other through a bookkeeping computer.

CENTRAL REGISTRATION DEPOSITORY. A computer system for filing the registrations of representatives, broker-dealer principals and agents.

CERTIFICATE. A document verifying security ownership. A certificate includes such information as the issuer's name and the terms under which the security was issued.

CERTIFICATED SECURITIES. The number of shares of a particular commodity that are certified and ready to be delivered on a futures contract.

CERTIFICATE FOR AUTOMOBILE RECEIVABLES. A short-term debt security backed by automobile loans, originating when lenders package the loans and sell to the public, thereby providing the lenders with more funds for use in additional lending. Cars are relatively safe investments, and the interest rates are usually higher than the interest rates of U.S. Treasury securities.

CERTIFICATELESS MUNICIPAL. One certificate is issued for an entire series of municipal bonds, instead of each bond having its own certificate of ownership.

CERTIFICATELESS TRADING. Trading securities that do not have certificates of ownership issued to the holder. The holder can prove ownership by requesting a nonnegotiable certificate issued in the name of the broker who originally executed the transaction.

CERTIFICATE OF ACCOUNTS. A certified public accountant's written evaluation of a company's financial records after he or she has audited the accounts.

CERTIFICATE OF ACCRUAL ON TREASURY SECURITIES (CATS). A U.S. Treasury bond that is sold at a deep discount from its face value. Although it pays no interest, it is redeemable for the full face value when it matures.

CERTIFICATE OF BENEFICIAL INTEREST. Designates non-voting securities with underlying assets of one corporation as debt securities of another corporation.

CERTIFICATE OF CLAIM. A contingent promise of the Federal Housing Administration to reimburse an insured mortgagee for certain costs incurred during a foreclosure of an insured mortgage provided the proceeds from the sale of the property are sufficient to cover those expenses.

CERTIFICATE OF DEBT. A document that shows a borrower still owes a balance on a loan or other debt obligation.

CERTIFICATE OF DEPOSIT (CD). A debt instrument issued by a bank that will pay interest, periodically or at maturity (set by competitive forces in the marketplace), and principal when it reaches maturity. Maturities range from a few weeks to several years.

CERTIFICATE OF DEPOSIT ROLLOVER. A person who buys a certificate of deposit on margin can deduct interest on the loan while moving income from the certificate to the next year to defer taxes.

CERTIFICATE OF INCORPORATION. The charter granted to a corporation's petitioners with which the corporation can legally transact business in the state issuing the certificate.

CERTIFICATE OF INDEBTEDNESS (CI). A defunct debt security issued by the U.S. Treasury that had a fixed coupon rate and matured within 90 days to a year. The Treasury replaced CIs with Treasury bills that mature in 180 days to a year.

CERTIFICATE OF PARTICIPATION. Investment companies issue such certificates in place of shares of a security to indicate how much interest a customer holds in a particular company.

CERTIFICATE OF TITLE. A title company provides a person selling property with verification that the seller does own the property.

CERTIFIED CHECK. A personal check that the issuing bank pledges to make good upon presentation. A certified check is not the same as a bank check, which the bank draws on itself.

CERTIFIED FINANCIAL PLANNER (CFP). A person who has passed examinations for a certification, who coordinates a customer's banking, estate, insurance, investment, and tax affairs. Some planners charge only fees while others may collect a smaller fee and a commission on products sold.

CERTIFIED PUBLIC ACCOUNTANT (CPA). An accountant who has passed certain exams and achieved a designated amount of experience, is licensed by his or her state of residence, and can prepare corporate and personal tax returns as well as usual accounting and auditing work.

CFP. *See* Certified Financial Planner.

CFTC. *See* Commodities Futures Trading Commission.

CHAIRMAN OF THE BOARD. The member of a company's board of directors who presides over board meetings. The chairman is the highest ranking officer in a corporation.

CHAMBER OF COMMERCE. A group of business executives that promotes the activities and interests of its members, often by promoting the group's home city in an attempt to draw new businesses to town or to attract tourism, both of which ultimately increase the city's tax base.

CHANCELLOR OF THE EXCHEQUER. The United Kingdom's version of the United States Secretary of the Treasury. The chancellor is responsible for his or her government's receipts and payments.

CHANGES IN STOCKHOLDERS' EQUITY. A section in a company's annual report that shows the stockholders' equity, which is the difference between their assets and their liabilities.

CHARITABLE LEAD TRUST. A trust fund with a charity as the beneficiary of income, and the remainder going to a noncharity beneficiary.

CHARITABLE REMAINDER. If a business venture ends or fails, any remaining interest in the venture goes to a charitable organization.

CHARITABLE REMAINDER ANNUITY TRUST. A trust fund with the stipulation that at least 5 percent of the initial fair market value of property held in the trust is to be distributed annually to a noncharitable beneficiary, with the remainder going to a charity.

CHARITABLE TRUST. A trust fund established to benefit an entire community without a specific, individual beneficiary. For example, a person can establish a trust to benefit a city's arts community, with proceeds from the trust fund going to help build a new art museum.

CHART. A pictorial display of data. Charts show the historical values of variables frequently used to spot trends that may be used to provide insights in projecting future values.

CHARTER. A document endorsed and approved by a branch of state government in a company's home state that gives the company legal status as a corporation.

CHARTERED FINANCIAL ANALYST. A person certified by the Institute of Chartered Financial Analysts as being proficient in accounting, evaluating financial data, and managing investment portfolios.

CHARTERED FINANCIAL CONSULTANT. A person certified by the American College of Bryn Mawr as being proficient in investments, real estate ventures, and tax shelters.

CHARTERED INVESTMENT COUNSEL. A person certified by the Investment Counsel Association of America as being proficient in accounting, economics, portfolio management, and taxation.

CHARTIST. A technical analyst who maps out stock, bond, and commodity patterns, looks for recurring patterns, and then recommends which securities should be purchased.

CHARTIST'S LIABILITY. The risk of buying or selling short a security when the transaction is based solely on a chartist's recommendation.

CHART OF ACCOUNTS. A list that shows the names of accounts and the order in which they appear on a company's ledger.

CHATTEL. Personal property, or all property that is not real estate. For example, land is real estate, but a house built on that land is chattel.

CHEAP. Used to describe a stock price as low compared to its present value. "Underpriced" is used when a stock price is low compared to its potential future value.

CHEAP STOCK. Corporate shares of stock that are distributed while the company still is in its experimental or speculative stage.

CHECK. A bill of exchange, or draft on a bank drawn against deposited funds to pay a specified amount of money. Considered cash and is negotiable when endorsed.

CHECKING THE MARKET. Surveying market-makers to find out what the best bid is for a specific security.

CHECK KITING. A person writes a check without having enough money in his or her account to cover it, but he or she expects to be able to deposit the money before the check reaches the bank.

CHERRY PICKING. Choosing the best stock while ignoring the less valuable.

CHICAGO BOARD OF TRADE (CBOT). The largest exchange in the United States for trading futures contracts. The Chicago Board Options Exchange is a subsidiary of the Chicago Board of Trade.

CHICAGO BOARD OPTIONS EXCHANGE (CBOE). The largest market in the United States for trading put and call options.

CHICAGO MERCANTILE EXCHANGE. The second largest commodities exchange in the United States.

CHIEF EXECUTIVE OFFICER. A corporate officer responsible for a company's activities.

CHIEF FINANCIAL OFFICER. A corporate officer responsible for signing checks, keeping the books, and planning the finances of the company.

CHIEF OPERATING OFFICER. A corporate officer responsible for a company's day-to-day management.

CHINESE MARKET. Investors are willing to pay more than the lowest offer for a stock, or sell for less than the highest bid, but only if a large number of the securities are included in the deal.

CHINESE WALL. An intangible barrier between the trading side of a broker-dealer firm and the finance and research side that prevents broker-dealers from taking advantage of the finance department's inside information.

CHUMMING. A person artificially inflates the stock market's volume to attract more orders in one competitive security issue.

CHURNING. Excessive trading in a customer's account in an effort to increase the broker's commissions. The customer will usually be worse off or in no better condition. Although difficult to prove, churning is illegal under the Securities and Exchange Commission's rules.

CI. *See* Certificate of Indebtedness.

CINCINNATI STOCK EXCHANGE (CSE). The first fully automated stock exchange in the United States. Exchange members trade securities through a computer network, not on a trading floor.

CIRCLE. An indication of how much interest will be expressed in a new security while the security is still in the registration process. Company representatives make lists of potential buyers, then circle the names of those who express an interest.

CIRCUMFIDUCIATION. Money, which was invested in certificates of deposit, is transferred to another investment.

CITIZEN BONDS. A certificateless municipal bond that may be registered on any of the stock exchanges.

CITY. London's counterpart to Wall Street in the United States. Most of England's financial services organizations are concentrated in The City, which is on London's East Side.

CLAIM ACCOUNT. A bank account in which a commodity can be deposited.

CLASS. Categorization of securities with similar features. For example, puts are one class and calls are another. Also, bonds are one class of security, and stocks are another.

CLASSIFIED STOCK. Equity securities are separated into groups such as Class A or Class B. The difference between the two will be determined by the provisions of the charter and bylaws. Differences can distinguish privileges in voting power, dividends, and liquidation procedures.

CLASS ONE RAILROAD. A United States railroad that has annual revenues of more than $10 million. Only railroads that are designated as Class One can use debt securities to borrow money without guarantees from a commercial bank or a parent company.

CLASS PRICE. Two different groups of people are charged two different prices for the same commodity, with the group less knowledgeable about the market charged a higher price.

CLASS SYSTEM. The stagger system of electing board directors in which only part of the board comes up for re-election in any one year.

CLAYTON ANTITRUST ACT. Federal statute passed in 1914 as an amendment to the Sherman Antitrust Act, prohibiting business monopolies and trade restraints in domestic industries.

CLEAN. If a block positioner can match buy orders and sell orders without taking the security into his or her inventory, thus taking a risk, the transaction is said to be "clean." (Also called "natural.") A clean balance sheet will be free of debt.

CLEAN ON THE PRINT. A block trade which can be executed on the floor without a broker-dealer firm acting as principal in the deal.

CLEAN OPINION. An auditing opinion stating that the auditor found a company's financial records to be accurate and reflective of the company's actual state.

CLEAR. Verifying the details of a security's trade before its settlement.

CLEARED. When the purchaser of a security pays for and receives the security.

CLEARING AGREEMENT. A document in which one broker-dealer agrees to execute and settle another broker-dealer's transaction for a fee.

CLEARING HOUSE. A place where deals between member firms are executed and settled.

CLEARING HOUSE FUNDS. Funds designated by a check that must clear a local or regional bank before the payee can receive credit.

CLEARING MEMBER. An exchange member who is granted membership in a clearing house.

CLEARING THE MARKET. Changing the price of a securities transaction to the satisfaction of the buyer and seller.

CLIENT SERVICE REPRESENTATIVE. A salaried person who acts as a registered representative in discount brokerage firms or handles walk-in clients and one-time transactions in the larger firms.

CLIFFORD TRUST. A trust fund established between two or more living people, with assets pledged for at least 10 years. Income from the assets is given to one party until the trust ends, at which time the assets revert to the grantor. The IRS considers income as a gift to the recipient.

CLIMAX. A time of heavy trading after a long rise or drop in market prices. The climax signals the top or bottom, so prices usually change directions following it.

CLIQUE. Several investors band together to form a group and agree to match orders and to sell short or wash sales in an effort to manipulate the price of a security. This act is now illegal.

CLONE MONEY-MARKET FUND. A type of money market fund that is readily created, but must put up a specific percentage of its assets as a reserve.

CLOSE. The final 30 seconds of trading on the stock exchange floor, designated by a bell that rings continuously for the 30 seconds.

CLOSE A POSITION. Eliminating an investment from a portfolio, usually by selling if a long position exists or by buying in the case of a short security position.

CLOSED ACCOUNT. A brokerage account that the customer or broker has terminated. Although the brokerage house by law retains transaction records, all securities and money involved are sent to the customer.

CLOSED-END INVESTMENT COMPANY. A company that keeps re-investing shareholders' money in securities instead of issuing new shares or redeeming existing ones.

CLOSED-END MANAGEMENT COMPANY. A management investment company that issues a specific number of shares which the holder usually cannot redeem at his or her option. The shares normally are redeemed through secondary market deals.

CLOSED-END MORTGAGE BOND. A bond issue that prohibits the property that secures it from being used as collateral on any future bond issues.

CLOSED-END MUTUAL FUND. A mutual fund that has a specific number of outstanding shares, is priced according to supply and demand, and is traded on the major stock exchanges. Ordinary mutual funds usually sell unlimited shares which normally can be redeemed for their net asset value.

CLOSED OUT. An investor who cannot meet his or her margin call or who cannot cover a short sale must liquidate his or her position.

CLOSED TRADE. A transaction closed when a security that was paid for earlier is sold.

CLOSELY HELD. Used to describe a company owned by a few stockholders. Closely held companies are tightly governed by law; the maximum number of shareholders and the transfer of shares are restricted.

CLOSE MONEY. When the price differences among successive stock transactions are fractional or when the spread between the bid and ask on the last trade is barely any different.

CLOSE PRICES. When the difference between bid and ask prices are fractional.

CLOSE THE BOOKS. When a company's board of directors declares dividends after temporarily closing the company's stock transfer books.

CLOSE TO THE MONEY. A put or call contract with a striking price that is close to the current market value of the underlying security.

CLOSING COSTS. The amount of money needed to transfer property from one person to another. Closing costs take care of title searches, attorney fees, insurance costs, and filing charges.

CLOSING OF TRANSFER BOOKS. A company's board of directors sets a date after which stock ownership cannot be transferred for a specific time period. During that time, dividends will be paid and meetings will be held. A company closes the transfer books in an effort to avoid confusion.

CLOSING PRICE. A security's last transaction price for the day.

CLOSING PURCHASE TRANSACTIONS. An option writer will purchase the same series, thereby creating a net zero position, thus closing the position.

CLOSING QUOTE. The final bid or offer on a security before the exchange closes for the day.

CLOSING RANGE. The range of a commodity's high and low prices in one trading day, indicating the amount of money it would cost to buy or sell the commodity.

CLOSING SALE TRANSACTIONS. Options deals in which contract holders liquidate their positions and end their obligations to buy or sell shares of the underlying securities.

CLOSING TRANSACTION. One securities deal that cancels another securities deal, both of which carry the same terms.

CLUB FINANCING. A number of banks that are about the same size band together to underwrite a security; each bank subscribes to equal amounts of the issue.

CMO. *See* Collateralized Mortgage Obligation.

CODE OF ARBITRATION. The National Association of Securities Dealers has established this set of rules and regulations to govern submitting and arbitrating disagreements among exchange members or between members and nonmembers.

CODE OF PROCEDURE. The National Association of Securities Dealers has established this set of rules and regulations to govern the submission and settlement of complaints that arise concerning possible violations of fair practice laws.

COD TRANSACTION. A broker buys a security for a client's account and delivers the security to the client's agent, who then pays for the purchase. Also known as "delivery against cost" and "delivery versus payment."

COEFFICIENT OF DETERMINATION. A gauge that determines the amount of market-imposed risk on a specific security.

COINCIDENT ECONOMIC INDICATORS. An economic gauge that follows an industry sector or the economy in general.

COINSURANCE. The sharing of an insurance risk. This is typical when a claim may be of a substantial size that one company may not want to underwrite the entire risk.

COLD CALL. A broker or agent of a broker calls a potential investor for the first time in an effort either to sell a security or to set up a meeting in which a security will be discussed.

COLD CANVASSING. Making up a list of potential investors without any prior knowledge of the customers or whether they have ever purchased securities. One example of cold canvassing is pulling names from a telephone book.

COLD IN HAND. A person with no money to invest.

COLLAPSE. Either the sudden drop in a stock's price or the failure of a business venture.

COLLAR. The lowest interest rate a bond purchaser can accept or the lowest price the issuer can accept from the underwriters.

COLLAR PRICING. A company agrees on a specific price range in which a stock will be priced instead of establishing an exact cost per share.

COLLATERAL. An asset such as an automobile or a piece of property that a person uses to take out a loan, promising to give the asset to the lender if loan payments cannot be met.

COLLATERAL BOND. A bond that is used to secure a loan.

COLLATERALIZED MORTGAGE OBLIGATION (CMO). A security which pools together mortgages and separates them into short-, medium-, and long-term positions. This system provides interest and principal in a more predictable manner.

COLLATERAL SURETY. Commercial paper such as a stock or a bond that is used to secure a loan.

COLLATERAL TRUST BOND. A bond secured by securities owned by the issuing company. A trustee holds the securities for the bond holder.

COLLATERAL TRUST NOTES. Bonds (usually issued by holding companies, investment trusts, or railroads) that are secured by other stocks or bonds.

COLLECTIBLE. An item that has an additional value because of its beauty, rarity, or historical representation. Rare coins, antiques, and old baseball cards are considered collectibles.

COLLECTION RATIO. Divide a company's accounts receivable total by its average daily sales to come up with the number of days it takes to turn a dollar entered under accounts receivable into a dollar entered under cash.

COLLECTIVE BARGAINING. Union members, representing workers at a particular company, negotiate with company management to arrive at fair and equitable salaries, safe working conditions, and acceptable fringe benefits for the employees.

COLLECTIVE INVESTMENT FUND. An investment trust with pension and profit-sharing funds commingled following Internal Revenue Service approval.

COLLECTIVE OWNERSHIP. Several individuals or companies own an asset, with no one entity owning any specific portion of the asset.

COLOR. The specifications, such as market conditions, investor preferences, and yield spreads for a particular security.

COMBINATION. The position of a group of options other than a straddle, which is made up of puts and calls.

COMBINATION BOND. A government-issued debt instrument fully backed by the issuer and by revenues from the project for which it paid, such as toll from a toll road or entrance fees from a city zoo.

COMBINED FINANCIAL STATEMENT. A financial statement that adds the assets and liabilities of at least two affiliated companies, but that does not necessarily reflect investment strength or credit responsibility.

COMEX. A commodity exchange in New York City formed by the merger of four past exchanges. This exchange trades futures in sugar, coffee, petroleum, metals, and financial instruments.

COMFORT LETTER. A document the issuer or seller of a security provides his or her underwriter or agent with in which the issuer or seller promises to repay any expenses incurred because of litigation, tender offers, or omissions in the registration.

COMING TO ME. Over-the-counter traders who give a price quote that is not their own. While the price does represent another dealer's market, it does not necessarily reflect the over-the-counter trader's final offer.

COMMERCE. The congressional labor legislation basis for trade, communication, etc., between states and nations.

COMMERCIAL BANK. A banking corporation which accepts deposits and makes loans to businesses regardless of its other services.

COMMERCIAL BAR. A brick of a precious metal that is used for nonmonetary purposes. For example, a brick of silver that will be melted down to make jewelry is a commercial bar, while a brick of silver that will be used to make dimes is not.

COMMERCIAL BORROWER. A person who borrows money for a business venture.

COMMERCIAL CREDIT. Credit extended to businesses for the production of goods and services. This is distinguished from personal, investment, agriculture, and bank credit.

COMMERCIAL DISCOUNTS. Discounts given to encourage prompt payments.

COMMERCIAL EXCHANGE OF PHILADELPHIA. A commodities exchange that deals in feeds, flour, and grains.

COMMERCIAL HEDGER. A company that tries to stabilize the price of a commodity by taking a position in the commodities markets because it must use the commodity in producing its own goods. For example, ABC Paint Company may take a position in petroleum futures because they want to lock in prices at which they buy raw materials or sell their products.

COMMERCIAL LETTER OF CREDIT. A document that lends its credit to a customer to permit him or her to finance a business transaction. This allows the customer to draw drafts on the bank under the agreed upon terms.

COMMERCIAL LOAN. Short-term financing to act as a company's working capital.

COMMERCIAL MORTGAGE. A loan that has real estate as collateral and is used for a business venture.

COMMERCIAL PAPER. An unsecured short-term debt instrument issued by a company with only its credit rating backing the security.

COMMERCIAL PAPER HOUSE. A dealer who buys commercial paper at one price, then tries to sell it at another.

COMMERCIAL STOCKS. Stocks owned by the U.S. Department of Agriculture, representing grain at major grain centers.

COMMERCIAL WELLS. Drilling sites that produce enough oil and gas to be workable as a corporate venture.

COMMINGLING. Mixing an investor's securities with those owned by a company in the company's proprietary accounts.

COMMISSION. Fees charged by a firm for executing trades.

COMMISSION BROKER. An agent, usually a floor broker who executes the public's trades for a commission.

COMMITMENT FEE. A person planning to issue securities gives money to investors to motivate them to buy the securities when they are issued. By paying a commitment fee, the issuer is assured the funds will be available later for the investors to buy the shares.

COMMITTEE. A group of exchange employees responsible for admissions and the conduct of members.

COMMITTEE FOR AN INCOMPETENT. A person appointed to handle the financial affairs for someone else who has been deemed physically or mentally unable to handle his or her own money.

COMMODITIES EXCHANGE CENTER. An organization used by New York's four commodities exchanges for clearing transactions and checking quotations.

COMMODITIES FUTURES CONTRACT. A document in which an investor agrees to buy or sell a specific amount of a commodity on a specific future date.

COMMODITIES FUTURES STRADDLE. A transaction in which an investor buys a commodity to be delivered in one month, then sells a contract for the same commodity to be delivered in another month in an effort to profit from any price differences.

COMMODITIES FUTURES TRADING COMMISSION (CFTC). A panel established to regulate commodities exchanges and futures trading.

COMMODITY. An agricultural product, mineral, or other tangible asset that investors trade on a cash or futures basis.

COMMODITY-BACKED BOND. A debt instrument that is closely connected to an underlying commodity, such as gold or silver, and that pays interest dividends based on the commodity's current price, thus providing the investor with a hedge against inflation.

COMMODITY EXCHANGE INCORPORATED. A New York commodity exchange that trades in coffee, financial instruments, futures, petroleum, precious metals, and sugar.

COMMODITY FUTURE. A contract to buy or sell a specific commodity at a specified price at a certain future date.

COMMODITY FUTURES TRADING COMMISSION. A committee that regulates commodity exchange trading.

COMMODITY PAPER. A loan with a commodity as its collateral.

COMMODITY POOL OPERATOR. A person who pools funds to be used to trade in commodities futures contracts to benefit the people who put money into the pool.

COMMODITY STANDARD. A monetary system in which commodities are exchanged for a standing currency base such as gold or silver.

COMMODITY TAX STRADDLE. An individual profits from a commodity investment, then looks for a capital loss with which to offset the profit in the current tax year.

COMMODITY TRADING ADVISOR. A futures expert who advises investors on how and when to buy and sell futures contracts.

COMMON LAW. Any legal precedent that has been set by a history of court decisions as opposed to a precedent set by a specific ruling.

COMMON MESSAGE SWITCH. A computer that connects members with the New York and American stock exchanges over which order instructions are transmitted.

COMMON STOCK. A unit of ownership in a public company for which the holder can vote on matters and receive dividends from the company's growth, but he or she is the last to receive assets if the company liquidates. It differs from preferred stock in that preferred stock has a set dividend rate.

COMMON STOCK EQUIVALENTS. Securities that can be converted into common stock of the same company.

COMMON STOCK FUND. A mutual fund with a portfolio consisting of only common stock.

COMMON STOCK INDEX. The average current price of a stock versus its average price at an earlier date.

COMMON STOCK RATIO. The percentage of a company's permanent capital that comes from common stock, paid-in surplus, and retained earnings. When added together, the bond ratio, preferred stock ratio, and common stock ratio equal 100 percent.

COMMON TRUST FUND. A fund held by a bank or trust company in which the money is collectively invested and profits are reinvested.

COMMUNISM. A political system in which the government controls production and distribution of goods and services.

COMMUNITY PROPERTY. Property and assets acquired during a marriage that are owned equally by each spouse. To dispose of the assets, both spouses must consent. If the couple were to break up, the assets would be divided 50-50.

COMPARATIVE STATEMENTS. Financial documents that cover different time periods (but similar in content), used to compare a company's financial situation and to predict where the company is heading.

COMPARISON RETURNS. Comparing the return of a taxable investment versus a non-taxable investment.

COMPENSATING BALANCE. The amount of money a bank requires a depositor to have in an account before the bank will have credit available for the depositor.

COMPETITIVE BID. The awarding of an underwriting contract to the highest bidder based on the best price and terms.

COMPETITIVE TRADER. An exchange member who trades stock for an account in which he or she holds some interest.

COMPLETE AUDIT. A thorough study of a firm's accounts, internal controls and subsidiary records to make sure the firm is obeying the law, keeping accurate financial records, and using appropriate accounting practices.

COMPLETION PROGRAM. A limited partnership that takes over an oil-drilling operation when it becomes apparent the well has enough to support a commercial venture. Completion programs allow limited partnerships to profit from the oil industry without spending money for exploratory drilling.

COMPLIANCE DEPARTMENT. A broker-dealer department responsible for ensuring all members adhere to Securities and Exchange Commission regulations.

COMPLIANCE REGISTERED OPTIONS PRINCIPAL (CROP). The person who audits a brokerage firm and must determine if the firm is trading options in accordance with federal and state law and with the rules and regulations of the Securities and Exchange Commission and the self-regulatory organization.

COMPONENT OPERATING FIRM. A company owned or controlled by a holding company system that functions as a unit of that system.

COMPOSITE. An average that measures results using information from several different sources. For example, the Dow Jones Composite uses industrial, transportation, and utility averages.

COMPOSITE COMMODITY STANDARD. A system in which a monetary unit is defined in terms of a specific number of commodities instead of gold or silver, which normally serve as the currency base.

COMPOSITE LIMIT ORDER BOOK. A proposed central computer that would show all buy and sell orders of securities, and ultimately could eliminate the need for exchanges because brokers could execute orders directly through the computer.

COMPOSITION. Creditors agree to accept partial instead of full payments from a person or business that cannot pay off debts. By doing this, the troubled business can avoid bankruptcy, and the creditors are assured some payment. If the business were to go through bankruptcy, some of the creditors might not receive any payments, or the payments may be lower.

COMPOUND ARBITRAGE. When arbitrage is achieved using at least four different markets.

COMPOUND GROWTH RATE. A number indicating how much a company will grow; profits are taken for each of the last five years and compounded every year. Analysts use this method to determine whether a company is a worthwhile investment.

COMPOUND INTEREST. Interest that is computed on the original amount plus all accumulated interest.

COMPOUND INTEREST BONDS. Municipal bonds that are issued at a price which is much lower than their face values, and which pay no periodic interest. These bonds can be redeemed at par when they mature.

COMPOUND INTEREST METHOD OF DEPRECIATION. A system in which the salvage value of a capital asset, at the time it will be discarded, is subtracted from the asset's original cost, with the difference spread into equal installments for the duration of the asset's life. During each installment, the depreciation amount is reduced by the amount of interest it would earn.

COMPTROLLER OF THE CURRENCY. A U.S. official who charters, examines, liquidates, and supervises the nation's banks.

COMPUTER ASSISTED EXECUTION SYSTEM. A communication network, sponsored by the National Association of Securities Dealers, that connects broker-dealers to over-the-counter market makers and through which the broker-dealers can order the execution of certain transactions.

COMPUTER INFORMATION SERVICES. A network through which broker-dealers and commodity futures merchants buy processing, reporting, and surveillance services.

COMPUTERIZED MARKET TIMING SYSTEM. A computer network that compiles information about buys and sells, then evaluates trends so the user can decide when and if to invest in particular funds.

CONCESSION. The amount paid per share or per bond to members of a selling group in a corporate underwriting.

CONDENSED STATEMENT. A financial document in which minor details are grouped together in one section so the public can study the document more easily.

CONDITIONAL SALES AGREEMENT. The issuer of an equipment trust certificate pledges a minimum amount of equity, but does not acquire title to the equipment until the entire debt is retired.

CONDOR SPREAD. A vertical bull and bear spread on either put or call options and without any duplicate strike prices.

CONDUIT THEORY. An investment organization passes along interest, dividends, and capital gains to investors so that they, rather than the company, will have to pay the federal and state taxes.

CONDUIT-TYPE CUSTOMER. The customer of a broker-dealer who does not reveal his or her customers' identities. Financial institutions often are conduit-type customers.

CONFIRMATION. Indicates that at least two indexes verify a market trend or turning point.

CONFIRMATION SLIP. Verification that a broker sends to a client acknowledging a transaction.

CONFLICT OF INTEREST. A person who is supposed to be objective in a specific transaction places his or her personal interests above that of the customer by taking a beneficial interest in the outcome of the transaction. For example, a city council member who owns stock in a company would have a conflict of interest if the council voted to give the company a zoning variance.

CONFORMED COPY. A document copy that contains all of the legal features of the original, such as a notary seal and a signature.

CONGLOMERATE. The merging or combination of unrelated companies.

CONGLOMERATE MERGER. The joining of two companies involved in unrelated businesses.

CONSENT TO SERVICE. A document that authorizes one individual to act as an attorney on behalf of another individual in accepting legal processes.

CONSERVATIVE PORTFOLIO. A group of investments chosen because they are safe, with the investor not entering any risky ventures.

CONSERVATOR. A person appointed by a court to handle the financial interests of another person who has been deemed incompetent because of age or some physical or mental inadequacy.

CONSIDERATION. Cash or securities with which a person buys title to an issuer's equity or debt securities.

CONSOL. British bonds issued during the Napoleonic wars which paid a fixed coupon rate and never matured.

CONSOLIDATED BALANCE SHEET. A financial statement that shows a parent company's total assets and liabilities without breaking the numbers down to show the assets and liabilities of the company's subsidiaries.

CONSOLIDATED MORTGAGE BOND. A debt instrument that has only one coupon rate of interest. This type of bond is issued in an effort to obtain money to refund previously issued mortgage bonds with different interest rates and maturity dates.

CONSOLIDATED QUOTATION SYSTEM. Gathers current bid and asked prices of listed securities from all of the different exchanges, then distributes the figures to subscribers.

CONSOLIDATED SINKING FUND. A sinking fund designed to serve at least two bond issues.

CONSOLIDATED STATEMENT OF FINANCIAL POSITION. A document in which a company's current financial status is reported.

CONSOLIDATED TAPE. A network that continuously reports on all securities transactions on every exchange.

CONSOLIDATED TAX RETURN. The combined tax returns of all of a company's affiliates and subsidiaries.

CONSOLIDATION. Two or more companies combine to form one new company.

CONSOLIDATION LOAN. A loan that combines all of a person's or business's debts into one so that only one payment needs to be made. A consolidation loan usually is taken out to reduce interest rates: the person or business would be paying interest on only one loan, instead of on five or six.

CONSORTIUM. A group of companies or organizations with members pooling their resources toward one common goal.

CONSTANT DOLLAR PLAN. A method in which an individual invests a fixed amount of money in a security at set intervals. More shares will be purchased when the price is lower and less when the price is higher.

CONSTANT DOLLARS. A hypothetical unit of purchasing power, measured as the number of dollars in a company's base year. Dollars of other years are adjusted against the constant dollars to determine the company's actual purchasing power.

CONSTANT FACTOR. The total amount of principal and interest a person or business must pay to retire a debt.

CONSTANT RATIO PLAN. A system in which a specific dollar ratio is maintained in two different types of investments. For example, if an investor had $100,000 and wanted a 50-50 ratio maintained in stocks and bonds, $50,000 would be invested in each. If the investment rose to $150,000, adjustments would be made so that $75,000 would be invested in stocks and $75,000 would be invested in bonds.

CONSTRUCTION AND DEVELOPMENT REIT. A real estate trust fund from which developers can borrow to build a commercial or residential development.

CONSTRUCTION LOAN. A short-term loan used to pay for building a real estate project, with loan funds disbursed to the borrower as needed and repaid after the project is completed. While the interest rate on construction loans usually is higher than the prime rate, the effective yield also tends to be high, and the lender can maintain a secure interest in the property.

CONSTRUCTIVE RECEIPT. The actual date a taxpayer receives income, as defined by the Internal Revenue Service. Constructive receipt is the actual date the income is available, even if the taxpayer doesn't actually exercise his or her right to take possession of the money. For example, if an investor receives an interest check on December 30, he or she must report it as income for that year, even if the check isn't cashed until after January 1.

CONSUMER CREDIT PROTECTION ACT OF 1968. Also known as the Truth in Lending Act, this law requires lenders to tell borrowers the annual percentage rates, the total cost of the loan including interest, and all loan terms.

CONSUMER DEBENTURE. An investment note that the issuing financial institution markets directly to the public in an effort to raise money to make loans.

CONSUMER PRICE INDEX (CPI). The primary gauge of inflation in the United States, the CPI is calculated by establishing the price of a fixed basket of goods and services, which are selected because of their direct impact on average citizens. Included in the basket are such things as food, gasoline, housing, and medical care. Increases in the costs of such items indicate a rise in the inflation rate.

CONSUMPTION. Using a product until it has no further value.

CONTANGO. When commodities futures prices rise as maturities lengthen thus creating negative spreads as contracts go further out. These increases usually reflect costs involved in handling the goods.

CONTINGENT IMMUNIZATION. An active bond management system that involves a minimum compound annual return and in which strategies are applied to the portfolio as long as its value is more than that needed to achieve the minimum return.

CONTINGENT LIABILITIES. A bank's responsibility to honor letters of credit or other obligations, and the responsibility of a customer, whose account will be charged, if he or she opens a line of credit.

CONTINGENT ORDER. An order to buy one security and sell another only if the deal can be made at a stipulated price difference.

CONTINUED BOND. A bond that never matures and continues to pay dividends indefinitely.

CONTINUOUS MARKET. A security that is frequently sold, has a narrow spread, experiences minimal price changes, can be promptly executed, and is liquid.

CONTINUOUS NET SETTLEMENT. The National Securities Clearing Corporation becomes the intermediary between two brokers involved in a securities transaction, thus creating a securities balance account. Depending on whether the firm was buying or selling, the account is adjusted up or down each day. Most securities deals are settled in this manner.

CONTRA BROKER. The broker handling the other side of a trade. When buying, the seller is the contra broker.

CONTRACT. An agreement between two or more individuals for which certain rights and acts are exchanged and bound by law.

CONTRACT BROKER. One stock exchange member who trades for other exchange members.

CONTRACT GRADES. A commodity that can be traded on a futures contract, with superior grades that carry a premium, and lower grades that sell at a discount.

CONTRACT SHEET. The Securities Industry Automation Corporation prepares this sheet daily from information provided to it by brokers. The sheet covers transaction information, including whether there are problems or disagreements over the pending settlement.

CONTRACTS IN FOREIGN CURRENCY. A document in which investors agree to buy and sell a specific amount of one country's currency for another country's currency at an agreed upon rate.

CONTRACTUAL PLAN. A plan in which mutual funds are used to buy additional fund shares, with the investor agreeing to buy a specific dollar amount and paying on an installment basis.

CONTRARIAN. An investor who does the opposite of most other investors. This investor believes that if others say the market is going up, they are only saying so because they are fully invested, which means the market actually is at its peak and will begin to decline. In addition, when others say the market is going down, the contrarian believes they are saying this only because they have sold out, therefore the market actually will go up.

CONTROLLED ADJUSTABLE RATE PREFERRED STOCK. A preferred stock with a dividend that changes according to the varying Treasury security rate. The issuer maintains an asset base to make sure the company can pay changing dividends, thus making it "controlled."

CONTROLLED COMMODITIES. The trading of commodities futures are federally regulated to prevent fraud and manipulation in the market.

CONTROLLED CORPORATION. One company controlled by another company, with the controlling company owning at least 51 percent of the other company's stock.

CONTROLLED FOREIGN CORPORATION. A foreign company that has five or fewer U.S. citizens with voting shares.

CONTROLLER OR COMPTROLLER. The division of a brokerage house responsible for preparing financial statements, complying with the SEC, and supervising internal audits.

CONTROLLING INTEREST. When a person, family, or group owns more of a company's voting shares of stock than anyone else. Controlling interest is either more than 50 percent, or can be less than 50 percent if no other investor holds a higher amount of shares. For example, if Janet Jeffries owns 30 percent of the voting stock, but the remaining 70 percent is divided among 10 other people, with no one person holding more than 29 percent, Janet Jeffries still has controlling interest because no one else has enough shares of stock to out vote her.

CONTROL STOCK. Securities owned by those who have a controlling interest.

CONVENIENCE SHELF. A registration statement for a security that will be offered publicly for sale. While this particular registration does not require information concerning the price or the underwriter, it does stipulate the maximum number of shares that can be sold.

CONVENTIONAL LOAN. A mortgage loan secured by real estate instead of by a government agency, and with a fixed interest rate and fixed loan payments for the life of the loan.

CONVENTIONAL MORTGAGE. A residential mortgage loan with a fixed interest rate and term, having regular monthly payments due usually for 20 or 30 years, and is secured by the property itself. A conventional mortgage is not insured or guaranteed by the Federal Housing Administration or the Veterans Administration.

CONVENTIONAL OPTION. A put or call option that was negotiated outside of a listed option market.

CONVENTIONAL PASS THROUGH. A security issued by a financial institution that represents a part of a mortgage pool. The government does not guarantee interest or principal.

CONVERGENCE. The price of a futures contract moves toward the price of its underlying cash commodity as the contract nears expiration. Because of its time value, the contract price is higher at the beginning, but then goes down.

CONVERSION. The exchange of one type of security for another.

CONVERSION CHARGE. Some mutual funds require the investor to pay a fee if he or she switches from one fund to another within the same class.

CONVERSION PARITY. The dollar values of a convertible security and the security into which it can be converted are the same.

CONVERSION POINT. When the amount of money it takes to convert a stock or bond is equal to the security's current market price plus any accrued interest.

CONVERSION PREMIUM. The difference of a convertible security's market value above the price of its underlying stock.

CONVERSION PRICE. An underlying security's value after it has been converted into common stock at the conversion ratio.

CONVERSION RATE. The dollar amount of a bond's par value that can be exchanged for one share of common stock.

CONVERSION RATIO. The number of company shares a convertible security can be converted into. For example, if one share of a security can be converted into 50 shares of Trumbell stock, then the conversion ratio is 50:1.

CONVERSION VALUE. The value of the number of shares into which a convertible security can be exchanged. The conversion rate multiplied by the current market value equals the conversion value.

CONVERTIBLE CURRENCY. Money that can be exchanged easily for a precious metal or another currency.

CONVERTIBLE DEBENTURES. A security that carries a fixed interest rate and has a specific maturity date, can be traded for stock at any time, but also provides the issuer with the right to call it in or redeem it for cash or common stock at any time.

CONVERTIBLE HEDGE. When an investor sells short his or her shares of a company's common stock, while at the same time creating a long position with convertible bonds from the same company.

CONVERTIBLE MORTGAGE. A mortgage, usually on commercial properties, in which pension funds receive interest, appreciation is based on any rent increases, and the fund carries an option that allows for conversion into equity ownership.

CONVERTIBLE SECURITY. Corporate securities that can be exchanged easily for common stock in the same company upon demand by the stockholder.

CONVEYANCE. A property deed, and therefore ownership, which is transferred from one person to another.

COOKED BOOKS. Falsified financial records used to entice investors to buy more shares of stock by making the records look like the company will be making outstanding profits when, in reality, it will not.

COOLING OFF PERIOD. A period of time, usually 20 days, that must elapse between the filing of a registration statement with the SEC and the offering of securities to the public.

COOPERATIVE. An organization owned by its members, who pool their resources to achieve a common goal. In a food cooperative, for example, a group of people get together so they can buy large quantities of food at discount prices.

COOPERATIVE APARTMENT. A multi-unit residential complex in which each tenant has an interest in the complex, but does not own his or her apartment unit.

COOPERATIVE BUILDING. Building tenants own stock in the corporation that owns the building. Instead of paying rent, the tenants pay a proportionate fixed rate to cover the building's maintenance and operating costs.

CO-ORIGINATOR. The customers of several surety companies get together to invest in a specific security. Each customer is a co-originator.

CORNERING THE MARKET. Holding enough shares of a security to be able to manipulate the price.

CORPORATE AGENT. A trust company that acts as a corporation's or government's agent in a variety of investment transactions.

CORPORATE BOND. A corporation-issued, long-term debt instrument.

CORPORATE BOND UNIT TRUSTS. A trust unit similar to that of the Government National Mortgage Association, but that has no principal or monthly return.

CORPORATE EQUIVALENT YIELD. The yield from a corporate bond selling at par must equal the yield from a government security selling at a discount.

CORPORATE FINANCING COMMITTEE. A panel that works with the National Association of Securities Dealers' Board of Governors in reviewing documents that underwriters file with the Securities and Exchange Commission to make sure the underwriters' markups are fair.

CORPORATE INCOME FUND. A fixed-unit investment trust containing fixed-income securities and paying net investment income each month.

CORPORATE INDENTURE. A document in which a bank, protecting the interest of the lender, agrees to act as an intermediary between a company issuing bonds and the investors buying the bonds.

CORPORATE RE-ACQUISITION. A company tries to buy back its own securities through a tender offer.

CORPORATE SHELL. A company that has no fixed assets other than its cash, name, and stock exchange listing.

CORPORATE TAX EQUIVALENT. The rate of return a par bond must carry to have the same aftertax yield to maturity as a given bond.

CORPORATION. An association owned by its shareholders and considered to be a legal entity. Chartered by a U.S. state or the federal government, this "legal person" may own property, incur debts, and may sue or be sued. The owners have limited liability.

CORPUS. The principal amount of a debt security, or the underlying assets in a trust agreement.

CORRECTION. The reversal, usually short-term, of a security's price. Reversals are common in any long-term price trend.

CORRELATION COEFFICIENT. A statistical measure of how two market movements are related.

CORRESPONDENCY SYSTEM. The manner in which independent loan correspondents establish and administer mortgage loans for investors.

COST ACCOUNTING. Gives a company's management the figures needed to evaluate production costs.

COST BASIS. The original cost of an asset less depreciation.

COST-BENEFIT ANALYSIS. Determining whether the benefits of a specific decision will outweigh its costs. For example, a company will use the cost-benefit analysis to determine whether buying a copying machine will cost more money than it will save in labor.

COST FACTORS. A consumer credit supplier's business expenses upon which his or her fees are based.

COST LEDGER. A subsidiary's financial statement with each job, operation, process, and other expenses given a separate, detailed listing so they ultimately can be verified and reconciled with the parent company's general accounting books.

COST OF CAPITAL. The amount of money a company could make if it invested in another venture with an equal risk.

COST OF FUNDS. A percentage of the average amount of money saved or borrowed is paid or accrued in interest or dividends on that money.

COST OF GOODS SOLD. The amount of money spent during a specific accounting period on labor, material, and production.

COST-OF-LIVING ADJUSTMENT. Based on the Consumer Price Index, a company adjusts the salaries of its employees to compensate for changes in the amount of money it takes to live at a certain level. For example, if a company did not make cost-of-living adjustments, an employee making $15,000 in 1975 would not be able to live in the same style in 1990 if he or she still was making $15,000. Because it costs more to live each year, the employee, in essence, would be making less.

COST-PLUS CONTRACT. A document in which a product's selling price is based on its production costs added to a fixed fee. Such contracts are common on new products that have no pricing history. For example, if a company designed a machine that could translate a dog's barks into human words, the company would use a cost-plus contract because it has no other way of determining how much to charge for the machine since nothing like it has existed before. On the other hand, if the company designed a new flea collar, the price probably would be based on what flea collars have sold for in the past.

COST PURCHASE ACCOUNTING. A system allowing a company that owns less than one-fifth of another company's stock to include the stock's dividends in its own income.

COST-PUSH INFLATION. When the costs of labor and materials go up, the prices of the goods also go up.

COST RECORDS. Documents that verify the amount of money a company spent to produce goods or to provide services, including vouchers and invoices.

COSTS THEORY OF CAPITALIZATION. A system in which a company's capitalization is determined by the amount of out-of-the-pocket money that was invested in its fixed assets and by the amount of money it takes to run the company.

COSURETY. A surety company of a group executing a bond.

COUGARS. Certificates on government receipts which show interest in principal or in coupon payments to be made later on particular U.S. Treasury bond issues.

COUNCIL OF ECONOMIC ADVISORS. A panel of economists, selected by the president of the United States, that advises him on economic policies and helps him draw up a budget.

COUNTER-CYCLICAL SECURITIES. Corporation-issued securities in which earnings are always going in the opposite direction of the general economy.

COUNTERMAND. Canceling an order or command before the order or command has been executed.

COUNTERSPECULATION. In an effort to counteract investor influence on prices, the government (in a controlled economy) determines what prices would prevail if the buyers and sellers imposed no restrictions. The government guarantees the estimated amount, then reaches the price by buying sales.

COUPON. A certificate that accompanies a bond and carries the amount and the date interest is due. The certificate is torn off and presented when the investor wants an interest payment.

COUPON BOND. A debt instrument with a detachable coupon. Anyone who has physical possession of the coupon can present it to an agent for payment of any interest due.

COUPON RATE. A bond's annual rate of interest, expressed as a percentage of the bond's face value.

COUPON ROLLOVER DATE. The day a new interest rate on a floating-rate security will be established.

COUPON YIELD. Divide a bond's yearly interest rate by its face value, which equals the coupon rate.

COVARIANCE. The relationship between two variables multiplied by the standard deviation of each.

COVERAGE RATIO. The ratio between debt instrument payments and income before taxes, indicating whether or not a company will be able to cover its debt service.

COVER BID. The second highest bid in a competitive distribution.

COVERED ARBITRAGE. An investor uses forward cover—a contract for future delivery—to eliminate the exchange risks involved in an arbitrage between different currencies.

COVERED FORWARD SALE. The owner of a commodity sells the commodity for delivery and payment at a later time.

COVERED INTEREST PARITY. A forward exchange rate differential will equal the difference between foreign and domestic currency interest rates, which will bring the differential to near zero.

COVERED MARGIN. The interest rate margin between two different currency instruments after considering the cost of the forward cover.

COVERED OPTION. When a person who is selling an option owns either the underlying security or another option with the same terms, the sold option is considered a covered option.

COVERED WRITER. An investor who owns a stock sells options against that stock so he or she can collect premium income. If a person writes a call option and the stock price drops, the investor can hold onto the stock. If the price goes up, the investor probably will have to give it up to the person buying the option.

CPA. *See* Certified Public Accountant.

CPI. *See* Consumer Price Index.

CPI-W FUTURES CONTRACT. A commodity futures contract that is based on the government's monthly urban wage and salary index.

CRASH. A dramatic drop in the securities market and in the economy in general.

CREDIT. Any money lent through loans and bonds or money owed for the payment of goods and services.

CREDIT AGREEMENT. A contract between a broker-dealer and client when the client uses credit to purchase securities. The contract stipulates terms of the credit and the amount of margin to be maintained, as well as how interest will be charged.

CREDIT ANALYST. A person who studies and interprets an individual's or a company's financial history to see if the individual or company is creditworthy. Analysts also look at the issuer of a corporate or municipal bond to decide the bond's credit ratio.

CREDIT DEPARTMENT. An area within broker-dealer firms where margin accounts are maintained and supervised, and where the financial history of a client seeking credit is investigated.

CREDITOR. Anyone to whom money is owed.

CREDITOR'S COMMITTEE. A panel that represents the creditors of a company facing bankruptcy. The panel also will represent the creditors of a smaller company that is having financial problems in an effort to resolve the trouble and avoid bankruptcy.

CREDIT RATING. The financial history of an individual or a company, indicating whether the person or business can repay debts. The credit rating is based on the number of outstanding debts and whether debts have been repaid in a timely manner in the past.

CREDIT RISK. The risk that an obligation will not be completed with the result being a loss.

CREDIT SALES. A sale in which time is given for the buyer to make payment.

CREDIT SPREAD. When the value of the long option on a security is less than that of the short option on the same security, the investor gets credit in his or her brokerage account.

CREEPING TENDER OFFER. One person, or a group working together, buys a large percentage of a newly issued stock in an effort to get control of the company without first issuing a proxy statement.

CROP. The principal in an options transaction who must make sure the firm is abiding with options regulations (*see* Compliance Registered Options Principal).

CROP YEAR. In the commodities market, the time between one agricultural harvest and the next. The crop year is different for each crop.

CROSSED MARKET. When one broker's bid is higher than another's lowest offer. While crossed markets sometimes occur, the National Association of Securities Dealers Automated Quotations prohibits brokers from intentionally crossing the market.

CROSS HEDGE. An investor owns one security, then buys or sells a different security that has similar market reaction in an effort to keep from losing money.

CROSS ORDER. One client asks a broker to buy a security, and another client asks the same broker to sell the same security. Such orders cannot be directly paired, and must be executed through the stock exchange.

CROSS PURCHASE. When a broker improperly executes a cross order directly without going through the stock exchange.

CROSS SHAREHOLDING. Two or more companies hold shares of stock in each other.

CROWD. Group of exchange members gathering around the same post to seek executions that are not readily available.

CROWDING OUT. When the government borrows heavily at the same time that businesses and individuals want to borrow, the government, in effect, closes out the latter two groups' ability to borrow. The government, which can afford to pay any interest rate, crowds out individuals and businesses who cannot pay the higher rates, thus slowing down economic activity.

CROWN JEWEL. A company's most valuable asset, with the term used primarily in attracting or dissuading takeover attempts.

CROWN JEWEL DEFENSE. A company's management agrees to sell the company's most valuable asset to another party in an effort to avoid a hostile takeover by a third party. By selling off its most valuable asset, the company becomes less attractive to the party threatening the hostile takeover.

CRUMMY TRUST. A trust fund with a beneficiary who can continually accept valuable assets from anyone and, in turn, give that person an annual exclusion of up to $10,000 from federal gift taxes.

CRUNCH. Financial pressures or actions which produce a financial crisis lead to poor economic conditions in a specific market or in the economy in general.

CRUSH MARGIN. The amount of money a processor earns from selling the derivatives of a product, minus the cost of the product. For example, if a processor made oil and soybean meal, the crush margin would equal the gross amount the processor made after subtracting the amount he or she paid for the soybeans.

CRUSH SPREAD. A futures trader believes discrepancies exist between related products, such as soybeans and their derivatives, and therefore takes a spread position in the market in an effort to profit from the differences.

CRWNS. Currency-related warrants to buy some U.S. Treasury securities that expire in one or two years.

CSE. *See* Cincinnati Stock Exchange.

CSVLI. *See* Cash Surrender Value.

CUFF QUOTE. Without checking the current market conditions, a person takes an educated guess at what he or she believes the bid and ask prices will be on a securities issue.

CULPEPPER SWITCH. A computer based in Culpepper, Virginia, that transfers federal funds and U.S. Treasury securities between the U.S. Federal Reserve System and member banks.

CUM DIVIDEND. An investor buying a stock cum dividend receives the dividend that was declared but not yet paid.

CUM RIGHTS. An investor buying a stock with cum rights receives the rights that were declared but not yet paid.

CUMULATIVE DIVIDEND. A dividend from cumulative preferred stock that has not yet been paid.

CUMULATIVE PREFERRED STOCK. A preferred stock issue on which all dividends that have not been paid will accumulate for the shareholders and will be paid before holders of common stock receive their dividends.

CUMULATIVE RATE OF RETURN. A rate of return that has been compounded for more than one year.

CUMULATIVE VOTING. Stockholders can have as many votes for each share they own as there are directors to be elected. For example, if there are three directors to be appointed, each stockholder is allowed three votes per share of stock.

CURB EXCHANGE. The original name of the American Stock Exchange, so named because securities were traded on the street.

CURRENCY. Any form of money that is in public circulation.

CURRENCY DEVALUATION. The dollar's exchange rate drops because of market or government action. With devaluation, Americans can buy less from other nations with the same dollar.

CURRENCY FUTURES. Futures contracts on major currencies (e.g., the British pound, the German mark and the U.S. dollar) that are held by companies doing worldwide business in an effort to reduce their risks by hedging the value of their home country's currency.

CURRENCY IN CIRCULATION. Paper money and coins that are exchanged widely and daily, as opposed to money in circulation (this also includes checking account deposits, etc.).

CURRENT. In budget and accounting practices this designates the operations of the present fiscal period.

CURRENT ACCOUNT. A bank account from which the depositor can withdraw funds at any time.

CURRENT ASSETS. All of a company's assets that probably will be converted into cash within the company's fiscal year. For example, accounts receivable are considered current assets.

CURRENT COUPON BOND. A debt instrument that has a coupon interest rate that is near its yield to maturity. Such bonds have a competitive cash flow and interest rates that are less likely to change.

CURRENT LIABILITIES. All of a company's debts that are payable within the company's fiscal year. For example, a mortgage payment is considered a current liability.

CURRENT MARKET VALUE. The value of a security based on its closing price of the previous day.

CURRENT MATURITY. The amount of time left on a bond before it matures.

CURRENT PRODUCTION RATE. The maximum interest rate that may be placed on current Government National Mortgage Association mortgage-backed securities. These securities will normally pay half a percentage point below the current rate to cover clerical expenses.

CURRENT RATIO. A company's current assets divided by its current liabilities, which provides a measure of liquidity.

CURRENT SINKER. In an operative bond with a sinking fund obligation, the company must retire part of the outstanding bond issue by exercising a call or through an open market purchase.

CURRENT VALUE ACCOUNTING. An accounting system in which a person's assets are measured according to current prices instead of the prices the person paid when buying the assets.

CURRENT YIELD. A security's dividend divided by its current market value.

CURTSY. The legal interest a man has in any property in his deceased wife's estate.

CUSHION BOND. A callable bond with a market price that is artificially suppressed because of its call price, which helps the bond remain stable during a time of intense interest rate changes.

CUSIP NUMBER. A number assigned by the Committee of Uniform Security Identification Procedure that appears on the face of all securities documents. Each security is given its own number so it can be easily identified.

CUSTODIAL ACCOUNT. An account that an adult creates for a minor child. Since the social security number used on the account is that of the minor, all returns are listed on the child's income tax documents. Minors can only make transactions with the custodian's consent. These may only be cash accounts, not margin.

CUSTODIAN. An agent such as a broker or a bank that stores a customer's investments.

CUSTOMER'S FREE CREDIT BALANCE. The amount of money an investor has in his or her brokerage account that is available for use.

CUSTOMER'S MAN. Synonymous with *Registered Representative* and *Account Executive*, but rarely used as more women enter the industry.

CUSTOMER'S NET DEBIT BALANCE. The New York Stock Exchange provides credit to its member firms so the firms can, in turn, finance their own customers' securities purchases.

CUTOFF POINT. The smallest amount of return allowed on an investment.

CUTTING A LOSS. An individual takes his or her money out of an investment that is losing money and accepts the loss instead of leaving the money in and losing even more.

CUTTING A MELON. Profits, either from securities or employee bonuses, are distributed by either cash or stock dividends.

CYCLE. A constant pattern of reversals.

CYCLICAL STOCK. Securities such as those in automobile manufacturing plants and real estate ventures that rise quickly when the economy is on the upswing and fall when the economy drops. Noncyclical stocks include those in companies that produce items people need no matter what the economy is doing, such as food and drugs.

D

D. Lowercase, it appears in stock transaction tables and indicates the stock has reached its lowest price in the last year.

DAILY ADJUSTABLE TAX EXEMPT SECURITIES. A municipal industrial development revenue bond with interest calculated daily and distributed monthly. It also provides that the holder can redeem the bond at any time for its face value plus any accrued interest.

DAILY BOND BUYER. A daily newspaper directed toward the municipal bond industry, with additional news included for fixed-income investors.

DAILY TRADING LIMIT. The maximum rise or decline permitted by many commodity and option markets in one trading session.

DATED DATE. The effective date of a new bond issue, after which accrued interest is calculated. If the dated date is December 2, for example, and the issue is settled on Dec. 14, the buyer pays the issuer 12 days of accrued interest, but will get the money back when he or she receives the first interest payment.

DATED EARNED SURPLUS. The amount of a company's retained earnings that have accumulated since the company reorganized. This date must be included when the company reports its retained earnings.

DATE OF MATURITY. The designated day an obligation must be paid.

DATE OF RECORD. The last day a new purchaser will be entitled to a dividend. If an investor buys stock before the date of record, he or she will be entitled to receive a dividend from the stock.

DATE OF TRADE. The day a buy or sell order is executed.

DATING. A financial institution extends a company's line of credit further than the institution's usual terms. Financial institutions commonly will do this with companies that have seasonal businesses so the companies can continue operating during the lean months.

DAWN RAIDS. A British company quickly buys a large block of another company's stock at a premium price.

DAYLIGHT TRADING. Buying a security and then selling it the same day (*see* Day Trade).

DAY LOANS. Money that banks or other financial institutions lend to brokers, which brokers need to use as working capital for that particular day.

DAY ORDER. A buy or sell order that expires when the exchange closes for the day. Usually, all buy and sell orders are day orders unless otherwise specified.

DAY-TO-DAY REPO. An open-ended repurchase agreement that expires after one day. If it is not canceled, it is renewed automatically at an adjusted interest rate.

DAY TRADE. The purchase and sell of a stock in one day (*see* Daylight Trading).

DEAD MARKET. A market with little trading and little interest or activity.

DEALER. A person who buys and sells securities for his or her own account and at his or her own risk. A company also can be a dealer.

DEALER ACTIVITIES. Usually refers to a bank that takes on the responsibilities of a dealer by trading and underwriting securities.

DEALER BANK. A bank that continuously deals in government and agency securities.

DEALER FINANCING. A bank or other financial institution that loans a market maker money so that the market maker can carry an inventory of stocks and bonds.

DEALER LOAN. A bank loans a market maker money to finance its trading position.

DEALER MARKET. A market in which all securities are traded between principals for their own accounts, not for the accounts of clients.

DEALER PAPER. Commercial paper an issuer sells to a broker-dealer, who then marks it up and sells it to institutional investors.

DEALER'S TURN. A broker-dealer's profit when he or she buys a security at bid and sells at the offer price.

DEALING FOR NEW TIME. In England, a security is bought or sold in the last two days of an account trading period for the next period.

DEALING WITHIN THE ACCOUNT. In England, either a buy and a sell, or a short securities sale and an agreement to buy the securities back within the same accounting period.

DEATH SENTENCE. All utilities companies must be registered with the Securities and Exchange Commission, and no utility company can have more than three levels (i.e., the parent company, a subsidiary, and a sub-subsidiary). Any other existing affiliate or holding company must be dissolved.

DEATH STOCK. The stock of a company facing bankruptcy or liquidation.

DEBENTURE. A long-term, corporate debt instrument issued without collateral.

DEBENTURE BOND. A long-term debt instrument that has no collateral other than the issuing company's general credit.

DEBENTURE STOCK. A security that has fixed payments at designated intervals. As with a preferred stock, a debenture stock's liquidity is in its equity, not in its debt like a normal debenture.

DEBIT. A bank account entry subtracting a specific amount of money. The opposite of a credit.

DEBIT SPREAD. When an option sold is cheaper than an option bought, thus creating a debit in the investor's brokerage account.

DEBT DISCOUNT. When the proceeds of a loan are lower than the note's face value.

DEBT-EQUITY RATIO. Divide a company's long-term debt by stockholders' equity to determine the level of risk involved in the company's financial structure.

DEBT-EQUITY SWAP. One securities issuer exchanges a new issue from another company for an outstanding bond from that same company. By lowering the company's amount of long-term debt, such a swap often can increase the company's earnings.

DEBT FINANCING. Notes or bonds that are issued so a company can meet its financial obligations.

DEBT INSTRUMENT. Any certificate that represents a loan.

DEBT LIMIT. The maximum amount of money the government can legally owe.

DEBT MONETIZING. The Federal Reserve System issues new fiat money (U.S. currency) to pay-off government debt.

DEBT RATIO. A company's total debt divided by its assets.

DEBT RETIREMENT. A financial obligation that has been repaid in full.

DEBT SECURITY. Any security that represents a loan.

DEBT SERVICE. The annual principal and interest payment on a debt, as required by the debt issuer.

DEBT SERVICE FUND. A fund that pays for an account held to receive interest and principal on general obligation debts.

DEBT SERVICE REQUIREMENT. The amount of money needed to pay interest on a debt, the serial maturities of a serial bond, and money paid to a debt service fund.

DEBT-TO-EQUITY RATIO. A gauge that measures the amount of leverage a company's financial structure has, usually achieved by dividing the par value of the company's preferred stock by its common stock equity, and adding that quotient to the company's long-term debt.

DECAPITALIZE. Withdrawing an investment from a company.

DECAY. The gradual loss of premium over time in an options or futures contract. Also a client disclaiming connection with responsibility for a trade.

DECLARATION DATE. The day a company announces it will pay dividends, when it will pay them, and how much they will be.

DECLARE. A company's board of directors authorizes the company to pay a dividend on a particular day.

DEDICATED BOND PORTFOLIO. An investment portfolio, such as a re-tirement fund, aimed at making future payments with the most cash flow possible from the bonds contained in the portfolio.

DEDUCTION. An IRS-allowed subtraction of an expense from one's adjusted gross income in determining a person's taxable income. These expenses may include charitable contributions, state and local taxes and interest paid.

DEEP BID. A significant, away-from-the-market bid.

DEEP DISCOUNT BOND. A debt instrument issued at par and currently selling for less than 80 percent of its par value.

DE FACTO CORPORATION. A company formed in good faith that in some way failed after there was an act of corporate power.

DEFALCATION. When a fiduciary or representative misappropriates funds.

DEFAULT. When a debtor fails to either pay interest or repay the principal of a loan.

DEFEASANCE. A government or corporation erases a debt from the balance sheet by floating a second bond to retire the first.

DEFEASED BOND-EQUITY SWAP. A bond guarantor swaps its common stock for the same amount of U.S. Treasury securities, which are put in escrow until maturity or until their earliest call date, when they are used to retire the first debt. The dealer who arranged the swap pays for the U.S. Treasury securities by selling the common stock.

DEFENSIVE INDUSTRY. A company that does not suffer financially when the economy is poor, such as a utilities company, and therefore does better than the general market during a recession.

DEFENSIVE INVESTING. Putting money into securities that are safe and stable, even though the profits may not be as great, to avoid risking a loss.

DEFENSIVE PORTFOLIO. A group of investments that probably won't go up or down much, with emphasis placed on the safety of the investments.

DEFENSIVE STOCKS. Stocks that tend to be more stable in times of recession or economic uncertainty in regard to terms of dividends, earnings, and market performance.

DEFERRAL OF TAXES. A company or person can put off paying certain taxes until a later year.

DEFERRED ACCOUNT. Any account, such as an Individual Retirement Account, on which taxes can be paid in a later year.

DEFERRED ANNUITY. An annuity that will not make payments until a specified future date.

DEFERRED ASSET. An asset that cannot be converted easily into cash.

DEFERRED CHARGES. Expenditures on an asset carried forward over a period of time. These are usually monies a company spends to improve the long-term outlook of its business.

DEFERRED GROUP ANNUITY CONTRACT. A single premium deferred annuity is bought for each person covered in an insured pension plan. The amount of the annuity is equal to the amount the person has accrued in benefits for each year.

DEFERRED INTEREST BOND. A bond such as a zero-coupon bond that does not pay interest until a later date.

DEFERRED PAYMENT ANNUITY. An annuity agreement in which the annuitant deposits premiums in a lump sum or in installments at a later date.

DEFERRED PAYMENT NOTE. A debt security with a fixed rate that requires a 25 percent initial payment, with the final payment due several months later.

DEFERRED PROFIT-SHARING PLAN. A company-sponsored retirement plan, with the company donating either 20 percent of the employee's wages or $3,500, whichever is greater, thus reducing taxable income for the year.

DEFERRED SPECIAL ASSESSMENTS. An amount of money that has been assessed against a company or an individual, but has not yet come due.

DEFERRED STOCK. A security with a dividend that will not be paid until after a specific date or until after a designated event has occurred.

DEFICIENCY LETTER. A letter the Securities and Exchange Commission provides a security issuer during registration of a security. The letter advises the issuer that the registration is inadequate, and changes in the registration must be made before the SEC can approve the security.

DEFICIT. A company's liabilities and debts exceed its income and assets, or a company's spending exceeds its budget.

DEFICIT FINANCING. The government borrows money to issue bonds in order to compensate for a revenue shortfall. This procedure strengthens the general economy temporarily, but ultimately becomes a drain because it pushes up interest rates.

DEFICIT NET WORTH. Liabilities exceed assets and capital stock.

DEFICIT SPENDING. The government spends more money than it takes in. This deficit must be financed through borrowing.

DEFINED BENEFIT PLAN. A pension plan stipulating the exact amount of money the beneficiary will receive.

DEFINED CONTRIBUTION PLAN. A pension plan stipulating the exact amount of money the participant must contribute.

DEFINITIVE SECURITY. A permanent security issued to replace a temporary certificate, which may have been offered on a new issue.

DEFLATION. A drop in general price levels, usually caused by increased demand for money that isn't offset by an increased money supply, or a drop in the money supply that isn't offset by a drop in the demand for money.

DEFLATOR. Used to adjust the difference between one value and the same value as it is affected by inflation.

DEFLECTION OF TAX LIABILITY. One person's tax burden is shifted to someone else.

DEGREE OF COMBINED LEVERAGE. Combining a company's operating leverage and financial leverage creates a gauge of the company's earnings per share variability.

DEGREE OF FINANCIAL LEVERAGE. A company's fixed financing costs create a gauge of the company's earnings per share variability.

DEGREE OF OPERATING LEVERAGE. A company's fixed operating costs create a gauge of the company's earnings before interest and taxes.

DELAYED DELIVERY. A securities contract is settled after a regular-way delivery of the security, which usually is after five business days.

DELAYED ITEMS. Transactions that occurred in a previous year.

DELAYED OPENING. The opening of trading for a security is delayed temporarily, usually when there are a lot of buy and sell orders for it and the market specialist wants to maintain an orderly market.

DEL CREDERE AGENCY. An agency that tries to guarantee a client that a buyer will pay off his or her debt.

DELINQUENCY. Failure to meet a financial obligation.

DELIST. A company's rights to list its securities on the exchange is withdrawn, usually because the firm has stopped meeting the minimum requirements. After delisting, the security still can be traded over the counter.

DELIVERABLE BILLS. Treasury bills that meet the requirements on the exchange on which it is traded.

DELIVERY. An options exercise or a futures contract is fulfilled by handing over the stock certificates or the commodity.

DELIVERY AGAINST COST. *See* COD Transaction.

DELIVERY DATE. The specific day a futures contract will be delivered.

DELIVERY NOTICE. The seller confirms that he or she will deliver a stock or commodity on a specific day at a specific place.

DELIVERY POINT. Where a commodity that is covered by a futures contract can be delivered to fill the contract.

DELIVERY PRICE. The amount for which a commodities contract is settled.

DELIVERY VERSUS PAYMENT. Payment for a security must be made when the security is delivered. Usually, the payment is made to a bank, which in turn pays for the stock certificates.

DELTA. The change in an option premium for each single point of change in the underlying security's price. For example, a delta of 0.5 means a stock's premium goes up by half of a point for each point the underlying stock goes up.

DEMAND. The amount of interest in a security or commodity.

DEMAND AND SUPPLY CURVES. A graph of the highest buying and lowest selling prices on a specific security at a particular time and place.

DEMAND DEPOSIT. A customer's deposited assets that are available to be drawn upon by a check or a draft. For example, if a customer deposited an amount of money in his or her checking account, that amount would constitute a demand deposit.

DEMAND FOR MONEY. The portion of a person's wealth that he or she holds in money, as opposed to investing it.

DEMAND LINE OF CREDIT. A bank customer can borrow a predetermined amount of money from the bank each day.

DEMAND LOAN. A loan that has no maturity date and must be repaid immediately upon the lender's demand.

DEMAND MORTGAGE. A mortgage that must be repaid in full upon the lender's demand.

DEMAND NOTE. A loan that is due immediately upon demand.

DEMAND PRICE. The most amount of money a buyer will pay for a specific security or commodity.

DEMAND-PULL INFLATION. When demand is greater than supply, inflation results. Increased demand causes prices to go up, which causes wages to go up, and thereby causes the costs for goods and services to go up.

DEMOGRAPHIC TRENDS. A gauge that measures how population trends will affect specific industries.

DEMONETIZATION. A currency or currency base that is taken out of circulation.

DEMONSTRATION. A sudden and unexpected change in a security's activities.

DENOMINATION. The number of shares appearing on the face of a security, or the principal amount appearing on the face of a bond.

DEPLETION. A figuratively stated amount of money that a company sets aside from its annual earnings to replace a natural asset—such as lumber from a forest or oil from a well—that is being used up and cannot be replaced. Because the asset cannot be replaced, the company usually gets a tax break on the amount.

DEPLETION ALLOWANCE. The Internal Revenue Service allows companies to take a tax deduction for wasted assets.

DEPLOYMENT. Money from a fund is distributed into asset categories.

DEPOSIT ACCOUNT. A bank account with withdrawal restrictions that normally provides a higher rate of interest than regular accounts.

DEPOSIT ADMINISTRATION CONTRACT. An insurance company's unallocated account which is held for active participants in a pension plan. The participants receive annuities after they retire.

DEPOSITORY. A bank that accepts deposits of securities and government funds.

DEPOSITORY INSTITUTIONS DEREGULATION COMMITTEE. An ad-hoc panel that creates government-insured, interest-bearing deposit accounts at financial institutions to compete with mutual funds.

DEPOSITORY PREFERRED STOCK. A preferred stock with a high par value is deposited with a bank, which then issues more shares of a preferred stock with a lower par value. The lower-valued stock is entitled to a portion of the deposited security's interest.

DEPOSITORY TRUST COMPANY. A firm through which members can use a computer to arrange for securities to be delivered to other members without physical delivery of the certificates. A member of the Federal Reserve System and owned mostly by the New York Stock Exchange, the Depository Trust Company uses computerized debit and credit entries.

DEPRECIATED COST. A fixed asset's original cost minus all accumulated depreciation.

DEPRECIATED CURRENCY. The exchange value of a currency drops, and the currency no longer can be accepted at face value.

DEPRECIATION. An amount of money that represents a tangible asset's drop in value over time. The amount is subtracted from the asset's purchase price to give its residual value. For example, an automobile depreciates each year the more it is used. In other words, the more miles racked up, the greater the depreciation.

DEPRECIATION FUND. Money or securities set aside and designated to replace depreciating fixed assets.

DEPRESSED PRICE. A security's price is lower than it should be when considering the issuing company's financial condition.

DEPRESSION. A long-term decline in living conditions.

DEPTH. The amount of general interest investors show in the market, representing the number of issues traded compared to the number of issues listed. Logically, the more issues traded, the greater the market depth. Depth also describes the market's ability to absorb a large buy or sell order without a dramatic change in the security's price.

DEREGULATION. Stopping or cutting down the control government has over a particular industry in an effort to free the market and promote competition.

DERIVATIVE SUIT. A stockholder sues the issuing corporation, charging that the officers did not protect the best interest of the corporation. In essence, the stockholder is suing the corporation on behalf of the corporation.

DERIVED DEMAND. The need for a good or service as a result of the demand for another good or service.

DESCENDING TOPS. A bearish chart pattern in which each new high price for a security is lower than the security's last high price.

DESIGNATED CONCESSION. A syndication order for a number of securities that designates nonmembers of the account who will receive the concession for the securities' sale.

DESIGNATED NET. Someone who is not a member of the Municipal Securities Rulemaking Board gives an order, to be executed at the public offering price. The order, given to a municipal security syndicate, directs that the concession be credited to the accounts of at least three syndicate members. Municipal investors often use designated net to reward account members who have come up with valuable ideas.

DESIGNATED OPTIONS EXAMINING AUTHORITY. A panel responsible for overseeing individual broker-dealers.

DESIGNATED ORDER TURNAROUND. A computer New York Stock Exchange members use to route market orders for 1 to 499 shares directly to a market specialist, who represents the orders. If the specialist cannot find a contra broker, he or she executes the order against the book. If the specialist can make the deal immediately, he or she does not charge the member a fee.

DESTINATION CLAUSE. A contract that allows an oil monopoly to designate what nations will get its oil, which in turn keeps the oil out of the spot market.

DETAILED AUDIT. When all of a company's internal control systems, financial ledgers, and subsidiary records are examined extensively for accuracy.

DETERMINATION DATE. The last day in a month that a person can deposit money in a savings account and still earn interest from the first day of the month.

DETROIT STOCK EXCHANGE. This exchange is used primarily for trading unlisted securities.

DEUTSCHEMARK. West German currency, commonly referred to as a mark.

DEVALUATION. One country's currency drops in value when it is exchanged for another country's currency. For example, if the U.S. dollar was worth 1,200 Italian lire yesterday and 1,100 today, a person with lire could buy more American goods today than he or she could have bought yesterday, marking a devaluation of the dollar.

DEVELOPMENTAL DRILLING PROGRAM. Drilling for oil and gas in an area that previously has produced oil and gas. While the program usually provides a stable income, it normally does not yield enormous profits.

DIAGONAL SPREAD. An investor takes long and short positions in the same class of options with different strike prices and different expiration dates.

DIAMOND INVESTMENT TRUST. A trust fund that invests in diamonds, but the investors do not have physical possession of the stones.

DIARY. A listing of financial instruments' maturity dates.

DIFFERENTIAL. A dealer is paid, usually 1/8 of a point, for completing an odd lot transaction, or the dealer increases his or her quoted fee to a customer because the customer is buying or selling a small amount of securities.

DIFFERENTIAL DUTY. Two blocks of the same commodity may be subject to different duties, depending on their place of origin, the type of labor involved in their production, or some other factor.

DIGESTED SECURITIES. Securities owned by an investor who plans to hold onto them for a long time.

DIGITS DELETED. A designation on the exchange tape that appears when the tape has been delayed, displaying only the variations instead of the variations and the digits.

DILUTION. When a company issues additional shares of stock even though its income has not increased, the company's equity ratio, earnings per share, and book value per share will drop.

DIME. Equal to 10 basis points, or 0.1 percent, on a debt security's yield.

DINGO. Nickname for Australia's discounted investment in negotiated government obligations, which are government-issued securities that do not carry coupons and are sold at a discount.

DIP. A slight drop in securities prices in an upward trend, usually marking a good time to buy.

DIRECT EARNINGS. Earnings of a parent company without the upstream dividends of its subsidiaries.

DIRECTED TRUST. A fund, such as a pension plan, that allows the owner to tell the trustee how to invest the money.

DIRECT FINANCING. Raising money without using an underwriter.

DIRECT INVESTMENT. Equity is invested in property, securities and service companies.

DIRECTOR. A person who serves on a company's board.

DIRECT PAPER. Commercial paper a company sells directly to the public without going through a broker-dealer.

DIRECT PARTICIPATION PROGRAM. A partnership agreement that calls for tax consequences to flow through to participants.

DIRECT PLACEMENT. An issuer sells a new security directly to institutional clients without using a broker.

DIRECT REDUCTION MORTGAGE. A mortgage that is liquidated in equal payments throughout the life of the loan. As regular payments reduce the amount of principal, the interest rate drops accordingly.

DIRTY. A British stock that is cum divided and is near the date when interest will be paid.

DISBURSEMENT. Funds paid in the discharge of an expense or debt.

DISBURSING AGENT. A person responsible for paying interest or dividends to stockholders.

DISC. Created by a U.S. corporation, the Domestic International Sales Corporation enables American companies to compete with subsidized foreign companies by providing tax advantages to foreign exporters of American goods.

DISCHARGE OF BANKRUPTCY. An order that ends a bankruptcy procedure and frees the debtor from all financial responsibilities.

DISCLOSURE. A company must report all of its management practices, its financial situation, and its legal involvements when it could influence an investment decision.

DISCONTINUOUS MARKET. Securities that are not listed form a separate market.

DISCOUNT. The difference between a security's redemption value and its current market price.

DISCOUNT BOND. A bond that initially sold near par, but now sells for less.

DISCOUNT BROKER. A broker who charges a lower fee because he or she executes transactions, but provides clients no other services, such as investment advice.

DISCOUNTED CASH FLOW. The value of expected cash receipts and expenses on one specific day. A discount rate is based either on the marginal cost of capital to future cash flow, or on the current value of future cash flow to the original cost of the investment.

DISCOUNTED VALUE. The current value of future obligations, as determined by a specific interest rate.

DISCOUNT ON SECURITIES. The difference in amounts when a security is traded for less than its par value.

DISCOUNTING THE NEWS. When the price of a stock or the level of one of the markets moves up or down in anticipation of good or bad news.

DISCOUNT RATE. The interest rate member banks pay the Federal Reserve when they use securities as collateral. Banks use the rate to determine the lowest interest rate they will charge loan customers. For example, if the bank is paying the Federal Reserve 9 percent interest, it will not loan a customer funds with an interest rate below 9 percent.

DISCOUNT WINDOW. A place provided by the Federal Reserve where member banks borrow against collateral at the discount rate.

DISCOUNT YIELD. Achieved by dividing a security's discount by its face value, and multiplying that number by the approximate number of days in the year (360) divided by the number of days left to maturity. The figure provides the interest on a security's face value instead of on the amount of money invested.

DISCRETIONARY ACCOUNT. A brokerage account that allows an employee of an exchange-member firm to make investment decisions on the client's behalf, such as buying and selling, choosing securities, when to buy or sell and at what price to buy or sell.

DISCRETIONARY INCOME. The money a person has available after paying all of his or her bills.

DISCRETIONARY ORDER. An employee of an exchange-member firm agrees to a buy or sell order because he or she has only a limited power of attorney over a client's account.

DISCRETIONARY POOL. One group of people authorizes another group of people to buy and sell securities on the first group's behalf.

DISCRETIONARY TRUST. A trust fund or mutual fund that can be invested in any way, and is not limited to a particular security.

DISHONORED. A financial instrument that is rejected after it is offered for payment.

DISINFLATION. A time when price inflation drops without going below zero.

DISINTERMEDIATION. An investor who deposited money with a portfolio intermediary withdraws the money and directly invests it in securities.

DISINVESTMENT. Capital goods are eliminated or capital assets are not maintained or replaced, thus reducing the capital investment.

DISPOSABLE INCOME. All money a person has left after paying taxes. Disposable income includes money used to pay bills as well as discretionary income.

DISPROPORTIONATE IN QUANTITY. When more than 100 shares, or bonds, with face values totaling more than $5,000, are sold to anyone representing or associated with the underwriter, or to officers of financial institutions.

DISSOLUTION. When a company disbands, either voluntarily or through a government order, after its charter expires.

DIST. Appears on exchange tapes to represent an exchange distribution.

DISTRESS SELLING. Selling a security out of necessity.

DISTRIBUTING SYNDICATE. A group of brokers or banks that unite to distribute a large block of securities.

DISTRIBUTION AREA. A security has not changed in price much in a long time. The area is that narrow price range.

DISTRIBUTION DATE. The day a company pays its stockholders interest or dividends.

DISTRIBUTION OF RISK. An investment is spread out over several areas instead of being concentrated on one specific security, which could prove financially disastrous if that one security bottomed out.

DISTRIBUTION STOCK. After a shelf registration, the issuer's affiliates publicly sell the stock.

DISTRIBUTOR. Wholesaler or middleman of securities to the retailers.

DISTRICT BUSINESS CONDUCT COMMITTEE. A panel, appointed by district members of the National Association of Securities Dealers, that hears complaints of unfair trade practices lodged against either an NASD member or someone associated with an NASD member.

DIVERGENCE. When market trends go in a different direction than market indicators predicted, usually signaling the onset of a trend change.

DIVERSIFICATION. An investor reduces his or her financial risk by spreading his or her investment over a large number of securities, instead of risking it all in one area.

DIVERSIFIED. When 75 percent or more of a management investment company's assets are in four different types of cash or securities, no more than 5 percent of its total assets can be invested in one issuer's security, and the company holds no more than 10 percent of any issuer's voting shares.

DIVERSIFIED COMMON STOCK FUND. An investment firm that holds a diversified stock portfolio, with the portfolio value following the market's general trends.

DIVERSIFIED HOLDING COMPANY. One company that controls several other companies, but that does not participate in the other companies' management or day-to-day operations.

DIVEST. To sell or get rid of an investment.

DIVESTITUTE. One company that was holding a large block of stock in another company distributes the stock.

DIVIDED ACCOUNT. Each member of an underwriting syndicate is responsible for his or her allocation only, and not the allocation of any other member. (Also known as an eastern account.)

DIVIDEND. The amount of money or securities distributed out of net profits to the company's shareholders.

DIVIDEND APPROPRIATIONS. The amount of a company's retained income that will be paid in dividends for outstanding preferred or common stock.

DIVIDEND CAPTURE. A company buys stock shares right before the dividend is paid, holds it for a while, and then sells it without losing any money. The company profits greatly because it pays only a minimal amount of taxes on dividend income.

DIVIDEND CLAIM. A person buying stock asks the registered holder for the amount of the dividend because the trade was made before the ex-dividend, but the actual transfer was not completed until after the record date.

DIVIDEND DEPARTMENT. The area in a broker-dealer's firm where employees accept and pay clients those dividends from securities for which the firm is responsible.

DIVIDEND DISBURSING AGENT. A financial institution that pays clients interest and dividends on certain securities.

DIVIDEND EXCLUSION. The dollar amount of dividends that is not taxable.

DIVIDEND ON. A person buys stock with the understanding that he or she will receive the next dividend payment.

DIVIDEND ORDER. A document asking the issuing corporation to send dividend checks to a specific address.

DIVIDEND PAYOUT RATIO. Divide the amount of a company's earnings that is available for common stock by the annual common stock dividend. The quotient provides a gauge for comparing different companies. For example, a company with a low ratio probably is considered a growth company.

DIVIDEND PRICE RATIO. The difference between the current dividend rate and the stock's market price.

DIVIDEND RECORD. Standard & Poor's publishes a newsletter listing dividend payments and the dividend policies of securities issuers.

DIVIDEND REINVESTMENT PLAN. Instead of receiving cash dividends, investors can put the money into buying more shares of the security.

DIVIDEND REQUIREMENT. The amount of money a company needs to earn annually in order to pay the required dividends on preferred stock.

DIVIDEND ROLLOVER PLAN. Stocks are bought shortly before the announcement that dividends will be paid, then sold shortly thereafter. By doing this, the investor can make a small profit and collect the dividend.

DIVIDENDS PAYABLE. The exact dollar amount of a dividend.

DIVIDENDS PER SHARE. The amount of money an investor receives in dividends for each share of stock he or she owns.

DIVIDEND WARRANT. A document ordering a corporation to pay dividends to stockholders.

DIVIDEND YIELD. Divide a stock's market price per share into its dividend per share.

DNE. An acronym for discretion not exercised which appears on order tickets after a client has given a broker a discretionary order, but ultimately made the deal without the broker.

DOCUMENTED DISCOUNT NOTES. A Federal Reserve Discount Bank member bank qualifies this commercial paper as collateral as long as it is accompanied by a different commercial bank's letter of credit or an unrelated private insurance company guarantee.

DOG AND PONY SHOW. A broker-dealer firm puts on a seminar to introduce a company's new product or service in an effort to attract the interest of its representatives.

DOLLAR BONDS. A long-term municipal debt instrument that is quoted in dollars instead of its yield to maturity; or foreign bonds denominated in U.S. dollars.

DOLLAR CONTROL. A company guides its inventory based on the amount of money it has, instead of on the number of tangible assets it has.

DOLLAR COST AVERAGING. *See* Constant Dollar Plan.

DOLLAR CREDIT. A bank issues this document so that a customer can draw drafts in dollars.

DOLLAR DRAIN. The amount that a foreign country's U.S. imports exceed its U.S. exports. Because the country pays more for the American goods it takes in than it receives for its own goods going to the U.S., the country's dollar supply dwindles.

DOLLAR PREMIUM. British investors must pay this additional fee when they buy dollars to invest outside of the country.

DOLLAR PRICE. A bond's cost is expressed as a percentage of its face value. For example, a bond with a face value of $1,000 is quoted at 95 1/2, so the bond's dollar price would be 95.5 percent of the face value, or $955.

DOLLAR SHORTAGE. A foreign country that imports American goods runs out of dollars and must borrow money from the U.S. before it can import anything else from the U.S.

DOLLAR STABILIZATION. The government tries to stop fluctuations in the U.S. dollar's foreign exchange rate.

DOLLAR STOCKS. British description of U.S. securities.

DOLLAR WEIGHTED RATE OF RETURN. A gauge of an investment fund's growth rate, measuring the cash flow's weight on the fund's assets during a specific time period.

DOMESTIC CORPORATION. An American company, or a company operating in the same country in which it was created.

DOMESTIC INTERNATIONAL SALES CORPORATION. *See* DISC.

DONATED CAPITAL STOCK. Stockholders donate capital stock shares back to the issuing company.

DONATED SURPLUS. A stockholder's equity account is credited when the stockholder donates stocks back to the issuing company.

DONOGHUE'S MONEY FUND AVERAGE. A weekly listing, published in many newspapers, of seven- and 30-day money market fund yields, along with money fund portfolio maturities, with short maturities indicating that interest rates will go up.

"DON'T FIGHT THE TAPE". Some analysts say it is not wise to trade securities against the general market trend.

DORMANT ACCOUNT. A brokerage account that has not had any activity for a long time.

DORMANT PARTNER. A person who is a partner in a specific business and who financially benefits from profits and suffers from losses, but who is not publicly associated with the business.

DOUBLE AUCTION MARKET. Buyers and sellers constantly vary their prices in an attempt to make the market. When the investor making the highest offer and the seller with the lowest asking price agree on a price, a transaction is made.

DOUBLE-BARRELED. The interest and principal of a municipal revenue bond is guaranteed by a municipality, which will make payments out of its tax revenues if necessary. For example, if the school board issues a bond to build a children's museum, but the museum ultimately does not bring in enough money to pay the principal and interest, the city will use its tax revenues to make up any differences.

DOUBLE BOTTOM. When a stock drops to the same low price twice. Analysts use the double bottom to determine if a stock will continue a decline. Usually, they will predict further decline if the stock drops to that level a third time.

DOUBLE DECLINING BALANCE METHOD. A method of calculating accelerated depreciation with the IRS permitting twice the rate of annual depreciation as the straight-line method.

DOUBLE DIGIT INFLATION. Inflation reaching 10 percent or more.

DOUBLE DIPPING. A company issues industrial revenue bonds so it can build a project in the same city that issued the bonds. The company raises the finances at lower rates, then uses accelerated depreciation to get the money back.

DOUBLE ENDORSEMENT. A note or other negotiable instrument with two signers so that if one fails to meet the obligation, the other will become responsible. Both signers are equally responsible for the instrument.

DOUBLE ENTRY. When one financial account entry shows an increase, another entry must show either an increase or decrease so that all of the debits equal all of the credits.

DOUBLE EXEMPTION BOND. A bond, usually municipal, with the holder and issuer in the same state, that is free from federal and state taxes.

DOUBLE TAXATION. The government taxes shareholders' dividends after it already has taxed the corporation's profits from which the dividends were drawn.

DOUBLE TOP. When a stock hits the same peak high price twice. Analysts use the double top to determine if a stock will continue to go up. Usually, they will predict further increases if the stock reaches that peak a third time.

DOUBLE WITCHING HOUR. From 3 p.m. to 4 p.m. on the third Friday of eight months of the year, institutional traders have their last chance to close out June stock-index options and futures positions before the options expire.

DOW JONES AVERAGE. A composite of the price movement of 65 stocks, including 30 industrials, 20 transportation, and 15 utilities.

DOW JONES BOND AVERAGE. An index of six bond groups that represents the general bond market's strength.

DOW JONES COMMODITY FUTURES INDEX. An index of 12 commodities that represent the strength of the commodities market. The index is based on such data as average prices, trading volume, etc.

DOW JONES INDUSTRIAL AVERAGE. A composite of the price movement of 30 actively traded industrial stocks which purports to reflect the overall stock market movement.

DOW JONES MUNICIPAL INDEX. The average weekly market value of discounted municipal bonds.

DOW JONES TRANSPORTATION AVERAGE. An index of 20 transportation companies that measures the transportation market's strength.

DOWN-AND-OUT OPTION. A block of 10 or more call options with the same exercise price and expiration date, stipulating that if the underlying security's price drops a specific amount, the contract is canceled.

DOWNDRAFT. A stock market decline.

DOWN GAP. When the lowest price in a given market day is higher than the highest price of the next day, an open space appears on the stock chart.

DOWN MARKET. A trend of declining market prices.

DOWN REVERSAL. A sudden drop in prices after the prices had been moving up.

DOWNSIDE PROTECTION. The range a security's price must drop before the investor starts to lose money.

DOWNSIDE RISK. A prediction of what a security's lowest value probably will be in the future.

DOWNSIDE TREND. A security's price continues a long-term drop.

DOWNSTAIRS MERGER. A parent company merges with one of its subsidiaries.

DOWNSTREAM. A corporation's financial activity, such as a loan, that flows from the parent company to its subsidiary.

DOWNSTREAM BORROWING. A company borrows money using the credit standing of one of its subsidiaries.

DOWNTICK. An exchange-listed security is sold for less than the last regular-way transaction involving the same security.

DOWN TREND. A security's price is dropping, and it looks like it will continue to go down.

DOWNTURN. A financial cycle that begins to go down. For example, when a bullish market becomes bearish, the market is experiencing a downturn.

DOWN UNDER BONDS. A Eurobond from Australia or New Zealand that is not registered in the U.S. American investors can buy down under bonds only after they have been traded in Europe for a long time.

DOWPAC. An over-the-counter, Dow Jones option contract that allows the holder to buy or sell a block of eight stocks, most of which usually are the blue-chip stocks Dow uses to calculate its industrial averages.

DOW THEORY. No market trend will last longer than a year unless such a trend is indicated by the movements of the industrial, transportation, and utility averages.

DRAFT. An instrument used to transfer money from one person's account to another's, with the debit appearing only after the instrument is presented for payment.

DRAINING RESERVES. The Federal Reserve System cuts down the amount of available money banks can loan out by decreasing the money supply. This is usually done through raising reserve requirements, increasing the interest rates at which banks borrow money from the government, and selling bonds at attractive rates.

DRAWBACK. The syndicate manager has taken back some of the issues the underwriter was selling to his or her customers so that the manager can sell the shares to institutional accounts.

DRAWN SECURITIES. A security ready to be redeemed.

DREW'S ODD-LOT THEORY. Garfield Drew advised investors to sell if odd-lotters were buying, and to buy if odd-lotters were selling because odd-lotters' actions are indicators of general market trends.

DRIED UP. A buying or selling order is removed from the market.

DRIVE. Sellers try to manipulate the market by forcing prices down, which is illegal.

DROP LOCK. A feature on a floating-rate note that allows the holder to convert the note into a fixed-rate note if overall interest rates drop to a predetermined level.

DROP LOCK SECURITY. A feature on a floating rate security that allows the holder to exchange the security for a fixed-rate security if the popular interbank loan rate drops to a predetermined level.

DRT. The abbreviation of disregard tape that appears on orders when the buyer or seller wants the floor broker to use his or her own discretion in determining when to execute the transaction and how much the price should be.

DRY HOLE. A well that does not produce enough oil or gas to be profitable.

DUAL BANKING. American banks are chartered either by the state or the federal government, creating differences in regulations and services provided to customers.

DUAL CURRENCY YEN BONDS. A Japanese security with interest paid in yen and the principal paid in a different currency.

DUAL EXCHANGE MARKET. When the same people operate two exchange markets, using one for specific types of underlying transactions, and the other for dealing in the foreign exchange market.

DUALLY LISTED. A security that is listed on more than one stock exchange.

DUAL MUTUAL FUNDS. A fund with portfolios invested in capital growth issues and income investments.

DUAL PURPOSE FUND. A closed-end mutual fund with one type of share that gives holders all dividends and interest income, and a second type that gives holders the benefits of capital gains earned when the securities are sold.

DUAL-PURPOSE INVESTMENT COMPANY. A closed-end investment firm that issues income shares and capital shares, with the owners receiving all of the interest, dividends, and profits.

DUAL SAVINGS PLAN. Two different authorities can post savings deposits and account withdrawals.

DUAL SERIES ZERO-COUPON DEBENTURE. In an effort to attract two different markets, a company issues a short-term, zero-coupon note as well as a long-term, fixed-coupon bond at the same time.

DUAL TRADING. An investor trades the same security on two different exchanges at the same time.

DUE ANNUITY. A clause requiring annuity payments to begin immediately.

DUE BILL. A broker selling a security attaches this document, which gives the buyer title of ownership to the security when it is delivered.

DUE ON SALE CLAUSE. A mortgage clause stating that if the property is sold, the entire balance of the loan must be paid immediately, eliminating the possibility of a mortgage assumption.

DUE DILIGENCE. Representatives of an underwriting syndicate who make sure that all available information on a new issue is released.

DUFF AND PHELPS. A Chicago firm that numerically rates banks, finance companies, and industrial and utility securities.

DULL. When securities' prices do not change much and trading is relatively inactive.

DUMMY. A person who acts on behalf of someone else in a business situation, but not on behalf of himself or herself. The dummy controls the other person's votes, but has no personal financial interest or ownership.

DUMMY INCORPORATORS. A group of people who act as incorporators at a company's inception, then resign and transfer their interest to the real owners.

DUMMY STOCKHOLDER. A person who holds stock in his or her name when the stock actually belongs to someone else. By doing this, the actual owner's name is kept confidential.

DUMP. To sell a security at a reduced price just to get rid of it.

DUMPING. Selling a large number of stocks with little concern about their market price.

DUN & BRADSTREET. A firm that deals in collection services and credit reporting, used primarily by brokers and dealers.

DUN'S NUMBER. The Dun's Market Identifier, or the Data Universal Numbering System, is included in a list of companies. The list contains identification numbers, firms' names, addresses, numbers of employees, corporate affiliations, etc.

DU-OP SECURITY. A dual option security in which the holder can have his or her choice of an issue of common stock or an issue of preferred stock.

DURABLE POWER OF ATTORNEY. One person acts on behalf of another, even if the other becomes mentally or physically disabled.

DURATION. The difference between a bond's price change and the change in its yield to maturity, which gives the investor an indication of how interest rate changes will affect the bond's price.

DUTCH AUCTION. A theory that says a bidder will not bid higher to buy a security, but the seller will come down in price until the two reach an agreement.

DUTCH AUCTION RATE TRANSFERABLE SECURITIES. An adjustable rate, preferred, nonconvertible stock with a dividend rate that is reset every 49 years through competitive bidding.

DUTY. A tax on imported or exported goods.

DYNAMITER. A broker who uses the telephone to try to sell unregistered or outright fraudulent stocks and bonds.

E

E. Appears in newspaper stock listings to designate that an item has been either declared or paid within the last year.

EACH WAY. Commissions earned by a broker on the buy and the sell of a trade.

EAGLE. A restricted and tightly controlled computer system at the New York Stock Exchange containing corporate information.

EARLY EXERCISE. A person holding an options contract decides to exercise the contract before it expires.

EARLY OWNERSHIP MORTGAGE. Contains the provision that the first six years of payments are sufficient to pay off the loan in 30 years, and after the six years, the loan payments will increase, but the interest rate will stay the same. With this type of mortgage, the loan will be paid off in less than 30 years.

EARLY WITHDRAWAL PENALTY. If a person holding a fixed-term investment withdraws his or her money before the investment matures, the person is charged this fee.

EARNED GROWTH RATE. The yearly compounded internal rate that reinvesting earnings causes a company's per share equity to grow.

EARNED INCOME. Any income from wages or taxable gifts.

EARNED SURPLUS. The amount of money a company keeps in its business after dividends are paid.

EARNEST MONEY. To seal a deal, one person signing a contract gives the other signer this money, which is forfeited if the person who gave the money fails to honor the contract.

EARNING ASSETS. The loans and investments that comprise most of a bank's profits.

EARNING POWER. The amount of money an asset or security is expected to earn and the current value of those earnings.

EARNINGS. A company's profits after paying all expenses, but before paying dividends.

EARNINGS BEFORE TAXES. The amount of money a company has after it pays dividends but before it pays taxes.

EARNINGS PER SHARE (EPS). A company's net profit minus its preferred stock obligations, with the difference divided by the number of outstanding shares of common stock.

EARNINGS PRICE RATIO. The relationship between a security's earnings per share and its current price. This earnings yield compares the benefits of and differences between bonds, money markets, and stocks.

EARNINGS REPORT. A document that provides an accounting of all of a company's income, expenses, profits, and losses.

EARNINGS STATEMENT. A written review of a company's earnings, such as an income statement.

EARNINGS YIELD. A security's earnings divided by its market price.

EARN-OUT. Future payments that must be made after someone buys a business if that business's profits exceed a predetermined limit. The buyer pays the seller if such rights are specified in the contract.

EASIER. Bid prices are dropping.

EASTERN ACCOUNT. Also known as a divided account, this is an underwriting system, usually with municipal bonds, wherein an entire syndicate assumes responsibility for the success of the distribution of that amount, for example, if one firm has 20% participation but sells more, that firm will be responsible for 20% of any remaining securities.

EASY MONEY. An expanded money supply, which creates an economy in which money is readily available for loans.

EBIT. Designates a company's earnings before it pays any interest or taxes.

ECONOMETRICS. The relationship among such economic forces as government policies, labor, interest rates, and capital expressed in mathematical terms derived from a computer. Through these terms, economic changes can be tested. For example, an econometric theory may study the relationship between the government's policy on agriculture and food prices at the supermarket.

ECONOMIC GROWTH RATE. The annual percentage change in the Gross National Product. If the growth rate drops during two consecutive quarters, the country is experiencing a recession. If the growth rate increases during two consecutive quarters, the country's economy is expanding.

ECONOMIC INDICATORS. Gauges of the nation's economic strength, such as wages and prices, with emphasis on whether that strength will grow or dwindle in the future.

ECONOMIC LIFE. When a fixed asset can be depreciated against a company's current earnings; the life of the asset's usefulness.

ECONOMIC RECOVERY TAX ACT OF 1981. Among other things, this legislation provided an across-the-board tax cut to U.S. citizens, indexed tax brackets to interest rates, lowered the marriage penalty tax, reduced estate and gift taxes, and lowered the rates of exercising stock options.

EDGAR. The Electronic Data Gathering, Analysis, and Retrieval is a Securities and Exchange Commission computer that allows registered securities issuers to file reports with the SEC by computer instead of having to file physical documents.

EFFECTIVE ANNUAL YIELD. The amount of money an investment makes as expressed in its equivalent simple interest rate.

EFFECTIVE DATE. The day a newly registered security can be offered for sale, which normally is 20 days after the registration statement is filed.

EFFECTIVE DEBT. The total amount of money a company owes.

EFFECTIVE EXCHANGE RATE. A spot exchange rate the public has either paid or received, including taxes, subsidies or banking commissions paid on the transaction, with all rates falling within the allowed margin near par.

EFFECTIVE GROSS REVENUE. A company's total income minus any collection losses, contingencies and vacancies, but before the company deducts any amount for operating expenses.

EFFECTIVE LIFE. The amount of time left on an unexecuted order, or the expected duration of a self-amortizing security.

EFFECTIVE NET WORTH. A company's net worth added to its subordinated debt, which is money owed after other, more important, financial obligations are met.

EFFECTIVE PAR. A preferred stock's par value that corresponds to a specific dividend rate.

EFFECTIVE RATE. The yield on a debt security based on the coupon rate, price, time between interest payments, and the amount of time to maturity. This rate determines the overall yield.

EFFECTIVE SALE. The amount of a round-lot sale, which usually is 100 shares of stock, determines the price of the next odd-lot transaction, with 1/8 of a point tacked on as the odd-lot differential. For example, if a round-lot transaction involved stock selling at 42, the next odd-lot purchase would be at 42 1/8.

EFFICIENT MARKET HYPOTHESIS. Theory that in a free market, with competition for profits, all knowledge and expectations are accurately reflected in market prices.

EIGHTH STOCKS. Odd-lot stocks on which the odd-lot differential also is applied to the next round-lot sale.

EIGHTY-FIVE PERCENT EXCLUSION. When one company receives cash dividends from another company, 85 percent of the total is excluded as taxable income in some cases.

EITHER/OR ORDER. An investor advises his or her broker to have one of two orders executed. When one is executed, the other alternative is automatically canceled.

EITHER WAY MARKET. When a bid on a security is identical to an offer price.

ELASTICITY OF DEMAND AND SUPPLY. The demand for luxury items or for nonessentials is elastic because it can jump dramatically or drop if prices go up or down. Necessities such as drugs, food, electricity, are not elastic because people need to buy the products and services regardless of their costs. Elasticity of supply refers to the increase in supply as production and prices go up.

ELBOW. On a graph, a sharp shift in a yield curve slope resembles an elbow.

ELECT. A round-lot transaction that causes a round- or odd-lot stop order to become a market order. For example, if an odd-lot request is in for 60 shares of ABC Paper Co. with a stop order at 42, and the previous round-lot trade of

ABC went for 41 7/8, the broker can make the odd-lot deal without passing the stop limit, thus the stop order is elected and becomes a buy order.

ELECTRONIC ACCESS MEMBER. For a fee, the New York Stock Exchange gives some people the right to use electronic communications to buy and sell securities on the trading floor, even though they are not exchange members.

ELEEMOSYNARY INSTITUTION. A philanthropic, nonprofit, tax-exempt charity.

ELIGIBLE INVESTMENT. An investment that earns money and that Federal Reserve System banks can rediscount.

ELIGIBLE LIST. A list of securities that banks and other financial institutions can buy.

ELIGIBLE PAPER. Commercial paper, notes, and other financial issues that Federal Reserve System banks can submit to the Federal Reserve System for discounting.

ELIGIBLE STOCK. A security in which charities and financial institutions can invest.

ELLIOTT WAVE THEORY. Created by Ralph Elliott in 1938, this system predicts future trends and pinpoints the next probable broad market movement by counting and measuring price changes in the Dow Jones Industrial Average.

ELVES. A gauge of 10 market indicators that test economic conditions, investors' psychology, and the stock market's current momentum.

EMBARGO. The government bans the exportation of specific goods, an approach usually taken during war time or to protest another country's social or foreign policies.

EMBEZZLEMENT. The theft or misappropriation of a customer's or company's assets, checks, or securities.

EMERGENCY HOME FINANCE ACT OF 1970. Legislation that created the Federal Home Loan Mortgage Corporation to build interest in developing a secondary mortgage market. The corporation puts together and sells mortgages guaranteed by the Federal Housing Administration and the Veterans Administration with investors buying the packages as pass-through securities.

EMINENT DOMAIN. The government can take possession of an individual's assets for the general public welfare after it has paid the individual a fair price.

For example, the government can force a person off his or her land if the government decides to put a highway through that particular property.

EMPLOYEE RETIREMENT INCOME SECURITY ACT (ERISA). A law established in 1974 which governs the operations of most private pension and benefits plans to protect the interests of the participants.

EMPLOYEE SPENDING ACCOUNT. Employees designate up to 50 percent of the money they earn in profit-sharing to reimburse themselves for benefit expenses or for medical insurance.

EMPLOYEE STOCK OWNERSHIP PLAN. A company plan that allows employees to buy shares of the company's stock through a contribution system.

EMPLOYEE STOCK REPURCHASE AGREEMENT. A company's employees can buy shares of the company's stock, but the company retains the right to buy the shares back.

ENCUMBERED. An asset owned by one person, but subject to another's claim. For example, if one took out a mortgage to buy a house, the house would be encumbered because even though the property is owned, the bank holds an interest in it until the mortgage is paid.

ENDIGUER. French for hedging an investment.

ENDORSE. The act of placing a name on a certificate to legally transfer ownership.

ENDORSED BOND. A bond issued by one company, but guaranteed by another.

ENDORSEMENT FEE. An options broker pays a New York Stock Exchange member firm to guarantee a customer's performance in an over-the-counter option.

ENERGY ISSUES. Securities issued by a company involved in energy research, production, or related field.

ENERGY TRENDS. An analysis of how and where future energy sources will be tapped and how it will affect industry.

ENFORCED LIQUIDATION. When the holder of a security fails to keep enough equity in his or her margin account.

ENGLISH AUCTION. Broker-dealers independently bid on a specific number of securities issued during a public offering at a price the broker-dealers feel is fair. The issuer distributes all of the issues to the best bid.

ENTREPRENEUR. A business owner, and the person who takes the greatest amount of risk in the business venture.

ENVELOPE. A graduated listing of securities' price extremes.

EOM. All purchases made through the 25th of one month must be paid within 30 days of the end of the next month. For example, if ABC Corporation purchased $10,000 worth of pharmaceuticals from Dow Chemical on February 10, with the sale marked with an EOM designation, that $10,000 would be due by the end of April.

EPS. *See* Earnings Per Share.

EPUNTS. In Europe, a payment guarantee that is expressed in terms of gold, with its value based in gold. Each unit weighs about 0.9 gram of gold. If someone owns a bond that is expressed in epunts, the holder can ask that it be paid in any one of 17 different currencies. Epunts, which stands for the defunct European Payments Union, were originally created to ease the difficulties in exchanging foreign currencies.

EQUAL COVERAGE. If a company issues bonds for a second time, this clause provides that the second issue will carry the same protection as the company's first issue.

EQUAL CREDIT OPPORTUNITY ACT. Legislation that outlaws sex, religious, and racial discrimination in the granting of credit. The lender also cannot discriminate if the person is receiving public assistance. Enforced by the Federal Trade Commission, this act became law in the mid-1970s.

EQUALIZING DIVIDEND. When changes occur in a dividend's normal dividend dates, this is paid to correct any irregularities.

EQUALIZING SALE. A short sale executed at either a lower price than the previous sale, or the same price as a previous sale, which was lower than the sale before.

EQUILIBRIUM PRICE. When the supply of a particular good or service equals its demand, this is the item's cost.

EQUIPMENT LEASING PARTNERSHIP. A limited partnership formed to buy computers, machinery and other equipment and, in turn, lease the equipment to other companies. While these partnerships profit from the lease payments, they also receive the tax advantages of the equipment's depreciation.

EQUIPMENT OBLIGATIONS. Any bond or note that is secured solely by the lien on a specific piece of equipment or machinery.

EQUIPMENT TRUST CERTIFICATES. A debt certificate that a company issues when it needs to buy mechanical equipment, with the equipment serving as the debt's collateral.

EQUITY. A company's value after all of its liabilities have been discharged.

EQUITY CAPITAL. Money a company earns by selling shares of its stock. Equity capital reflects ownership, while a bond represents a debt.

EQUITY EARNINGS. A portion of a subsidiary's surplus earnings that exceed dividend payments and that the parent company does not report.

EQUITY EQUIVALENT LOANS. A loan with property as collateral that provides the lender with the associated option of buying a percentage of the property.

EQUITY FINANCING. A company issues equity shares of stock usually at a time when the stock is trading at a high price.

EQUITY INCOME. A company's loan interest subtracted from its operating income.

EQUITY INCOME FUND. A fund that holds stocks and bonds, with both earning high dividends and interest.

EQUITY INVESTMENT. Any investment that does not carry a guarantee that the investor definitely will earn a specific amount of money.

EQUITY KICKER. An offering of debt securities that can be converted into the common stock of the company. Because of this feature, a company will pay less interest.

EQUITY MORTGAGE. A loan in which the lender reduces interest rates in exchange for part of the profits the owner earns when he or she sells the property. The percentage the lender receives equals the percentage by which the lender reduces the interest rate.

EQUITY NET WORTH. The amount of interest a company's stockholders own based on capital, retained earnings, and surplus.

EQUITY NOTES. Debt instruments that automatically convert to shares of common stock after a predetermined time. The common stock is issued by the same company as the debt instrument.

EQUITY PURCHASE ACCOUNTING. A company that has at least 20 percent of another company's stock can include a percentage of that company's income in its own net income. The percentage the company can include must equal the percentage it owns. For example, if the ABC Company owns 23 percent of XYZ Company's stock, ABC can include 23 percent of XYZ's income in its own net reported income.

EQUITY REIT. A real estate investment trust that buys and leases property using stockholder equity. Investors profit from the rental income and appreciation.

EQUITY RISK PREMIUM. The difference between the rate of return on risk-free assets and risky common stocks.

EQUITY SECURITY. Any stock that represents ownership in the issuing company, including common stock, preferred stock, and warrants.

EQUITY-TYPE SECURITY. A security that is not common or preferred, but can be converted or exercised for either.

EQUITY TURNOVER. Used to figure common equity's rate of return, this is the relationship between sales and the holder of common stock's equity.

EQUIVALENT BOND YIELD. Comparison of discount yields and the yields on bonds that pay interest. For example, if a 90-day Treasury bill is sold for $970, the yield to $1000 is 12.54%, based on 365 days.

EQUIVALENT TAXABLE YIELD. The amount of money an investor must earn from a taxable investment to get the same amount of money he or she would have earned on a tax-free investment.

ERISA. *See* Employee Retirement Income Security Act.

ERR. A designation in the futures market that indicates quotations have been erratic.

ERRORS AND OMISSIONS ACCEPTED. "E & OE" appears on customers' statements and relieves broker-dealers from responsibility if the statements contain mistakes.

ESCALATOR CLAUSE. A contract stipulation that cost increases will be passed on, whether the contract is for wages, in which case an employee would receive a raise if his or her employer's profits went up, or for a rent agreement, in which case the tenant would have to pay a higher rent if the property owner's costs went up.

ESCHEAT. The ownership of property reverts to the state if the property is abandoned, but in most cases the owner can claim the property later.

ESCROW. Money or assets involved in a contract are placed with a third party to make sure both sides fulfill their parts of the contract.

ESCROW AGREEMENT. Two people or two firms agree to place a specific amount of money with a third person or firm, with the money to be delivered only after all terms of the agreement are satisfied.

ESCROW ANALYSIS. A mortgagee reviews escrow accounts to make sure monthly deposits are enough to pay for insurance, taxes, and other expenses.

ESCROW RECEIPT. A depository guarantees it will deliver the securities involved in an option contract as soon as the contract is exercised.

ESCROW RECEIPT DEPOSITORY PROGRAM. The Options Clearing Corporation administers this book-entry program, which allows a custodian bank to easily deposit, move, or withdraw escrow receipts that are held as collateral on different series of the same class of option. The program cuts down on the issuing and reissuing of escrow receipts.

ESTATE. All the possessions one owns at the time of death.

ESTATE TAX. An excise tax imposed by a state or federal government to be paid before assets are transferred to heirs.

ESTIMATED BALANCE SHEET. An estimate of what a company's assets and liabilities will be at the end of the company's next fiscal year.

ESTIMATED TAX. The amount of money a financial officer believes his or her company will have to pay in taxes after tax credits are subtracted.

EUROBILL OF EXCHANGE. A bill of exchange expressed in terms of a foreign currency and payable outside of its country of origin.

EUROBOND. A company issues a bond through the international market, with interest and principal payments due in the currency in which the bond was issued.

EUROCREDIT SECTOR. A part of the European sector in which banks continuously roll over shorter-term loans with rates that fluctuate according to the cost of funds so the banks can act as long-term lenders.

EURO CLEAR. An organization in Brussels that provides transaction clearing services for member banks dealing in Eurobonds and Yankee bonds.

EUROCURRENCY. Currency deposited in a foreign bank with one of the parties not necessarily being European. For example, U.S. dollars deposited in Germany and Japanese yen deposited in Canada would both be considered Eurocurrency.

EURODOLLAR BONDS. American or European bonds that pay interest and principal in dollars.

EURODOLLAR CERTIFICATE OF DEPOSIT. A certificate of deposit purchased in dollars and deposited in a bank outside of the United States.

EURODOLLARS. U.S. dollars deposited in banks outside of the United States, with the foreign banks usually paying higher interest rates.

EURODOLLAR SECURITY. A U.S. or foreign security denominated in U.S. dollars, with the dollars deposited in European banks.

EUROLINE. A foreign bank offers a line of credit to an American, with the credit terms available in the foreign country's own currency.

EUROPEAN COMPOSITE UNIT. A private account unit with a specific amount of currency from each European community, with the amount of currency based on the significance of the country.

EUROPEAN CURRENCY UNIT. A weighted package of Common Market nations' currency, with the packages adjusted regularly to represent the different countries' trade balances.

EUROPEAN DEPOSITORY RECEIPT. A document issued in place of stock shares that represents ownership of the shares and makes it easier to deal in foreign securities because the actual stock certificates do not have to be physically transferred.

EUROPEAN ECONOMIC COMMUNITY. Belgium, France, Italy, Luxembourg, the Netherlands, and West Germany entered this alliance, called the Common Market, in 1957, to create an environment of cooperation in trade. Duties were standardized and barriers were torn down. Since then, Great Britain, Denmark, Greece, and Ireland have joined, as have several dependencies in Africa and the Caribbean.

EUROPEAN OPTION. A put or call contract that must be exercised within five days of the expiration date.

EUROPEAN TERMS. The amount of foreign currency needed to buy $1. For example, if it takes 2.5 Swiss francs to buy one American dollar, the franc would be worth 40 cents, and it would be called "2.5 in European terms."

EVALUATION. The process used to determine an investment portfolio's value, with exchange-listed stocks valued at their closing price the previous day, and over-the-counter stocks at their bid price.

EVALUATOR. An independent party without a beneficial interest that assigns a resale value to an asset which has a limit market.

EVEN-BASIS SWAP. An investor sells one fixed-income security from his or her portfolio and buys another without the portfolio's yield changing at all. The average maturity or face values in the portfolio, however, may change.

EVENING UP. A person profits from an investment, with the profit equaling— thus offsetting—a previous loss.

EVEN KEEL. The Federal Reserve System's monetary policy will stay the same.

EVEN LOTS. Stocks sold in blocks of 100 shares, or in multiples of 100 shares.

EVEN-PAR SWAP. One block of bonds is sold and another is bought at the same time with the same nominal principal, regardless of any net cash difference.

EVEN SPREAD. A spread position wherein an investor's premium on his or her long position equals the premium he or she has to pay on a short position.

EVERGREEN LOAN. A loan to a country to pay for any sovereign lending loss that might be caused by continuous rollovers or by the government's own reluctance to enter bankruptcy.

EVERGREEN PROSPECTUS. A securities issue registered with the Securities and Exchange Commission that will be offered continuously, such as a share in an open-end investment company.

EXACT INTEREST. Financial institutions pay interest based on 365 days per year, instead of the usual 360 days when calculating the daily interest accrued on large deposits.

EX-ALL. A security is sold without any rights, dividends, warrants, or other privileges.

EX-ANTE SAVING. A planned savings that may be either more or less than the planned investment.

EXCEPT FOR OPINION. An accountant's designation that an audit could not be completed in a specific area of a public company because the information available was not sufficient for the auditor to form an opinion.

EXCESS EQUITY. An account's cash value exceeds the amount needed for buying securities on margin.

EXCESS INTEREST. The amount by which the interest actually credited exceeds a dividend's lowest acceptable interest rate.

EXCESS MARGIN. Equity in a margin account that exceeds the lender's requirement. The excess amount can be invested or withdrawn.

EXCESS MARGIN ACCOUNT SECURITIES. A client's securities that exceed the value of that needed to pay the debit balance in his or her margin account. If the securities are worth more than 140 percent of the debit, the debit balance must be segregated in case the broker becomes insolvent.

EXCESS PROFITS TAX. Because of a certain historical base, the government can determine that a company's profits are too great and tax the amount that exceeds a certain limit.

EXCESS RESERVES. Federal Reserve System bank deposits that exceed the Federal Reserve Board's minimum requirements.

EXCESS RETURN. A security's return minus the return from a no-risk security during the same time period.

EXCHANGE. The physical location where brokers transact business for their clients.

EXCHANGE ACQUISITION. An order to buy a large block of stocks is combined with several orders to sell the same security, with the deal being put together on the exchange floor.

EXCHANGE CONTROL. A government prohibition of importing or exporting financial instruments, including bank deposits and notes.

EXCHANGE DISTRIBUTION. An order to sell a large block of securities is combined with several orders to buy the same stock, with the deal being put together on the exchange floor.

EXCHANGE FLOOR. The physical area of a stock exchange where securities deals are put together.

EXCHANGE FOR FUTURES. A person buying a cash commodity transfers the cash commodity of a long futures position to the seller, with any difference between the futures contract and the spot paid out in cash.

EXCHANGE FOR PHYSICAL PROGRAM. A method of trading index futures and their component stocks in which a computer shows deviations between the futures and the stocks in a spread. The trader then tries to buy the index future and sell the stocks short, or vice versa. After the deviations disappear, and the spread returns to normal, the trader closes out the positions for a profit.

EXCHANGE OF SPOT FOR FUTURES. Two investors swap a specific amount of a cash commodity for the same quantity of futures.

EXCHANGE PRIVILEGE. A stockholder can convert his or her mutual fund into another fund in the same family at no additional charge.

EXCHANGE RATE. How much of one currency is worth another. For example, if 1,000 Italian lira is worth one U.S. dollar, that would be the exchange rate.

EXCHANGES. Any financial instrument given to a clearing house for collection.

EXCHANGE SEAT. Stock exchange membership, with a limited number of seats available.

EXCHANGE SUPERVISORY ANALYST EXAMINATION. Employees of stock exchange-member firms who are responsible for reviewing research reports which will be issued to the public, must pass this test, which determines an employee's knowledge of financial analysis and exchange research standards.

EXCHANGE-TRADED OPTION. An option that is listed on one of the exchanges.

EXCHANGE-TYPE COMPANY. Now illegal, management companies formerly allowed their clients to trade in the securities they owned for diversified mutual fund shares without paying capital gains taxes.

EXCISE TAX. A federal or state tax placed on the manufacture of a commodity.

EX-CLEARING HOUSE. When two contrabrokers complete a transaction without using a clearing house.

EXCLUSION. Any item not covered in a contract, or a specific item that is listed as not being covered by the contract. For example, some expenses for which a person does not have to pay taxes are considered exclusions.

EX-COUPON. A stock sold without a coupon.

EX-DIVIDEND. The buyer of a stock will not receive a dividend that has been declared for that quarter, but the seller will. The trade will be ex-dividend because the settlement date will be after the record date, which determines which holder is entitled to the dividend.

EX-DIVIDEND DATE. The specific day a security begins to be traded without paying a current dividend. Only the person who owned the stock before this day is entitled to the current dividend.

EXECUTION. Filling a buy or sell order, or completing a securities transaction.

EXEMPTION. The government allows a taxpayer to deduct a certain amount from his or her total annual earnings for each family member, as long as the taxpayer can prove he or she paid at least half of that family member's support. The government also allows specific deductions for those with some physical impairments.

EXEMPT SECURITIES. Securities such as government and municipal bonds that do not have to be registered or that do not have to comply with some securities laws, such as those governing margin, dealer registration, and reporting requirements.

EXERCISE. The investor holding a put or call option decides to proceed with the transaction.

EXERCISE ASSIGNMENT. Notifying the person who wrote an options contract that the option is being exercised.

EXERCISE CUT-OFF TIME. The time frame in which the holder of an options contract must exercise the option, after which the contract is canceled.

EXERCISE LIMIT. Options exchanges prohibit investors and groups of investors working together from exercising more than 2,000 options in each class within five days.

EXERCISE NOTICE. A broker advises the Options Clearing Corporation that a long-option contract must be exercised, after which the OCC assigns another broker to fulfill the contract.

EXERCISE PRICE. The price for which a call holder can buy, or a put holder can sell, the underlying security.

EXERCISE RATIO. The number of common stock shares an investor is allowed to exchange for each warrant he or she owns.

EXERCISE VALUE. On a call option, this is the amount of money by which the underlying security exceeds the exercise price. On a put option, it is the amount of money that the exercise price exceeds that of the underlying security.

EXHAUSTION GAP. A gap that reverses a market trend.

EXIT. The time period in which an investor can convert his or her holdings into cash or stock to be liquidated over a designated period of time.

EXIT FEE. A bank fee designed to discourage investors from transferring their accounts to another trustee.

EX-LEGAL. A municipal security that is not accompanied by a bond counsel's legal opinion, the buyer must be advised of this fact before purchase.

EXPECTED YIELD. The amount of money an investor expects to earn from a specific security divided by the total investment, usually expressed in a ratio or percentage.

EXPENDABLE FUND. A fund designed to hold cash or assets to be used for administrative actions or other predetermined purposes.

EXPENDITURE. A payment or the promise to make a future payment.

EXPENSE. The amount of money it costs to make money.

EXPENSE RATIO. Mutual fund expenses are compared to the average net asset value of outstanding shares. The ratio normally is expressed as a number of cents for $100 of investment. For example, if the expense ratio is 58 cents, the investor is paying 58 cents per $100 to pay for the expenses incurred in operating the fund.

EXPIRATION. The last day an option can be exercised.

EXPIRATION CYCLE. One of three times in which options can be traded. One cycle includes January, April, July, and October; the second includes February, May, August, and November; and the third covers March, June, September, and December.

EXPIRATION DATE. Equity options normally become void at 11:59 p.m. Eastern Standard Time on the Saturday following the third Friday of the contract.

EXPIRATION MONTH. The specific month an option contract expires, after which its terms cannot be exercised.

EX-PIT TRANSACTION. A commodities deal traded off the floor of the exchange or away from the place where such deals normally are consummated.

EXPLORATORY DRILLING PROGRAM. A limited partnership engaged in a risky venture to find oil or gas at a sight that previously has not been drilled.

EXPORT-IMPORT BANK OF THE UNITED STATES. Established in 1934 and commonly referred to as the Eximbank, this is an independent federal agency that borrows money from the U.S. Treasury to finance U.S. exports and imports.

EX-POST. Variables that have had an effect on securities in the past, but no longer carry any importance other than providing a historical perspective.

EXPOSURE. The highest line of credit a broker-dealer will extend to a customer between the trade and settlement dates of a securities transaction.

EX-RIGHTS. Securities that previously were traded with specific rights, but the rights have been removed.

EX-STOCK DIVIDENDS. The time between when the payment of a dividend is announced and the day the actual payment is made. If an investor buys a stock during this period, he or she is not entitled to the forthcoming dividend.

EXTENDABLE DEBT SECURITY. A debt security in which the holder can redeem the note at face value at maturity or hold it for a specified time, after which the interest rate will be adjusted.

EXTENDED. A rise or fall in a security's price that continues a trend.

EXTENSION SWAP. An investor buys one debt security and sells another, with the new security giving the investor more time before maturity.

EXTERNAL FUNDS. Any infusion of capital into a company which does not come from the company's own sources. Bank loans and the proceeds of a bond sale are both considered external funds.

EXTERNALIZATION. A broker buys and sells securities for clients by sending the orders to the exchange floor for execution. This is the most common practice in securities trading.

EXTRA DIVIDEND. When a special dividend that is not included in the annual dividend amount is paid to investors with no guarantee that they ever will receive such a bonus again.

EXTRA-MARKET COVARIANCE. Prices of related securities move together, but not in line with the rest of the market.

EXTRAORDINARY ITEM. Either income or an expense that probably will not recur.

EX-WARRANTS. Securities that previously were traded with warrants, which give the holder the right to buy more shares at a certain price, but the warrants have been removed.

F

F. Describes large, rapid, price fluctuations in the commodities market.

FACE AMOUNT. The principal amount of money involved in a financial agreement or designated on a financial instrument.

FACE-AMOUNT CERTIFICATE COMPANY. An investment firm that issues fixed-rate debt securities, but no other types. The owner of a face-amount certificate makes periodic payments to the issuer, who agrees to pay the owner either the certificate's face value at maturity or the certificate's surrender value if it is presented before it matures.

FACE VALUE. The amount of money for which a coin, note or other financial instrument can be redeemed in cash, or the amount of money for which a financial instrument can be redeemed for cash at maturity.

FACILITATING AGENCY. Any company, such as a stock exchange or a brokerage house, that helps people or other companies obtain ownership of goods, services, securities, etc.

FACILITATION ORDER. An order for a broker-dealer's proprietary account that is crossed with a customer's order.

FACSIMILE SIGNATURE. A mechanically reproduced and stamped signature on a financial instrument.

FACTORING. An investor borrows against securities he or she owns to finance another position in the securities market.

FADED. Prices that were quoted earlier have been either adjusted down or withdrawn altogether.

FAIL FLOAT. The cash balance left after a securities transaction falls through because the security was not delivered by the settlement date.

FAIL POSITION. A broker-dealer cannot deliver securities to the buyer because the broker-dealer's client has not delivered the securities to him or her.

FAILS. A broker is unable to complete a transaction by the agreed upon settlement date.

FAIL TO DELIVER. An overdue agreement in which the seller has not delivered the security to the buyer.

FAIL TO RECEIVE. An overdue agreement in which the buyer has not paid for a security because the seller has not delivered the security.

FAILURE. When a person or company cannot meet financial obligations.

FAIR CERTIFICATE. An affordable, federally insured savings certificate that is not subject to federal income tax and pays significant returns.

FAIR CREDIT REPORTING ACT. A law that gives people the right to view their credit bureau credit reports, challenge any items they believe to be inaccurate, and submit a letter of explanation for any negative marks.

FAIR MARKET VALUE. The amount at which the buyer and seller, both with all available information, decide to complete a transaction, with neither having any leverage over the other, and with neither exerting any unfair influence upon the other.

FAIR PRICE. A regulation that requires a bidder to make the same offer for all shares of the same security he or she purchases during a specific time.

FAIR RATE OF RETURN. The maximum amount the federal government allows a public utilities company to earn as profit, with the amount based on how much the company must pay in dividends and interest, in maintaining equipment and covering overhead expenses.

FAIR RETURN. Considering the amount of money invested and any risks involved, this is the amount of profit a person can expect from an investment.

FAIR TRADE ACTS. Acts which allow manufacturers to set minimum retail prices for their products in an effort to diminish competitive price-slashing.

FAIR VALUE. A company's board of directors must determine a fair price, one that is reflective of worth, for any securities or assets that do not have market quotations readily available.

FAIRY GODFATHER. A prospective supporter or investor in a particular company.

FALL. The seller does not deliver the securities to the buyer by the specified delivery date.

FALLEN ANGEL. A well-known company's security with a value that dropped suddenly after a negative development or news report.

FALL OUT OF BED. A market that suddenly drops lower than at any other recent time.

FAMILY OF FUNDS. A group of mutual funds that are directed by the same investment manager, but have different objectives.

FANNIE MAE. Nickname for the Federal National Mortgage Association.

FARM CREDIT ADMINISTRATION. A division of the U.S. Department of Agriculture with the responsibility of aiding farmers during difficult times by offering credit or financial assistance.

FAQS. *See* Firm Access Query System.

FARMER'S HOME ADMINISTRATION. A unit of the Department of Agriculture. The FHA loans money for community centers, farms, and homes in rural areas.

FAR OPTION. The stock spread position that expires last.

FASB-8. The statement of Financial Accounting Standards No. 8 governs how companies account for and report foreign currency transactions.

FASCISM. An economic system in which the government controls private industry as the producer and distributor of goods and services.

FATE. The question of whether a bill of exchange has been accepted, paid, or has some other current status.

FAVORABLE TRADE BALANCE. When a country exports more than it imports.

FAVORITE FIFTY. The fifty largest equity holdings of all institutional investors.

FDIC. Formerly the Federal Deposit Insurance Corporation *(see* Bank Insurance Fund).

FEDERAL AGENCY SECURITY. A federally issued debt instrument that has a higher safety rating because it is government sponsored.

FEDERAL CREDIT AGENCIES. Any government unit that loans money to financial institutions, companies, or segments of the country's populace.

FEDERAL CREDIT UNION. A cooperative in which people can deposit money for savings, take out loans at low interest rates, and request other types of financial assistance.

FEDERAL DEBT LIMIT. The total face amount that the United States can legally issue in outstanding obligations, or can guarantee in principal and interest.

FEDERAL DEFICIT. The amount by which a country's spending exceeds its revenue. The U.S. Government normally floats long- and short-term loans to cover the deficit, which reached historic proportions in the 1980s. Economists blame high interest rates and inflation for the mountainous deficit.

FEDERAL DEPOSIT INSURANCE CORPORATION (FDIC). *See* Bank Insurance Fund.

FEDERAL FARM CREDIT BANKS. Consolidation of the Federal Intermediate Credit Bank, Banks for Cooperatives, and Federal Land Banks, which joined to reduce financing costs. They provide credit services to farmers.

FEDERAL FARM CREDIT SYSTEM. Provides short-term, discounted notes in increments of $50,000 to agriculture and agribusiness enterprises through 12 regional districts, each of which has a Bank for Cooperatives, a Federal Intermediate Credit Bank, and a Federal Land Bank.

FEDERAL FINANCING BANK. A government-owned bank created to reduce the costs of federal agencies with government-guaranteed obligations.

FEDERAL FUNDS. The amount of money that exceeds the Federal Reserve System's requirement for daily trading by member banks. These funds can be lent out overnight to other member banks.

FEDERAL FUNDS RATE. The interest rate charged when one Federal Reserve bank borrows money from another Federal Reserve bank.

FEDERAL HOME LOAN BANK. A corporation, sponsored by the U.S. government, that issues bonds, with the proceeds providing mortgages to the home building industry. The bank was established to promote home financing during the Great Depression.

FEDERAL HOME LOAN BANK CONSOLIDATED DISCOUNT NOTES. A short-term issue with no fixed offering schedule, sold in $100,000 denominations with maturities of 30 to 270 days, and sold without government guarantees.

FEDERAL HOME LOAN MORTGAGE CORPORATION (FHLMC). Commonly referred to as Freddie Mac, this government-sponsored company buys conventional residential mortgages from company members, then assures the mortgage and resells it publicly.

FEDERAL HOUSING ADMINISTRATION. Government unit that sponsors insurance for residential mortgage loans.

FEDERAL HOUSING INSURED LOANS. Private financial institutions that are insured by the U.S. Department of Housing and Urban Development insure mortgages to promote residential home-buying.

FEDERAL INTERMEDIATE CREDIT BANK. A unit of the U.S. government that issues bonds, with the proceeds directed toward farming and other agricultural interests.

FEDERAL INTERVENTION HOUR. Usually right before noon, the Federal Reserve System enters the market to conduct its own business.

FEDERAL LAND BANK. A corporation, sponsored by the U.S. government, that issues bonds, with the proceeds providing mortgages for farming interests.

FEDERAL LOAN BANKS. Twelve district banks that issue equitable long-term mortgages to farmers so the farmers can own their own farms.

FEDERAL NATIONAL MORTGAGE ASSOCIATION (FNMA). Commonly referred to as Fannie Mae, the FNMA is a government-sponsored corporation that buys and sells Farmers Home Administration, Veterans Administration mortgages, and some nongovernmentally backed mortgages.

FEDERAL OPEN MARKET COMMITTEE. A panel that makes short-term decisions in an effort to meet long-term Federal Reserve System objectives. The committee either sells securities to cut down on the money supply, or buys government securities to increase the money supply. The panel is made up of the Board of Governors and the presidents of six Federal Reserve banks.

FEDERAL RESERVE AGENT. A federal reserve bank's board chairman who maintains the collateral for all of the federal reserve notes held in his or her bank.

FEDERAL RESERVE BANK. One of the 12 banks that make up the Federal Reserve System. These banks monitor commercial and savings banks in their regional district to make sure they abide by Federal Reserve rules and regulations; they also provide emergency loans to the institutions. The 12 banks are in Atlanta, Boston, Chicago, Cleveland, Dallas, Kansas City, Minneapolis, New York, Philadelphia, Richmond, St. Louis, and San Francisco.

FEDERAL RESERVE BANK RESERVE REQUIREMENT. The amount of uninvested money a Federal Reserve bank must have in reserve, expressed as a percentage of the bank's demand deposits.

FEDERAL RESERVE BOARD. The Federal Reserve System's presidentially elected Board of Governors, administers the system's regulations and supervises its 12 banks. It also sets margin and bank requirements, as well as the system's discount rates.

FEDERAL RESERVE CHECK COLLECTION SYSTEM. The process by which a bank that accepts an out-of-town check sends the check to the Federal Reserve System, which in turn sends the check to its bank of origin and credits the bank on which the check was drawn.

FEDERAL RESERVE CREDIT. All of the Federal Reserve System's credit based on the amount that member banks have supplied to their reserves, mostly earning assets.

FEDERAL RESERVE CURRENCY. The Federal Reserve Bank issues this paper money for general circulation to be used as legal tender.

FEDERAL RESERVE NOTE. The most prevalent form of paper currency, ranging in denominations from $1 to $10,000, in the United States.

FEDERAL RESERVE REQUIREMENTS. The amount of money that Federal Reserve member banks must have deposited with a Federal Reserve Bank so the member bank can back up any outstanding loans.

FEDERAL RESERVE SYSTEM. An organization of 12 banks, with the group serving as a central bank that is overseen by a Board of Governors. The United States is divided into 12 districts, with one Federal Reserve Bank in each.

FEDERAL SAVINGS AND LOAN ASSOCIATION. A federally chartered organization that collects individual savings accounts and uses the money to make residential mortgage loans. These savings and loans are owned either by stockholders or depositors, and are members of the Federal Home Loan Bank System.

FEDERAL SAVINGS AND LOAN INSURANCE CORPORATION (FSLIC). *See* Savings Association Insurance Fund.

FEDERAL TRADE COMMISSION. A government agency that promotes fair competition and works to eliminate monopolies and unfair practices that lead to restraint of trade.

FEDERATION INTERNATIONALE DES BOURSES DE VALEURS. A Paris-based international stock exchange federation, to which the New York Stock Exchange belongs, that allows international investing.

FED WIRE. A computer system that connects the Federal Reserve System with its banks and with some dealers in government securities. Banks can use the computer to transfer the ownership of some securities.

FEEDING THE DUCKS. An investor sells his or her stock as the stock's price is going up.

FEEMAIL. The fees attorneys charge to settle shareholders' suits that try to stop the company's management from ransoming those shares of stock that are held by corporate raiders.

FEE OWNERSHIP. The same person owns both the royalty and working interest in a mineral ownership.

FEES AND ROYALTIES FROM DIRECT INVESTMENTS. Represents income that U.S. companies receive from their foreign affiliates, in which the U.S. companies are directly invested, which pays for such things as licensing costs, patent royalties, and management expenses.

FENCE SITTER. An investor who can't decide whether or not to invest in a particular venture.

FEVERISH MARKET. When market prices fluctuate so erratically that no common direction can be detected easily.

FIAT MONEY. Currency that cannot be converted into gold or silver, but is designated as legal tender. The currency has no tangible backing such as gold, but it is backed by a government's good faith. All U.S. currency is fiat money.

FICTITIOUS ORDER. A person orders a broker to buy or sell a security, but never intends to honor the contract. The buy or sell order is filed only to manipulate prices by making it look like there is a lot of activity in the market.

FIDELITY BOND. Insures employees, officers, and partners of broker-dealer firms against misplaced money or misplaced securities, forged checks, forged securities, and fraudulent trading.

FIDUCIARY. A person or firm entrusted with another person's or another firm's assets.

FIDUCIARY ACCOUNT. An account in which a bank holds assets for a client.

FIDUCIARY LOAN. A loan that is made without collateral.

FIELD GOAL. Nickname for the U.S. Fidelity & Guaranty Corporation, the stock symbol for which is FG.

FIFO. *See* First In, First Out.

FILL. An order to execute a buy or sell order for securities.

FILL OR KILL ORDER. A broker is ordered to trade an order entirely as soon as it reaches the trading post. If it is not executed immediately, it is canceled automatically.

FINAL DIVIDEND. In Great Britain, the last payment given to investors in a specific year. Because final dividends are required, they do not necessarily reflect other dividends paid earlier in the year.

FINANCE AND CONTROL. The gauge of a company's financial activities, including future plans, goals, and intended directions.

FINANCE BILL. A domestic bank draws this draft on a foreign bank against securities held in the foreign bank.

FINANCE COMPANY. Any financial institution that is not a bank, yet loans money to companies and individuals.

FINANCE PAPER. The credit that some companies issue to their own customers, like General Motors issues to its clients through the General Motors Acceptance Corporation.

FINANCIAL ACCOUNTING STANDARDS BOARD. A panel of certified public accountants that reviews and offers opinions on bookkeeping practices, with most companies following the board's recommendations when putting together their financial statements and reports.

FINANCIAL AND OPERATIONS PRINCIPAL. The person who is responsible for keeping financial records and approving financial reports. The individual must be tested and certified under the regulations of the National Association of Securities Dealers and the Municipal Securities Rulemaking Board.

FINANCIAL FLEXIBILITY. In a need to take care of unexpected costs or opportunities, this is the degree to which a company can effectively change the amount and timing of its future cash flow.

FINANCIAL FUTURES. An agreement to trade a financial instrument, such as a Treasury bill, at a specific price and on a specific future date.

FINANCIAL GUARANTY. A bond-insurer guarantees the bond will pay a fixed amount of money.

FINANCIAL GUARANTY INSURANCE COMPANY. A group of banks and brokerage firms that guarantees municipal securities and unit investment trusts.

FINANCIAL INSTRUMENT. Any financial document that has a monetary value or that verifies a financial transaction.

FINANCIAL INTERMEDIARY. A financial institution that smooths the flow of funds, such as redistributing savings, between units where income exceeds consumption and units where consumption exceeds income. Normally, individuals are seen as having income that exceeds consumption, and businesses and the government are seen as having consumption that exceeds income.

FINANCIAL PYRAMID. A structure, representing a pyramid, that investors aim for in setting up a risk structure. For example, an investor may want the bulk of the portfolio in safe liquid instruments with the tip of the pyramid in high-risk investments.

FINANCIAL RATIOS. Relationships between various items appearing on balance sheets, income statements, and other items to measure and evaluate a company's condition and effectiveness.

FINANCIAL STRUCTURE. All of a company's long- and short-term financing.

FINANCIAL SUPERMARKET. A large retail company or organization that offers a wide range of financial services, such as stocks, bonds, real estate, and insurance.

FINDER'S FEE. The fee given to a person who refers business to someone else.

FINENESS. The degree to which a piece of gold or silver actually is gold or silver.

For example, some bars of silver bullion have a fineness of .999, which means that 99.9 percent of the bar is pure silver.

FINITE LIFE REAL ESTATE INVESTMENT TRUST. An investment trust with real estate as the underlying asset. The assets must be liquidated at a future date, with the profits distributed to the beneficiaries.

FIREWORKS. A security's price shoots up quickly.

FIRM. The acceptance of an obligation.

FIRM ACCESS QUERY SYSTEM (FAQS). A computer network that the National Association of Securities Dealers offers to its customers so they can review pending securities registrations as well as the results of qualification tests.

FIRM BID. A bid that pledges a specific amount of money for a definite number of securities, with the bid binding on acceptance.

FIRM COMMITMENT. In a securities offering, the underwriter will assume the risk of selling the entire offering.

FIRMING OF THE MARKET. When, after a downturn, the prices of securities stabilize.

FIRM MAINTENANCE EXCESS. The minimum equity required of a margined security's long market value, usually about 30 percent at most firms.

FIRM MARKET. A nonnegotiable asking or selling price.

FIRM ORDER. An investor tells his or her broker to buy or sell a specific quantity of securities at a specific limit price.

FIRM PRICE. A broker tells a client that a specific cost for a security is non-negotiable and will be good only for a limited time.

FIRM QUOTE. The amount offered for a security that the market maker is willing to accept for a round-lot order.

FIRST BOARD. An established date that futures will be delivered.

FIRST CALL DATE. The first day a bond issuer can redeem all or part of an issue.

FIRST COUPON. This is used if the first interest payment on a newly issued bond will be anything other than six months from the issue date. Subsequent interest payments, however, will be made every six months.

FIRST IN, FIRST OUT (FIFO). For accounting and tax purposes, inventory and assets are presumed to be sold in the same order in which they were purchased. Therefore, inventory costs begin with the oldest asset, and move forward toward the most recent purchase.

FIRST MORTGAGE BOND. A long-term debt instrument with the first mortgage on the issuer's property serving as the bond's collateral.

FIRST NOTICE DAY. The first day a person can notify a short-position seller that a delivery will be made through a commodities clearing house.

FIRST PREFERRED STOCK. A stock that holds the primary claim on dividends and assets, with priority over common stock and other preferred stock.

FIRSTS. Any asset's highest quality issue.

FIRST SINKING FUND DATE. The earliest day a bond issuer can begin making sinking fund payments.

FIRST-YEAR REPUBLICAN JINX THEORY. A theory that the market will drop in the first year of any Republican president's incumbency.

FISCAL AGENCY SERVICES. Federal Reserve banks, acting on behalf of the federal government, maintain accounts for the U.S. Department of Treasury, cash checks drawn on the Treasury, sell and redeem securities, and perform a variety of other functions for the government.

FISCAL AGENT. A bank or trust company that acts, under a corporate trust agreement with a corporation, in the capacity of general treasurer. The agent will perform duties like making dividend payments, paying rents, redeeming bonds and coupons at maturity, and handling taxes relating to the issuance of bonds.

FISCAL POLICY. Congress' manner of managing taxes and public spending.

FISCAL YEAR. A company's bookkeeping year, which can begin at any time during the year.

FISH. When one dealer tries to identify the buyer or seller working with another broker-dealer who is trying to trade a large block of securities.

FITCH INVESTORS SERVICES. A firm that rates corporate bonds so investors can judge them as investment risks.

FITCH SHEETS. Fitch Investors Services provides a list of consecutive trade prices for specific securities.

FIVE HUNDRED DOLLAR RULE. A broker-dealer doesn't have to liquidate part of a client's account that has a cash deficiency if that cash deficiency is less than $500.

FIVE PERCENT RULE. Set by the National Association of Securities Dealers, this is an ethical standard for markups, markdowns, and dealers' commissions on securities transactions.

FIXATION. Establishment of a commodity's current or future price.

FIXED ANNUITY. An insurance product in which the recipient regularly deposits money, which later will be paid back out to the recipient or the recipient's beneficiary as income. Such annuities protect the person's principal, allow the annuitant to defer taxes on the interest, and exclude the income from any probate proceedings.

FIXED ASSET. Any asset a company expects to use in its current operations for at least a year.

FIXED-BALANCE BONUS ACCOUNT. A savings account that pays higher interest rates as long as the holder maintains a specific minimum balance for a specific time period.

FIXED CAPITAL. The capital that securities investors invest in fixed assets, as opposed to current assets, such as land, buildings, machinery, etc.

FIXED CHARGE COVERAGE. Compares a company's income before paying interest and taxes with the amount the company spends on its yearly interest on funded debts. The result provides a gauge of the bond's safety.

FIXED COST. A company's expense that does not change with business volume, such as salaries, interest, and rent.

FIXED-DOLLAR SECURITY. A nonnegotiable debt instrument that the holder can redeem for the amount established in a fixed-price schedule.

FIXED EXCHANGE RATE. A narrow range in which the exchange of two countries' currencies must fall when trading on the open market.

FIXED-INCOME INVESTMENT. An investment that pays a predetermined, regular rate of return until it matures, such as a coupon bond that pays a fixed rate of interest.

FIXED-INCOME MARKET. A debt-bearing instrument such as a money market, a corporate bond, or a financial future.

FIXED-INCOME SECURITY OPTIONS PERMIT. An American Stock Exchange license that allows the holder to trade interest rate options for his or her own account.

FIXED INTEREST RATE. An interest rate on a debt instrument that remains the same until the debt is retired.

FIXED LIABILITIES. A debt obligation that will mature in a year or more.

FIXED OBLIGATION. A debt that was fixed at the time of settlement, remaining fixed during the obligation's life.

FIXED PRICE. An amount the underwriting syndicate establishes as the public price of a new securities issue. The amount will not change unless the syndicate is dissolved.

FIXED RATE. A loan interest rate that does not fluctuate with changing market conditions. Because borrowers are protected from fluctuations, these rates are normally higher than variable interest rates.

FIXED RETURN DIVIDEND. A dividend that does not change during the life of an investment, such as that on a preferred stock.

FIXED TRUST. A trust with a portfolio that is made up of specific types and numbers of a security.

FIXING THE PRICE. Arbitrarily establishing a price on something in advance rather than via the free market.

FIXTURE. Any permanent structure or item attached to a piece of property that if removed from the property would cause permanent damage, such as electrical wiring or plumbing.

FLASH REPORTING. When transaction reporting at a stock exchange falls six minutes behind the market activity, the prices of 15 stocks are given every five minutes with "FLASH" preceding the prices.

FLAT. Used to describe a bond that is traded without any interest, such as a bond in default or one which is tied directly into the earnings at a company.

FLAT SCALE. When the short-term and long-term yields of a municipal bond are about the same.

FLAT TAX. A tax that is applied at the same rate to all income levels instead of higher income levels paying higher rates.

FLEXIBLE BUDGET. A report outlining a company's expected revenues and expenses, with costs varying according to sales and output levels.

FLEXIBLE EXCHANGE RATE. Where foreign exchange rates change because of supply and demand, not because any government is trying to manipulate the rate.

FLEXIBLE LOAN INSURANCE PLAN. A mortgage in which part of the buyer's down payment is put into a savings account, with the lender drawing on the account over a period of time to supplement the buyer's low monthly payments.

FLEXIBLE MANAGER. An investment manager with the ability to change the investments in a client's portfolio, both in the cash amount involved and in the types of securities held.

FLEXIBLE-PAYMENT MORTGAGE. A loan in which the first five years of payments are slightly lower because they cover only interest. After five years, the payments must be fully amortizing.

FLEXIBLE REPURCHASE AGREEMENT. A long-term contract, with securities as collateral, between a lender and borrower in which the borrower is required to buy the collateral back in the future. During the life of the loan, the principal and interest is adjusted according to current market conditions.

FLIER. A person who normally doesn't invest, or who invests conservatively, puts money into a highly speculative investment.

FLIGHT OF CAPITAL. Capital, or liquid assets that were converted from capital, that moves in such a way so as to cut losses or to increase profits.

FLIGHT OF THE DOLLAR. An investor uses the dollar exchange to buy foreign securities and thereby avoid the effects of inflation or some other financial force.

FLIGHT TO QUALITY. An investor who is trying to protect his or her portfolio in an unsettled market immediately moves his or her money to a safe investment.

FLIP MORTGAGE. A loan in which payments are graduated.

FLIP-OVER PROVISION. With this contractual stipulation, a company's preferred stock shares can be converted either into the company's common stock or into common shares of any corporation that takes the company over. With this stipulation, takeovers are less attractive because the percentage of new ownership can be drastically cut, with many shares remaining with the original holders of preferred stock.

FLIPPER. A trader in the market who is in and out of stocks usually in a matter of days.

FLOAT. The number of shares of a corporation that have been issued and are available for trading by the public.

FLOATER. A note with a variable interest rate that is tied to another interest rate.

FLOATING AN ISSUE. Distributing a new securities issue.

FLOATING CHARGE. A business loan, with assets instead of a particular piece of collateral as security, in which the lender is paid first from the assets after a receiving order is made against the firm.

FLOATING CURRENCY. A currency with its value based on market forces instead of on the variety of exchange rates, but that can be affected by official government intervention.

FLOATING DEBT. A continuously renewing debt.

FLOATING EXCHANGE RATE. An exchange rate that fluctuates and is not dependent on government activities.

FLOATING INTEREST RATE. An interest rate that changes according to market conditions, Treasury bills, and the prime rate.

FLOATING RATE NOTE. A bond with its interest rate adjusted according to the interest rates of other financial instruments.

FLOATING RATE PREFERRED STOCK. A preferred stock with a dividend that is adjusted according to another rate, such as a Treasury bill rate.

FLOATING SECURITIES. An investor buys a security in his or her broker's name and sells it immediately to make a quick profit.

FLOATING SUPPLY. The number of shares of a security that normally is available to be traded.

FLOOR. The physical area of an exchange where securities are traded.

FLOOR BROKER. A person who executes security or commodity orders, as agent, on the floor of an exchange.

FLOOR OFFICIAL. An exchange employee who settles auction disputes.

FLOOR PARTNER. The officer of an exchange member firm who is responsible for securities transactions on the exchange floor.

FLOOR REPORT. After an order has been executed on the exchange floor, the price, number of shares, and the name of the security are confirmed.

FLOOR TICKET. Entered by an investor's broker, this contains all the information necessary to complete a buy or sell order.

FLOOR TRADER. An exchange member who trades only for his or her own account or for accounts in which he or she holds some financial interest.

FLOTATION COST. The expense involved in issuing a new security. Normally, the flotation costs are higher for stocks than for bonds because distribution is wider and common stocks generally are more volatile.

FLOWER BOND. A Treasury bond that can be redeemed at par value when the owner dies so the proceeds can be used to pay any inheritance taxes.

FLOW OF FUNDS. A statement of how municipal revenue from a bond resolution will be spent and how priorities will be set as to what will be funded first, second, third, etc.

FLUCTUATION. Changes in a security's market price between transactions, with the movements caused by such factors as supply and demand.

FLUCTUATION HARNESSING. Dollar Cost Averaging in which an unchanging dollar amount is regularly invested.

FLUCTUATION LIMIT. Commodities exchanges limit the height and depth of daily price changes. If the price of a commodity reaches the limit, it cannot be traded any more during that day.

FLUID SAVINGS. Money that has not been invested.

FLURRY. A security's trading volume suddenly takes a sharp jump, albeit temporary, usually because of a newspaper or magazine report.

FMAN. Some classes of listed options expire quarterly in February, May, August, and November.

FNMA. *See* Federal National Mortgage Association.

FOCUS REPORT. Broker-dealers must submit Financial and Operational Combined Uniform Single reports to self-regulatory organizations monthly and quarterly. The statements must include the firm's earnings, capital, trade information, etc.

FOOTSIE. Nickname for the Financial Times Stock Exchange Index, which includes the 100 largest publicly owned stocks listed on the London Stock Exchange. Footsie is Great Britain's answer to the Dow Jones indexes in the U.S.

FOR A TURN. An investor commits to a particular stock for a small, fast profit.

FORBES 500. A list published in Forbes magazine of the 500 largest U.S. companies based on sales, assets, profits, and other requirements.

FORCED CONVERSION. Because the underlying shares of a convertible security are above market value, the convertible security is selling above its call price. The security's issuer calls the security at its call price so the holder must convert to common shares, sell it, or take the loss by accepting the lower call price.

FORECASTING. Projections in the market or economy by implementing existing data.

FORECLOSURE. The lender takes the home and property from a mortgagee who has failed to make timely payments.

FOREIGN BUY-SELL RATIO. The total foreign purchase of American securities divided by total foreign sales of American securities provides a gauge of how foreign investors perceive the American securities market.

FOREIGN CORPORATION. A company created in another country and incorporated under that country's laws. A foreign corporation also can refer to a company formed under the laws of another state. For example, a foreign corporation in Ohio could be a company incorporated in New York.

FOREIGN CROWD. Members of the New York Stock Exchange who trade foreign bonds.

FOREIGN CURRENCY. Paper money and coins issued by another country. In Germany, for example, the U.S. dollar is considered foreign currency.

FOREIGN CURRENCY OPTION. A put or call option on a package of individual foreign currency bought or sold on the Philadelphia Stock Exchange.

FOREIGN CURRENCY OPTIONS PARTICIPANT. A person certified by the Philadelphia Stock Exchange who can do business in particular foreign currency options.

FOREIGN DIRECT INVESTMENT. A foreign citizen buys most of an American company's stock.

FOREIGN EXCHANGE. The handling of foreign trades, including the physical movement of currencies from one country to another to complete a transaction.

FOREIGN EXCHANGE RATE. The amount of money one country's currency is worth compared to another's. For example, the number of francs it takes to buy one U.S. dollar would be the franc's foreign exchange rate.

FOREIGN INVESTMENT COMPANY. A company created and headquartered outside of the United States, but with Americans or American residents holding the majority of stock, and with securities comprising most of the company's assets.

FOREIGN INVESTORS TAX ACT. Established a 30 percent tax limit for foreign citizens who invest in U.S. securities. The legislation was designed to increase the number of foreigners who invest in U.S. securities, which could help lower America's international account deficit.

FOREIGN PERSONAL HOLDING COMPANY. A company created and headquartered outside of the United States, which has less than six Americans or American residents owning more than 50 percent of the company's stock, and with most of the company's income coming from investments.

FOREIGN SECURITIES. A security issued by a company incorporated outside of the United States which does most of its business outside of the United States.

FORGERY. The act of altering any document or signature with the intent to defraud or prejudice an individual. This is a statutory crime.

FORM 3. An officer, director, or investor who has at least 10 percent of a company's equity must file this report, which states security ownership, with the Securities and Exchange Commission.

FORM 4. An officer, director, or investor who has at least 10 percent of a company's equity must file this report, which states changes in security ownership, with the Securities and Exchange Commission.

FORM 8-K. A company files this report with the Securities and Exchange Commission within a month after an event occurred which changed the company's financial situation.

FORM 10-K. An annual report, released publicly, that all companies with registered securities must issue. The report must include such information as sales, revenue, and operating income.

FORM 10-Q. A quarterly report a company must file with the Securities and Exchange Commission; copies must also be sent to stockholders.

FORM S-1. Before publicly selling a securities offering, a company files this form with the Securities and Exchange Commission. In the form, the company provides detailed information about itself, the securities, and the manner in which the securities will be sold.

FORM S-2. Before publicly selling a securities offering, a company that has been reporting to the Securities and Exchange Commission for three years files this form with the SEC. Less detailed than Form S-1, Form S-2 provides the company's latest financial statements.

FORM S-3. Before selling personally owned stock, a company official files this form with the Securities and Exchange Commission.

FORMULA PLANS. Any predetermined system of investing, such as dollar cost averaging or constant ratio investing, that outlines a program based on investing a specific amount of money or investing during a specific time period. Through formula investing, a person can eliminate the risks involved in making financial decisions based on emotion.

FORTUNE 500. A list published by "Fortune" magazine which names the 500 largest U.S. industrial corporations ranked by sales.

FORWARD. A financial instrument an investor sells for future delivery. This act is in direct violation of federal securities laws. A mortgage-backed security, for example, cannot be sold this way.

FORWARD BUYING. An investor purchases commodities at the current market price for future delivery. An investor would forward buy if he or she expected the commodity's price to go up.

FORWARD CONTRACT. An agreement in which an asset s price is determined now, but the asset will be delivered in the future.

FORWARD COVER. A forward foreign exchange agreement that protects the buyer or seller of foreign currency from unexpected changes in the exchange rates.

FORWARD EXCHANGE TRANSACTION. Buying or selling foreign currencies with the price fixed at a current price, but with delivery to be made later.

FORWARD-FORWARD. An investor enters into a contract to be effective on a future date, with the instrument—often a certificate of deposit—maturing on an even further future date.

FORWARD INTEREST RATE. The most common interest rate for a specific forward futures contract.

FORWARD MARGIN. The difference between a currency's cost today and its cost at a specific future date.

FORWARD MARKET. When all transactions are made at the current market price with delivery to be made later.

FORWARD PRICE. The amount of money an asset costs when it will be delivered and paid for in the future.

FORWARD PURCHASE UNDERWRITING. A company raises money by issuing stock at a price higher than the prevailing rate with the understanding that the company will not collect the money until later.

FORWARD RATE. The dollar amount a commodity, currency, or bond will cost on future delivery.

FORWARD SELLING. An investor is selling a commodity at the current market price with the commodity to be delivered later. An investor would forward sell if he or she expected the commodity's price to drop.

FOUNDATION. A private, nonprofit, tax-free organization that collects and distributes money for charities.

FOUNDERS' SHARES. Capital stock, usually with special restrictions, issued to the people who created a company.

FOUR C GRADING SCALE. The four determinations of a diamond's value: carat weight, clarity, color, and cut.

401-K PLAN. An employee can deposit up to 10 percent of his or her gross salary in a company fund, with the fund invested in stocks, bonds, or money markets. Income tax is deferred on the amount the employee puts into the fund.

FOURTH MARKET. When two large institutions execute a securities deal without using a broker.

FRACTION. Less than one share of a stock. Holders normally do not receive dividends.

FRACTIONAL DISCRETION ORDER. A broker has the right to buy or sell for a client using the broker's own discretion, up to a certain order or price limit.

FRACTIONAL RESERVE BANKING. A system in which the money a bank must pay depositors on demand is invested or lent to other clients. Therefore, the bank could not pay 100 percent of the money it owed if 100 percent of its customers tried to withdraw all their money.

FRACTIONAL SHARES. Factors including stock splits, investment plans, and stock dividends create a security share that actually is less than one whole share.

FRAGMENTATION. Determining the primary market for a specific security is difficult because orders for it are flowing through several different exchanges.

FRANCHISE. A manufacturer or franchiser gives a dealer the right to sell his or her products in a specific area.

FRANCHISE TAX. A state tax that state-chartered corporations must pay to do business under their corporate names.

FREDDIE MAC. Nickname for the Federal Home Loan Mortgage Corporation.

FREE CREDIT BALANCE. The amount of money an investor has in his or her brokerage account that can be withdrawn.

FREE CROWD. The group that most actively trades bonds on the New York Stock Exchange.

FREED UP. Underwriting syndicate members no longer have to sell securities at the previously agreed upon price.

FREE MARKET. A system of voluntary transactions, with deals made according to unregulated supply and demand.

FREE RIDE. After a person makes a buy order, the stock price goes up and he or she sells the stock before actually paying for the buy order. This illegal practice allows a person to profit without actually risking any money.

FREE RIGHT OF EXCHANGE. An investor can change his or her security from bearer to registered, or from registered to bearer, without having to pay a fee.

FREE SUPPLY. When the total number of stocks in the commodities industry is less than that owned by the government.

FREE SURPLUS. The part of retained earnings that can be used to pay common stock dividends.

FREE WHEELING. After breaking a resistance area on the chart, a security's price increases even further.

FRIEDMAN THEORY. Economist Milton Friedman theorized that a country's monetary controls directly affect the country's economic condition, with the economy moving in direct proportion to an expanding or decreasing money supply.

FRIVOLITY THEORY. Hypothesizes that future market trends can be predicted by looking at the amount of money Americans spend on eating and drinking. If the amount is above 36 percent or below 33 percent of a household's income, the market will drop. The theory is that if the percentage does not fall within 33 and 36, Americans are too frivolous or not frivolous enough.

FRONT-ENDING ORDER. A broker-dealer agrees to buy part of a block order as long as he or she is allowed to act as the agent for executing the rest of the block.

FRONT-END LOAD. A sales charge of up to 8 percent that investors must pay when buying shares of a mutual fund.

FROZEN ACCOUNT. Any account in which no transactions can be made, usually because the bank or carrier of the account has accused the holder of some rules violation, or because of account discrepancies.

FROZEN ASSET. An asset that cannot legally be liquidated during a specific time period.

FULL. A bond that is trading with accrued interest.

FULL-BODIED MONEY. A commodity currency such as gold that is worth its face value.

FULL COUPON BOND. A debt instrument with a coupon rate higher than the market's current interest rate.

FULL DISCLOSURE. All pertinent facts about a security and the issuing company must be revealed when the security is offered for sale as required by the Securities and Exchange Acts of 1933, 1934, and the major stock exchanges.

FULL FAITH AND CREDIT. The promise to pay a debt secured only by credit history, not by collateral.

FULL FAITH AND CREDIT BOND. A financial instrument secured only by the issuers' credit history, not by collateral.

FULL-SERVICE BROKER. A broker who provides varied services to clients, such as offering advice, tax shelters, and partnerships.

FULL SERVICE FUND. A mutual fund in which the investor's dividends are automatically reinvested in the fund.

FULL STOCK. Any equity stock that has a par value of $100.

FULL TRADING AUTHORIZATION. A person other than the investor is permitted to trade on the investor's account.

FULLY DILUTED EARNINGS PER SHARE. A company's earnings figured as if all of the company's convertible securities had been changed into shares of common stock.

FULLY DISTRIBUTED. When a public securities offering has been completely sold to investors, either private or institutional, but not with large quantities sold to dealers or traders.

FULLY INVESTED. All of an investor's available money already is invested, so he or she cannot seek additional investments until liquidating some of his or her existing holdings.

FULLY MANAGED FUND. A mutual fund that puts money in several types of investments, such as common stocks, preferred stocks, and bonds.

FULLY MODIFIED PASS-THROUGH SECURITIES. A debt instrument with fractional claims on a multi-mortgage portfolio, with the issuer distributing guaranteed principal and interest to the holder. If the payments were not guaranteed, the securities would not be fully modified.

FULLY PAID SECURITIES. Securities an investor has paid for, or legal issues for which a company has received cash, goods, or services equal to its par value.

FULLY REGISTERED BOND. A bond's holders are registered with the issuing company. Any interest or maturity redemptions are automatically mailed to the holders.

FULLY TAX-EXEMPT SECURITY. A municipal debt with interest payments that are not taxable.

FULLY VALUED. The point at which a stock has reached a price that accurately reflects its underlying company's actual earning power. If the price goes above this price, it is overvalued, and if it drops below this price, it is undervalued.

FUND. An asset or sum of money that is set aside and designated for one specific purpose.

FUNDAMENTAL ANALYSIS. An analysis method in which only sales, earnings, and the value of a company's assets are considered.

FUNDAMENTALIST. An investor who places more importance on a company's conditions and on the conditions of the economy in general than on the market's technical factors or the technical factors of a specific security.

FUNDAMENTAL PRODUCT. A market offering, such as a savings account, that can be immediately recognized as what is being sold.

FUNDAMENTALS. A theory that one can forecast stock market activity by looking at the relative data and statistics of a stock, the company's management and its earnings.

FUNDAMENTAL VALUE. An asset's capital value, taken from its value as income plus interest, or from its use.

FUND BALANCE. The amount by which assets exceed liabilities and reserves.

FUNDED DEBT. Money raised when a long-term debt obligation, such as a bond, is issued.

FUNDED DEBTS TO NET WORKING CAPITAL. Divide the funded debt by net working capital to determine whether the long-term debts are in the proper proportion. The ratio should not be higher than 100 percent.

FUNDED DEBT UNMATURED. A funded debt that matures in a year or more from the date it is issued.

FUNDED DEFICIT. A government issues bonds for the sole purpose of retiring a deficit.

FUNDED RESERVE. A reserve that is invested in an interest-earning security.

FUND GROUP. A collection of funds that share similar purposes, classes, or characteristics.

FUNDING. Refinancing a debt before the debt matures, or providing capital for a business or organizational venture.

FUNDS MANAGEMENTS. A bank's balance is continuously adjusted and rearranged to increase profits as long as the liquidity is kept intact and the investments are safe.

FUNDS RATE. The interest rate a bank charges when loaning money to another bank or to a government securities dealer.

FUNNEL SINKING FUNDS. A sinking fund in which the issuer has combined payments from several issues so the profits can be used to retire the most expensive of the issues.

FURTHEST MONTH. The month that is the furthest away from settling an options or commodities contract, or the last month it can be settled.

FUTURE INCOME GROWTH SECURITIES. A bond issued by Paine Webber at discount which, after a specific number of years, pays a fixed interest rate based on a $1,000 par value.

FUTURES. Commodities which are sold to be delivered at a future date.

FUTURES CALL. Commodities are sold at the request of an investor who holds an option to buy the commodities at a certain price as long as the option is exercised by a predetermined date.

FUTURES COMMISSION MERCHANT. A business that handles buy and sell orders for commodities futures contracts or exchange-traded commodity options.

FUTURES CONTRACT. An agreement to sell or buy a specific amount of a commodity or security at a specific time, with the contract executed on one of the exchanges.

FUTURES EXCHANGE. A securities or commodities exchange designed to handle the trading of futures contracts only.

FUTURES MARKET. A market where futures contracts on commodities and securities are traded.

FUTURES SPREAD. Buying one commodities contract and selling another at the same time to take advantage of price differences between the two contracts.

FUTURE VALUE OF A DOLLAR. The rate at which a dollar will grow with a specific interest rate compounded over a designated length of time.

FUTURE WORTH. The amount an item is expected to be worth at a future date.

G

G. In newspaper stock listings, this designates earnings in Canadian dollars.

GAIN. An investment's realized or unrealized profits.

GAIN ON DISPOSAL. Selling an asset, which wasn't expected to be sold or converted to cash, for more than its book value.

GALLOPING INFLATION. A time when prices and wages are going up so quickly that the trend cannot be controlled by any normal means.

GAMBLING. Buying and selling securities without checking into the wisdom of investing in those particular issues.

GAP. A period when a stock's high and low prices do not overlap its high and low prices from the previous day during which no trade was made. This will occur when some extraordinarily positive or negative news is received on a stock or a commodity.

GARAGE. A nickname given to the New York Stock Exchange's annex floor, which is north of the exchange's primary trading floor.

GARNET ST GERMAIN DEPOSITORY INSTITUTIONS ACT. The Depository Institutions Deregulation Committee must authorize the issuance of money market deposit accounts, and the accounts must be equal to money market mutual funds. The accounts cannot have a minimum maturity, and must have up to three automatic and three third-party transfers a month.

GARNISHMENT. The withholding of wages by a court order. If a court has entered a judgment against a person for failure to pay a debt, the court also can order the person's employer to withhold all or part of that person's wages until the debt has been completely paid.

GATHER IN THE STOPS. Selling enough shares of a stock to force the price down to the level of stop orders. When the stop orders are activated, the price is driven down even farther, to the level of even more stop orders, thereby creating a snowballing effect.

GEARING. As England's version of leverage, this is the difference between fixed-interest capital and equity capital.

GENERAL ACCOUNT. A customer's margin account in which a broker makes equity transactions for that customer.

GENERAL BONDED DEBT. A government's outstanding bond indebtedness excluding utility and special assessment bonds.

GENERALISTS. Securities that trade at more than $100 a share, so named after the General Electric Company because its stock formerly traded above this price.

GENERAL LEDGER. A balance sheet that contains all of a company's financial statements, including the offsetting credit and debit accounts.

GENERAL LIEN. A claim against a person's personal property, excluding real estate, that carries the stipulation that the holder of the lien can take possession of the personal property to satisfy a debt. The property to be seized is not limited to the property which caused the debt.

GENERAL LOAN AND COLLATERAL AGREEMENT. A contract with which a broker-dealer can borrow money from a bank using listed securities as collateral so he or she can buy inventory, finance a new securities issue, or carry a customer's margin account.

GENERAL LONG-TERM DEBT. A government unit's long-term debt that can be paid from general revenues.

GENERALLY ACCEPTED ACCOUNTING PRINCIPLES. The procedures and rules that govern accepted accounting practices as defined and supervised by the Financial Accounting Standards Board, a self-regulatory organization.

GENERAL MANAGEMENT INVESTMENT COMPANY. An investment firm that does not specialize in any particular type of investment, so it can diversify when market conditions make doing so wise.

GENERAL MANAGEMENT TRUST. A trust fund that is not fully invested or limited to investing in one particular type of security.

GENERAL MORTGAGE. A blanket loan that covers all of a borrower's property and carries a lower priority in liquidation than mortgages that cover specific parcels.

GENERAL MORTGAGE BOND. A bond that the issuing company secures with all or most of its property, even if the property already is mortgaged.

GENERAL MOTORS BELLWETHER. A theory which says that when the common stock of General Motors reaches a new high, the general market will go up for four months; if it reaches a new low, the general market trend will follow suit for four months. If, within those four months, the General Motors stock does not set another high or low, the general market trend will reverse.

GENERAL OBLIGATION BOND. A municipal bond with the issuer fully backing, in credit and in faith, the obligation.

GENERAL PARTNERSHIP. An unincorporated business owned by at least two persons, with each being liable and each profiting in compliance with a predetermined plan.

GENERAL REVENUE SHARING. The federal government provides a certain amount of money to all centralized government entities, such as the 50 states, cities, villages, townships, Indian tribes, and counties, with each entity allowed to do whatever it wants with the funds.

GENERAL SERVICES ADMINISTRATION. A federal agency that buys, sells, manages, and maintains the government's property, as well as stockpiling strategic materials. The GSA sometimes issues government-backed participation certificates that are subject to federal taxes, but are exempt from local and state taxes.

GENSAKI. A short-term Japanese money market.

GENSAKI RATE. A rate applied to repurchase agreements involving Japanese bonds that are traded in yen.

GIFTS TO MINORS ACT. Allows an adult to act as custodian of a minor's investment account without being appointed by a court. The purchases, dividends, and interest all are in the child's name. Because the stocks are considered gifts, they cannot be revoked.

GIFT TAX. A tax assessed against a person who gives money or an asset to another person without receiving fair compensation; there is an annual exclusion of $10,000 per recipient. For example, if Donna Schmidt gave Daniel Schwarz a $100,000 car, but charged him only $1 for it, Donna Schmidt would have to pay a tax based on $89,999—$100,000 minus the $1 he paid equals $99,999, and $99,999 minus the $10,000 exclusion equals $89,999. The tax was designed to prevent people from transferring ownership to avoid taxes or to protect property from any pending legal action, such as bankruptcy.

GILT. A British word used to connote a debt obligation from the United Kingdom.

GILT-EDGED. Describes securities issued by a company that historically has achieved high profits and has proven its ability to make interest and dividend payments.

GINNIE MAE. Nickname for the Government National Mortgage Association.

GINNIE MAE CERTIFICATE UNIT TRUST. A government-backed mortgage with a maturity of 12 years or less which carries a reinvestment option. A broker will take all of the monthly interest and principal payments and put them into a market-rate money fund.

GINNIE MAE MORTGAGE-BACKED SECURITIES. Mortgage bank-issued securities backed by Ginnie Mae bonds and protected by the full faith and credit of the government.

GINNIE MAE TRUSTS. A closed-end investment trust made up of Ginnie Maes, with units available in lower denominations than the regular Ginnie Maes.

GINNIE MAE II. Serviced through Chemical Bank, this security is based on a number of different mortgage pools with varying rates and maturities from various parts of the United States.

GINZY. An illegal futures contract arranged at a price that is not favorable to the executing broker.

GISCARDS. A bond backed by the French government.

GIVE AN INDICATION. An investor enters a firm buy order for a specific number of a newly issued security, thereby expressing an interest in the issue.

GIVE AN ORDER. An investor tells his or her broker to buy or sell a specific number of a particular security, often with a predetermined price limit.

"GIVE ME A LOOK AT". A phrase brokers use when asking for a price and size quote on a particular security.

GIVE-OUT ORDER. An investor tells his or her broker to have a specialist execute a particular order for securities or commodities.

GIVE UP. When one broker executes an order for another broker's client, they split the commission, but the client does not have to pay anything extra.

GIVE-UP ORDER. An underwriter refuses to directly sell a security.

GLAMOUR STOCKS. Securities that are popular because investors believe the prices will go up faster than the general market. Glamour stocks normally have high price/earnings ratios, and usually sell at prices beyond their projected potentials.

GLASS-STEAGALL ACT. Prevents commercial banks from underwriting corporate securities and from owning broker-dealer affiliates.

GLOBAL CERTIFICATE. The total debt of a foreign debt security offering.

GLOW WORM. Nickname for the stock of Corning Glass, the stock symbol for which is GLW.

GLUT. To oversupply.

GNMA. *See* Government National Mortgage Association.

GNOME. Either technical analysts or a technical analysis of the market.

GNOMES OF ZÜRICH. A nickname the British gave to Swiss bankers involved in foreign exchange speculation during the 1964 sterling crisis.

GNP. *See* Gross National Product.

GO AROUND. When the Federal Open Market Committee accepts bids from those banks and investment houses that are allowed to directly buy and sell.

GO-GO FUND. A mutual fund invested in highly speculative common stocks, with investors looking for high, short-term profits.

GOING AHEAD. Brokers unethically trade for their own accounts before settling deals for their customers' accounts.

GOING AWAY. One or more municipal bond serial maturities that an institutional account purchased in a block, or another deal bought to use as inventory for future sales.

GOING BUSINESS. A company that has been continuously fiscally responsible and profitable and is expected to continue in the same manner.

GOING-CONCERN VALUE. The value one company has to another company or to individuals. When this value is greater than the value of its assets, the difference is described as goodwill, which is an intangible asset.

GOLD BOND. A bond issued by a gold-mining operation, with interest tacked on to the price of gold.

GOLD BRICK. A security that originally looks like a sound investment, but later turns out to be worthless.

GOLD BUG. An analyst who is partial to gold investing, recommending to investors that gold is a safe place to put money because a depression or hyperinflation could push up its price. In reality, gold is a safe investment because it holds value, but it's not usually very profitable. For example, one ounce of gold 50 years ago would buy a high-quality wool suit. Today, that same ounce of gold will buy that same suit because the price of each has risen equally.

GOLD CERTIFICATE. Legal tender that can be converted to gold on demand because it is backed by gold. Few countries today actually back their currency with gold.

GOLD CERTIFICATE ACCOUNT. Backed by government-owned gold and serving as legal reserve, these documents are what is on hand and due from the U.S. Treasury.

GOLDEN HANDCUFFS. A contract in which a broker agrees to stay with the same firm and receive profitable commissions and bonuses; or upon leaving the firm, agrees to repay a lot of the money he or she earned while with the firm. Such agreements were designed to deter brokers from continuously changing firms and taking their prior clients with them.

GOLDEN PARACHUTE. If a company is taken over, this provides the company's executives with profitable benefits (such as a large severance check and stock allowances) so that they will be financially secure in the event that they are let go.

GOLD EXCHANGE STANDARD. A system in which only central banks and foreign governments are allowed to convert a particular currency into gold.

GOLD FIX. When dealers in precious metals set the price of gold.

GOLD HOARDING. People convert their cash and other assets into large quantities of gold bullion in an effort to hedge inflation. The hoarders believe the value of the dollar will drop, so they invest in gold, which historically has held its value and has increased in value in tandem with inflation.

GOLD MARKET. A foreign exchange market specializing in gold trading.

GOLD MUTUAL FUND. A mutual fund with investments divided among shares of gold mining companies.

GOLD POINTS. The difference between the foreign exchange rates of gold standard countries, with the points equal to the exchange's par rate plus or minus the cost of transportation.

GOLD POOL. Representatives from the seven Central Banks try to keep the price of gold stable by trading gold within a specific price range. The seven representatives are from Belgium, Italy, the Netherlands, Switzerland, the United Kingdom, the United States, and West Germany.

GOLD SHARES. Stock issued by a company that mines gold.

GOLD STANDARD. When a government agrees to convert any or all of its currency into a specific amount of gold on demand. In other words, the country's currency is backed by an amount of gold equal to the currency's face value.

GO LONG. When an investor buys stock because he or she either needs to cover a short position or expects the price to go up.

GOOD BUYING. When investors buy securities based on sound, reasonable information.

GOOD DELIVERY. A stock certificate that is in good condition, is properly endorsed, and is accompanied by any required legal documents when presented to transfer the stock's ownership from one investor to another.

GOOD FAITH CHECK. Included with all bids on a bond sale. If the bonds are awarded to a syndicate that does not follow through on the agreement, this check is held to be used as liquidated damages. Losing bidders' good-faith checks are returned to them.

GOOD FAITH DEPOSIT. When an investor establishes an account with a brokerage firm, the firm usually requires a deposit of 25 percent of the purchase price; this is because the firm is unfamiliar with the investor's credit.

GOOD MONEY. A nickname for federal funds, so named because the holder can use the money immediately instead of waiting for it to clear a bank.

GOOD NAME BROKER. When a mismatch exists between the buying and selling broker, the Securities Industry Automated Clearing will suggest the name of this contrabroker so an easier and quicker settlement can be reached.

GOOD QUALITY. The stock of a company that has good financial status and historically has made prompt dividend and interest payments.

GOOD-THIS-MONTH ORDER (GTM). An investor tells his or her broker to buy or sell a specific amount of securities within a specific price limit, with the order expiring at the end of the month.

GOOD THROUGH. An investor tells his or her broker to buy or sell a specific amount of securities, usually with a specific price limit, within a predetermined time frame.

GOOD TICKET. Financially successful.

GOOD-TILL-CANCELED ORDER (GTC). An investor makes an order to buy or sell a specific number of a particular security, with the order remaining effective until the order is filled or until the investor cancels the order.

GOOD TO THE LAST DROP. If a clearing house member fails to transfer the debits and credits from a day's trading, the other clearing house members must make good on the transactions.

GOODWILL. An intangible asset between the book value of a company and the price at which the company is purchased. A company can build goodwill when they treat their customers well.

GOOSE JOB. A trader who faces a limited supply of a stock illegally tries to push the price up to increase its demand.

GO PRIVATE. In accordance with Securities and Exchange Commission rules, a company buys back all of its outstanding shares of stock in an effort to change the company's status from publicly held to privately held.

GO PUBLIC. A privately owned company becomes a publicly held company by selling shares of ownership publicly after registering with the Securities and Exchange Commission and meeting the SEC's requirements.

GORDON MODEL. A standard developed by Myron Gordon in which a stock's theoretical value can be determined by using equity investors' required rate of return to discount the stock's expected cash dividends.

GO SHORT. An investor who expects a particular stock's price to drop sells shares of that stock, even though he or she does not actually own the stock.

GOVERNING COMMITTEE. The governing unit of any securities or commodities exchange.

GOVERNMENT AGENCY SECURITIES. Debt securities, such as Ginnie Maes, issued by branches of the U.S. government, but not guaranteed by the government.

GOVERNMENT BILLS. U.S. government-issued debt securities that mature in a year or less.

GOVERNMENT BOND. A 10 year or longer U.S. government-issued debt security that carries the highest rate available.

GOVERNMENT NATIONAL MORTGAGE ASSOCIATION (GNMA). A government corporation that buys Veterans Administration and Federal Housing Administration mortgages, then issues bonds on pools of the mortgages. An investor in such a bond, commonly referred to as a Ginnie Mae, receives monthly dividends through the mortgagee's payments on principal and interest.

GOVERNMENT NATIONAL MORTGAGE ASSOCIATION MORTGAGE-BACKED SECURITIES DEALERS ASSOCIATION. An organization of Ginnie Mae dealers that pools its resources for training, lobbying, trading, and other industry-oriented topics for people interested in Ginnie Maes.

GOVERNMENT NATIONAL MORTGAGE ASSOCIATION STANDBY. A put option on a Ginnie Mae.

GOVERNMENT NOTES. Conservative, U.S. government-issued debt securities that trade easily and mature in one to 10 years.

GOVERNMENTS. Nickname for U.S. Treasury securities.

GRACE PERIOD. The time between the date a loan payment is due and the date the loan will be called in or canceled, or when the borrower will be considered guilty of default.

GRADING OF SECURITIES. Securities are rated according to the issuing company's financial strength, management ability, and stability so they can be compared against other securities.

GRADUATED PAYMENT ADJUSTABLE MORTGAGE LOAN. An adjustable-rate mortgage with low early payments that increase over time and level off after a few years. With the adjustable rate, both the borrower and the lender share the risk of changing interest rates.

GRADUATED PAYMENT MORTGAGE. A real estate mortgage that has a fixed interest rate, but monthly payments that rise during the first 10 years. The 10 years of payment increases reduces the principal, which ultimately reduces the life of the loan.

GRADUATED SECURITY. A security that has been moved from one exchange to a more prestigious exchange in order to widen its trading range. For example, a security that was moved from a regional to a national exchange would be a graduated security.

GRAHAM-DODD METHOD. Benjamin Graham and David Dodd theorized that investors should buy securities that had undervalued assets because the assets' prices eventually would increase to their true value. They also said investors should buy stock in companies with assets that exceed liabilities and long-term debt, and with low price-earnings ratios. In addition, Graham and Dodd said investors should market their shares when the shares reach a profit of 50 to 100 percent.

GRAIN. A measure equal to 0.002 troy ounce or 0.0648 gram.

GRAIN PIT. The area of a commodities exchange where brokers transact business; different areas represent different contract periods.

GRAM. A metric measure equal to 0.03215 troy ounce or 15.432 grains.

GRAMM-RUDMAN ACT. Federal legislation that requires the national deficit to be erased by 1991.

GRANDFATHER CLAUSE. A stipulation included in most new rules, regulations, and laws that protects people who already are engaging in the practice outlined in the law from being restricted by the law. For example, if Joe Smith owned a store in a neighborhood that later was zoned for residential use only, he still could maintain his store because he was conducting business at the location before the new zoning law took effect. New businesses, however, could not be established in the area. In the securities industry, if a new examination is required of people wishing to be financial advisors, those who already serve as financial advisors don't have to take the test.

GRANNY BOND. A government savings bond available in England to retired citizens and citizens receiving money from the government.

GRANTOR. The primary person who establishes or puts money into a trust.

GRATUITY FUND. When a member of one of the stock exchanges dies, his or her next of kin receives a benefit from this fund, which ranges from $20,000 to $100,000. The fund is made up of contributions from exchange members.

GRAVELLED. The London equivalent to bottoming out. It is when a stock's price starts to go up after it has hit a low, which then sparks interest in the security because of its low price.

GRAVEYARD MARKET. A bear market in which investors who sell their shares lose money, and other potential investors stay away from the market altogether. The market is so named because the people who are inside can't get out, and the ones who are outside don't want to get in.

GRAY CHIPS. Stocks of small- and medium-sized companies, as opposed to blue chips.

GRAY KNIGHT. The second bidder in a corporate takeover attempt, who hopes to take advantage of any hostilities that may exist between the first bidder and the corporation. The corporation has not solicited this second party.

GRAY MARKET. A broker-dealer buys shares of an open-end mutual fund above the net asset value so he or she can resell the shares to his or her clients.

GREAT DEPRESSION. When the U.S. stock market crashed on October 29, 1929, almost every nation in the world plunged into a depression, with supplies exceeding demands, businesses failing, and the job market squeezing closed. The Great Depression, seen by many as the worst financial crisis in America's history, continued until the mid-1930s.

GREED INDEX. A system of grading portfolio managers. The lower the score, the more bearish, thus more preferable, the manager. A manager can receive up to 10 points in each of 10 categories which include: institutional activity, preference of stocks to bonds, money manager of personal investments, and invests for aggressive growth.

GREENMAIL. An investor buys a large block of stock with the intention of selling it to a corporate raider at a premium, or selling it back to the company at a higher premium to keep it out of the hands of the corporate raider.

GREEN SHOE. This underwriting agreement clause allows the syndicate to buy more shares at the original offering price so it can safely cover shares it sold short.

GRESHAM'S LAW. Sir Thomas Gresham, an English economist, theorized that if a country has two forms of currency, citizens will hoard the currency with the higher intrinsic value, thus forcing it out of circulation.

GROSS. The total amount of cash or assets before taxes are paid.

GROSS ESTATE. The total value of a person's assets before any deductions for taxes, funeral expenses, attorney fees, or administration costs. After these items are deducted, the remainder is the person's net estate.

GROSS LEASE. Typically a short-term rental agreement, in which the owner agrees to pay all expenses such as utilities, insurance, and repairs.

GROSS NATIONAL PRODUCT (GNP). A measure based on the current market prices of the total of all goods and services produced in the United States, with the amount expressed in dollars.

GROSS PROFIT. The amount of money an investor profits before paying taxes or commissions.

GROSS SALES. A company's total sales, with no deductions for customer returns, discounts, or adjustments.

GROSS SELECTION. Any choice made before the final choice.

GROSS SPREAD. The amount an underwriter charges the seller when the underwriter resells a block of securities; the fee includes management costs, underwriting fees, and selling concessions.

GROSS UNDERWRITING SPREAD. The difference between the cost of a new security and the amount that goes to the issuer.

GROSS YIELD. A discounted bond's yield to maturity before any taxes are paid.

GROSS YIELD TO REDEMPTION. A British term used to describe a security's interest yield plus its annual capital gain if it is redeemed.

GROUP AVERAGES. An entire industry's average of market prices, price/earnings ratios, and earnings per share.

GROUP NET. The manager of a municipal securities syndicate is given a buy order in which the buyer, who is not a member of the syndicate, agrees to pay the public offering price and promises to leave the entire spread in the syndicate's account for the syndicate's benefit.

GROUP OF TEN. The 10 largest free industrialized nations, which work together to keep the world economic scene stable. The nations are: Belgium, Canada, France, Italy, Japan, the Netherlands, Sweden, the United Kingdom, the United States, and West Germany.

GROUP SALE. The sale of a block of securities to an institutional investor, with the securities coming from the underwriting syndicate's pot.

GROUP SALES. A syndicate manager sells offerings registered with the Securities and Exchange Commission to institutional investors, with the shares being pulled from the syndicate's pot.

GROWING EQUITY MORTGAGE. A home real estate mortgage with the first principal and interest payments based on 25 years, then increasing 4 percent per year. The increase helps reduce the principal amount, so the equity is increased and the mortgage actually is amortized in 15, not 25, years.

GROWTH FUND. A mutual fund that invests in stocks with a long term capital appreciation objective.

GROWTH INDUSTRY. A business or an entire industry that is reaching higher profit and sales levels than the general market, with the trend expected to continue.

GROWTH IN EARNINGS PER SHARE. Primary earnings per shares' annual percentage growth for a restated five-year period.

GROWTH PORTFOLIO. A securities portfolio comprised of stocks that are expected to increase quickly in price.

GROWTH STOCK. A stock that financial experts predict will rise quickly in price because the issuing company is in an expanding industry or in the midst of some new and potentially popular technology.

GSA. *See* General Services Administration.

GTC. *See* Good-Till-Canceled Order.

GTM. *See* Good-This-Month Order.

GUARANTEE. To be liable for paying a debt if the person originally responsible for the debt defaults.

GUARANTEED ACCOUNT. One brokerage client guarantees another client's account, with the equity from the guarantor's account used in the account he or she is guaranteeing.

GUARANTEED BOND. A bond that is issued by one company, but backed by another.

GUARANTEED CERTIFICATE OF DEPOSIT. A bank-issued certificate of deposit with flexible terms, guaranteed principal, and reinvestment rates.

GUARANTEED DEBT. A public company's debt that the federal government guarantees as a contingent liability.

GUARANTEED INCOME CONTRACT. An insurance company contract in which a corporation makes a large capital investment through its pension and profit-sharing plans, and the insurance company guarantees a specific rate of return on the invested capital over a period of three to 10 years. The insurance company takes on all interest, market, and credit risks involved with the security that serves as collateral for the obligation.

GUARANTEED INSURANCE TRUST. Created for small- and medium-sized retirement funds, a broker will use a group of these trusts to form a unit trust, then sell participation units with face values as low as $1,000.

GUARANTEED INVESTMENT CONTRACT. A short-term, public bond with a fixed rate of return.

GUARANTEED MORTGAGE CERTIFICATE. A security with income passed from the debtor, through an intermediary, and to the investor, with the owner of the security holding an undivided interest in a parcel of conventional mortgages bought by the Federal Home Loan Mortgage Corporation.

GUARANTEED SPREAD. A customer agrees to buy a new security at a price to be determined, and the broker-dealer, in turn, agrees to buy the securities the customer already is holding at a spread somewhere between the two prices.

GUARANTEED STOCK. A preferred stock with dividend payments guaranteed by a company other than the issuer.

GUARANTEE LETTER. A commercial bank issues this document on behalf of a customer who has written a put option. The letter guarantees that the dollar amount involved will be paid if the option is exercised.

GUARANTEE OF SIGNATURE. A bank or brokerage house issues a document certifying that a customer's signature is genuine. Such documents usually are required when a security's ownership is transferred from one person to another.

GUERILLA. A syndicate that tries to out-bid an independent bidder on a new municipal bond issue.

GUERILLA GROUP. A municipal underwriting group with only a few members who assume large financial risks.

GUN JUMPING. Illegally soliciting orders for a security before the Securities and Exchange Commission has approved the issue, or buying a security after receiving inside information that is not available to the public.

GUNSLINGER. An investor who puts money into speculative ventures.

GUY TO THE HEAD. Used to draw attention away from plans to take over a company, often when the takeover would be a friendly one.

H

HAIRCUT. A way of computing a broker-dealer's net capital by valuating securities; the manner varies depending on the type of security and its market risk.

HAIRCUT FINANCE. A person borrows money using securities as collateral.

HALF-HEDGED OPTION. An option writer sells two option contracts for every 100 shares of the underlying stock he or she owns.

HALF STOCK. Any stock that has a $50 par value.

HAMMERING THE MARKET. The persistent selling of stocks to drive the prices down.

HANDLE. The total percentage amount of a bid or asked price. In most cases the handle is omitted because industry professionals presumably already know the percentage amount involved. For example, if a bid is quoted as "8–14," the professional will know the price actually is 87 8/16 bid and 87 14/16 asked because he or she knows the security's current market price.

HANDLING CHARGE. A brokerage fee for handling small orders.

HAND SIGNALS. The manner in which brokers formerly signaled price quotes and executions on the American Stock Exchange.

HANG SENG INDEX. Similar to the Dow Jones Average but more reflective, this index charts the price movements of 33 stocks listed on the Hong Kong Stock Exchange.

HARD CURRENCY. A national currency from an economically and politically stable nation, such as Switzerland, France, or the United States, with the currency holding worldwide confidence.

HARD DOLLAR. Payments made by a customer for services such as research and investigations.

HARD MONEY INVESTMENTS. Investments in gold, silver, or a foreign currency that has undergone little inflation.

HARD SPOT. Securities that remain strong in a weak market.

HART-SCOTT-RODINO ACT. A law requiring a corporation that is trying to buy into another company to notify the Federal Trade Commission and the Justice Department if the firm is planning to spend more than $15 million or buy 15 percent or more of that other company.

HEAD AND SHOULDERS. When a security's central price peak is higher than the surrounding peaks.

HEART ATTACK MARKET. After President Dwight D. Eisenhower suffered a heart attack in 1955, the Dow Jones Industrial Average dropped 6.5 percent.

HEAVY. A lot of offers to sell a particular security, which will cause its price to drop.

HEAVY INDUSTRY. An industry which manufactures basic products such as steel, oil, or mining.

HEAVY MARKET. When sell orders exceed buy orders, securities and commodities prices drop.

HEDGE. A measure used to offset losses or potential losses. For example, gold and oil often are used as investments to hedge, or offset, inflation.

HEDGE CLAUSE. A disclaimer that absolves a writer, who has obtained information from a presumedly sound source, from responsibility if information in letters or research documents is found to be inaccurate.

HEDGED TENDER. When a seller believes the buyer will accept less than the full amount of a stock tendered, he or she will sell a portion short for protection.

HEDGE FUND. A mutual fund that involves speculative investing in stocks and options, while selling short other companies engaged in the same industry.

HEDGER. A person who, in order to avoid losing his or her cash position in the market, tries to offset potential losses.

HEDGING. Selling foreign currency forward to local currency to protect the money against any changes in the exchange rate.

HEMLINE THEORY. A theory that securities prices move in accordance with the hemlines on women's skirts.

HERFINDAHL INDEX. A statistical analysis for determining when an industry is so saturated that a merger would be anti-competitive.

HICCUP. A temporary market drop.

HIDDEN ASSETS. A company's assets that are not readily apparent by studying the company's balance sheet.

HIDDEN INFLATION. The quality of goods and services drops, while prices may not rise. While hidden inflation affects the economy, it does not appear on any of the major indexes.

HIGHBALLING. A dealer illegally buys a customer's securities above the current market value so the dealer doesn't have to take a loss. When the customer exchanges his or her holdings for other holdings, which also are sold above the market value, the dealer takes the loss on the purchase, thereby giving the dealer a gain on the sale.

HIGH CREDIT. The maximum one-time trade credit a company receives from a supplier.

HIGH FLYERS. A speculative security that goes either up or down in price by several points on any given trading day.

HIGH-GRADE BONDS. A bond that has been classified as AAA or AA by Standard & Poor's rating service. Such rankings are given to bonds issued by strong, stable companies with high levels of proven management ability.

HIGH-LOW INDEX. Predicts market pattern changes by defining the year's highs and lows on a moving average.

HIGH-PREMIUM CONVERTIBLE DEBENTURE. A bond that protects the holder against inflation by providing higher returns and a long-term equity kicker.

HIGH-QUALITY STOCK. The stock of a company that historically has paid dividends in a timely manner, has shown good management, and has demonstrated fiscal responsibility.

HIGH-RATIO LOAN. A mortgage that is more than 80 percent of the sales price.

HIGH-RISK STOCK. An investment in a security with a volatile price, usually stock of a company with a high price-earnings ratio and a small capital structure.

HIGHS. The total number of stocks that have made a new 52-week high in a daily session.

HIGH-SPECULATION SECURITY. A security from a company that has a high price-earnings ratio is considered a risky investment.

HIGH TECH. A company that manufactures or is connected with the sale or distribution of highly advanced computers, machines, or concepts.

HISTORICAL COST. All of the data on financial statements must be detailed with each entry's original cost to the company.

HIT. The dollar amount lost on any particular investment.

HOLD. A stock an investor buys and keeps because it is expected to have growth.

HOLDER IN DUE COURSE. A person or firm takes on an obligation that is complete and regular with the provision that he or she takes possession before the obligation is overdue and with the verification that it has not been dishonored.

HOLDER OF RECORD. The person who holds a stock on the close of business on the record date. That person will be entitled to receive the dividends.

HOLDING COMPANY. One company owns enough shares of another company to hold voting control.

HOLDING COMPANY AFFILIATE. One company owns enough shares of a bank to hold voting control over the bank's board of directors.

HOLDING PAGE. A brokerage account that shows all of a client's transactions and holdings.

HOLDING PERIOD. The length of time a person holds on to an investment or a company holds on to an asset.

HOLDING PERIOD YIELD. Add the dividend yield to the percentage change in a stock's capital value during a specific time period to obtain this figure, which provides a measure of an investment's return.

HOLDING THE MARKET. An investor buys enough shares of a security to increase interest and thereby cut down on a price decline.

HOME. A term a seller uses for a buyer when looking for a buyer in a tight market. For example, a seller would say, "I'm looking for a home for 15,000 shares of ABC stock."

HOME LOAN BANK BOARD. A panel that oversees the Federal Loan Bank System.

HOMEOWNER'S EQUITY ACCOUNT. A homeowner can borrow on the equity in his or her home through a line of credit.

HOME RUN. An investor makes a significant profit in a short time.

HONEYCOMBED WITH STOPS. When the securities market contains a lot of stop orders.

HORIZON ANALYSIS. Measures an investment's discounted cash flow by studying changes from the time of the investment's maturity. The analysis provides a comparison with different types of investments so investors can fill their individual portfolio needs appropriately.

HORIZONTAL MERGER. When one company buys another company that is involved in the same type of business.

HORIZONTAL SPREAD. Buying and selling the same types of option contracts with the same underlying security and the same striking price, but with different expiration dates.

HOSPITAL REVENUE BOND. A city- or state-issued, tax-exempt bond taken out to finance the construction of a new hospital or nursing home, which subsequently will be operated as a nonprofit organization.

HOT ISSUE. A newly issued stock that is in demand and rises quickly in price.

HOUSE. A broker-dealer company or a firm involved in investment banking.

HOUSE ACCOUNT. The account a brokerage firm uses for its own transactions.

HOUSE CALL. A broker notifies a customer that the equity in the customer's account has dropped below the maintenance level. If the customer fails to bring the account to a higher level, the broker can liquidate the account.

HOUSE MAINTENANCE REQUIREMENT. What a brokerage firm determines is the lowest level a customer's margin account can hit before further collateral is required.

HOUSE OF ISSUE. An investment bank that underwrites and distributes securities.

HOUSE PAPER. A subsidiary or affiliate accepts a commercial bill of exchange drawn by the parent company.

HOUSE RULES. A broker-dealer firm's rules regarding how customer accounts should be handled.

HOUSING AND URBAN DEVELOPMENT. A federal agency that guarantees loans and takes other measures to provide housing for low- and middle-income citizens.

HOUSING BOND. An uncallable bond issued by a housing authority and used to finance construction of low- and middle-income housing, factories, or pollution-control plants.

HOUSING STARTS. One of the 12 leading economic indicators, with changes that can drastically affect banking, construction, and other industries.

HULBERT RATING. Hulbert Financial Digest outlines how well different investment advisories fared in accuracy over the years, who followed the recommendations, and how much the advisories' followers profited or lost.

HUMAN ACTION THEORY. The foundation of the Austrian school of economics, this theory states that every human action is motivated by a person's desire for a higher level of mental well-being.

HUMPTY DUMPTY FUND. A unit investment trust made up of shares of American Telephone and Telegraph and its regional companies.

HUNG UP. An investor's money is tied up in securities that have dropped below the original purchase price. If the investor sells the shares, he or she will suffer a great financial loss. However, if he or she holds on to the shares, they may drop even lower.

HURDLE RATE. The minimum rate of return on an investment.

HYBRID ANNUITY. An insurance firm allows an investor to mix the benefits from fixed-rate and variable-rate annuities.

HYPERINFLATION. Out-of-control inflation that cannot be reined by ordinary means.

HYPOTHECATED ASSET. An asset that has been pledged, but physical possession and title have not be transferred.

HYPOTHECATED STOCK. A stock that was pledged as collateral on a loan.

HYPOTHECATION AGREEMENT. A client signs this document to open a margin account, pledging securities so that money can be borrowed against those securities.

I

I. Appears in stock listing to indicate that a dividend already has been paid or has been omitted or deferred.

I BUY. Used by over-the-counter brokers to acknowledge a transaction for a security in his or her own account. The expression stresses the broker's role as a dealer.

IDEAL PORTFOLIO. The perfect portfolio an investor would hold if all of his or her assets were available to be invested.

IDENTIFIED SHARES. The portion of an investor's multiple holdings of the same security, purchased at different prices, that the investor wants to sell off.

IDLE MONEY. Money in cash available for investing.

IF COME ORDER. A customer order to buy a bond issue if the broker-dealer can obtain the bond from its current holder.

IFX OPTION. *See* International Option.

IMMEDIATE ANNUITY. An annuity that begins making payments one period after a lump sum has been purchased.

IMPUTED VALUE. A reasonable or logical value a company does not record in its books, including those not yet available.

INACTIVE ACCOUNT. A brokerage account in which there has been no activity over a long period of time.

INACTIVE ASSET. An asset a company does not continuously use in its production processes, such as a backup generator.

INACTIVE BOND CROWD. Exchange-listed bonds that trade infrequently.

INACTIVE MARKET. When the market's trading volume drops below its normal level.

IN-AND-OUT TRADE. An investor buys a security and then sells it immediately in the hopes of making a short-term profit.

INCENTIVE FEE. A bonus paid to commodities trading advisors for providing outstanding services or for producing outstanding results.

INCENTIVE STOCK OPTION. Executive compensation in which the executive pays no tax when exercising a stock option. If the executive holds the stock for more than a year, the difference between the exercise price and the sale price is considered a long-term capital gain.

INCHOATE. Not completed, or recently begun.

INCHOATE INTEREST. Indicates the person has a future interest in a piece of property.

INCOME ACCOUNT. Part of a portfolio that is devoted to holding onto money that is available for spending.

INCOME AVERAGING. Personal income tax is computed by averaging the current year's income with the income received during each of the three previous years. By using this method, a taxpayer is not hit with a large tax increase if his or her income rises by 140 percent or more in a year.

INCOME BASIS. The amount of interest or dividend dollars compared to the amount the investor paid for a security.

INCOME BONDS. A bond issued by a reorganized company, with interest paid out only when, and if, enough interest is accumulated.

INCOME DIVIDENDS. The amount paid to mutual fund investors, with dividends, interest, and short-term capital gains earned and paid from the fund's portfolio securities after operating expenses are deducted.

INCOME FUND. A mutual fund that provides investors with short-term high income instead of long-term principal growth.

INCOME INVESTMENT COMPANY. A management investment firm that tries to provide the highest income possible to its fund holders.

INCOME LIMITED PARTNERSHIP. A limited partnership designed to achieve high income, which then uses tax shelters to protect its profits from taxes.

INCOME PORTFOLIO. Securities designed to provide investors with short-term high income instead of long-term growth.

INCOME STATEMENT. A part of a company's annual report that tells how much money the company made or lost in the previous year after all expenses are deducted.

INCOME STOCKS. Usually considered conservative securities with returns in the form of dividends rather than capital gains.

IN CONCERT. Two or more people join forces to reach a specific investment goal.

INCONVERTIBILITY. When a security or other investment cannot be exchanged for another security or for cash.

INCREMENTAL COST OF CAPITAL. The weighted average of additional costs raised in a specific time period associated with debt issues and equity classes composing the firm's capital structure.

INCURRED LOSSES. The number of transactions in which a company or an individual has lost money, with the transaction occurring within a specific time period.

INDENTURE. The part of a bond that specifies its terms and obligations.

INDEPENDENT AUDIT. An audit conducted by someone not within or associated with the firm undergoing the audit.

INDEPENDENT BROKER. A member of the New York Stock Exchange who executes orders on behalf of overworked floor brokers.

INDEX. A statistical composite that tracks changes in the economy or in the financial markets.

INDEX CALL. A bond issue stipulation in which the issuer can retire the bond at a price connected to the prevailing government bond rate instead of the more commonly used fixed-dollar price.

INDEX FUND. A fund made up of securities that parallel a major market index. The portfolio carries most of the same securities that are listed in the index and carries them in the same proportion. This type of investing is also known as an index program.

INDEX FUTURES. A promise to buy or sell a standard amount of stock index by a particular date through a broker licensed by the Commodity Futures Trading Commission.

INDEXING. The organizing and weighing of a person's investments in line with one of the major stock indexes.

INDEX OF COINCIDENT ECONOMIC INDICATORS. Compiled from a collection of indicators issued by the U.S. Department of Commerce. This index uses such items as retail sales and personal income to come up with a value that many believe accurately reflects the current state of the economy.

INDEX OF INDUSTRIAL PRODUCTION. A federal index that measures the state of the economy by comparing changes in U.S. industrial, mining, and utility production.

INDEX OF LAGGING ECONOMIC INDICATORS. Compiled from a collection of indicators issued by the U.S. Department of Commerce. This index uses such items as outstanding business loans and trade inventories' book values to come up with a value that many believe accurately reflects the former state of the economy.

INDEX OF LEADING ECONOMIC INDICATORS. Compiled from a collection of indicators issued by the U.S. Department of Commerce. This index uses such items as unemployment and factory orders to come up with a value that many believe will accurately reflect the future state of the economy.

INDEX OPTIONS. An option that is based on a stock index instead of on an underlying security, with the option paying in cash instead of shares when exercised. The Options Clearing Corporation issues index options.

INDEX PROGRAM. *See* Index Fund.

INDICATED ORDER. An expressed interest in buying or selling a security. Following an indicated order, the broker can try to find a contra buyer or seller, but cannot execute the transaction without a binding order from the person who originally expressed the interest.

INDICATED YIELD. The amount a stock is expected to yield during a specific time period based on market projections for that specific security.

INDICATION. The price range in which a security can be traded.

INDICATORS. Factors that accurately depict financial trends are also used to predict future economic movements.

INDIRECT EXPENSE. Any business expense that is not associated with a particular department or function, such as rent, utilities, insurance, and taxes. Such costs usually are distributed evenly over a company's departments because all of the departments benefit equally from them.

INDIRECT LABOR COSTS. The amount of money a company spends on employees who are not involved in the actual production of the finished products. Indirect labor costs could be associated with the salaries paid to maintenance workers, secretaries, or inspectors.

INDIVIDUAL ACCOUNT. Any account that carries only one person's name.

INDIVIDUAL IDENTIFICATION. The method by which brokers segregate fully paid and excess-margin securities. Through this method, brokers register the securities in the customer's name or tag the securities with identification marks.

INDIVIDUAL RETIREMENT ACCOUNT. Employed persons make deductible payments of up to $2000 into this tax-sheltered fund, from which withdrawals will be made to the owner without a penalty between the ages of 59 1/2 and 70 1/2.

INDIVIDUAL RETIREMENT ACCOUNT ROLLOVER. A person who loses his or her job and receives a pension distribution in a lump sum can reinvest the amount in his or her IRA within 60 days. The amount, therefore, falls under the IRA's tax shelter.

INDORSEE. The person to whom a financial instrument is payable.

INDORSOR. The person to whom a negotiable instrument is payable, but who signs that payment over to another person.

INDUSTRIAL. Companies that produce and distribute goods and services. Those that are followed closely by market analysts such as Dow Jones, will be used to devise indexes to determine market trends.

INDUSTRIAL BOND. A bond issued by a company that produces and distributes goods and services. The money raised from the debt will be used for expansion, working capital, or the retirement of other debts.

INDUSTRIAL COLLATERAL. Brokers who borrow in the call money market present this stock exchange collateral, represented by the broker's traded stocks, to the lender.

INDUSTRIAL PRODUCTION. A Federal Reserve Board statistic that is released once a month and provides the total amount of U.S. output from mines and factories.

INDUSTRIAL REVENUE BOND. A municipal bond issued to raise money for construction of a corporate building, factory, or other venture. Principal and interest on the bond are paid through the venture's proceeds.

INDUSTRIAL STOCKS. An industrial corporation's common stock, excluding the common stock of banks, railroads, or utilities companies.

INDUSTRY. A specific segment of business, with all related businesses falling into the same segment. The businesses, while following their own financial paths, generally experience the same overall market trends that other businesses within the same industry experience. For example, while Shell and Mobile Oil compete, they also both are hurt by low import prices and helped by oil embargoes.

INDUSTRY FUND. A mutual fund with most of its investments in preferred stocks and bonds derived from industrial companies with the objective of high income and preservation of capital.

INFANT INDUSTRY ARGUMENT. Some new industries say they need protection from imports or other international competition while they are trying to establish themselves. They seek help from their government by asking that import duties and tariffs be imposed.

INFLATION. The rise in the costs of goods and services, with the value of the currency going down.

INFLATION ACCOUNTING. A company's ledger reflects the effects inflation has had on its business.

INFLATIONARY GAP. The difference between the amount of private and public investment funds available and the total amount of savings. Many believe the inflationary gap sets the pace for inflation.

INFLATIONARY RISK. The potential an investment has for losing purchasing power during its lifetime. The risk is that the investment will be worth less once it is liquidated.

INFLATION HEDGE. An investment that is expected to go up in value enough to offset the declining value of the dollar during inflation.

INFLATION-PROOFING. A person protects his or her savings and other fixed-income investments from the effects of inflation by tying the investments to a standard that reflects any changes in purchasing power, such as an index.

INFLATION RATE. The rate of change at which prices rise.

IN FOR A BID. An institutional investor asks a broker-dealer for a bid on a block of securities from the broker-dealer's proprietary account. The commitment becomes binding following negotiations as long as the broker-dealer can execute the deal on the exchange floor.

INFRASTRUCTURE. A nation's physical foundation based on road maintenance, bridges, electrical systems, transportation, communication, and other aspects, all of which provide the nation with millions of jobs.

IN GEAR. The even and parallel rise in two or more economic indicators, such as two of the Dow Jones averages.

INGOT. A bar of precious metal, such as gold or silver.

IN HAND. A firm order a broker must execute for a customer within a specific, limited time frame, usually during the same morning or afternoon.

INHERITANCE TAX RETURN. A document the executor or administrator of an estate must file with the state government to determine the amount of tax due on an inheritance.

INITIAL EQUITY. The amount of money or securities a brokerage house requires a customer to have to open a margin account.

INITIAL MARGIN. The amount a customer must have in his or her margin account to take a long or short position in the market.

INITIAL PUBLIC OFFERING. The first time an equity securities issue is available for the public to buy.

INJUNCTION. Prohibits a person or company from participating in specific activities following an accusation that the person or company is violating the regulations of the Securities and Exchange Commission. The prohibition usually remains in effect until an inquiry can be completed.

IN-LINE TRANSACTION. Indicates a person buying or selling a block of securities is looking for a contra buyer or seller, and agrees to complete the deal at the prevailing market price.

INSCRIBED. A government bond with records held by a Federal Reserve Bank.

INSIDE DIRECTOR. A company director who holds a large block of the company's stock.

INSIDE INFORMATION. Information known by a company's directors and officers, but not available to the public. Generally, the facts concern conditions that could affect the price of a company's securities. Trading securities using the advantage of having inside information is illegal.

INSIDER BUYING AND SELLING. Officers or directors in a publicly traded corporation buy or sell securities from that corporation.

INSIDER TRADING SANCTIONS ACT. A federal law that allows the Securities and Exchange Commission to sue people who illegally trade securities. The law enables the SEC to seek up to three times the profit earned or three times the losses avoided by the person or company involved in the illegal activity.

IN SIGHT. The amount of commodities that are to be delivered to a specific place.

INSOLVENCY. A debtor cannot meet financial obligations, and his or her assets are not sufficient to meet those obligations, even after liquidation.

INSTALLMENT SALE. An asset is sold with payments to be made regularly over a specified period of time, or money is lent with the principal and interest to be repaid regularly over a specified period of time.

INSTALLMENT SALES CONTRACT. An agreement in which a property buyer receives possession of the property, but not actual title until the entire loan is paid.

INSTITUTIONAL BROKERAGE FIRM. A brokerage house that specializes in handling investments of large organizations that invest their assets.

INSTITUTIONAL BROKER'S ESTIMATE SYSTEM. A compilation of analysts' estimates of how much thousands of public companies are expected to make in the future.

INSTITUTIONAL BUY-SELL RATIO. Measures the enthusiasm of institutional investors by dividing institutional selling into institutional buying.

INSTITUTIONAL HOUSE. A brokerage firm that has financial institutions and profit-sharing plans, instead of individuals, as clients.

INSTITUTIONAL DELIVERY SYSTEM. A system that paves the way for trade notifications and settlements between broker-dealers' institutional investors. Through the system, transfers, payments, and deliveries are made between the custodian banks and the broker-dealers.

INSTITUTIONAL INVESTOR. A large organization that invests its assets and buys large blocks of securities.

INSTITUTIONAL LENDER. A financial institution that invests, directly or indirectly, in mortgages.

INSTITUTIONAL MARKET. Corporations and financial institutions use this market of short-term investments and commercial paper for investing large sums of money for short-term profits.

INSTITUTIONAL NETWORKS CORPORATION. A computer network subscribers use to complete transactions without using a broker.

INSTRUMENT. Any security.

INSTRUMENTALITY. Any federal agency, such as the Federal Land Bank, with obligations that are backed by the government's full faith and credit.

INSUBSTANTIAL QUANTITY. The limit, as prescribed by the National Association of Securities Dealers, that broker-dealers can allocate on hot issues.

INSURANCE. System whereby a party, whether an individual or a company, concerned about potential hazards, pays premiums to an insurance company. Pools of money are collected, categorized by the hazard, out of which losses sustained by the contributors are paid.

INSURED MUNICIPAL BOND. A municipal bond with principal and interest protected by insurance, which is paid for by the issuer. Such bonds carry higher ratings because of the protection involved.

INTANGIBLE ASSET. An item that is considered valuable, but that does not have a physical presence. A company's good reputation, for example, would be an intangible asset.

INTANGIBLE COST. A business cost that is tax deductible, such as those incurred in oil drilling, geological surveys, or management fees.

INTANGIBLE PROPERTY. The title and deed to a piece of personal property.

INTANGIBLE TAX. A state tax on individual bank deposits, including stocks and bonds.

INTANGIBLE VALUE. The total value of any corporation's intangible assets.

INTEGRATED MARKETMAKING. A dealer who continuously bids on equity securities and on over-the-counter options on the underlying securities.

INTENSITY. The degree to which the market, in a specific trading period, is filled with either overbuying or overselling.

INTER ALIA. Appears in legal complaints to indicate the specific charges and inferred other charges made against broker-dealers and their firms. Literally translated, the Latin words mean, "among other things."

INTER-AMERICAN DEVELOPMENT BANK. Owned by several Western nations, this bank promotes and advances the development of the member countries in Latin America.

INTERBANK BID RATE. The rate at which a clearing member buys, or offers to sell, U.S. dollars for immediate delivery from another member in exchange for transaction currency.

INTERBANK MARKET. A market wherein investors can spot and forward currency transactions.

INTERBANK RATES. The interest rates effective when one bank lends money or assets to another bank.

INTERCHANGE AUTHORIZATION. The amount an authorizing member can approve transactions on behalf of the issuer. The member can approve the transaction alone if the amount is at the specified amount or less than the specified amount. If it is more than the amount specified, the issuer must approve the transaction.

INTERCOMMODITY SPREAD. The price difference between the long and short positions of two different, but related, commodities, such as gold and silver.

INTERCORPORATE STOCKHOLDING. A form of restraint-of-trade in which one company holds stock in another company, and uses those share holdings to hinder its competition. Such activities are illegal.

INTERDELIVERY SPREAD. Buying one month of a commodity contract, and selling another month of the same contract.

INTEREST. The amount of money a lender loans a borrower to pay for using the borrower's principal.

INTEREST ACCRUED. The amount of interest that has been earned, but not yet paid.

INTEREST ASSUMPTION. That rate at which an investment in an investment plan's assets is expected to produce returns.

INTEREST BEARING. A debt instrument that pays interest instead of dividends.

INTEREST-BEARING NOTE. A note in which the issuer has agreed to pay the face value plus interest.

INTEREST CHARGES. The cost of carrying a customer's margin account, including brokerage fees.

INTEREST DIFFERENTIAL. The difference between one interest rate and another.

INTEREST EQUALIZATION TAX. A defunct 15 percent tax on interest that foreign borrowers of U.S. capital had to pay in the 1960s and early 1970s. The tax led to the development of the Eurobond.

INTEREST ON INTEREST. Compound interest, which is computed with each forthcoming interest payment based on the principal plus the previous earned interest amount. With simple interest, payments are based only on the principal amount.

INTEREST RATE FUTURES MARKET. A market for trading financial futures contracts on some government securities, commercial paper, and currencies.

INTEREST RATE OPTION. An options contract on a financial instrument.

INTEREST WARRANT. A document in which a company asks an issuer to pay all interest due on the issuer's notes and other debts.

INTEREST YIELD. The interest rate on a security, computed using the price at which the security was purchased to amortize premiums paid or to accrue discounts received.

INTERIM BORROWING. Selling short-term paper while expecting a bond to be issued.

INTERIM CLOSING. A company's account books are closed before the end of the company's fiscal year without computing profits and losses.

INTERIM DIVIDEND. Generally a quarterly dividend, this is declared and paid before earnings have been announced.

INTERIM REPORT. A regular report, issued monthly or biannually, that updates stockholders on progress and developments within the company. Like the interim statement, the report acts as a supplement to the company's annual report.

INTERIM STATEMENT. A company puts out a financial report that covers only part of its fiscal year to supplement its annual report. A quarterly statement, for example, would be an interim statement.

INTERLOCKING DIRECTORATE. A person serves as a director on the boards of two or more companies, which is legal as long as the companies do not compete with each other.

INTERMARKET. Trading the same security on at least two different stock exchanges, or selling one type of bond while buying another type.

INTERMARKET SPREAD. Buying a commodity that is deliverable on one exchange while selling the same commodity deliverable on another exchange.

INTERMARKET TRADING SYSTEM (ITS). A computer network that connects six stock exchanges so brokers and market makers can contact each other to execute orders. The six exchanges are the American, Boston, Midwest, New York, Pacific, and Philadelphia.

INTERMEDIARY. A financial institution with the power to make or implement investment decisions for others.

INTERMEDIATE CREDIT BANK. One of 12 Federal Intermediate Banks that other financial institutions use for rediscounting intermediate-term agricultural paper.

INTERMEDIATE TERM. A time frame, usually between six and 12 months in regard to stocks and one to 10 years for debt instruments.

INTERMEDIATE-TERM CREDIT. Credit that has been extended for three to 10 years.

INTERMEDIATE TREND. A security's price movement that falls within a larger, general trend.

INTERMEDIATION. The process by which funds flow through a financial institution into investments or borrowers.

INTERMOUNTAIN POWER AGENCY. A political subdivision of Utah that issues municipal revenue bonds to finance its activities, which include owning, buying, building, and operating the electrical plants within the state.

INTERNAL AUDIT. A department of a company that conducts audits of that same company's financial records.

INTERNAL CONTROL. A company's system of maintaining an efficient and well-managed business with protected assets and well-regulated policies.

INTERNAL EXPANSION. The amount by which a company's assets grow through internally generated cash, accretion, or appreciation.

INTERNALIZATION. A broker buys or sells securities for a customer within his or her own brokerage firm without going to the exchange floor to execute a deal.

INTERNAL FINANCING. A company uses retained earnings to expand its business.

INTERNAL RATE OF RETURN. Because interest rates and depreciation cause shifts in property values, it is difficult to compute actual returns on a real estate investment. Therefore, this rate is computed by dividing net rents and the residual value, minus mortgage interest, into the actual dollar amount invested in the property.

INTERNAL REVENUE. All of the United States government's income from federal taxes except for money received through import or customs duties.

INTERNAL REVENUE SERVICE (IRS). The U.S. agency empowered to collect and administer the accumulation of all internal revenue taxes.

INTERNATIONAL BANK FOR RECONSTRUCTION AND DEVELOP-MENT. An agreement to help finance the reconstruction of Europe following World War II. The bank now helps developing countries to build an infrastructure.

INTERNATIONAL BANKING AND INVESTMENT SERVICES. A computer network based in Valley Forge, Pennsylvania, through which traders can buy securities for their own accounts. The network provides traders with confirmations, currency positions, credit information, and settlements.

INTERNATIONAL COMMERCIAL EXCHANGE. A commercial market for trading currency futures.

INTERNATIONAL CORPORATION. A company that does business in more than one country.

INTERNATIONAL DEPOSITORY RECEIPT. A receipt given for a foreign corporation's share certificates.

INTERNATIONAL FUNDS. Any funds that can be used to buy securities that are traded on foreign exchanges.

INTERNATIONAL MONETARY FUND. A United Nations financial agency that establishes currency exchange rates and tries to maintain a world balance of trade.

INTERNATIONAL MONETARY MARKET. The part of the Chicago Mercantile Exchange where futures contracts on precious metals, foreign currencies, and Treasury bills are traded.

INTERNATIONAL MONEY MANAGEMENT. A company that handles multinational investments uses this strategy to attain higher interest earnings and reduce risks by taking advantage of changes in exchange rates.

INTERNATIONAL MUTUAL FUND. A mutual fund with investments in international securities and foreign currencies.

INTERNATIONAL OPTION. An equal and transferable foreign currency option cleared by the Options Clearing Corporation and traded on the London and Philadelphia stock exchanges. This instrument is also known as an IFX option.

INTERNATIONAL SECURITIES. Listed and unlisted securities that are traded on exchanges throughout the world

INTERPOLATION. A statistical analysis used to determine a bond's price or yield when the bond's maturity falls between listed maturity dates. To find the price or yield, determine how far away the bond falls from the listed maturity, and adjust the price accordingly.

INTERPOSITIONING. This potentially unethical practice exists when one broker uses another broker to execute a deal between a client and the market. By doing this, the client ends up paying more and receiving less because he or she is paying for two agency transactions instead of one.

INTERPRODUCT COMPETITION. A company that offers different but similar goods to the same market, such as two different kinds of soft drinks.

INTERSTATE COMMERCE COMMISSION. A government agency that oversees interstate transportation companies and regulates equipment trust certificate offerings.

INTERSYMPATHY BETWEEN STOCKS. The prices of similar securities usually follow the same trends.

INTERVALS. A schedule of exercise prices, expressed in points, upon which options are introduced.

INTERVENTION. An agency that handles currency transactions can maneuver exchange rates between the currencies it handles.

INTERVENTION CURRENCY. The foreign currency a country uses to make sure the standard exchange rate margins are maintained.

INTER VIVOS TRUST. A trust established for transferring a piece of property from one person to another.

INTESTATE. When a person dies without leaving a last will and testament.

IN THE MONEY. An option contract that has a below-the-market strike price on the underlying stock for a call, and an above-the-market strike price for a put.

IN TOUCH WITH. When a seller knows someone is interested in purchasing a security, even though that potential buyer has not entered an actual order.

INTRASTATE SECURITIES OFFERING. A company in one state sells its securities only to citizens of another state.

INTREPRENEURIALISM. A large corporation invests in a new, small company to take advantage of any new technology that the new company may be developing.

INTRINSIC VALUE. In a call option, the amount the underlying security's current market value exceeds the option's strike price. In a put option, the amount the option's strike price exceeds the underlying security's current market value.

INTRODUCING BROKER. A futures commission broker and National Futures Association member who gives another member a customer execution and clearance.

INVENTORY. A balance sheet entry that represents all materials involved in a company's manufacturing processes, including all goods produced as well as all raw materials.

INVENTORY FINANCING. A bank finances a dealer's inventory of consumer or capital goods. The dealer uses the inventory as collateral for the loan.

INVENTORY TURNOVER. A company divides the cost of its goods sold by its average inventory for the year. This ratio helps the company to determine how efficiently it is using its assets in its turnover of saleable goods.

INVERSE DEMAND PATTERN. When prices and trading volumes change at the same rate and at the same time and more securities are sold at higher prices than at lower ones.

INVERTED MARKET. When distant-month commodity futures contracts sell at lower prices than near-month commodity futures contracts.

INVERTED SCALE. A serial bond offering with short-term yields that are higher than the long-term yields.

INVERTED YIELD CURVE. A graph of yields from similar securities with short-term yields that are higher than their long-term yields.

INVESTED CAPITAL. The amount received in exchange for equity capital.

INVESTMENT. Cautiously using money to make more money, with the smallest amount of risk. Using money to make more money without regard to risk is considered gambling.

INVESTMENT ADVISORS ACT. Requires the registration of people and companies who provide investment advice and guidance for a fee.

INVESTMENT ADVISORY SERVICE. A company that provides advice and guidance in securities investing. Many companies, the advisors of which must be registered with the Securities and Exchange Commission, specialize in guiding clients toward specific types of investments, such as growth stocks.

INVESTMENT ASSETS. Cash, bonds, stocks, other assets, or other investments that will produce income for the investor or that will appreciate in value.

INVESTMENT BANKER. A person who acts as an intermediary between a company that needs money and a person who wants to invest in the company. To make the exchange, the banker aids in a number of functions, such as underwriting a securities issue.

INVESTMENT BANKERS ASSOCIATION. A national organization established in 1912 that is made up of bankers involved in investment activity.

INVESTMENT BANKING HOUSE. A firm that buys large blocks of corporate and government securities and then sells the securities to investors to finance the corporation's capital needs.

INVESTMENT BILL. A discounted bill of exchange that an investor buys and holds until maturity.

INVESTMENT CERTIFICATE. A document verifying that a person has money invested in a savings and loan association. The document indicates the investment amount, but it does not provide the holder with any stockholder rights, such as voting rights.

INVESTMENT CLUB. A group of people who do not invest as a profession, but who pool their money together to invest.

INVESTMENT COMPANY. A firm that pools investors' money and puts the funds into securities.

INVESTMENT COMPANY ACT. This act requires the registration of investment companies.

INVESTMENT COMPANY AND VARIABLE CONTRACT PRODUCTS. A limited Securities and Exchange Commission registration that allows a person to sell or manage either shares of an investment company or annuity contracts.

INVESTMENT CREDIT. A company that invests in specific asset categories can have a portion of its income tax liability reduced, as long as the credit is claimed in the same year the purchase is made.

INVESTMENT FEATURE. An investment's characteristics and qualities, including income and growth potential, financial safety, and tax advantages.

INVESTMENT GRADE. The rating of a bond from AAA down to BBB according to Standard & Poor's system is considered to be suitable for prudent investors.

INVESTMENT HISTORY. NASD term pertaining to sales of hot issues. The amount of shares purchased by an individual is governed by previous shares purchased in accordance with his or her investment history of a particular investment.

INVESTMENT INCOME. Any money earned from an investment.

INVESTMENT IN DEFAULT. An investment in which interest or dividend payments are in default.

INVESTMENT LETTER. A private contract between a buyer and seller in which the buyer promises that the security is being purchased as an investment and not for resale, so he or she therefore will hold on to it for a specific length of time, usually two years. This usually occurs in private placements.

INVESTMENT MANAGER. A person authorized to invest money for another person or for a corporation.

INVESTMENT OBJECTIVE. The amount of money an investor expects to realize on an investment. Also, the goals of a portfolio.

INVESTMENT POLICY STATEMENT. A statement that tells how much risk the fiduciaries are willing to assume with pension fund assets and that spells out desired courses of action.

INVESTMENT PORTFOLIO. The grouping of all securities a person owns.

INVESTMENT PROPERTY. Any real estate a person buys with the intent of making a profit, either through renting the property or through a quick sale.

INVESTMENT SECURITIES. All investments purchased for a portfolio instead of for a quick sale.

INVESTMENT SKELETON. A worthless, speculative security, or a speculative security that fails to meet a person's investment objectives.

INVESTMENT STRATEGY. A plan of investing among choices such as stocks, bonds, cash, commodities, and real estate.

INVESTMENT TAX CREDIT. When a person buys certain tangible assets, he or she can receive a 10 percent tax credit during that same year. The credit is provided to stimulate the purchase of assets that will increase employment or public service opportunities.

INVESTMENT TRUST. Any company or trust that invests its capital in another company or trust.

INVESTMENT VALUE. The amount a bond would be worth if it did not have a conversion feature. The value is determined by adding the value of the coupons to the principal amount after the principal amount is discounted by the current interest rate for a similar bond.

INVESTOR RELATIONS DEPARTMENT. An exchange-listed company will have a staff member responsible for acting as the intermediary between the company and an investor. While the duties of the person in charge vary from company to company, the job is similar to a public relations job in that the person disseminates pertinent information to the public and usually is responsible for showing the company in a good light.

INVESTORS SERVICE BUREAU. A service offered by the New York Stock Exchange that answers questions regarding all types of securities investments.

INVOLUNTARY INVESTOR. An investor who paid a high price for a security and because the price later dropped, he or she cannot sell the security without losing a lot of money.

INVOLUNTARY LIEN. A lien, such as property tax increases, placed on a person's property without that person's consent.

IO. An interest only bond. *See* Stripped Bond.

IOU. An informal agreement to repay a debt.

IRISH DIVIDEND. Nickname for when a stock split ends with fewer shares outstanding.

IRREVOCABLE LETTER OF CREDIT. A document in which an issuer agrees to accept drafts and to charge them against his or her own account during a specific time period.

IRREVOCABLE TRUST. A trust that the creator cannot alter or end unless the beneficiary agrees.

IRS. *See* Internal Revenue Service.

ISLAND REVERSAL. A gap that marks a number of trades on both the up and down side when those trades fall in the middle of a market trend reversal.

ISSUE. A security issued by a company that is at least partially public-owned.

ISSUED AND OUTSTANDING. Stock that is owned by the public or by the company's directors.

ISSUED CAPITAL STOCK. A company's capital stock that has been either sold publicly or traded for goods and services.

ISSUED STOCK. The total number of a company's publicly held stock shares plus the number of shares the company holds as treasury stock.

ISSUE PRICE. The price at which a new security will be sold to the public.

ITS. *See* Intermarket Trading System.

J

JAJO. Represents January, April, July, and October, which are the expiration months of successively offered option contracts. It also represents interest and dividend payments that are due quarterly.

JAMES BOND. Nickname for a U.S. Treasury bond that matures in the year 2007, so named because the maturity date is James Bond's agent number in the fictional series of movies.

JAPANESE DEPOSITORY RECEIPT. A receipt that represents ownership of a certain number of stock shares of a non-Japanese company. The JDR is the Japanese equivalent to the American Depository Receipt.

JARGON. Terms and vocabulary that are particular to one general field or industry.

JDR. *See* Japanese Depository Receipt.

JELLY ROLL SPREAD. A long and short position in the same index option with different classes—a put and a call—having different expiration dates.

JEOPARDY CLAUSE. A stipulation in a Eurocurrency agreement that guarantees certain actions will be taken to protect the market if some events curtail the lender's activities or Euromarket operations.

JOB. A foreign bank that deals with other banks on its own behalf.

JOBBER. A London market maker similar to a U.S. exchange specialist.

JOBBER'S TURN. In England, the difference between a jobber's bid and ask prices, the equivalent to a spread on the American market.

JOB LOT. A trading unit of commodities or securities that is less than a round lot, which usually is equal to 100 shares of stock, and varies in the futures market with each individual commodity.

JOHN DOE. The legal name given to anyone whose given name is unknown.

JOINT ACCOUNT. An account held by two or more people, with each person equally sharing all profits, privileges, and liabilities associated with the account.

JOINT ACCOUNT AGREEMENT. All people who hold a joint account must sign this document, which authorizes each person to make transactions on the account.

JOINT AND SURVIVOR ANNUITY. An annuity that pays dividends to two or more people, usually a husband and wife. After one of the beneficiaries dies, the other continues to receive his or her share of the payments, but not those of the decedent's.

JOINT BOND. A bond that is issued by one party, but guaranteed by another, or a bond that has more than one issuer.

JOINT CONTRACT. An agreement in which two or more people consent to be joint obligators to another party.

JOINT ENDORSEMENT. Two or more signatures are required on a financial instrument that has been made payable to those two or more people. The instrument is nonnegotiable without the signatures of everyone named as a payee.

JOINT TENANCY. Two or more people jointly and equally own a piece of property. If one of the owners dies, his or her share is divided proportionately among the other owners.

JOINT TENANCY WITH RIGHT OF SURVIVORSHIP (JTWROS). A joint account held with a brokerage firm or a bank with the agreement that if one should die, the ownership of the account assets would be transferred to the joint tenant(s).

JOINT VENTURE. Two or more people unite to form a business.

JOINT VENTURE TENDER. Two or more companies combine their resources and capital to takeover another company, after which the companies will share in the venture equally.

JTWROS. *See* Joint Tenancy With Right of Survivorship.

JUDGMENT CURRENCY CLAUSE. A stipulation in a Eurocurrency credit agreement guaranteeing lenders that they will not lose any money if the loan is made in one currency and a court passes judgment in a different currency with an unfavorable exchange rate.

JUMBO CERTIFICATE OF DEPOSIT. A certificate of deposit with a denomination of at least $100,000, usually purchased by institutional investors.

JUNIOR. An investor exchanges securities that mature in one to five years for securities that mature in five or more years.

JUNIOR BOND. A debt instrument that falls subordinate to other bonds from the same issuer if that issuer defaults or becomes subject to financial claims.

JUNIOR REFUNDING. Issuing securities that mature in five or more years to refinance a government debt that matures in one to five years.

JUNIOR SECURITIES. A stock or bond that falls subordinate to other claims on the issuer's cash or assets. For example, preferred stock is junior to a debenture, and common stock is junior to preferred stock.

JUNIOR STOCK PLAN. A benefit plan that provides an executive with the right to exchange specially issued shares of stock for common stock after the executive has been with the company for a specified length of time.

JUNK BOND. A speculative bond with a rating of BB or lower from Moody's or Standard & Poor.

JUNK FINANCING. Using unsecured, high-interest securities with low credit ratings to raise capital.

JURY OF EXECUTIVE OPINION. A panel of experts combine knowledge to make individual forecasts, which later form a composite prediction.

K

K. Follows a number to indicate that the number should be multiplied by 1,000.

KAFFIR. Any gold mining company in South Africa, or South African gold mining shares.

KANSAS CITY BOARD OF TRADE. A Kansas City, Missouri, commodities exchange with brokers specializing in futures contracts and agricultural commodities.

KARAT. A measure of gold content, with one karat equal to 1/24 pure gold. For example, 24-karat gold would be pure gold.

KEEP IN MIND. A customer tells a market maker at which quantities and prices he or she would be willing to buy or sell a security.

KEEP WELL AGREEMENT. A contract between one company and another in which the first company agrees to make sure its subsidiary maintains a minimum financial ratio and net worth to protect a future deal between the subsidiary and the second company.

KEOGH PLAN. A self-funded, tax-sheltered, invested pension plan available to self-employed people and to people who work for unincorporated businesses without company-sponsored plans. Nearly any investment, except for collectibles and precious metals, can be used in a Keogh.

KERB DEALING. Commodities market transactions that transpire after the exchange has closed for the day.

KEY INDICATOR OPERATIONAL REPORT. A weekly report from New York Stock Exchange members who carry and clear customer accounts to the exchange. The exchange can tell if any of the members are having business problems that could effect the members' net capital.

KEY INDUSTRY. An industry that is vitally important to the country's economy, such as the defense and automobile industries.

KEYNESIAN ECONOMIC THEORY. John Maynard Keynes theorized that investment capital and the multiplier effect of such investments influence economic growth and income.

KICKBACK. A cash reward for dealers who discount installment purchase paper, or the illegal practice of secretly paying a seller for awarding a contract.

KICKER. A security feature or stipulation providing added rights, benefits, or liabilities.

KILL. To cancel an order.

KILLER BEES. A team of specialists a corporation will hold on retainer to protect the company from a hostile takeover by using such tactics as issuing tender offers or holding proxy contests.

KILLING. To make outstanding profits from investments in the stock market.

KIND ARBITRAGE. Profitably buying and selling identical securities in the same market at about the same time, with the profit coming from the price differences in separate trading values.

KINKED DEMAND. An industry that has only a few companies and no price leader often has a demand curve that becomes continuous at the market price.

KITING. A company sustains credit or raises money by making prices skyrocket.

KIWIS. Nickname for the United States' Student Loan Marketing Association, also referred to as a Sallie Mae, which is a five-year floating rate note with the interest rate denominated in New Zealand dollars.

KNIFE. Nickname for the New York Futures Exchange, derived from the exchange's initials NYFE.

KNOCKED DOWN. A price that has been reduced.

KNOW YOUR CUSTOMER RULE. On the New York Stock Exchange, brokers are instructed to know all pertinent facts about a customer and their customer's accounts before they allow the customer to open a brokerage account.

KONDRATIEFF WAVE THEORY. Soviet economist Nikolai Kondratieff theorized in the 1920s that Western capitalistic societies would go through rising and declining supercycles that lasted 50 to 60 years each. Kondratieff said he predicted the 1929 stock market crash, which led to the Great Depression, because the American economy also crashed in 1870.

KRUGERRAND. A South African gold bullion coin with one troy ounce of gold.

L

L. The symbol for a pound sterling, which is Great Britain's primary currency.

LABOR INTENSE INDUSTRY. A company or industry that requires a large number of employees compared to its total capital investment.

LAFFER CURVE. Economics professor Arthur Laffer theorized that economic output would increase if marginal tax rates were reduced. The curve is used to describe supply-side economics.

LAGGING ECONOMIC INDICATORS. An economic measure used to confirm, after the fact, the financial condition and stability of a particular industry or the economy in general.

LAISSEZ-FAIRE CAPITALISM. French for "let do," this is a capitalistic theory that says the economy works best when market forces are allowed to operate freely and without intervention.

LAND DEVELOPMENT LOAN. A person or company uses a mortgage to obtain a financial advance to improve a piece of land so that the site will be ready for construction.

LANDOWNER ROYALTY. The person who owns the land from which oil or gas is drawn receives a fee for the drilling find, but does not actually own part of the oil or gas because the owner has not contributed financially to the development of the well. The owner normally receives a share—usually 12.5 percent—of the well's gross production.

LAPPING. An individual solicits people to take part in an investment opportunity, fraudulently takes their money, then uses their money to repay people who were recruited into the scheme earlier. Known also as a Ponzi scheme, such a scheme could continue indefinitely.

LAPSED OPTION. A worthless, expired options contract that was never exercised.

LAST IN, FIRST OUT (LIFO). A company lists the production costs of the items most recently added to its inventory first on its inventory balance sheet, as opposed to the first in, first out method.

LAST SALE. A security's most recent transaction, often used to describe the closing sale on the last trading day.

LAST TRADING DAY. The last and final day a futures contract can be settled.

LATE TAPE. When an exchange's announcement of trades and prices falls behind trading activity.

LAUNDER MONEY. To transfer money through a number of different financial institutions and businesses to conceal its illegal source.

LAY UP. The easy execution of a buy or sell order, so named for the seemingly effortless basketball move.

LBO. *See* Leveraged Buy Out.

LEADING ECONOMIC INDICATORS. A measure, represented by such indicators as the unemployment rate, used to predict the financial condition and stability of a particular industry or the economy in general.

LEADS AND LAGS. The manner in which international payments are made. A lead occurs if experts predict a country's currency will drop in value. Upon such a prediction, importers with overseas currency obligations will rush to pay their debts so they will not increase after the currency devaluates. A lag occurs when the exporters, under the same circumstances, do not rush to convert export receipts in foreign currency because of the potential devaluation.

LEAD UNDERWRITER. The first insurance underwriter to accept a line on a risk.

LEASEHOLD IMPROVEMENT. The changing or modification of a leased piece of property, with the modification costs added to the fixed assets.

LEASE-PURCHASE AGREEMENT. A contract that applies a portion of the lease payments toward purchase of the same property.

LEASE UP. To fill a commercial building with paying tenants who sign lease agreements.

LEDGER. The final bookkeeping entry record which accounts for every type of transaction and has an entry for every transaction within every account.

LEDGER DEBT BALANCE. The amount of money a customer owes his or her broker for all fees, including commissions and interest.

LEFT-HAND FINANCING. To borrow money using assets listed on the left side of the corporate balance sheet in double-entry bookkeeping. By using this method and these assets, asset-rich companies can get money at lower costs.

LEG. One side or the other of a straddle option position.

LEGAL. A New York Stock Exchange computer network used for customer complaints, enforcement information, and the results of audits conducted on member firms.

LEGAL ASSET. Any asset a person or company can use to pay a debt. For example, securities would be considered a legal asset.

LEGAL CAPITAL. The portion of a company's capital surplus that makes up its par value. The capital surplus is the difference between the common shares' aggregate par value and the price at which they were sold.

LEGAL INVESTMENT. The investments, usually high grade, that are appropriate for a fiduciary to buy for portfolios he or she manages.

LEGAL LIST. A state-approved list of investment alternatives that are appropriate for fiduciaries and regulated companies, such as financial institutions, to invest in.

LEGAL MONOPOLY. A company, such as a utilities company, that has the exclusive legal right to provide a specific service within a geographical area as long as the company agrees to have its rates and policies regulated.

LEGAL TRANSFER. A security registered to such an extent that several documents are required before the security can be transferred. Most selling brokers must be responsible for putting the documents in order because most buying brokers won't accept a security that requires a legal transfer.

LEG INTO A HEDGE. An investor tries to create an offsetting position in a security by executing one side of a straddle option position (leg) now, then executing the other side later when a better price prevails.

LEHMAN INVESTMENT OPPORTUNITY NOTE (LION). This security, marketed by Lehman Brothers Kuhn Loeb, represents ownership interest in the future interest and future principal payments of some U.S. government securities. The security is more commonly known as a LION and is similar to

Treasury Investors Growth Receipts and Certificate of Accrual on Treasury Securities, commonly referred to as TIGRs and CATS, respectively.

LENDER OF LAST RESORT. Federal Reserve banks can borrow against securities to fulfill reserve requirements with fewer restrictions than imposed by the Federal Reserve System, so the system therefore becomes the lender of last resort.

LENDING AGREEMENT. An investor signs an agreement with his or her broker that allows the broker's firm to lend out securities held in the investor's margin account.

LENDING FLAT. When a borrower doesn't pay a fee and a lender doesn't pay interest; typically done when a person borrows securities using cash as collateral.

LENDING SECURITIES. The securities a client borrows from his or her broker to make a short sale, with a cash amount equal to the value of the securities delivered to the buyer's broker.

LESSEE. A person who pays to rent an asset or property from another person for a designated period of time.

LESSEE MEMBER. A person who pays an exchange member for use of the membership for a specific time period.

LESSOR. A person who owns an asset or property and allows someone else to use that asset or property for a specified amount of money and a designated period of time.

LETTER BOND. A debt instrument that was sold privately, with the buyer allowed to transfer or resell the instrument under terms stipulated in an investment letter.

LETTER OF ADMINISTRATION. A court will issue this document to authorize a court-appointed administrator to settle the estate of a person who died without leaving a will.

LETTER OF CREDIT. Through this document, a commercial bank authorizes a broker-dealer to borrow money, as needed, to meet its obligations. In turn, the broker-dealer pays the bank an annual fee based on a percentage of the amount.

LETTER OF FREE CREDIT. Through this document, a broker-dealer attests that a client has enough money to pay for the securities he or she has purchased.

The buying broker-dealer delivers this document on behalf of his or her client to the selling broker-dealer.

LETTER OF INDEMNIFICATION. One party in a business contract agrees to pay the other party for any losses that the other party incurs in the proposed venture.

LETTER OF INTENT. An investor buying into a mutual fund signs a document agreeing to buy enough shares of the fund during the next 13 months to qualify for a reduced sales charge.

LETTER SECURITY. A stock or bond not registered with the Securities and Exchange Commission which, therefore, cannot be sold in a public exchange. A company privately issues a letter security to certain key people with the stipulation that the stock cannot be resold or transferred publicly.

LETTER TESTAMENTARY. A court issues this document authorizing the executor of an estate to settle the estate as quickly as possible under the terms of the will.

LEVEL. The price at which a security can be bought or sold.

LEVEL 1 SERVICE OF NASDAQ. A computer subscription service, available to brokerage firms, that provides the highest and lowest price offers of securities traded through the National Association of Securities Dealers Automated Quotation.

LEVEL 2 SERVICE OF NASDAQ. A computer subscription service, available to institutional investors and traders, that provides the names of market makers and their bids on securities traded through the National Association of Securities Dealers Automated Quotation.

LEVEL 3 SERVICE OF NASDAQ. A computer subscription service, available to registered market makers, that provides the names of market makers and their bids on securities traded through the National Association of Securities Dealers Automated Quotation.

LEVEL ACCRUAL. Earned income is recognized by dividing the number of months before maturity into the interest balance.

LEVEL CHARGE PLAN. A program used for buying additional shares of a mutual fund over a specified length of time, with the sales charge assessed each time additional shares are purchased and with that sales charge based on the total dollar amount of each purchase.

LEVERAGE. In investments, this is the control of a large amount of money by a smaller amount of money, such as buying on margin. In finance, this is the relationship of debt to equity on a company's balance sheet in the form of the debt-to-equity ratio.

LEVERAGED. A company that borrows money at a fixed-interest rate to obtain a higher rate of return on its total invested capital.

LEVERAGED BUY OUT (LBO). A person, company, group of company employees, or entity that borrows money to buy controlling interest in a company. This is usually done by using the company's assets as security for the loans taken out by the acquiring party and repaying the loans from the company's cash flow.

LEVERAGED COMPANY. A company that has both equity and debt accounting for its total capital.

LEVERAGED EMPLOYEE STOCK OPTION PLAN. A plan into which a company deposits payments each year out of its revenue, deducting the full amount from taxable income. Shares of stock are distributed among the employees' accounts as the loan is paid off. This method helps to alleviate the threat of an unwanted corporate takeover.

LEVERAGED HEDGE. An investment that can produce unproportionately high profits compared to its original purchase price.

LEVERAGED INVESTMENT COMPANY. A dual-purpose fund that has income as well as capital shares, with dividends going to income shares and capital gains going to capital shares. The charter of the open-end investment company allows the borrowing of capital from a bank or other lender.

LEVERAGED LEASE. An equipment lease financed by a nonrecourse loan so that the lessee can use the equipment without putting out any money and the lessor can retain the residual depreciation value when the lease expires.

LEVERAGED STOCK. A stock that can produce unproportionately high profits compared to its original purchase price.

LEVERAGE FACTOR. The ratio of a leveraged security's price to its working assets.

LEVERAGE FUND. A mutual fund that borrows money to increase the number of securities it can buy so it can increase its returns.

LEVERAGE TRANSACTION MERCHANT. A futures commission merchant who can deal in certain over-the-counter futures instruments as long as they were doing business before June 1, 1978, which is when off-exchange futures trading was made illegal. Aside from qualifying under the grandfather clause, such merchants also must be registered with the Commodities Futures Trading Commission.

LIABILITY. Any debt, both current and potential.

LIBOR. *See* London Interbank Offering Rate.

LIFE CYCLES. A system used to study and analyze different companies and products as they progress through the developmental phases of pioneering, expansion, stabilization, and decline.

LIFE INSURANCE. The payment of a stipulated sum of money, upon the death of the insured, to the designated beneficiary.

LIFE OF CONTRACT. The time period extending from the first day to the last day of a futures contract.

LIFE OF DELIVERY. The time between when a commodities trade is initiated and the last transaction's delivery date.

LIFT. A market-average measure of a security's price increase.

LIFT A LEG. Closing one side of a straddle option position while leaving the other side open.

LIFT A SHORT. An investor closes a short position by buying a futures contract for the same commodity with the same delivery date.

LIFO. *See* Last In, First Out.

LIGHT BID, LIGHT OFFER. An equity trader uses this to indicate his or her bid is not equal to or better than the best prevailing bid or offer. Market movements up or down will create institutional interest.

LIKE KIND ASSETS. Two or more assets that are so similar that the selling of one and the buying of the other cancel each other out so that for tax purposes, in essence, no transaction at all has taken place.

LIMIT. The highest price fluctuation that the commodities exchange will allow from an item's previous settlement price. Each exchange sets its own limits.

LIMITED ACCESS TO BOOKS AND RECORDS. A person who holds stock in a company is allowed to inspect some of the company's records.

LIMITED AUDIT. Selected items are examined to determine the effectiveness of a company's internal controls, mathematical accuracy, legality, and the completeness of all transactions, with the results of the selected items' analysis generalized to cover all items, even those not examined.

LIMITED COMPANY. The British equivalent to a U.S. company that has been incorporated.

LIMITED DISCRETION. A customer authorizes his or her registered representative to make certain trades without any authorization.

LIMITED DIVIDEND CORPORATION. A company with a ceiling on the amount of dividends it can pay on its capital stock.

LIMITED EXERCISE OPTION. An options contract that cannot be exercised until the fifth business day before the contract expires.

LIMITED LIABILITY. A stockholder or partner in a partnership or corporation who holds liability for only as much as his or her investment.

LIMITED PARTNERSHIP. A partnership with at least one of the partners holding only a limited liability.

LIMITED TAX BOND. A municipal bond based on the taxation value of the municipality's real estate.

LIMITED TRADING AUTHORIZATION. *See* Limited Discretion.

LIMIT ORDER. An investor tells his or her broker to buy securities or commodities at or below a specific maximum price, or to sell securities or commodities above or at a specific minimum price.

LIMIT ORDER INFORMATION SYSTEM. An electronic system that gives the location, number, and prices of specialists' offers and bids on the different exchanges.

LIMIT-OR-MARKET-ON-CLOSE ORDER. An investor tells his or her broker to buy a specified number of shares of a certain security at a certain price. If the broker cannot execute the order as specified, he or she is to execute it as a market order as close to the specifications as possible and as close to the end of the trading day as possible.

LIMIT PRICE. The maximum amount at which a broker can buy a security for a client, or the minimum amount at which a broker can sell a security for a client, with the client determining that amount.

LIMIT SYSTEM. A computer network through which subscribers can find out about securities traded on all participating exchanges, and including information such as the specialist, the number involved in the deal, and the bid and offer prices.

LIMIT UP, LIMIT DOWN. The most a commodity's price is allowed to move during one trading day.

LINE CHART. A graph that charts a security's or the general market's price changes during a specific time period, with one line connecting the prices.

LINE OF CREDIT. An arrangement between a person and a financial institution that allows the person to borrow up to a certain amount of money for a predetermined time period without providing any additional credit information.

LION. *See* Lehman Investment Opportunity Note.

LIPPER MUTUAL FUND INDUSTRY AVERAGE. The average performance of all mutual funds, as reported quarterly and annually by Lipper Analytical Services.

LIQUID. Having enough assets that easily can be converted to cash to retire all short-term debts.

LIQUID ASSETS. Assets that easily can be converted into cash such as money market fund shares, treasury bills, and bank deposits.

LIQUIDATING DIVIDEND. The distribution of assets from a company that is going out of business.

LIQUIDATING MARKET. A market in which securities are aggressively sold at relatively low prices.

LIQUIDATING VALUE. The amount of money an asset is expected to cost when the company that owns it goes out of business.

LIQUIDATION. Selling an asset, or closing a company and turning all of the company's assets into cash.

LIQUIDITY. The degree to which assets of a company or an investment can easily be sold or converted into cash.

LIQUIDITY DIVERSIFICATION. A portfolio manager invests in bonds which all have different maturities.

LIQUIDITY FUND. A California company will pay a limited partner 25 to 30 percent below the appraised value for interest in a real estate limited partnership.

LIQUIDITY RATIO. Comparison of a company's cash and marketable securities to its current liabilities.

LIQUID MARKET. A market in which securities or commodities are easily bought and sold because of the willingness of interested buyers and sellers to trade large quantities at reasonable prices.

LIQUID SAVING. A savings of either a person, a company, or a trust is in cash or assets that can easily be converted into cash.

LIQUID SECURITIES. Stocks and bonds that are easily converted to cash.

LIQUID YIELD OPTION NOTE. Also known as a LYON, this callable, zero-coupon security combines the capital needs of an investment banking customer with the investment needs of a retail customer. Put and call options on the note become operative in the third year after it is issued, with the put and call prices reflecting fixed interest rates. The put and call prices, therefore, increase over time.

LISTED OPTION. A put or call option that a particular securities exchange has approved for trading.

LISTED OPTION CONTRACT. A stock option contract that is traded in an organized auction market on a member-exchange's floor, and has a preset strike price and expiration date.

LISTED SECURITIES. Any security that a particular registered exchange has accepted for trading.

LISTING. Achieved through meeting all of an exchange's trading requirements and through receiving that exchange's approval for trading.

LISTING AGREEMENT. A company and a stock exchange sign such a contract when the company wants its shares listed for trading on that exchange.

LISTING REQUIREMENTS. Rules and regulations a security must meet before it can be traded on a particular exchange.

LITIGATION. Involvement in a civil lawsuit.

LITTLE BOARD. Nickname for the American Stock Exchange, which has the second-largest trading volume of all exchanges. The Big Board is the New York Stock Exchange, which has the largest trading volume.

LOAD. The commission fee (up to 8.5 percent) charged for buying shares of an open-end mutual fund to cover expenses.

LOAD FUNDS. A mutual fund that a brokerage firm sells for a sales charge.

LOADING. Funds are added to the prorated market price of the underlying securities to cover fees and overhead costs.

LOADING CHARGE. Up to an 8.5 percent fee charged on open-end investment funds when new securities are sold. The fee is used to cover all selling costs.

LOAD SPREAD OPTION. A contractual plan for paying the sales charge on mutual funds.

LOAD UP. An investor speculatively buys a security or commodity and pays up to his or her financial limit.

LOAN-CLOSING PAYMENTS. The expenses involved in setting and finalizing a mortgage loan.

LOAN CONSENT AGREEMENT. A contract, required by the Securities and Exchange Commission, authorizing a securities broker to lend securities carried in a customer's account.

LOAN CROWD. Members of a stock exchange who either lend or borrow securities to cover their brokerage customers' short sales.

LOANED FLAT. A loan without interest.

LOANED STOCK. A brokerage firm lends stock to an investor who is selling short in order to cover delivery of the shares to the buyer.

LOAN VALUE. The maximum amount a brokerage firm can lend to a client for buying securities on margin.

LOAN-TO-VALUE RATIO. The ratio of a property's appraised value to the amount of the mortgage.

LOBSTER TRAP. Used by companies with outstanding convertible securities to stop unfriendly takeovers. A lobster trap prevents a person who holds 10 percent or more of the company's voting shares from converting their holdings into common shares of stock. The system is so named after the real lobster traps, which net large lobsters while allowing smaller fish to escape through the net.

LOCAL. A commodities exchange trader who works in the pit and sells for his or her own account.

LOCAL BILL. A document that verifies an investor's transactions.

LOCKED-IN. A position an investor is in when he or she has not held onto a security for a long enough period and therefore cannot sell it to his or her advantage: i.e., (1) benefit from a capital gains treatment, (2) an owner of a low-interest bond during a period of rising interest rates, (3) an investor in a commodities position when the exchange has established an up or down limit per day and he or she cannot get out, etc.

LOCK AWAY. A long-term security in England.

LOCKED MARKET. When bid and offer prices are the same in a highly competitive market.

LOCKED OUT. Current market conditions are preventing an investor from taking advantage of buying potentially profitable securities.

LOCKUP. A security that has been pulled out of circulation as a long-term investment and placed in a safe deposit box.

LOCO. A term used to identify the place a commodity is being traded.

LOLLIPOP TACTIC. A method a company uses to stop an unfriendly takeover bid. With this method, some stockholders can tender shares at a premium price if the unwanted bidder buys a predetermined number of the outstanding shares. The deal, therefore, becomes profitable to everyone except the person attempting the takeover.

LOMBARD RATE. The interest rate that Germany's central bank charges to other commercial banks when the banks borrow money using German securities as collateral. The Lombard rate is Germany's equivalent to the U.S. Federal Reserve System's discount rate.

LOMBARD STREET. England's financial district.

LONDON INTERBANK BID RATE. In England's Eurodollar market, this is the interest rate at which American dollar deposits can be retraded within the British banking community.

LONDON INTERBANK OFFERING RATE (LIBOR). In England's Eurodollar market, this is the interest rate banks charge each other on short-term money.

LONDON INTERNATIONAL FINANCIAL FUTURES EXCHANGE. A British futures exchange where arbitrageurs, hedgers, and speculators can trade selected financial instruments that are subject to interest rate changes.

LONDON METAL EXCHANGE. An exchange where members trade in metals such as lead and copper.

LONDON OPTIONS. English options contracts for commodities such as cocoa.

LONDON STOCK EXCHANGE. A major European stock exchange.

LONG BOND. A bond that doesn't mature for at least 10 years.

LONG CALL. Ownership of a call option contract on an opening purchase.

LONG COUPON. A newly issued bond with the first coupon not redeemable for at least six months.

LONG HEDGE. An investor locks in a future yield on a fixed-income security by buying a futures contract, whereby he or she could lose money if interest rates increase, or by purchasing a call option, whereby he or she could lose money if interest rates do not drop.

LONG INTEREST. Collectively holding on to a specific security or a group of securities as an investment.

LONG LEG. The position of an investor who holds an offsetting position.

LONG MARKET VALUE. The daily market value in an investor's margin account, as determined by the value of its long-position securities.

LONG OF EXCHANGE. A trader trades foreign bills in an amount that exceeds his or her outstanding bills.

LONG ON THE BASIS. An investor buys currency or spot goods and hedges them by selling futures.

LONG POSITION. An investor achieves a long position through buying a security (ownership) before selling because of an expected price increase.

LONG PUT. An investor buys a put option contract on an opening purchase transaction.

LONG SALE. Any time an investor sells securities he or she owns.

LONG SIDE. A long interest.

LONG SQUEEZE. Occurs when prices drop and people holding long positions are forced to liquidate their positions.

LONG STOCK. Securities an investor buys because he or she believes the prices will go up.

LONG-TERM CAPITAL GAINS. The amount of money an investor earns by holding on to an investment for more than a year.

LONG-TERM CAPITAL LOSSES. The amount of money an investor loses by holding on to an investment for more than a year.

LONG-TERM CORPORATE DEBT. An obligation that will not be due for more than a year after the contract is signed.

LONG-TERM DEBT. A debt obligation that does not mature for at least 10 years.

LONG-TERM FINANCING. An obligation that will not be due for at least a year.

LONG-TERM INSTITUTIONAL EQUITY. An institution can create a longer term stake by financing with additional preferred stocks and convertible debts.

LONG-TERM INVESTMENT. An investor buys a security and holds on to it for more than a year because its growth potential is much greater than its short-term profits through a sale would be.

LONG-TERM LIABILITY. A debt that falls due in more than a year, but usually indicating an obligation that will last 10 or more years.

LONG-TERM MORTGAGE. A home mortgage with a life of 40 years or more.

LONG-TERM RECEIVABLES AND INVESTMENTS. Long-term debts owed to a company plus the company's investments.

LONG-TERM TREND. The direction prices are expected to move during a specific future time period.

LOOK BACK. A company's past records are audited in a search for mistakes that already have become obvious to a bank's auditing department.

LOOPHOLE. The process of circumventing the law without violating its letter. A tax-sheltered investment exploits a loophole in the tax law.

LOOK-BACK OPTION. A commodities put or call option that allows the holder to buy or sell at the best available price during the option's life.

LOOPHOLE CERTIFICATE OF DEPOSIT. A federally insured bank can pay the market interest rate, as pegged to the weekly Treasury bill auction, on deposits of $10,000 or more. The bank lends a customer the difference between his or her deposit amount and $10,000. The loan is a paper transaction, so the customer never actually receives the money which the bank deposits in his or her account and then withdraws six months later.

LOSS RESERVE. An account established to provide for defaulted loans or other account receivables.

LOST OPPORTUNITY. An investment that does not earn as much as the current interest rate.

LOT. A trading unit *(See* Odd Lot; Round Lot).

LOW. The lowest price a security, or the market in general, reached during a specific time period.

LOW GRADE. A securities rating that indicates a particular security is not worth investing in because the issuer probably will not be able to meet financial obligations and has a poor reputation in the industry.

LUXURY TAX. The taxes assessed against all nonessential items, such as hot tubs or built-in swimming pools.

LYON. *See* Liquid Yield Option Note.

M. The abbreviation for one thousand; when following a number, it indicates the number is to be multiplied by 1,000. For example, 3M would equal 3,000.

M1. A money supply category consisting of currency in public circulation, credit union share account balances, NOW account balances, automatic transfer account balances, demand deposits, and travelers checks.

M2. A money supply category consisting of all money in the M1 category plus Eurodollar deposits, savings and other small deposits, and private holdings in money market mutual funds.

M3. A money supply category consisting of all money in the M1 and M2 categories, plus large deposits and institutional shares in money market mutual funds.

M4. A money supply category consisting of all money in the M1, M2, and M3 categories, plus banker's acceptance, commercial paper, and U.S. savings bonds.

MACROECONOMICS. A nation's inflation rate, price levels, unemployment figures, and industrial production, among other data, used to study the country's economy as a whole.

MACROHEDGE. An investment hedge that reduces an organization's net portfolio risk.

MAE WEST SPREAD. A strategy that brings the investor profits when the market is stagnating, and involves a combination of a short straddle and a long strangle.

MAGIC MORTGAGE. Promoted by the Mortgage Guarantee Insurance Corporation, this is a method that allows a person to buy a house with a low down payment as long as the buyer pays a yearly interest fee to the loan's insurer.

MAGIC SIXES. A group of undervalued stocks, with each trading at less than 60 percent of its book value, having a price-earnings ratio of six or lower, and having an annual yield higher than 6 percent.

MAINTENANCE. The amount of cash and securities an investor has deposited in his or her account to fulfill his or her margin requirements.

MAINTENANCE BOND. A financial obligation with materials and workmanship that are guaranteed after a contract has been filled, with the guarantee lasting a predetermined time.

MAINTENANCE CALL. A broker's request for cash or securities when the equity in his or her client's margin account falls below the brokerage firm's maintenance requirements. Unless the client deposits enough cash or securities to bring the account up to the required level, the broker can sell some of the client's securities to make up for the deficit.

MAINTENANCE EXCESS. The amount a client's equity exceeds the minimum maintenance requirements in his or her margin account.

MAINTENANCE FEE. The cost a brokerage firm charges yearly to maintain some accounts.

MAINTENANCE MARGIN. A margin sale must occur below this margin or level, which is set by the lender.

MAINTENANCE OF INVESTMENT ORGANIZATION. The income charges and administration expenses of the firm which carries investments in leased property or securities.

MAJOR BOTTOM. When market prices have dropped to the lowest expected value.

MAJOR-BRACKET UNDERWRITER. An investment banking group that continuously subscribes to the largest portion of a new securities issue.

MAJORITY-OWNED SUBSIDIARY. A subsidiary with more than 51 percent of its outstanding stock owned by the parent company.

MAJORITY SHAREHOLDER. The person who holds the most voting shares of a company's stock. If a person owns 51 percent of the stock, he or she automatically is the majority shareholder. However, if ownership of the shares is widely scattered among many different stockholders, the majority shareholder may own a lot less than 50 percent, as long as he or she owns more shares than anyone else.

MAJOR TREND. The general direction that stock prices are moving, disregarding any minor, temporary shifts.

MAKE A LINE. When a security's price movement remains in a narrow range for a long time.

MAKE A MARKET. The maintaining of firm bid and offer prices on a specific security by always being ready to buy and sell round lots of the security at the prices quoted publicly. The dealer on the over-the-counter market is called the market maker and is called a specialist on the exchanges.

MAKER. The person or company who signs a check or other obligation.

MAKING UP PRICE. A delivered security's price.

MALFEASANCE. An illegal action.

MALONEY ACT. A law that regulates over-the-counter securities and holds the registered securities' associations responsible for supervising and making sure the regulations are obeyed.

MANAGED ACCOUNT. One or more people hold such an investment account, with a bank trust department or an investment firm entrusted with deciding what investments to make and when to make them. The investors share in paying management fees in any profits or losses, with each person responsible for an amount that is in proportion to the amount he or she invested.

MANAGEMENT AUDIT. The overall analysis of a management's performance.

MANAGEMENT COMPANY. A firm that handles other people's investments and supervises their portfolios.

MANAGEMENT FEE. An investment manager charges investors this cost for handling their portfolios or mutual funds, or for taking care of shareholder relations and administration. The charge is based on a percentage of the particular fund's asset value.

MANAGEMENT STOCK. Those shares of stock owned by a company's management.

MANAGER. The bank that manages a Eurocredit or a security issue.

MANAGER'S FEE. The underwriter in a public offering imposes this charge on the issuer in return for handling the new series.

MANAGING UNDERWRITER. The investment banking firm for an underwriting group, which formed to buy and distribute a new securities issue. An agreement among underwriters gives this agent authority to buy, carry, and distribute the issue, to ensure compliance with federal and state laws, to determine how many shares each group member receives, to sell at discount to the selling group, and to initiate the public market offering.

MANIPULATION. The illegal buying or selling of a security to create the false impression that active trading exists in an effort to convince other people to buy more shares or sell the ones they own. Manipulation is done to influence prices so the person doing the manipulating can achieve a more advantageous market.

MAPLELEAF SERIES. A Euro-Canadian warrant to buy a particular amount of a Canadian government bond issue. Created by the Merrill Lynch Capital Markets Inc., this product is not available to investors in the United States.

MARGE A TERME. A forward margin in France.

MARGIN. The amount of money a client deposits with his or her broker and against which the client can borrow when he or she wants to buy securities.

MARGINABLE SECURITIES. Securities that can be used for buying on margin.

MARGIN ACCOUNT. The brokerage account established for a client who wants to buy securities. The client borrows against the account.

MARGIN AGREEMENT. The document that provides the rules and regulations concerning margin accounts, including the amount of money and securities the client must maintain in the account.

MARGINAL ACTIVITY. A company with revenues that barely meet its obligations.

MARGINAL ANALYSIS. The amount a value increases when one variable is increased by one unit of another variable.

MARGINAL BORROWER. A person who will borrow money as long as the interest charge is not increased.

MARGINAL BUYER. A person who will buy an item as long as the price is not increased.

MARGINAL COST. The potential increase or decrease in a company's total costs if it had one more or one less unit of output. In most companies, these costs drop as volume increases because of bulk discounts and the more efficient use of equipment. For other companies, the cost may go up because increased production requires additional employees. Even those companies whose costs drop reach a point where the cost will begin to rise because additional personnel are needed and more intense supervision is required.

MARGINAL EFFICIENCY OF CAPITAL. The annual percentage yield a company's last additional unit of capital earns, which represents the market interest rate at which undertaking a capital investment becomes profitable. If the market rate is 12 percent, it would not be profitable to undertake any project that has less than a 12 percent rate of return.

MARGINAL LENDER. A person who will lend money as long as the interest charge is not lowered.

MARGINAL PAIR. The marginal seller and marginal buyer, along with the first seller whose offer is above the current market price and the first buyer whose bid is below the current market price.

MARGINAL REVENUE. The degree to which a company's total revenue would change by adding one unit of output. The marginal revenue is determined by the difference between the total revenue produced before the unit was added and the total revenue produced after the unit was added. If the price of the unit does not change, the marginal revenue will equal the unit's price.

MARGINAL SELLER. A person who will sell a security as long as the price is not reduced.

MARGINAL TAX RATE. The amount of additional tax imposed on a company with each additional dollar of income because of the U.S. progressive income tax system.

MARGINAL TRADING. A person borrows part of the money necessary to buy a security or commodity.

MARGIN BUYING. An investor uses a broker's credit to buy securities.

MARGIN CALL. A broker's request for a customer to deposit enough money in the customer's margin account to bring the balance back up to the initial margin requirement. If the customer fails to do so, the broker is allowed to liquidate the account.

MARGIN DEPARTMENT. A brokerage firm department responsible for making sure customers comply with the firm's margin rules and regulations, and for monitoring margin debits, credits, short sales, and purchases.

MARGINED SECURITIES. Securities an investor buys on credit and holds as collateral in his or her margin account.

MARGIN LOAN. A call loan with an investment as collateral.

MARGIN MINIMUM REQUIREMENT. Set by the Federal Reserve Board, this is the minimum amount of money or marginable securities an investor must have deposited in his or her margin account to buy more securities on margin. The minimum is a percentage of the total value of the securities the investor wants to buy.

MARGIN OF PROFIT. The ratio of a company's net sales to its gross profits. To obtain the margin of profit, a company would divide its net sales into its gross profits. The margin provides an indication of the company's operating efficiency and pricing policies.

MARGIN OF SAFETY. The difference between a bond issue's price and the value of its underlying property.

MARGIN REQUIREMENT. The minimum amount a brokerage firm requires a customer to have deposited in his or her margin account.

MARGINS. The par value's range within which the spot exchange rate of a member nation's currency is permitted to move.

MARGIN SALE. When assets are sold to fill a margin call requirement.

MARGIN SECURITY. A security a customer can buy or sell in his or her brokerage margin account.

MARK DOWN. The amount that a security's selling price is reduced to cover commissions to a market maker in the over-the-counter market. A reduction in the price of an underwriter's municipal bond offering to entice buyers when there is a lack of interest at the original price.

MARKET. Where products, services, and securities are sold to the public. Market also indicates the general supply and demand for a particular security.

MARKETABLE LIMIT ORDER. An investor tells his or her broker to buy at or below a maximum price, or sell at or above a minimum price, with the specified prices better than the current market. The orders, therefore, can be executed immediately.

MARKETABLE SECURITIES. Stocks or bonds that easily and quickly can be bought and sold.

MARKETABILITY. The speed and ease with which a specific security can be bought and sold.

MARKET ANALYSIS. A study followed by a prediction of the movement expected from a particular security or commodity, or from the market in general, with emphasis placed on supply and demand.

MARKET AREA. The area where a commodity purchase or sale directly affects the prevailing price of that commodity.

MARKET AUCTION PREFERRED STOCK. A variable rate issue that a Dutch auction resets every 49 days. The security is immediately callable.

MARKET AVERAGE. The measure of a group of securities to gauge the market movement as a whole. The term often refers to the Dow Jones Industrial Average.

MARKET BOTTOM. The lowest point a market indicator reaches during a specific time period.

MARKET BREADTH. The number of shares of a particular security that are traded during a particular time period. Generally, this term refers to the overall strength and trading volume of the market by such measures as advance/decline figures and volume momentum.

MARKET CAPITALIZATION. A company's worth as indicated by the price of its outstanding shares of stock.

MARKET CYCLE. When an increase in prices follows a period of lower prices, or when a drop in prices follows a period of higher prices.

MARKET DATA SYSTEM. A communications system that displays a summary of trading volumes on the New York Stock Exchange.

MARKET EQUILIBRIUM. Occurs after buyers and sellers refuse to trade at the prevailing prices.

MARKET EXCESS RETURN. The percentage that a predicted return exceeds the risk-free rate of return.

MARKET IF TOUCHED ORDER (MIT). An investor's order to buy or sell a security or commodity as soon as it can be bought or sold at a predetermined market price. When it reaches that price, it is considered a market order.

MARKET INDEX. A group of numbers (with arbitrary values assigned to proportionately represent real values) that provide a gauge to track specific securities, industries, and markets.

MARKET INSTINCT. The ability to understand, interpret, and use market signals such as volume trading and price shifts.

MARKET IS OFF. Indicates that the prices of securities dropped after a previous closing.

MARKET LEADERS. When the stock of a major, influential company is considered a reflection of the market in general.

MARKET LETTER. A newsletter sent to brokerage clients. The newsletter examines market trends, interest rates, and the economy. The newsletter also may make investment recommendations.

MARKET LIQUIDITY. Occurs when an investor can buy or sell a security near the price at which the security last sold.

MARKET MAKER. A dealer who continually buys and sells round lots of a security on the over-the-counter market.

MARKET MAKER IDENTIFIER. A four-letter acronym or code the National Association of Securities Dealers uses to represent broker-dealers who actively use the NASD's Automated Quotations.

MARKET MULTIPLE. A price-earnings ratio. The market multiple helps an investor determine whether a stock is overpriced or underpriced.

MARKET-ON-THE-CLOSE ORDER. An investor's order to his or her broker to buy or sell a security at the close of the trading day, or as near to the close as possible.

MARKET-ON-THE-OPENING ORDER. An investor's order to his or her broker to buy or sell a security at the opening of the trading day, or as near to the opening as possible.

MARKET OPENING. The first transaction of the day on an exchange.

MARKET ORDER. An investor's order to buy or sell a security or commodity at the best price.

MARKET ORDER SYSTEM OF TRADING. A computer system that connects the Toronto Stock Exchange with the American Stock Exchange and through which orders for dual-listed stocks can be automatically executed at the best price.

MARKET OUT CLAUSE. A stipulation in some underwriting agreements that releases underwriters from the purchase commitment if some development negatively affects the overall securities market.

MARKET OVERSIGHT SURVEILLANCE SYSTEM. A computer surveillance system that monitors market activity for the Securities and Exchange Commission.

MARKET POTENTIAL. The amount of a commodity or security that is expected to sell during a specific time period.

MARKET PRICE. The last price at which a security or commodity publicly sold.

MARKET REPORT. A verbal or written statement from the exchange floor that a transaction has been executed at a specific price.

MARKET RESEARCH. A study and analysis of a prospective company's or product's size, characteristics, and market potential. In the securities market, market research refers to the study and analysis of volume, price changes, and market potential, all of which indicate potential price movements.

MARKET RISK. The risk an investor takes when owning securities because the prices could go up or down, with all movements beyond the investor's control.

MARKET SECURITIES. Stock or bonds that are publicly traded.

MARKET SENTIMENT. Positive or negative public attitudes that affect trends in the securities or commodities markets.

MARKET SHARE. The percentage of an industry's total sales that belong to a specific product or a particular company.

MARKET STABILIZATION. An organization tries to hinder the market to affect prices. The Securities and Exchange Commission normally prohibits this practice.

MARKET SWING. A cyclical shift in a security's price.

MARKET TIMING. When economic factors indicate the economy is strong and interest rates are favorable for buying or selling securities.

MARKET TONE. When traders are willing to deal actively, with minimal price differences between bid and ask prices.

MARKET TOP. The highest point a market indicator reaches during a specific time period.

MARKET TREND. The general market movement, either up or down.

MARKET UNCERTAINTY. An investor's opinions and attitudes change in such a way that the investment's market price changes.

MARKET VALUE. The last price for which a security or commodity was bought or sold.

MARKET VALUE-WEIGHTED INDEX. An index with components that are stressed according to the total market value of their outstanding shares.

MARKET VERSUS QUOTE. A security's market price at the last price it was executed versus the current bid and ask.

MARKET VOLUME. The number of shares traded in one day on a particular exchange.

MARKING. At the close, an investor executes an option contract that does not reflect the contract's fair value, with the execution bringing the investor's account into a better equity position.

MARK TIME. When the prices of a number of transactions in the commodities and securities markets fail to indicate any trend.

MARK TO THE MARKET. A securities portfolio is weighted to make sure the investor's margin account complies with his or her margin account requirements.

MARK UP. The amount a dealer adds to a security's actual price to arrive at the purchase price to cover commissions to the market maker in the over-the-counter market.

MARRIED PUT. An investor buys a put option to sell a specific number of a security at a specific price by a specific time. The option is purchased from the same underlying company at the same time the investor buys the securities, so the investor can hedge the price he or she paid for the securities.

MASSACHUSETTS RULE. A rule that governs trust fund investing. Included in the rule are limitations on those securities in which a fund can be invested.

MASSACHUSETTS TRUST. A form of business organized as a trust and in which shareholders have a limited liability.

MASTER LIMITED PARTNERSHIP. An investment that offers some tax shelter advantages as well as publicly traded securities.

MASTER NOTES. Paper that a large company with good credit can issue to a bank, but not to another company.

MASTER TRUST. A pool of trusts, or a pool of assets involved in one trust agreement.

MATCHED AND LOST. When two securities brokers are competing against each other to execute a trade, with both representing the same price, a coin is flipped, and this is the report of that coin toss for the broker who lost. The losing broker tells his or her client the security was not available in sufficient quantity to execute the deal at the price the client stipulated.

MATCHED BOOK. A securities dealer's account when his or her borrowing costs equal the interest he or she earned for loaning money to customers and other brokers.

MATCHED MATURITIES. A financial institution coordinates the maturities of a customer's loans and certificates of deposits to ease the problems that result when interest rates rise or fall sharply.

MATCHED ORDERS. In a practice that the Securities and Exchange Commission prohibits, an investor offsets buy and sell orders in a particular security to create the false impression that the security is being actively traded, which causes its price to go up.

MATCHED SALE PURCHASE TRANSACTION. The Federal Reserve Bank of New York sells government securities to a securities dealer against the payment of federal funds, after which the dealer must agree to sell the securities back by a predetermined date. In turn, the Federal Reserve Bank pays the dealer an interest rate equal to the discount rate.

MATCH FUNDS. A person who borrows money has the same repayment date as a loan which that person makes out to someone else. For example, the person borrows money that is to be repaid by January 16, then lends someone else money, with that loan to be repaid by January 16.

MATCHING. Assets are denominated in a specific currency to lower the risks involved in foreign exchange rates.

MATRIX TRADING. Two brokers trade bonds in different classes, or in the same class but with different ratings, in an effort to take advantage of differences in the yield spreads.

MATURED. A contract or other obligation that has been completely paid and the terms of which have been completely fulfilled.

MATURE ECONOMY. The economy of a country with a stabilized or declining population and with stabilized economic growth. While consumer spending increases, government spending on roads and factories drops. Many Western European economies have reached maturity.

MATURITY. The date the principal amount of a bond or other debt instrument becomes due, or the date an installment loan must be completely paid.

MATURITY BASIS. A ratio that compares the interest, in dollars, due on a bond to the bond's maturity value. In calculating the maturity basis, no consideration is given to any discounts or premiums that were in effect when the bond was purchased.

MATURITY DISTRIBUTION OF LOANS AND SECURITIES. Provides the amounts of loans, acceptance holdings, and government securities due within a specific time period.

MAXIMUM CAPITAL GAINS MUTUAL FUND. A mutual fund directed at achieving the highest returns for its investors, with a policy of investing in smaller, fast-growing companies with volatile stock. While the fund may earn large, quick profits for the investors, it also is subject to quick, dramatic losses.

MAY DAY. Fixed minimum brokerage commissions became prohibited in the U.S. on May 1, 1975, after which brokers could charge whatever fee they wanted. The change created an opening for both discount brokers and a diversified and specialized brokerage industry.

MBS. *See* Mortgage-Backed Security.

MCFADDEN ACT. A federal law that allows each state to regulate commercial banks within that state.

MCIC INDEMNITY CORPORATION. An MGIC Investment Corporation subsidiary that insures some municipal bonds.

MEAN RETURN. The expected returns of all of the investments in a portfolio, an analysis of which determines the relationship between risks and returns.

MEASURING GAP. A price gap that copies the most recent movement.

MECHANIC'S LIEN. A claim the state can hold against a building until contractors, laborers, and suppliers involved in the construction are paid in full. If the company that contracted for the building liquidates before these people are paid, the state can give them priority over any other creditors.

MEDIUM OF EXCHANGE. Any negotiable instrument that is commonly accepted as payment for goods or services or for settling a debt. The instrument is accepted without any consideration given to the person's creditworthiness. For example, U.S. dollars are a medium of exchange.

MEDIUM OTHER THAN CASH. Any negotiable instrument other than cash that is commonly accepted as payment for goods or services or for settling a debt. For example, checks, notes, and credit are considered medium other than cash.

MEDIUM-TERM BOND. A debt instrument with a maturity of two to 10 years.

MEDIUM-TERM NOTE. An unsecured obligation that matures in nine months to 15 years.

MEETING BOND INTEREST AND PRINCIPAL. Principal and interest payments are being made when they fall due.

MEGAGOTH. A company that has the ability to offer more services than any similar firm, and that has capital totaling at least $25 billion.

MEMBER BANK. A bank that is a member of the Federal Reserve System.

MEMBER CORPORATION. A company registered as a broker or as a dealer that has at least one employee as a member on one of the securities exchanges.

MEMBER FIRM. A brokerage firm or a company that is a member of an organized stock exchange.

MEMBERSHIP CORPORATION. A company that members can join by paying a fee, but that does not issue any stocks.

MEMBERSHIP DUES. The annual fees that exchange members pay to remain members of the exchange.

MEMBER'S RATE. The commission an exchange member must pay when the member is not also a member of the clearing association.

MEMBERS' SHORT SALE RATIO. Achieved by dividing all short sales into all shares that members sold short for their own accounts during a specific time period.

MEMBER TAKEDOWN. When an underwriting syndicate member agrees to buy bonds at a discount from the member's account and sell them to the customer at the public offering price.

MERCANTILE AGENCY. An agency that provides one company with the credit ratings of another company when that first company expects to do business with the other. A mercantile agency also collects overdue accounts.

MERCHANT BANK. A British commercial bank. A merchant bank is different from an American commercial bank because a merchant bank is allowed to underwrite new issues of corporate securities, and an American commercial bank is not.

MERGER. When two or more companies voluntarily combine to form one company, with only one of the companies maintaining its identity.

MERGER CONVERSION. When the depositors of a mutual institution can vote on a merger, even though the acquiring company does not give them any money or stock shares. The depositors will be offered the stock first in an offer that equals the mutual's market value.

MESSAGE SWITCHING. A computer network that connects the different trading areas of an exchange to direct orders and transmit prices to member firms.

MEZZANINE BRACKET. An underwriter who, next to the major underwriters, subscribes to the next largest portion of the issue.

MEZZANINE FINANCING. A takeover is financed through preferred stock or convertible subordinated debentures to expand the company's equity capital and to satisfy creditors that the new owners are making a substantial financial commitment to the company.

MEZZANINE LEVEL. The time right before a company goes public when venture capitalists enter with a lower risk than if they had entered earlier. Investors who enter at this time can expect early capital appreciation because market values can increase at the initial public offering.

MGIC INVESTMENT CORPORATION. A company that provides insurance on some municipal bonds, mortgages, and commercial leases.

MICROECONOMICS. A study of an economy's individual parts, such as an individual industry.

MICROHEDGE. A hedge that reduces the risk of owning a security or asset.

MID-AMERICA COMMODITY EXCHANGE. A commodities exchange in Chicago.

MIDDLE-OF-THE-ROAD STAND. To avoid predicting or voicing an opinion on how securities prices probably will change. Such a stand is neither bullish nor bearish.

MIDGET. A Government National Mortgage Association mortgage pool with a 15-year maturity. Other than the maturity—the average Ginnie Mae has a 30-year maturity—the midget is the same as a regular Ginnie Mae.

MIDWEST STOCK EXCHANGE (MSE). A securities exchange that handles transactions of its own listed securities as well as some of those traded on the New York Stock Exchange. The MSE is in Chicago.

MIDWEST STOCK EXCHANGE AUTOMATED EXECUTION SYSTEM. An electronic system that connects the Midwest Stock Exchange with the Intermarket Trading System and through which dual-listed stocks can be immediately executed at the best price.

MILL. Equal to 0.1 percent.

MINI MANIPULATION. A manipulative deal on a stock option contract that is small enough to be difficult to detect, but large enough to change the option position. When the manipulator holds a large position in an underlying option, the movement can be multiplied many times.

MINIMUM LENDING RATE. The interest rate the Bank of New England charges British banks to borrow.

MINIMUM MAINTENANCE. The least amount of equity a brokerage firm requires a customer to maintain in his or her margin account.

MINIMUM PRICE CHANGES OMITTED. An announcement that appears on a stock exchange's tape if the reporting of trades are 10 or more minutes late. After the announcement, only prices that have gone up or down more than 1/8 of a point from the previous transaction are printed.

MINIMUM VARIATION. One-eighth of a point in securities transactions, and 1/32 of a point in transactions of bonds and government notes.

MINIMUM YIELD. Whichever is less, the yield to call or the yield to maturity.

MINI-WAREHOUSE LIMITED PARTNERSHIP. Two or more people form a partnership to invest in small warehouses and then rent space in the warehouses for people to store furniture or other belongings. While most of the profits come from rents, the partners also receive tax benefits from depreciation and capital gains after the warehouse is sold.

MINNEAPOLIS GRAIN EXCHANGE. A commodity exchange in Minneapolis.

MINORITY INTEREST. Ownership of stock shares with no voting control, or with less than controlling interest.

MINORITY INVESTMENT. A person's holdings in a company when those holdings total less than 50 percent of the company's voting shares.

MINORITY STOCKHOLDER. An investor who owns less than 50 percent of a company's voting shares.

MINOR TREND. Small, daily price changes in the securities or commodities markets.

MINT PAR OF EXCHANGE. Divide the weight of one country's monetary unit, such as gold or silver, by the weight of the similar metal of another country's monetary unit.

MINT PRICE OF GOLD. The price a government will pay for gold when that gold is delivered to the mint.

MINT RATIO. The difference between the weight of one metal to another along with each metal's national currency unit equivalent.

MINUS. The discount at which a closed-end mutual fund sells below the fund's net asset value.

MINUS TICK. A transaction executed at a price lower than the previous transaction.

MINUS YIELD. A convertible bond selling at a premium that is higher than the bond's interest yield.

MINUTE BOOK. A company's official record of its stockholder and board of directors meetings.

MISCELLANEOUS LIABILITIES. A bookkeeping entry that represents liabilities for which payments, for tax or legal reasons, have not been determined yet.

MISCELLANEOUS STOCK. The securities of a company that is not part of any particular industry.

MISSING THE MARKET. An investor's limit order that a broker could not fill because the security's market price jumped too far from the investor's limit price.

MIT. *See* Market If Touched Order.

MIXED. A market that follows no trend and that has many price shifts, with some prices going up and others going down.

MIXED ACCOUNT. A margin account that holds both long and short positions in the securities market.

MIXED COLLATERAL. In securing a loan, a borrower uses a variety of different types of securities as collateral.

MIXED CURRENCY. A currency that contains both notes and precious metals.

MIXING RATES. A variety of foreign exchange rates that are used in specific categories of items traded overseas.

MM. The abbreviation for one million; when following a number, it indicates the number is to be multiplied by 1,000,000. For example, 3MM would equal 3,000,000.

MO. Follows some newspaper stock listings to indicate the stock is listed and traded on the Montreal Stock Exchange.

MOBILE HOME CERTIFICATE. A Government National Mortgage Association security that represents a mortgage on a mobile home. The securities carry shorter maturities, but the same guarantees as the normal Ginnie Maes.

MODELING. An economic system model is designed and manipulated so that any possible changes and the impact of those changes can be analyzed.

MODERN PORTFOLIO. An investment theory in which investment managers classify, estimate, and control investment risks and returns.

MODIFIED LEGAL LIST. Allows fiduciaries in some states to put most of the money in funds on the legal list and the rest of the money in securities that are not on the list.

MOMENTUM. The pace and the strength of a specific security's, industry's or market indicator's price movements. In the stock market, technical analysts measure momentum by charting the trends of prices and volume.

MOMENTUM INDICATOR. A gauge that uses prices and trading volumes to determine the market's strength and its general health, and to find possible market turning points.

MONETARISM. An economic system with the theory that changes in the money supply prompt economic and price fluctuations.

MONETARY AGGREGATES. Money supply.

MONETARY INDICATOR. A gauge used to determine what effect the Treasury Department and Federal Reserve will have on equity and on the bond market.

MONETARY INFLATION. When the money supply increases.

MONETARY POLICY. The way in which the money supply is managed. In the United States, for example, the Federal Reserve Board establishes the monetary policy.

MONEY BROKER. A financial institution that acts as an intermediary between borrowers and lenders.

MONEY CENTER BANK. A bank in one of the world's major financial centers, such as London, Tokyo, or Chicago, that has large lenders, money market buyers, and securities purchasers. A money center bank also lends money to governments and international corporations.

MONEY FUNDS. A mutual fund in which an investor owns shares, usually at $1 each, in an account that is similar to a bank account.

MONEY MARKET. An international market for dealers who trade short-term government and corporate financial instruments such as a banker's acceptance, commercial paper, negotiable certificates of deposit, or Treasury bills.

MONEY MARKET ACCOUNT. A savings account with a higher interest rate for a time savings account with a minimum required balance.

MONEY MARKET BROKER. A financial institution that buys, sells, and transfers short-term credits and instruments.

MONEY MARKET CENTER BANK. A large, metropolitan bank that actively issues and trades short-term financial instruments such as commercial paper, bankers' acceptance, and certificates of deposit.

MONEY MARKET CERTIFICATE. A savings instrument with a minimum face value of $10,000 and a 26-week maturity, and with the interest rate tied to a six-month Treasury bill.

MONEY MARKET DEPOSIT ACCOUNT. A bank account that requires a minimum deposit of $1,000, allows the drawing of only three checks a month, while permitting unlimited transfers through automatic teller machines, and has an interest rate comparable to that found on money market mutual funds.

MONEY MARKET FUND. A mutual fund with investments directed in short-term money market instruments only, which normally can be withdrawn with 24-hour's notice without penalty.

MONEY MARKET INSTRUMENT. A short-term bill or note that is easily marketable and carries little risk of default.

MONEY MARKET PREFERRED STOCK. An equity security with a dividend paid every 49 days, at which time the rate is changed to reflect the current market rate.

MONEY MARKET RATES. The current interest rates on a variety of different money market instruments. Typically, the rate is based on the particular fund's security, liquidity, size, and maturity.

MONEY MARKET SECURITIES. High-quality securities with market prices that are tied more closely to the prevailing interest rates than to the underlying company's general economic health.

MONEY MULTIPLIER SECURITY. A zero-coupon offering that offers the investor a choice of maturities. Because long-term securities cost less than short-term securities, investors can profit greatly because all can be redeemed at par at maturity.

MONEY PRICE. The amount it costs to buy one unit of a commodity.

MONEY RATE. The interest rate a lender charges a borrower.

MONEY RATE OF RETURN. Divide the value of assets into the annual dollars received through those assets.

MONEY SPREAD. A vertical spread, occurring when a client buys a long option while simultaneously selling another option in the same class and with the same expiration dates, but with different strike prices.

MONEY SUPPLY. Bank deposits that can be withdrawn on command, and any currency held outside of a commercial bank.

MONEY SUPPLY INDICATOR. The percentage of change in the money supply when it is adjusted for the percentage change in the Consumer Price Index. The indicator is useful when the money supply steadily increases and inflation remains low; at this time, the prices of securities normally increase.

MONOPOLY. A company or group of connected companies controls all of the production and distribution of a product or service without competition. Because of the lack of competition, prices generally are high and little concern is given to the needs of consumers. Most monopolies are illegal.

MONTHLY INVESTMENT PLAN. Offered by the New York Stock Exchange, this method allows smaller investors to buy stocks by paying a specified minimum amount each month.

MONTHLY STATEMENT. A report a brokerage firm sends each client monthly, with the report outlining such information as the dates, amounts, credits, debits, and balances involved in each individual transaction.

MONTREAL EXCHANGE REGISTERED REPRESENTATIVE ORDER ROUTING AND EXECUTION SYSTEM. A computer network that connects the Montreal Stock Exchange with the Boston Stock Exchange and through which traders can execute orders in U.S. dollars on whichever exchange offers the best price.

MONTREAL STOCK EXCHANGE. A securities exchange in Montreal.

MOOCH. A person who wants to make big money fast, so he or she invests in securities without first investigating the market.

MOODY'S INVESTORS SERVICE. A company that analyzes and rates securities, and provides a variety of other investment information to investors. MIG 1 is the highest rating, and MIG 4 is the lowest, but even MIG 4 represents an adequate rating of bank quality and investment grade.

MORAL OBLIGATION BONDS. A revenue-backed, state-issued municipal bond upon which the state will pay principal and interest in the event of default.

MORAL SUASION. The moral, but not legal, ability of the Federal Reserve System to ensure compliance with its policies through well-placed influence.

MORATORIUM. When a debtor legally can delay paying an obligation.

MORNING LOAN. The unsecured loan a bank makes to a stockbroker so the stockbroker can deliver stocks to a customer until the customer can pay the broker.

MORTGAGE. A loan, usually to buy property, with property used as collateral.

MORTGAGE-BACKED CERTIFICATES. A bank-issued certificate in a large denomination, usually owned by an institution, that covers a mortgage pool insured by a private mortgage insurance company.

MORTGAGE-BACKED SECURITY (MBS). A debt instrument with a pool of real estate loans as the underlying collateral.

MORTGAGE BANKER. The intermediary between the institution that originates the mortgage and the investor who buys the mortgage.

MORTGAGE BANKERS ASSOCIATION OF AMERICA. A professional organization that promotes better investor services.

MORTGAGE BANKING. The combining of property-backed mortgage loans to form a pool, with shares sold to investors. For a fee, the seller services the investment for the life of the loan.

MORTGAGE BANKING COMPANY. An expert or specialist in the buying and selling of government-backed mortgages.

MORTGAGE BOND. A corporate bond backed by the mortgage on a particular piece of property, with a first mortgage bond backed by the first mortgage, a second mortgage bond backed by the second mortgage, and a general mortgage backed by either the third or some other mortgage on the same property.

MORTGAGE BOND SECURITIES CLEARING CORPORATION. An organization that helps investors in mortgage-backed securities transfer ownership and allows trade comparisons by book entry debits and credits.

MORTGAGE BROKER. An agent who arranges property loans, but does not service the loans after the financing is set.

MORTGAGE CERTIFICATE. A document that verifies and provides the details of an interest in a mortgage or in part of a mortgage. The mortgage certificate is not a negotiable instrument or an obligation to pay.

MORTGAGE CHATTEL. A personal property mortgage.

MORTGAGE COMPANY. A mortgage or a mortgage agent for large mortgagees. The company collects payments and retains all relevant records.

MORTGAGE CORPORATION. A government-sponsored corporation that buys some conventional residential mortgages from corporation members, then packages the mortgages and sells them publicly.

MORTGAGE CORRESPONDENT. A lender's agent who processes loans.

MORTGAGE CREDIT CERTIFICATES. An annual credit offered by cities and states that provides a mortgage subscriber with a federal tax credit. Through this program, cities and states can promote housing projects and subsidize mortgage payments at the federal government's expense.

MORTGAGE DEPARTMENT. The area of a lending institution where counselors, loan officers, and recording employees handle all mortgage work.

MORTGAGEE CLAUSE. An insurance contract stipulation in which the proceeds will be payable to the mortgagee.

MORTGAGE IN POSSESSION. A creditor who takes over a mortgaged property's income if the debtor defaults on the mortgage loan.

MORTGAGE INVESTMENT TRUST. A real estate investment trust that puts money in long-term, usually guaranteed, mortgages, and makes short-term construction loans.

MORTGAGE LIEN. A mortgage that is used as collateral for a debt.

MORTGAGE LOAN LEDGER RECORD. A record of all principal, interest, and charges involved in a mortgage transaction.

MORTGAGE NOTE. Proof of indebtedness that outlines how the mortgage is to be repaid.

MORTGAGE PARTICIPATION CERTIFICATE. A mortgage purchased by the Federal Home Loan Mortgage Association and resold as a pass-through security. The security represents an undivided interest in a mortgage pool.

MORTGAGE PASS-THROUGH SECURITIES. A pool of residential mortgage loans, with the interest and principal distributed to the investor each month.

MORTGAGE PATTERN. The way in which mortgage payments are arranged.

MORTGAGE POOL. A group of mortgages on the same class of property with the same interest rates and maturities.

MORTGAGE POOL ORIGINATOR. A mortgage banker who groups together similar classes of mortgages and then issues securities to reflect fractional interests in the pool. The originator also distributes interest and principal payments to certificate holders.

MORTGAGE PORTFOLIO. All of the mortgage loans a bank holds and claims as assets.

MORTGAGE PREMIUM. When the legal interest rate is lower than the prevailing market rate on mortgages and when mortgage money is in short supply, a bank or other lender will charge this fee for providing a mortgage.

MORTGAGE REAL ESTATE INVESTMENT TRUST. Uses investors' funds as a leveraged investment, with the trust lending money it borrowed from a commercial bank. Investors in the trust hope to profit from the difference between the bank's and borrower's interest.

MORTGAGE SERVICING. The supervision and administration of a mortgage loan. The person or institution who services a mortgage collects payments, monitors principal and interest payments, handles all escrow duties, and forecloses when necessary.

MOST ACTIVE LIST. A list of the securities that traded the heaviest volume in one day.

MOTHER GOOSE. A short, simple summary that explains a company's prospectus.

MOVABLE EXCHANGE. An instrument that is quoted in the currency of the nation being owed a payment instead of the nation paying the debt.

MOVEMENT. Any upward or downward shift, no matter how large or how slight, in a security's price.

MOVING AVERAGE. A price average that is continuously adjusted, with each new added price changing the overall average, during a particular time period, and therefore accurately reflects values.

MSE. *See* Midwest Stock Exchange.

MULTICURRENCY CLAUSE. A Eurocurrency loan stipulation that allows the borrower to repay the loan in a different currency as long as he or she takes out another Eurodollar loan immediately.

MULTIMANAGEMENT SYSTEM. A plan sponsor uses at least two investment managers to provide diversification.

MULTINATIONAL CORPORATION. A company that conducts business throughout the world and has fixed assets in at least one foreign country.

MULTIPLE CAPITAL STRUCTURE COMPANY. A corporation with several different classes of securities outstanding.

MULTIPLE COMMODITY RESERVE DOLLAR. To set a reserve of some items, an investor will try to keep a constant dollar ratio between gold and other commodities. The investor redeems dollars for gold or for the reserved items, and the gold and the items are always converted into dollars.

MULTIPLE CURRENCY PRACTICE. When at least two exchange rates are effective at the same time, with one at least 1 percent higher or lower than the par value.

MULTIPLE CURRENCY SECURITIES. Stocks or bonds for which the owner can choose the currency of the payments.

MULTIPLE CURRENCY SYSTEM. When foreign exchange is controlled to such an extent that foreign currency can be exchanged only through the government or through a controlled bank.

MULTIPLE EXCHANGE. Occurs when three or more people or companies are involved with several different pieces of property.

MULTIPLE OPTION PUT SECURITY. A municipal bond with a 30-year maturity and with two-, three-, and five-year put options. Because of the put options, the bond will trade as close to par as if it were a short-term bond.

MULTIPLIER EFFECT. A theory that even a minor event can cause great changes in another area because everything economic is, in some way, connected, so even a small change will cause a domino effect.

MUNICIPAL ASSISTANCE CORPORATION FOR THE CITY OF NEW YORK. A government agency that provides financial assistance to New York City by issuing bonds to keep the city from going through bankruptcy. The corporation can redeem city obligations, incur debt, and oversee the city's financial situation.

MUNICIPAL BOND. A city- or state-issued debt instrument. Interest on such instruments is exempt from federal income tax. If the bond was issued in the bondholder's state of residence, state and local taxes will be exempt.

MUNICIPAL BOND COMPARISON SYSTEM. A system that takes the Municipal Securities Rulemaking Board's trade information and clears the transactions by getting a contra party to accept the trade terms and by offering book entry debits and credits, where possible, to promote a settlement.

MUNICIPAL BOND FUND. A mutual fund that concentrates investments in tax-exempt municipal obligations.

MUNICIPAL BOND INSURANCE ASSOCIATION. A group of insurance companies that insure interest and principal on some municipal bonds.

MUNICIPAL IMPROVEMENT CERTIFICATE. A local government issues this tax-exempt certificate in lieu of bonds to finance such improvements as widening sidewalks or street repairs. The obligation is paid from special assessments made against the people who benefit from the improvements.

MUNICIPAL INSURED NATIONAL TRUST. A tax-free bond fund, offered by Moseley, Hallgarten, Estabrook, and Weeden, that offers monthly payments from a portfolio containing municipal securities.

MUNICIPAL INVESTMENT TRUST. A unit trust of diversified portfolio investments concentrated in municipal securities. Such trusts provide investors with tax-exempt monthly income.

MUNICIPAL NOTE. A municipal-issued, short-term debt instrument.

MUNICIPAL OPTION. One dealer offers to sell bonds to another dealer at a specific price, with the offer good only for a specific time period.

MUNICIPAL REVENUE BOND. A government bond issued to pay for such projects as bridges or sewers. After the project is completed, revenues from the project, such as tolls or other user fees, are used to pay off the bond.

MUNICIPAL SECURITIES RULEMAKING BOARD. A panel that issues the rules and regulations of registering municipal bonds.

MUNIFACTS. A service that provides available data on newly issued municipal bonds.

MUTILATED SECURITY. A security with a certificate that has the name of the issue or the issuer obscured, or with a portion of the certificate missing so the security cannot be identified. With such a security, the transfer agent must guarantee all ownership rights for the buyer.

MUTUAL ASSOCIATION. A savings and loan that is owned by its depositors, with deposits representing ownership shares. Such associations do not issue stocks.

MUTUAL COMPANY. A company with ownership and profits distributed among members, with the amount each member receives directly related to the amount of business each member does with the company.

MUTUAL FUND. An investment company that puts investors' money in a variety of areas, usually securities, and that must redeem the shares at net asset value upon demand.

MUTUAL FUND CASH RATIO. A percentage comparison of a mutual fund's cash to the fund's total assets. A high ratio of cash to assets is favorable because it means the investor has more funds available for investing.

MUTUAL FUND CORPORATION. A trust company or commercial bank that holds onto a mutual fund's securities, makes transfers, and pays and collects stockholders' investments.

MUTUAL FUND CUSTODIAN. A commercial bank or other institution that holds a mutual fund's assets for safekeeping.

MUTUAL SAVINGS BANK. A savings bank organized for the benefit of depositors, with income distributed to the depositors after expenses are deducted.

MUTUAL WILLS. An arrangement in which a husband and wife agree to leave everything to each other.

N

N. Used in stock listings to designate that a security's primary market is the New York Stock Exchange.

NAKED OPTIONS. The person selling (writing) a put or call option does not own the underlying security.

NAKED POSITION. A long or short position the holder has not hedged as prices fluctuate. The write of a call option, for example, is naked if the investor doesn't own the underlying security, and is partially hedged if he or she does own the underlying security because the potential risk is much greater if the price rises.

NAME. A participant in a foreign exchange market transaction.

NARROWING THE SPREAD. Occurs when a broker-dealer bids higher than the last bid price, or offers a lower price than the last offer price. By doing this, the broker-dealer narrows the price spread between bids and offers.

NARROW MARKET. Occurs when securities are traded with little difference between the bid and asked prices.

NASD. *See* National Association of Securities Dealers.

NASDAQ. *See* National Association of Securities Dealers Automated Quotations.

NATIONAL ASSOCIATION OF INVESTMENT CLUBS. An organization that helps to establish investment clubs, through which investors pool their money and make common investments.

NATIONAL ASSOCIATION OF SECURITIES DEALERS (NASD). An organization of brokers and dealers who trade securities in the United States. Supervised by the Securities and Exchange Commission, the NASD regulates all over-the-counter brokers and dealers.

NATIONAL ASSOCIATION OF SECURITIES DEALERS AND INVESTMENT MANAGERS. A self-regulating organization of licensed securities dealers who do not have to apply for a license every year before they can deal in securities.

NATIONAL ASSOCIATION OF SECURITIES DEALERS AUTOMATED QUOTATIONS (NASDAQ). A national computer network through which securities dealers execute and post transactions and record prices. NASDAQ is the major method of over-the-counter trading.

NATIONAL ASSOCIATION OF SECURITIES DEALERS AUTOMATED QUOTATION INDEXES. Seven indexes that act as gauges and which average the trading prices of more than 3,000 American over-the-counter companies. The seven indexes cover banks, the industrials, insurance companies, other financial institutions, transportations, utilities, and a composite.

NATIONAL ASSOCIATION OF SECURITIES DEALERS AUTOMATED QUOTATION OPTIONS AUTOMATED EXECUTION SYSTEM. A computer network over which NASD members can trade and execute over-the-counter put and call options. The members can use the computer to trade up to three contracts on an option series.

NATIONAL ASSOCIATION OF SECURITIES DEALERS FIVE PERCENT POLICY. A nonbinding NASD recommendation that brokerage commissions, markups, and markdowns should be near five percent on most transactions. NASD members do not need to adhere to this policy when executing small transactions, transactions that are difficult to complete, or mutual fund transactions.

NATIONAL ASSOCIATION OF SECURITIES DEALERS FORM FR-1. A document that foreign broker-dealers who are not syndicate members sign when they want to subscribe to a hot issue. Upon signing the certificate, the broker-dealer agrees that he or she understands and will adhere to the National Association of Securities Dealers' rules on hot issues.

NATIONAL ASSOCIATION OF SECURITIES DEALERS RULES OF FAIR PRACTICE. NASD regulations that cover the ethics of brokers and dealers to make sure that they all deal fairly with their customers.

NATIONAL BANK. A commercial bank that is chartered with the U.S. Comptroller of the Currency instead of by the state in which it does business. Such banks must be members of the Federal Reserve System.

NATIONAL CRIME INFORMATION CENTER. A Securities and Exchange Commission computer network that registers lost or stolen securities. A broker-dealer will use the network to verify the ownership of a security for sale.

NATIONAL DEBT. The total amount of money the U.S. government owes, including all Treasury bills, Treasury bonds, and other debt obligations.

NATIONAL FARM LOAN ASSOCIATION. An agricultural cooperative that, when subscribing to a local Federal Land Bank, can secure financing for farm mortgages.

NATIONAL FUTURES ASSOCIATION. An organization that regulates the commodities industry and that requires membership of commodity pool operators, commodity trading advisors, and futures exchange members.

NATIONAL HOUSING ACT. A law that established the Federal Housing Administration, which insures home mortgages, provides home improvement loans and finances low-income housing projects. The law also established the Federal Savings and Loan Insurance Corporation, which insures member association accounts for up to $5,000.

NATIONAL INCOME. All of the income a nation earns through its goods and services.

NATIONALIZATION. Occurs when a government takes over a company's assets and operations.

NATIONAL MARKET ADVISORY BOARD. A 15-member panel, appointed by the Securities and Exchange Commission, that makes recommendations to the SEC on establishing, operating, and regulating the securities market. Members serve between two and five years with the majority coming from within the securities industry.

NATIONAL MARKET SYSTEM. A theoretical, nationwide computer network that links all markets for a particular security so that everyone can have access to all bid and ask prices and can execute transactions based on the best prices available.

NATIONAL PARTNERSHIP EXCHANGE. A Florida-based computer network that acts as a secondary market for those limited partnership securities that are registered with the Securities and Exchange Commission.

NATIONAL QUOTATION BUREAU. A Commerce Clearing House subsidiary that provides subscribers with daily over-the-counter quotes.

NATIONAL QUOTATION SERVICE (NQS). A National Quotation Bureau system that lists corporate bonds, over-the-counter securities, their market makers, and bid and ask prices. The NQS reports on those OTC stocks that are not quoted by the National Association of Securities Dealers Automated Quotation system.

NATIONAL SECURITIES CLEARING CORPORATION. An independent clearing organization that member firms use to execute transactions with other member firms.

NATIONAL SECURITIES EXCHANGE. Any securities exchange that has been registered with the Securities and Exchange Commission.

NATIONAL SECURITIES TRADE ASSOCIATION. An organization of over-the-counter brokers and dealers. Among other activities, the association provides lobbying services on behalf of brokers and dealers.

NATIONAL STOCK EXCHANGE (NSE). A third New York City Stock Exchange. The NSE was established in 1960.

NATURAL FINANCING. A transaction in which financing is not necessary because the seller pays the buyer in cash.

NATURAL INTEREST RATE. The interest rate at which the demand for loans equals the savings supply.

NATURAL MONOPOLY. A company that holds a monopoly when no other company is able to compete because of variables beyond either company's control. For example, an agricultural business that holds a monopoly on a particular produce item because no one else can farm that item holds a natural monopoly. Other companies may not be able to farm the item because of climate or because of a lack of available labor.

NATURAL SELLER. An investor who is selling a security he or she actually has in his or her portfolio.

NEARBY DELIVERY. The closest active month a commodities futures agreement can be delivered.

NEAREST MONTH. In a group of commodity futures or options contracts, this represents the contract that expires first.

NEAR MONEY. A debt instrument such as a bond that is near its redemption or maturity date.

NEAR OPTION. The side of a spread option position that expires first.

NEAR TERM. A market performance evaluation that indicates a period from one to five weeks.

NEGATIVE AMORTIZER. A home mortgage that is lower than the average current rate, with the difference added to the principal. Such mortgage payments increase in amount as time goes on.

NEGATIVE CARRY. When a security's percentage of return is less than the interest rate charged on the loan the investor used to buy the security. For example, if the investor is buying a bond that has a 10 percent rate of return using funds from a loan that charges an 11.5 percent interest rate, the bond would have a negative carry.

NEGATIVE CASH FLOW. Occurs when a company is spending more money than it is taking in.

NEGATIVE INCOME TAX. A subsidy that low-income residents receive to bring them up to the subsistence level when their yearly income is below that level. To receive the subsidy, the residents first must file a tax return that verifies their poverty-level income.

NEGATIVE INTEREST. Money that has been deducted from the interest amount.

NEGATIVE INTEREST TAX. The Swiss government imposes this tax every now and then on new bank accounts held by foreigners when the account balances exceed a particular level. That level usually is about 100,000 francs.

NEGATIVE PLEDGE CLAUSE. An indenture agreement stipulation in which the company guarantees that it will not pledge any of its assets if such a pledge would decrease debt-holders' security.

NEGATIVE WORKING CAPITAL. When a company's current liabilities exceed its current assets.

NEGATIVE YIELD. Occurs when savings returns are less than the inflation rate plus taxes.

NEGATIVE YIELD CURVE. The graph that occurs when charting the following situation: the interest rate on a short-term fixed-income security is higher than the interest rate on a long-term fixed-income security with the same class and rating.

NEGOTIABLE. Any instrument that can be sold or transferred easily.

NEGOTIABLE CERTIFICATE OF DEPOSIT. A negotiable money market instrument that trades on the open market with high returns and low risks.

NEGOTIABLE INSTRUMENT. An ownership certificate that can be transferred without registering that transfer with the original issuer.

NEGOTIABLE ORDER OF WITHDRAWAL ACCOUNT. An interest-bearing account on which the holder can draw checks. Such an account, which is a combination savings-checking account, is commonly referred to as a NOW account.

NEGOTIABLE PAPER. A negotiable instrument used to take out short-term business loans.

NEGOTIABLE SECURITY. A security with a title that can be easily transferred.

NEGOTIATED BID. As opposed to a competitive bid, this occurs when a security's issuer and the underwriting syndicate mutually agree on a price after holding meetings and discussions on the subject.

NEGOTIATED SALE. When two or more parties agree to a securities transaction price without going through any competitive bidding.

NEGOTIATED UNDERWRITING. The underwriting of a new securities issue when the issuing company and the underwriting manager negotiate the spread between the price paid to the issuer and the offering price, instead of having that spread determined through competitive bidding. Corporate stocks and bonds normally are issued through a negotiated underwriting, and utilities issues are issued through competitive bidding.

NELLIE MAES. *See* New England Education Loan Marketing Corporation.

NEST EGG. The assets and money a person conservatively invests or sets aside for his or her retirement.

NET. The difference between the value of a sale, whether positive or negative, and the cost of completing that sale.

NET ASSETS. The difference between a company's assets and its liabilities.

NET ASSET VALUE. Determined by subtracting the liabilities from the portfolio value of a fund's securities, and dividing that figure by the number of outstanding shares.

NET AVAILS. The money a borrower receives on a discounted note, with the amount equal to the note's face value, less the amount of the discount.

NET BALANCE. The amount that falls due after any refunds have been subtracted.

NET BONDED DEBT. The gross bonded debt, which is a government's direct debt in outstanding bonds, minus cash and assets.

NET BORROWED RESERVES. The amount of money borrowed minus any excess reserves.

NET CAPITAL. A company's net worth minus assets that cannot be sold at their full value.

NET CAPITAL REQUIREMENT. A Securities and Exchange Commission regulation that outlines the net capital ratio, which is the aggregate, customer-related indebtedness along with cash and other assets that can be converted easily into cash.

NET CHANGE. The difference between a security's current price and the price at which it closed after the last trading session.

NET CURRENT ASSETS. The amount by which a company's current assets exceed its current liabilities.

NET DOWN. Occurs when a taxpayer offsets short-term gains with short-term losses, and long-term gains with long-term losses to reach a final figure in both columns. If the investor ends up with a net loss in one column and a net gain in the other, he or she must offset the gains and losses again.

NET EARNINGS. The amount by which gross operating income exceeds gross operating expenses, then subtract the applicable taxes.

NET ESTATE. The amount an estate is worth after all management expenses have been subtracted.

NET FOR COMMON STOCK. A preferred stock's net income after dividends have been subtracted during a period of accrual.

NET FOREIGN INVESTMENT. The amount a country's foreign assets and liabilities change through trade, investment income, and cash gifts.

NET INCOME. The profit after all expenses have been deducted.

NET INCOME MULTIPLIER. An estimated property value achieved by dividing the monthly net rent into the selling price.

NET INCOME PER SHARE OF COMMON STOCK. The dollar amount of earnings from one common stock share after all costs, including taxes and depreciation, have been subtracted.

NET INTEREST COST. A debt security issuer's interest expense for the security's life.

NET INVESTMENT INCOME. The profit from an investment minus commissions and other expenses.

NET INVESTMENT INCOME PER SHARE. The average dollar amount of dividend and interest earnings an investment company receives from each individual security share after all costs, including taxes and depreciation, have been subtracted.

NET LEASE. A lease in which the tenant pays all maintenance costs, taxes, insurance, etc.

NET LIQUID ASSETS. The difference between a company's cash and marketable securities and its current liabilities.

NET LISTING. The commission amount a broker receives beyond the security's selling price.

NET LONG-TERM DEBT. The total long-term debt minus sinking fund investment assets and other reserve funds that are held for redeeming the debt.

NET NATIONAL PRODUCT (NNP). Gross national product minus the capital consumption allowances (depreciation).

NET OPERATING INCOME. A company's net operating income after minority interest and taxes and subtracted and before investment profits and losses and preferred dividend payments are added or subtracted.

NET OPTION. A contract that gives a buyer the right to buy a piece of property at a specific price.

NET OUT. A brokerage client's market position is established by determining how much margin he or she must post at the exchange.

NET POSITION. The difference between open contracts held long and open contracts held short in the same commodity.

NET PRESENT VALUE (NPV). An investment evaluation method in which the net present value of all cash outflows and inflows is calculated with a discount rate or a required rate of return. The net present value of a good investment is positive.

NET PROCEEDS. The amount of money an investor receives from selling a security, with the cost of completing the sale subtracted.

NET PROFIT. Earnings after all debts, expenses, and taxes have been deducted.

NET PROFIT ON NET SALES. To measure a company's profitability, divide its net sales into its net earnings.

NET PROFITS ON NET WORKING CAPITAL. Subtract a company's total current debt from its total current assets, which provides the owner's equity in the current assets. The difference represents the financial cushion with which the company can carry inventories and receivables and can pay for the business's day-to-day operations.

NET PROFITS ON TANGIBLE NET WORTH. To determine a company's profitability, divide its net profits after taxes by its tangible net worth, which is obtained by subtracting liabilities from assets, then subtracting the intangible assets.

NET QUICK ASSETS. After removing a company's inventory from its current assets, subtract the company's current liabilities from the remaining assets to compute its net quick assets.

NET REALIZED CAPITAL GAINS PER SHARE. An investment company's long-term capital gains from selling a security added to the net of its long-term capital losses, with the sum divided by the number of outstanding shares. The gains are distributed among stockholders each year, with the amount each stockholder receives in direct proportion to the percentage of the investment company portfolio he or she owns.

NET REVENUE AVAILABLE FOR DEBT SERVICE. To determine revenue bond issue coverage, subtract an organization's operating and maintenance expenses, not including bond interest or depreciation, from its gross operating revenue.

NET SALES. A balance sheet item that indicates sales receipts minus the cost of the sales.

NET SALES TO INVENTORY. To determine a company's stocks-to-sales ratio, divide its inventory into its annual net sales. The figure is compared with the ratios of other companies.

NET SALES TO NET WORKING CAPITAL. Divide a company's net working capital into its net sales. This is a gauge to determine the extent to which a company is implementing its working capital and its margin of operating funds.

NET SALES TO TANGIBLE NET WORTH. To measure a company's relative capital turnover, divide a company's tangible net worth into its net sales.

NET SHARES MARKET. In Europe, most U.S. equity securities are traded in dealer markets with banks and brokers as principals, so they are net of commissions.

NET SURPLUS. A company's total earnings after operating expenses, taxes, insurance, dividend payments, and other costs have been deducted.

NET TANGIBLE ASSETS PER SHARE. Subtract a company's intangible assets from its total assets to find its total tangible assets. Subtract all liabilities and the preferred stock's par value from the total tangible assets, then divide the remainder by the total number of outstanding common shares to obtain the net tangible assets per share.

NET TRANSACTION. When the buyer and the seller of a security are charged no additional fee in the transaction.

NET UNREALIZED APPRECIATION. The appreciation between a person's investment costs and the current market value of his or her holdings.

NET UNREALIZED DEPRECIATION. The depreciation between a person's investment costs and the current market value of his or her holdings.

NET VOLUME. The difference between the uptick and downtick volumes.

NETWORK A. A Consolidated Tape Association subscription service that reports on successive New York Stock Exchange-listed round-lot transactions, even if the transaction was not executed on the NYSE.

NETWORK B. A Consolidated Tape Association subscription service that reports on successive American Stock Exchange-listed round-lot transactions, even if the transaction was not executed on the ASE.

NET WORTH. The difference between a company's or individual's assets and liabilities.

NET YIELD. A security's rate of return minus all related out-of-pocket costs, such as commissions.

NET YIELD TO REDEMPTION. A company's gross yield to redemption, which is a security's interest yield plus the yearly capital gains it would earn if it were held to redemption, minus taxes.

NEUTRAL MONEY. When a dollar could be converted into a commodity at a specific price to stabilize the price level.

NEUTRAL SPREAD. In a market with a narrow spread, this is a long call at a lower price and two short calls at a higher price.

NEUTRAL TREND. When a security's price remains even, with the prevailing price trend moving laterally.

NEW ACCOUNT REPORT. A document that broker-dealers must prepare and update on customers' investment objectives, financial situation, and investment background.

NEW ENGLAND EDUCATION LOAN MARKETING CORPORATION. A private Massachusetts company that buys student loan notes issued through the U.S. Higher Education Act. The firm then publicly issues tax-exempt bonds, with the proceeds used to buy education loans from eligible lenders. These securities are commonly referred to as Nellie Maes.

NEW ENGLAND NEGOTIABLE ORDER OF WITHDRAWAL ACCOUNT. A NOW account, which is a combination checking-savings account, with a federally chartered association in Connecticut, Maine, Rhode Island, or Vermont. The NOW account authority was expanded in 1979 to include these areas.

NEW HIGH. A security has reached its highest price during a given time period.

NEW HIGHS. A group of securities has reached its highest price in a year.

NEW ISSUE. A security publicly offered for sale for the first time.

NEW ISSUE MARKET. The market in which new securities issues are publicly sold.

NEW LOW. A security has reached its lowest price during a given time period.

NEW LOWS. A group of securities has reached its lowest price in a year.

NEW MONEY. A new bond that has a greater par value than a bond that was retired after a call option was exercised or after it matured.

NEW MONEY APPROACH TO INVESTMENT INCOME. An investment method in which investment income from a group annuity contract is allocated according to the rate of return earned on new investments that were made in the same year each block of contributions was received.

NEW MONEY PREFERRED. Preferred stock that was issued after October 1, 1942, with the shares providing the holder with an 85 percent tax exclusion on cash dividends.

NEWS TICKER. A brokerage house machine that provides business news that could have an effect on securities prices.

NEW YORK CALL MONEY. Money that a brokerage firm borrows to meet financial obligations after extending credit to a client's margin account.

NEW YORK CASH EXCHANGE. A regional organization of commercial banks that uses a central computer network to provide customers with automated teller services.

NEW YORK COFFEE AND SUGAR EXCHANGE. The primary U.S. market for trading coffee and sugar futures contracts.

NEW YORK CURB EXCHANGE. The original name of the American Stock Exchange.

NEW YORK FUTURES EXCHANGE (NYFE). A New York Stock Exchange subsidiary that deals in the trading of financial futures contracts.

NEW YORK INSURANCE EXCHANGE. The primary market where insurance brokers carry out large transactions with numerous different underwriters.

NEW YORK INTERBANK OFFERED RATE. The interest rate that deposits in U.S. financial center banks trade in the United States.

NEW YORK MERCANTILE EXCHANGE. A New York commodities exchange that deals in futures contracts on agricultural products, currency, petroleum, and precious metals.

NEW YORK PLAN. A plan in which equipment ownership is transferred through equipment trust certificates.

NEW YORK STOCK EXCHANGE. The largest stock exchange in the United States, with over 1,500 security listings.

NEW YORK STOCK EXCHANGE AVERAGES. A composite market indicator that profiles the general market condition through the prices of 25 industrial and railroad stocks.

NEW YORK STOCK EXCHANGE COMMON STOCK INDEX. A composite indicator that profiles the common stock market through the prices of all common stocks listed with the NYSE. A new index is calculated continuously and printed every 30 minutes.

NEW YORK STOCK EXCHANGE COMPOSITE INDEX. A gauge which averages the trading prices of all of the common shares of companies listed on the New York Stock Exchange. The four subgroup indexes are the financials, industrials, transportations, and utilities.

NEW YORK STOCK EXCHANGE VOLUME. All shares traded on the New York Stock Exchange in one day.

NEXT DAY CONTRACT. A securities transaction in which the payment and delivery must be made the next day.

NICKEL. A move in the bond market of five basis points either up or down.

NIFTY FIFTY. Institutional investors' 50 favorite stocks.

NINE-BOND RULE. A New York Stock Exchange regulation that if a member firm receives an order for nine or fewer listed bonds, the order must be sent to the exchange floor. If the order cannot be filled on the floor within one hour, the firm can fill the order in the over-the-counter market.

NINETY-DAY SAVINGS ACCOUNT. A passbook savings account that pays interest based on 90-day deposits, with substantial interest penalties assessed if the money is withdrawn before the end of 90 days.

NNP. *See* Net National Product.

NO-ACTION LETTER. A letter sent to the Securities and Exchange Commission when the writer is considering taking civil or criminal recourse against another party, but is not sure that the other party's actions were really illegal or improper. The SEC provides an opinion on the situation, but takes no civil or criminal action against anyone involved.

NO LIEN AFFIDAVIT. A document in which a property-owner verifies that work on a piece of property has been completed, and that the property is not encumbered by any liens or mortgages.

NO-LIMIT ORDER. An investor's request to have his or her broker buy a security with no price restrictions.

NO-LITIGATION CERTIFICATE. A document in which a bond attorney verifies that no lawsuits are pending in connection with the validity of a bond issue.

NO LOAD. Without any sales charge.

NO-LOAD MUTUAL FUND. A mutual fund that carries no sales charge.

NOMINAL. A security's face value.

NOMINAL ACCOUNT. An account used for analyzing surplus account changes, including income accounts that are closed into surplus at the end of the fiscal year.

NOMINAL ASSET. An asset with little or no worth, or with a worth that is difficult to determine. Judgments and many intangible assets are considered nominal assets.

NOMINAL CAPITAL. The face value or par value of a company's issued securities.

NOMINAL EXERCISE PRICE. To determine a Government National Mortgage Association option contract's dollar value, multiply its strike price by a Ginnie Mae certificate's unpaid principal balance with an 8 percent interest rate.

NOMINAL INTEREST RATE. The coupon rate of a bond, which represents the amount of interest due to the bond holder.

NOMINALLY ISSUED. Certified securities that have been properly prepared for delivery.

NOMINALLY OUTSTANDING. Securities that the issuing company buys back, but keeps alive instead of retiring.

NOMINAL QUOTATION. A broker's bid and offer price that estimates a security's value when the broker refuses to execute the deal at the prices given.

NOMINAL YIELD. Divide a fixed-income security's par value into its annual payout to reach this yield, which is stated as a percentage.

NOMINEE. The name that appears on a security's certificate when that name is different from the beneficial owner.

NONASSENTED SECURITIES. Securities in which the owner refuses to agree to the term changes of a defaulted security.

NONASSESSABLE STOCK. A security in which the owner cannot be penalized or held accountable if the issuer becomes insolvent. Most stocks are non-assessable stocks.

NONBORROWED RESERVES. Reported weekly via the Federal Reserve System, this provides the total of member bank reserves less the member banks' discount window borrowings.

NONCALLABLE. A security that cannot be redeemed before it matures.

NONCARRY. A market that handles transactions involving perishable commodities.

NONCASH. Any financial instrument that is not currency.

NONCLEARING HOUSE STOCK. Any securities that have not been cleared through the New York Stock Exchange Clearing Corporation. Over-the-counter securities are considered nonclearing house securities.

NONCLEARING MEMBER. A member of the National Association of Securities Dealers or a member of a securities exchange who does not maintain his or her own operations. Such a person pays another member a fee to use his or her operations to execute settlements.

NONCOMPETITIVE BID. An individual applies for a new government securities issue; the cost is established at the average price paid by brokers submitting competitive bids.

NONCONTINGENT PREFERENCE STOCK. A synonym for a share of cumulative preferred stock.

NONCONTRIBUTORY. A group insurance policy in which the policy holder, instead of his or her employer, pays the entire premium.

NONCUMULATIVE DIVIDENDS. If a company fails to pay a dividend when it is due, it does not accrue, so the shareholder loses it forever.

NONCUMULATIVE PREFERRED STOCK. Preferred stock with omitted dividends that are not cumulative.

NONCURRENT ASSET. Any asset that will not be sold, converted to cash or transferred within a company's normal cycle, which usually lasts one year. Fixed assets, intangible assets, and leasehold improvements all are considered noncurrent assets.

NONCURRENT LIABILITIES. A claim that will not fall due for one year or more.

NONDIVERSIFIED MANAGEMENT COMPANY. A management investment firm that is not subject to asset allocation limits, but that also is not eligible for specific tax exemptions. Such firms must register their intentions with the Securities and Exchange Commission.

NO NEAR BID-OFFER. When the bid or offer price for a security is significantly above or below the last bid or offer price.

NONEXEMPT. A bond that cannot be redeemed for a specific time period.

NONFORFEITURE OPTION. One of four possible life insurance contract privileges, including a stipulation that allows the policy holder to cash the policy, and one that permits the policy holder to take out a loan for an amount up to the policy's cash value.

NONINSURED FUND. Any mutual fund or pension fund that is invested, but not with an insurance company.

NONINTEREST-BEARING BOND. A discounted bond or note that earns no interest, but is redeemable at its face value at maturity.

NONINVESTMENT PROPERTY. Any property that is not purchased to create income for the buyer.

NONLEDGER ASSET. Any asset a company does not list in its general ledger. Accrued dividends, for example, are considered nonledger assets.

NONLEGAL INVESTMENT. Any investment that cannot legally be used for trust fund investing.

NONMARKETABLE LIABILITIES OF THE U.S. GOVERNMENT. A foreign, medium-term, nonmarketable government security that cannot be paid before maturity except under special conditions. An export-import bank certificate of participation, for example, falls into this category.

NONMARKETABLE SECURITIES. Securities that are difficult to sell for some specific reason, e.g., their lack of a secondary trading market.

NONMARKET RISK. The volatility of portfolio securities, when that volatility is not reflective of any general market trend.

NONMEMBER BANK. A bank that is not a Federal Reserve System member.

NONMEMBER FIRM. A brokerage firm that is not a member of a specific securities exchange. For example, a company that is a member of the New York Exchange would be a nonmember at the American Stock Exchange.

NONNEGOTIABLE. An instrument or document that does not meet the requirements of negotiability. Such a document cannot be transferred without assignment.

NONNEGOTIABLE CERTIFICATE OF DEPOSIT. A nonnegotiable instrument that brings high returns with low risk, but cannot be withdrawn early without incurring heavy penalties.

NONNEGOTIABLE INSTRUMENT. An instrument that cannot easily be sold or transferred.

NONPARTICIPATING GROUP ANNUITY CONTRACT. An insurance company contract in which the company provides the policy holder with income.

NONPRODUCTIVE LOAN. A commercial bank loan that subsequently increases the economic spending power in the economy, but does not increase output. A loan to pay for a leveraged buyout would be considered a nonproductive loan.

NONPROFIT ORGANIZATION. A chartered, tax-exempt business in which an officer or stockholder cannot legally receive any profits.

NONPUBLIC INFORMATION. Any information about a company that could cause the company's stock to go up or down in price if it were released publicly. Corporate officers who are privy to nonpublic information cannot legally trade shares using the information because doing so would give them an unfair advantage over other investors.

NONPURPOSE LOAN. A loan that will not be used to trade securities subject to the Federal Reserve System's credit regulations, but that has securities used as collateral.

NONQUALIFIED. A document, instrument, or investment that does not meet the requirements for tax preference.

NONQUALIFYING ANNUITY. An annuity that is not bought in an Internal Revenue Service-approved pension plan, and thus is purchased with aftertax dollars. The annuity's original investment dollars can, however, still fall under an appropriate tax shelter.

NONQUALIFYING STOCK OPTION. An issuing company grants such an option, usually to an executive, to buy a specific number of shares of a security at a specific price by a specific date. The difference between the option price and the fair market value is considered earned income in the year the option is exercised, so the difference is taxable.

NONRECOURSE LOAN. When a limited partner borrows money to finance his or her part in the partnership using his or her partial ownership as collateral for the loan. If the borrower defaults on the loan, the lender can take the partial ownership, but no other assets. In a recourse loan, the lender also can take the assets.

NONRECURRING CHARGE. A one-time income or a one-time expense listed on a corporation's ledger.

NONREFUNDABLE. A bond with the stipulation that the issuer cannot retire the issue with funds from a second bond issue.

NONRESIDENT AFFIDAVIT. A document that says a brokerage account holder is not a resident of the state of New York. Such a document, which no longer is used, would make the owner exempt from stock transfer taxes. Today, the tax is subject to a 100 percent rebate, so the affidavit is no longer necessary.

NONRESIDENT-OWNED INVESTMENT CORPORATION. An open-ended company, most often Canadian, with stock shares and funded indebtedness owned exclusively by people who do not live in the country, and thereby promotes foreign investments in the country.

NONREVENUE RECEIPTS. A collection that does not represent revenue and in which the liability is recorded in the same fund that the proceeds and account receipts are placed.

NONSTOCK CORPORATION. A nonprofit company in which members do not own stock shares. A charitable corporation, for example, would be considered a nonstock corporation.

NONSTOCK MONEY CORPORATION. A financial institution or insurance company that does not issue stock. A credit union, for example, would be considered a nonstock money corporation.

NONTAXABLE DIVIDEND. Money paid out to stockholders as returns or as capital. The dividend is not taxable when it is distributed, but the security's cost basis must be reduced by the dividend amount.

NONTAXABLE SECURITY. A security that is exempt from some taxes. Some municipal securities, for example, are at least partially exempt from income taxes.

NONVOTING STOCK. A company's issued stock that contains no voting rights.

NO PAR VALUE. A security that has no face value.

NO PAR VALUE STOCK. A company's issued stock that holds no par value, but that has a value assigned in the company's ledgers.

NO PASSBOOK SAVINGS. A savings account in which no passbook is used. Instead, the teller issues receipts for deposits or withdrawals. A monthly transaction statement is mailed to the depositor for his or her records. Also called a Statement Savings Account.

NO REVIEW OFFERING. An accelerated public securities offering that can be used by large issuers who already have outstanding publicly held securities. After registering with the Securities and Exchange Commission, the issuer can make the offering in two to three days.

NORMAL BETA. The desired portfolio risk.

NORMAL EXERCISE OFFERING. An option that can be exercised any time before its expiration date.

NORMAL INVESTMENT PRACTICE. A practice in which hot issues can be ethically allocated to a decision maker's personal institutional account. For example, if a bank officer has made 15 purchases at $2,000 each from an underwriter in the past two years, the underwriter could ethically allocate $2,000 in a hot issue to the officer's account.

NORMAL RETURN. A specific investment's standard return.

NORMAL SALE. A usual real estate transaction in which all parties are satisfied and in which no unusual problems occur.

NORMAL TRADING UNIT. The minimum number of security shares that can be bought or sold. When fewer are involved in a transaction they are considered odd lots.

NORTH AMERICAN SECURITIES ADMINISTRATOR ASSOCIATION. An association of securities administrators from the U.S., Mexico, and Canada organized to provide cooperation, and to coordinate national and international securities regulations.

NOT A DELIVERY. When a document or instrument is invalid because it does not meet the necessary requirements to complete the transaction.

NOTARIAL ACKNOWLEDGMENT. A notary public's acknowledgment that a legal instrument was properly executed in his or her presence.

NOTARIAL CERTIFICATE. The document a notary public issues and signs to acknowledge that a legal instrument was properly executed in his or her presence.

NOTARIZED DRAFT. A withdrawal order that a notary public signs and confirms that the person who signed the draft personally signed it in the notary's presence, and that the person was, indeed, the indicated person.

NOTE. A legal document that is evidence of a debt and that requires payment within a specific time period.

NOTE ISSUANCE FACILITY. An underwriting organization that deals in transactions involving offshore Eurodollar notes and Eurodollar certificates of deposit.

NOT HELD ORDER. A market order or limit order that gives the floor broker the right to use his or her own discretion in the price and time of filling the order.

NOTICE ACCOUNT. A savings account in which the owner promises to tell the financial institution in advance before making a withdrawal. Such accounts earn higher interest rates than most other savings accounts.

NOTICE DAY. The day of or after a notice of intent is issued to a futures contract holder.

NOTING A BILL. After a notary public presents a bill of exchange and protests nonpayment, he or she adds this notation to the bill. Among other information, the notation includes the reason for nonpayment.

NOT RATED. Indicates that a recognized rating service has not rated a particular security.

NOT SUBJECT TO CALL. A bond or note that cannot be redeemed before maturity.

NOVATION. An investor substitutes one debt for another debt by paying the dollar difference between the two.

NPV. *See* Net Present Value.

NQS. *See* National Quotation Bureau.

NSE. *See* National Stock Exchange.

NUCLEAR WAR. When at least two companies compete with each other to take over a third company. The action is so named because it is usually destructive to all involved.

NUMERAIRE. A French standard of measuring values that is similar to international monetary system exchange rates.

NUMISMATIC. A coin that carries a premium over its metal content because of its rarity.

NYFE. *See* New York Futures Exchange.

NYSE. *See* New York Stock Exchange.

O

O. In newspaper stock listings, this indicates that the security is traded over the counter.

OBLIGATION. Any legal debt.

OBLIGATION BOND. A mortgage bond with a face value that is higher than the underlying property's value.

OBLIGATORY MATURITY. A compulsory maturity on a debt obligation that is not optional or does not carry the rights of early redemption.

OCC. *See* Options Clearing Corporation.

OCD. *See* Other Checkable Deposits.

ODD LOT. A quantity of stock that amounts to less than 100 shares. A deal involving 100 shares or more is considered a round-lot transaction.

ODD-LOT BUY/SELL RATIO. To determine odd-lot investors' attitudes toward the market, divide the odd-lot selling into the odd-lot buying.

ODD-LOT DEALER. An exchange member who buys odd lots from and sells odd lots to other exchange members.

ODD-LOT DIFFERENTIAL. A fee a broker charges to a customer for executing an odd-lot transaction.

ODD-LOT HOUSE. A brokerage firm that deals in odd-lot transactions, which are deals for fewer than 100 shares.

ODD-LOT INDEX. This composite average indicator, which measures odd-lot purchases, is used to determine odd-lot investors' attitudes toward the market.

ODD-LOT ORDERS. Any stock transaction that involves fewer than 100 shares of stock.

ODD-LOT SHORT SALE RATIO. To determine whether the odd-lot market is positive or negative, divide odd-lot sales into odd-lot short sales. If the figure is at least 3 percent, the market is considered to be positive.

ODD-LOT SHORT SALES. This composite average indicator, which measures odd-lot sales, is used to determine odd-lot investors' attitudes toward the market.

ODD-LOT THEORY. A theory which contends that record highs in odd-lot transactions will precede a drop in the general market because small investors are usually wrong.

ODD-LOT TRADER. A broker or dealer who handles transactions that involve fewer than 100 shares of stock.

ODD-LOT TREND. A market indicator that compares the volume of odd-lot buying to the volume of odd-lot selling. Some analysts believe that high odd-lot selling indicates that the market is on the rise, while high odd-lot buying indicates the market will drop.

OFF-BALANCE-SHEET FINANCING. A system of financing that is not clearly defined, described, or displayed on a company's balance sheet.

OFF-BUDGET AGENCY. A government-sponsored and government-guaranteed agency that does not appear in the federal budget, such as the Federal Home Loan Mortgage Association.

OFFER. To present for sale.

OFFERED DOWN. Securities sold at prices that are lower than the last price quote or the last transaction involving the same securities.

OFFERING. A security that is being presented for sale.

OFFERING CIRCULAR. The prospectus to which potential investors are entitled. A company offering a new securities issue for sale must provide this detailed financial statement to anyone interested in buying shares.

OFFERING DATE. The first day a security is publicly offered for sale.

OFFERING LIST. The document a security's seller provides with the quantity and price of the security to be sold.

OFFERING PRICE. The price for which a new securities issue will be sold publicly.

OFFERING SALE. The prices or yields to maturity at which an underwriter offers the different maturities of a serial bond issue.

OFFERING SCALE. The price at which an underwriter will sell each of a bond issue's serial maturities. The price is stated in points, fractions, or as a yield to maturity.

OFFER WANTED. A term used by a dealer who wants another dealer to make an offer on a particular security.

OFF-EXCHANGE. A commodities firm that is registered with the Commodity Futures Trading Commission, but that is not a member of one of the 10 regulated futures exchanges, which oversee members' daily activities.

OFF-FLOOR ORDER. An order made off of the New York Stock Exchange floor, usually taking precedence over orders made on the floor.

OFFICE OF MANAGEMENT AND BUDGET (OMB). A federal agency that prepares and submits to Congress the U.S. president's budget, helps prepare Congressional appropriations, and reviews the performance of other government agencies.

OFFICE OF SUPERVISORY JURISDICTION. A department or office that oversees National Association of Securities Dealers members to make sure that the members follow NASD procedures. Every NASD member must have at least one office of supervisory jurisdiction at its firm.

OFFICER. A person who has some limited legal and management rights and responsibilities to act on behalf of a company. Officers normally include the president, vice president, secretary and treasurer.

OFFICIAL EXCHANGE RATE. The monetary authority of one country applies this ratio to determine how much its currency is worth compared to the currency of another country.

OFFICIAL NOTICE OF SALE. Made by a municipal securities issuer who is soliciting competitive bids for an upcoming issue. The notice details such information as the security's par value and condition, and the name of the municipal official who can provide further information on the issue.

OFFICIAL STATEMENT. The prospectus for a new municipal bond offering.

OFFSET. To liquidate or close a futures position.

OFFSETS TO LONG-TERM DEBT. Reserve fund assets that are held for redeeming the long-term debt, and credit-fund assets that are pledged to redeem the debt incurred while financing the funds' loan activities.

OFFSHORE. Describes a financial institution, organization, or fund outside of the United States that is not restricted by U.S. securities laws unless its securities are sold in the United States.

OFFSHORE FUND. A mutual fund that has its headquarters in a foreign country.

OFFSHORE TRUST. A personal, foreign trust, usually in a country that does not significantly tax the trusts.

OFF THE BOARD. A securities transaction that is not completed on a particular exchange. An odd-lot transaction, for example, would be considered an off-the-board deal.

OFF THE CURVE. Describes a corporate debt security when the Treasury yield curve is used as a benchmark in the corporate debt security's pricing.

OFF-THE-RUN ISSUE. An equity security that is inactively traded and that attracts little interest.

OLIGOPOLY. A system in which a small number of companies control the total market supply of a specific good or service. The companies, therefore, can control the market price. In a perfect oligopoly, all companies produce the exact same item. In an imperfect oligopoly, the companies produce items that are similar, but not identical. In an oligopoly, price competition is essentially nonexistent, so prices tend to be higher than they would have been in a competitive market. The tobacco industry, for example, is an oligopoly, as are the airlines that serve the same routes.

OLIGOPSONY. A system in which a small number of large and powerful buyers control the purchasing power for a specific good or service. The companies, therefore, can control the purchase price, so oligopsony prices usually are lower than would be expected in a competitive market. Because tobacco companies, for example, buy all of the small tobacco growers' output, the companies can control the prices they pay the growers for that tobacco.

OMB. *See* Office of Management and Budget.

OMITTED DIVIDEND. A dividend a company was supposed to declare, but didn't. For example, if a company is having financial troubles, its board of directors may decide that saving money is more important than paying the stockholders. Omitted dividends usually cause the company's stock to drop in price.

OMNIBUS RECONCILIATION ACT. A federal law that restricts mortgage subsidy bonds.

ON. The number of points that represent how much higher a cash commodity is than a particular futures month.

ON ACCOUNT. An open account in which a seller expects payment after the security or commodity is delivered, with a note documenting the debt obligation.

ON A SCALE. Occurs when a customer buys or sells equal amounts of a specific stock at prices that are spaced by a constant interval as the market price goes up or down.

ON BALANCE. The difference between the quantity of securities involved in offsetting sales and purchases. For example, if a person sold 3,000 shares of a security, then bought 4,000 shares of the same security, he or she bought 1,000 shares on balance.

ON BALANCE VOLUME. The net of volumes of transactions executed at price increases and transactions executed at price decreases. When the former is higher, the net is considered positive.

ON BID. Occurs when a broker completes an odd-lot transaction by selling at the bid price or buying at the offer price instead of waiting for the next round-lot purchase in the security to determine the price.

ONE CANCELS THE OTHER. An alternative order in which a client wants one of two orders executed. When one order is executed, the other automatically is canceled.

ONE-MAN PICTURE. A price quote from only one market maker.

ONE PERCENT BROKER. A broker who charges a fee to arrange the borrowing and lending of securities between dealers and institutional investors. The fee is 1 percent of the interest rate the lender pays to use the cash collateral.

ONE-SIDE MARKET. Describes a broker who will buy or sell securities, but will not do both.

ON-FLOOR ORDER. An order that originates on an exchange floor.

ONGOING BUYER. A buyer who wants to accumulate a lot of shares of a specific security makes continuous purchases in that security. When done with limit or scale orders, the buyer usually will achieve a better average price than he or she would have by buying a large block at one time.

ONGOING SELLER. A seller who wants to distribute a lot of shares of a specific security makes continuous sales in that security. When done with limit or scale orders, the seller usually will achieve a better average price than he or she would have by selling a large block at one time.

ON LEND. In England, the lending of borrowed funds to another person or company.

ON MARGIN. Securities an investor buys when he or she has borrowed at least part of the purchase price from his or her broker.

ON THE MONEY. When the strike price in a put or call option equals the price of the underlying security.

OPD. A stock symbol used to indicate a security's opening transaction when that transaction is at a price that went up or down substantially from the previous closing price. OPD also can indicate the first transaction of the day following a delayed opening.

OPEC. *See* Organization of Petroleum Exporting Countries.

OPEN CONTRACT. A contract that was bought or sold even though the transaction involved in the contract was not completed by a subsequent sale, repurchase, or commodity delivery.

OPEN CREDIT. Credit that is given to a customer even though the customer hasn't yet proven that he or she is creditworthy.

OPEN-END CLAUSE. A mortgage clause in which the property is pledged against future additional cash advances or loans, with the lender agreeing to pay such advances.

OPEN-END INVESTMENT COMPANY. An investment firm that continually issues new securities to the public. The proceeds are then put into other investments. The company must buy back the shares on demand.

OPEN-END INVESTMENT TRUST. An investment trust in which the trustee can invest in securities that were not originally in the trust.

OPEN-END MORTGAGE. A bond collateralized by property and carrying the stipulation that further bonds can be issued with the same property used as collateral again.

OPEN-END MUTUAL FUND. A mutual fund that continually issues new shares to the public. The proceeds are then put into other investments. The company must buy back the shares on demand.

OPENING AUTOMATED REPORT SERVICE. A computer network that market specialists from the New York and American stock exchanges use to open and reopen the market for a specific security.

OPENING BLOCK. A security's first transaction during a particular trading session.

OPENING PRICE. The price of a security at its first transaction during a particular trading session.

OPENING PURCHASE. The transaction that creates or increases an investor's long position in an option trade.

OPENING RANGE. The difference between the highest and the lowest opening prices of a particular commodity; often, a commodity will have several opening and closing prices during one trading session. Orders can be filled within this range at any time during that trading session.

OPENING ROTATION. The trading rotation in which the price and volume of buy and sell orders are in balance.

OPENING SALE. The transaction that creates an investor's short position in an option trade.

OPENING TRANSACTION. Indicates the first time a particular futures or option contract has been bought or sold.

OPEN INTEREST. The total number of option and futures contracts that have not been closed, liquidated, or delivered.

OPEN MARKET. A public market that is open and available to all prospective buyers and sellers.

OPEN MARKET CREDIT. The short-term financing through which a commercial paper house can buy notes and then resell them publicly.

OPEN MARKET OPERATION. The market through which the Federal Reserve System publicly buys and sells government securities to expand or contract the credit supply.

OPEN MARKET PAPER. A note or a bill of exchange that is sold to financial institutions, which a person with good credit can draw upon and make payable to himself or herself.

OPEN MARKET RATES. When supply and demand directly affects the interest rates of debt instruments that trade on the open market. Rates established through a Federal Reserve System discount or through a bank's commercial loan rates, for example, would not represent open market rates.

OPEN MORTGAGE. A mortgage that can be paid off at any time before maturity.

OPEN ORDER. Any unexecuted order to buy or sell securities that has not been canceled; a good-till-canceled order.

OPEN OUTCRY. Occurs on a commodities exchange when traders shout their buy and sell orders. When one trader shouts a buy order and another trader responds to that buy order, or unknowingly shouts a sell order for the same commodity, the contact is recorded.

OPEN PROSPECTUS. A document used to seek financial backing without saying exactly how the money will be invested.

OPEN TRADE. A deal that has not been closed or canceled.

OPERATING ASSET. Any asset involved in a company's operations that directly and regularly creates income for a company. Stocks and real estate, while creating some income, are not considered operating assets because they do not produce income regularly, and they are not directly related to the company's production or operations.

OPERATING BUDGET. Any budget that covers all expenses except capital expenses.

OPERATING CAPITAL. Money a company uses to pay for its daily operations.

OPERATING COSTS. The amount of money a company needs to pay for equipment, utilities, and other necessities in maintaining its operations.

OPERATING INCOME. The total amount of money a company makes through its earning assets and services.

OPERATING INTEREST. In property development and operations, this is the royalty interest subtracted from the mineral interest.

OPERATING LOSSES. Any loss a company incurs during its normal operations.

OPERATING MARGIN. To determine this expense margin, divide a company's net sales into its operating costs.

OPERATING PROFIT. Any profit a company makes through its normal operations.

OPERATING RATIO. To determine this margin of profit gauge, divide a company's cost of goods sold into its operating income.

OPERATING RESERVES. A company's balance sheet accounts that represent the net accumulated balances for amortization, damages, injuries, pensions, and insurance.

OPERATING STATEMENT. A financial statement that includes the company's net costs, expenses, profits, and sales during a specific time period.

OPERATING SURPLUS. A company's profits after it subtracts its operating costs.

OPERATIONS. A broker-dealer's functions in clearing, executing, settling, and recording his or her customer's transactions.

OPINION SHOPPING. A company hires an auditor who will provide a positive auditing report, even if the audit results would not normally be positive.

OPPORTUNITY COST. The maximum profit an alternative plan of action would provide.

OPTIMUM CAPACITY. The level of a company's production that leads to the lowest price per unit. For example, if a company produces 10,000 staplers at $4 each, but can manufacture the staplers at $3 each if it mass produces 15,000, then the latter figure is its optimum capacity.

OPTION. A contract that provides the right, but not the obligation, to buy or sell a specific amount of a specific security within a predetermined time period. One call option contract gives the buyer the right to purchase, or a put buyer to sell, 100 shares of the underlying stock in exchange for a premium based on the time value. The one selling the contracts is called the writer.

OPTION ACCOUNT. A charge account through which a customer can pay either a percentage of the balance, with an additional service charge, or the entire balance amount after 30 days. Also, an account which has been approved to trade options.

OPTION ACCOUNT AGREEMENT FORM. A document that all options contract customers must sign to verify that they will abide by the Options Clearing Corporation regulations. The form also contains a customer's financial position and his or her investment background.

OPTIONAL DATE. The date a corporation or a government can redeem its note or other obligation if certain designated requirements are met.

OPTIONAL DIVIDEND. A dividend that the recipient can take in cash or have reinvested at his or her discretion.

OPTIONAL PAYMENT BOND. A bond in which the holder can choose to have either principal and interest payments or both made in foreign or domestic currencies.

OPTION CONTRACT. The document that gives the buyer the right to buy or sell a specific quantity of a security by a specific date at a specific price.

OPTIONS CLEARING CORPORATION (OCC). A company that processes options transactions.

OPTIONS CLEARING CORPORATION PROSPECTUS. The Securities and Exchange Commission requires that all options customers must be given this disclosure statement before the options contracts can be approved for trading.

OPTION DAY. The date an options contract expires.

OPTION MUTUAL FUND. A mutual fund that buys or sells options to increase its shares' value. Because of the leverage options create, such investments can multiply the fund's earnings several times over if the options are exercised properly and invested wisely.

OPTION ORDER. A detailed and specific order to establish or cancel an options contract, with all of the pertinent information outlined.

OPTION PREMIUM. The dollar price per share that an option holder pays the option writer for the option privileges.

OPTIONS CONTRACT. The agreement between the writer and the holder of a put or call option.

OPTION SERIES. A listed option class with a specific price and a specific expiration date.

OPTIONS MARKET. The market in which financial futures contracts are bought and sold.

OPTION SPREAD. Occurs when an investor simultaneously holds a long and short position in the same option class.

OPTIONS PRICE REPORTING AUTHORITY. A subscription service that reports option prices and transactions.

OPTIONS PRINCIPAL MEMBER. An investor who bought the right to buy and sell listed options. The investor can buy such rights from an exchange or from an exchange member, but can buy and sell the options only on that particular exchange.

OPTIONS TO PURCHASE OR SELL SPECIFIED MORTGAGE SECURITIES. A customized group of put and call options on mortgage-backed securities that are combined according to coupon, exercise price, expiration date, and issue. Created by Merrill Lynch Mortgage Capital Corporation, these securities normally are referred to as Opposms.

OPTION TENDER BOND. A variable-rate, tax-exempt bond with a put option in its indenture and with an interest rate that is adjusted twice a year. If the bondholder does not like the new interest rate, he or she can tender the bond at the end of the year for its full principal amount plus any accrued interest.

OPTION TRADING RIGHT HOLDER. A person who is licensed by the New York Stock Exchange to trade NYSE-listed index options, but who is not a member of the exchange.

OPTION WRITER. An option seller who gives the buyer the right to buy a security if it is a call option, or sell a security if it is a put option.

OR BETTER. An investor's limit order to buy or sell at the price indicated or at a better price, if possible.

ORDER. A customer's instructions to his or her broker for buying or selling a security. Such an order may specify price, time limits, or quantity.

ORDER BOOK OFFICIAL. A Pacific or Philadelphia stock exchange official who takes options orders that cannot be immediately executed, then trades them later and notifies the person who submitted the order after a transaction is finally made.

ORDER CONFIRMATION TRANSACTION. Permits members of the National

Association of Securities Dealers to negotiate over-the-counter option transactions for more than three contracts while using the National Association of Securities Dealers Automated Quotations Options Automated Execution System, which normally limits the number of permitted contracts to three.

ORDER DEPARTMENT. The broker-dealer's office that routes buy and sell instructions to the trading floors of different exchanges and executes over-the-counter transactions.

ORDER GOOD UNTIL A SPECIFIED TIME. A market order or a limit order that a broker will hold in the trading crowd or will execute until a specific time, after which any unexecuted portion will be canceled.

ORDER SUPPORT SYSTEM. A Chicago Board Options Exchange system for disseminating information about people's orders.

ORDER TICKET. A document that provides a customer's directions to the registered representative concerning each specific securities transaction.

ORDINARY ASSET. An asset a company regularly buys and sells as part of its business. For example, real estate would represent an ordinary asset to a real estate broker.

ORDINARY DISCOUNT. The difference between an item's current value, with an assumed interest rate that will accumulate to the value at maturity, and the item's value at maturity.

ORDINARY GAIN. The amount of money a company will make by selling an asset that is not a capital asset.

ORDINARY INCOME. Any and all income except that earned from capital gains.

ORDINARY INTEREST. Simple interest based on a 360-day year. The difference when figuring ordinary interest and exact interest, which is based on a 365-day year, can be substantial when a large sum of money is involved.

ORDINARY SHARES. British common stock.

ORDINARY STOCK. Common stock or equity stock.

ORDINARY VOTING. Occurs in board of directors elections when each stockholder gets one vote for each share he or she owns.

ORGANIZATION CHART. A chart of the relationship between authority and responsibility within a company. An organization chart, for example, maps out who has the most responsibility, and to whom each employee is answerable.

ORGANIZATION OF ARAB PETROLEUM EXPORTING COUNTRIES. An association of Arabian oil exporters that sets international oil prices and settles disputes among Arab nations. OPEC includes the members of the Organization of Petroleum Exporting Countries plus Bahrain, Egypt, and Syria, and excluding Ecuador, Gabon, Indonesia, Iran, Nigeria, and Venezuela.

ORGANIZATION OF PETROLEUM EXPORTING COUNTRIES (OPEC). An association of 13 Middle East, South American, Eastern, and African oil exporting countries that sets international oil prices.

ORGANIZED EXCHANGE. The place where securities or commodities are bought and sold according to a prescribed set of rules and regulations.

ORGANIZED MARKET. An organization of traders that operates under a specific set of rules and regulations and, using those guidelines, trades in commodities or securities.

ORIGINAL COST. All costs that were incurred when buying an asset.

ORIGINAL ISSUE. The first stock a company issues when it is first trying to raise capital for establishing business.

ORIGINAL ISSUE DISCOUNT. A bond with its par value discounted at the time it is issued. The difference between the purchase price and the adjusted price is considered income in addition to any interest that may be paid. If held to maturity, no capital gains tax will be paid since the gain is considered interest.

ORIGINAL MARGIN. The amount of money a brokerage customer is supposed to have when beginning a transaction.

ORIGINAL MATURITY. The time between a bond's issue date and the maturity date it carries at the time it is issued.

ORIGINATION FEE. A tax-deductible service charge assessed against the person or company that originates the mortgage loan processing.

ORIGINATOR. A financial institution that is the first to mortgage a pool of loans, with the descriptive term used only after the pool is resold.

OTHER CHECKABLE DEPOSITS. A component used to calculate the M1 category of the money supply. OCDs include automatic transfers, credit union accounts, and negotiable orders of withdrawal.

OTHER INCOME. Appears on a profit and loss statement to indicate income received from sources that would not normally be income sources. Other income can indicate a one-time profit, or income received infrequently.

OTHER LOANS FOR PURCHASING OR CARRYING SECURITIES. The loan one broker will make to another broker for buying or for carrying securities.

OTHER LONG-TERM DEBT. A long-term debt that is neither a mortgage bond nor a debenture. Serial notes, for example, would be classified as "other long-term debts."

OUTBID. To offer a securities seller a higher price than any other bidder.

OUT OF THE MONEY. Occurs when the strike price of a call option is higher than the price of the underlying investment, or when the strike price of a put option is lower than the price of the underlying security.

OUTRIGHT TRANSACTION. A forward exchange or a purchase sale that does not have a corresponding transaction spot.

OUTSIDE BROKER. A trader who deals in unlisted stocks and who is not a stock exchange member.

OUTSIDE DIRECTOR. A member of a corporation's board of directors who is not a company employee. Such directors can bring fresh and unbiased opinions to the board.

OUTSIDE FINANCING. When a company issues securities to finance expansion instead of using its own retained earnings.

OUTSIDER. Any investor who is a member of the general public, as opposed to a corporate officer who owns stock in his or her company.

OUTSIDE SECURITY. A security that is not listed on one of the major exchanges in the issuing company's region.

OUTSTANDING. Any instrument that has not been redeemed, paid, or canceled, or any stock issued to shareholders.

OUTSTANDING OPTION. An options contract issued by the Options Clearing Corporation that remains open—it has not expired, been exercised, or canceled.

OUTSTANDING STOCK. All of a company's ownership shares of stock that have been publicly purchased or that are owned by the company's officers.

Shares that the company has repurchased are not considered outstanding stock.

OUT THE WINDOW. Describes a new securities issue when it is marketed aggressively, quickly, and successfully to investors. Such issues tend to be hot issues after distribution.

OVERALL MARKET PRICE COVERAGE. A figure that provides the extent to which the market value of a security class is covered if the issuing company were liquidated. To obtain the coverage, divide a company's tangible assets by the sum of the security issue's market value and the book value of the company's liabilities, along with any security issues that have a prior claim.

OVERALLOTTING. Offering a security for sale publicly when more shares are confirmed than are available because the issuer mistakenly believed that some investors would not confirm their orders.

OVERBANKED. An underwriting in which the initial allotment to syndicate members is greater than the total number of shares to be offered.

OVERBOUGHT. Occurs when speculative buying pushes a security's bid price unreasonably high.

OVERCAPITALIZED. Occurs when a company's capital stock has a higher value than its corporate assets.

OVERHANG. A large block of securities or commodities contracts that would push prices down if released into the market.

OVERHEAD. A company's expenses that are not directly related to production, such as rent and utilities.

OVERHEATING. An economy that is growing and expanding so quickly that inflation may result. In such an economy, demand far exceeds supply, which pushes prices up.

OVERINVESTMENT THEORY. A theory that proposes that business managers will invest too much in the economy when they see increasing demands during an upswing, and then make major investment cuts during the ensuing downswing when they realize that they expanded too much.

OVERISSUE. Occurs when a company issues more stock shares than it was authorized to issue. The company's registrar must work to cancel the orders for enough shares to bring the number back to the allowable limit.

OVERLAPPING DEBT. Municipal securities with either two or more issuers or with two or more municipalities responsible for the issue.

OVERNIGHT POSITION. A broker-dealer's description of his or her securities inventory at the end of a trading day. The securities in inventory represent the broker-dealer's overnight long position in those securities.

OVERSOLD. Occurs when, during heavy selling, a security's price is higher than the established downside trend. Because the price is extended, an upward movement probably will occur.

OVERSOLD MARKET. This occurs when speculative long interest drops sharply, and the speculative short interest subsequently increases. Usually, the market increases again quickly following an oversold market.

OVERSPECULATION. Occurs when speculators cause the market activity to be unusually heavy.

OVERSTAY THE MARKET. Describes a person who has held on to a long position for too long and subsequently will suffer a financial loss.

OVERSUBSCRIBED. Occurs when investors want to buy more shares of a new security than will be available. When this happens, the price of the security immediately goes up.

OVER THE COUNTER. The market for securities that are not listed on one of the major exchanges. The National Association for Securities Dealers Automated Quotations provides prices for over-the-counter securities.

OVER-THE-COUNTER INDEX OPTION. An index of the 100 most highly capitalized, unlisted securities, which will provide profit for investors who correctly gauge short-term, over-the-counter price movements. It also provides investors with a hedge against other over-the-counter securities in their portfolio.

OVER-THE-COUNTER MARGIN STOCK. A stock that is sold only in the over-the-counter market, with the issuer meeting certain requirements so broker-dealers can extend credit on the short purchase or short sale.

OVER-THE-COUNTER OPTION. An option with negotiated premium, striking price, and expiration date.

OVER-THE-COUNTER STOCK INDEX FUTURE. An over-the-counter contract in which a customer agrees to a delivery date that is based on a stock price index's quoted value.

OVERTRADING. A dealer, who also is an underwriter, offers to pay more for a security than it is worth if the customer agrees to buy a portion of a new issue.

OVERVALUED. Describes a security with a current market price that is too high (considering the company's earnings, history, and price-earnings ratio). A security that is overvalued probably will drop in price.

OVERWRITING. Describes a call option with an underlying security that is overpriced and is therefore expected to drop in value. Because of the expected drop, the call writer does not expect the option to be exercised.

OWNER FINANCING. A home loan made by the property seller instead of by a financial institution. At times, the seller offers lower interest rates, or will finance a home when the buyer cannot qualify for a loan from a financial institution.

OWNER OF RECORD. The person whose name appears on a company's books as the owner of a specific quantity of the company's securities, and who is eligible for any benefits from those shares.

P

P. Appears in newspaper stock listings to designate a put option.

PACIFIC STOCK EXCHANGE. A California stock exchange with two centers (one in Los Angeles and the other in San Francisco) that are electronically connected.

PACKET. A British block of securities.

PAC MAN DEFENSE. To avoid a hostile takeover or merger, the target company tries to buy control of the raider.

PAID-IN CAPITAL. The amount above par value that a company received for selling its stock.

PAID-IN SURPLUS. A company's balance sheet entry of the difference between the dollar value actually received from issued shares and the shares' par value.

PAID-UP CAPITAL. The total of the par value of a company's stock and the given value of its no-par securities for which the company receives full consideration.

PAID-UP STOCK. Capital stock that the buyer has paid for in cash, goods, or services in an amount that equals or is greater than the stock's par value.

PAINTING THE TAPE. A form of manipulation in which a broker illegally enters matched orders to create the false impression of an active market and heavy trading in a particular security.

PAIRED SHARES. The common stock of two companies with the same management, with shares of the two companies sold as a unit.

PANIC. Occurs when the public suddenly loses confidence in the economy, resulting in massive bank withdrawals, stock sales, etc. A panic can lead to a depression.

PAPER. Short-term notes such as corporate commercial paper.

PAPER CAPITAL. A federally insured, low-interest, long-term note.

PAPER CLAIM. A promise-backed investment.

PAPER INVESTMENT. A paper claim, or a promise-backed investment.

PAPERLESS. Proof that a person owns a security electronically, even though the owner does not physically hold a certificate.

PAPER LOSS. The loss an investor would incur if he or she sold a security or closed his or her position, but that is unrealized because he or she holds on to the security.

PAPER MONEY. Bank notes or deposits that serve as money.

PAPER PROFIT. The profit an investor would make if he or she sold a security or closed his or her position, but that is unrealized because he or she holds on to the security.

PAPER TITLE. Although not a proper title, a paper title is written verification that proves ownership of a security.

PAPILSKY RULES. A National Association of Securities Dealers regulations modification concerning the allocation of new securities issues to related people, selling concessions made in exchange for research services, and securities that an underwriter takes in a trade. The modifications were made after an investor named Papilsky sued an investment adviser.

PAR. Any security whose market value is equivalent to its face value at the time of redemption. A bond with a face value of $1000 is at par when it is selling for $1000.

PARAMOUNT TITLE. A title that supersedes all other titles, such as an original title.

PAR BOND. A bond with a current market value that is equal to its redemption value.

PAR CAP. The seller of a Government National Mortgage Association security cannot deliver a substitute Ginnie Mae with an interest rate that requires the contract's dollar price to be adjusted above the security's par value.

PARENT CORPORATION. One company that owns another company, or that owns part of another company.

PARENT GUARANTEED. Describes debt securities issued by a subsidiary, but with principal and interest guaranteed by the subsidiary's parent corporation.

PARETO'S LAW. Hypothesized by Italian-Swiss economist Vilfredo Pareto, this proposes that the pattern of income distribution remains the same, despite the nation's policies on taxation and public assistance. According to the theory, 80 percent of a country's income benefits only 20 percent of the population, and 20 percent of the customers account for 80 percent of any business' sales volume. Pareto postulated that the only way to improve the economic lot of the poor people is to increase the country's overall output and income levels.

PAR EXCHANGE RATE. The amount one country's money is worth in another country's money.

PARIS BOURSE. France's national stock exchange.

PAR ITEM. Any instrument that can be redeemed for its par or face value on demand.

PARITY. Price or value equality. For example, if a bond is convertible into 100 shares of common stock, with the stock's market price at $5 per share, the bond, to be selling at parity, would have a value of $500.

PARITY CLAUSE. A mortgage clause in which no note obtained through the mortgage has priority over any other note obtained through it.

PARITY PRICE. The price for one commodity that is pegged to either another price or a composite average of prices.

PARKING. An investor will put money into a safe investment to protect it while looking into other investments.

PARTIAL COVERED WRITING. An options position with both covered and uncovered calls written on the same underlying security.

PARTIAL DELIVERY. A delivery against a contract sale with the delivery amount less than the contract's total amount.

PARTIAL EXECUTION. Occurs when only part of a round-lot order is executed with the investor's permission.

PARTIALLY AMORTIZED MORTGAGE. A mortgage paid in part by amortization and in part at maturity.

PARTIALLY PAID BONDS. The initial public offering of a dollar-denominated bond sold to a foreign investor when that investor pays 20 to 30 percent of the purchase price immediately and the balance at a specified future date.

PARTIAL WRITE. An investment strategy in which the investor writes a call option against some of the stock that he or she owns so that if the price stays low, he or she will keep the premium and increase his or her cash flow; if the price goes up he or she can buy back the option and, while the premium is lost, hold on to the stock that now is worth more.

PARTICIPANT. A member of an underwriting syndicate.

PARTICIPATE BUT DO NOT INITIATE. An investor's trading instructions in which his or her large order cannot initiate market activity, but can be filled in normal market trading. Large institutional investors often will use these instructions to avoid having the order negatively affect market prices.

PARTICIPATING BOND. An industrial bond that provides the owner with both debt and equity participation.

PARTICIPATING BROKER-DEALERS. Broker-dealers who are not members of the underwriting syndicate, but who do assist the syndicate in selling the new issue.

PARTICIPATING CERTIFICATE. A document that verifies partial ownership in a stock.

PARTICIPATING EXCHANGE. A national securities exchange that the Securities and Exchange Commission has approved to trade options issued by the Options Clearing Corporation.

PARTICIPATING GROUP ANNUITY CONTRACT. An insurance contract in which income is distributed to 10 or more participants and in which the company and participants share, in varying degrees, the mortality risk and the investment experience.

PARTICIPATING INCENTIVE PREFERRED STOCK. The convertible, participating, and nontransferable voting stock that a potential takeover target will issue to its business constituents to stop the raider from buying 100 percent of the equity. Issuing the securities thus protects the constituents' financial interests.

PARTICIPATING MORTGAGE. A mortgage that offers an interest in future income from the mortgaged property or some other form of participation.

PARTICIPATING PREFERRED STOCK. A preferred stock that pays additional dividends after all common stock dividends have been paid.

PARTICIPATING TRUST. A unit investment trust with shares that reflect interest in an underlying mutual fund investment.

PARTICIPATION CERTIFICATE. A security that reflects an undivided interest in a mortgage pool.

PARTICIPATION DIVIDENDS. Profits that a member of a cooperative receives, with the amount proportionate to the amount of business he or she has provided the cooperative.

PARTICIPATION LOAN. Two or more lenders make a loan, with one of the lenders administering the loan. Participation loans make it possible for a large borrower to obtain the needed capital, even if the loan amount exceeds each lender's legal lending limit. For example, a bank cannot lend an amount that exceeds 10 percent of its capital.

PARTLY PAID. Stocks held in an investor's margin account.

PARTNERSHIP. A company that is owned by at least two people, with each owner sharing in direction, responsibility, management, and debt liability.

PARTNERSHIP CERTIFICATE. A written document filed with a bank that verifies members of a partnership, including limited and silent partners, and that indicates how much of the business each partner owns.

PARTY AT INTEREST. Any person who has money invested in, or has some other financial interest in, a company.

PARTY IN INTEREST. A person who provides investment advice, buys or sells securities, or makes credit transactions for an employee benefit plan such as a retirement program.

PAR VALUE. The stated amount of a bond. If the bond sold above the stated amount, it would be selling at a premium; if it sold below that amount, it would be selling at a discount. The par value for a stock share would be the stock certificate's face value.

PAR VALUE OF CURRENCY. The currency values, or exchange rates, are determined through supply and demand according to the buying and selling of other countries that use the same currency. The par value of currency determines the ratio of one country's currency unit to the currency unit of another country.

PASSBOOK SAVINGS. A customer savings account with a bank, savings and loan, or other federally insured financial institution that allows the customer to withdraw money easily. A record of the transactions is kept in a small booklet, which the customer presents to the bank teller when making a deposit or withdrawal. The government allows the financial institutions to charge whatever interest rate they want.

PASSED DIVIDEND. Occurs when a company does not pay a regularly scheduled dividend because it wants to keep the earnings within the company as a result of financial problems, or because it needs the money to expand operations.

PASSIVE BOND. A debt security that pays no interest, such as those issued by a charitable corporation.

PASSIVE MANAGEMENT. An investment strategy that seeks an average performance, adjusted for risk.

PASS-THROUGH SECURITY. A debt instrument that reflects an interest in a mortgage pool, with monthly payments divided between the interest on the unpaid principal balance and the repayment of principal.

PATENT. A government-issued license that gives the holder a monopoly on the use of a new design, invention, or process.

PAY. A bond's currency denomination.

PAYABLE IN EXCHANGE. A negotiable instrument must be paid with its issuer's funds.

PAYABLES. All of a company's accounts or redeemable notes.

PAYBACK PERIOD. The length of time it takes to realize a profit from an investment.

PAYDOWN. Part, but not all, of the principal is repaid.

PAYING AGENT. The financial institution or company treasurer who is named in a bond indenture as the person or organization responsible for repaying principal and periodically paying the interest on behalf of the bond's issuer.

PAYMENT DATE. The day that dividends or stock is scheduled to be paid to stockholders.

PAYOUT. The amount of a company's holdings that are distributed as dividends to stockholders.

PAYOUT RATIO. The percentage of a company's earnings that holders of common stock receive in cash dividends.

PAYROLL-BASED STOCK OWNERSHIP PLAN. A fund that allows a company that contributed 0.5 percent of its payroll to take that same amount in a tax credit.

PAYROLL DEDUCTION PLAN. A plan that allows an employee to accumulate mutual fund shares or shares in some other investment by having his or her employer withhold regular payments directly from his or her paycheck.

PAY-THROUGH BONDS. A debt instrument with the issuer guaranteeing the bond through a mortgage pool it owns. The bond's monthly interest and principal payments have features similar to that of a pass-through security.

PAY TO ORDER. A stipulation in a negotiable instrument that names the person to whom the instrument is payable.

PAY UP. An investor pays an above-the-market price for a security that he or she believes is a wise investment.

P/E. *See* Price/Earnings Ratio.

PEAK. The highest point a security or a market indicator reaches during a specific time period. Prices will begin to drop after reaching a peak.

PEGGED PRICE. The fixed price of a commodity.

PEGGING. A security's offer price is maintained by a bid that is slightly below that price.

PEGGING THE MARKET. An illegal form of manipulation in which an underwriting syndicate sets up a fund to stabilize the stock's price by fixing a bid at the offering price during the offering's initial stages.

PENALTY CLAUSE. A contractual stipulation that imposes financial penalties if the contract terms are not obeyed or if a loan payment is late.

PENALTY PLAN. A critical name for a mutual fund, so named because of the penalties incurred if the investor does not complete the involved contract.

PENALTY SYNDICATE BID. A syndicate manager's stabilizing bid which carries the provision that selling concessions will be withheld from, and a penalty will be assessed against, any syndicate members whose customers offer to sell the securities back to the syndicate.

PENETRATION PRICING. A company issues shares at a low initial price in an effort to quickly gain a large portion of the market.

PENNANT. A security's chart pattern that forms a triangle, or pennant. Usually, this indicates that the security's price either will rise or fall as the apex is reached.

PENNY STOCK. A low-priced share of stock that is usually traded for less than $1 a share. These stocks are normally issued by speculative companies with a short or erratic revenue and earnings history.

PENSION. A French money market borrowing against securities that the lender holds in pension until repaid.

PENSION BENEFIT GUARANTY CORPORATION. A federal corporation that guarantees pension benefits in plans that clearly define benefits for more than 25 employees. The corporation administers terminated plans and places liens on the company's assets for any pension benefits that were promised but not delivered.

PENSION PLAN. A company- or government-sponsored plan that provides regular income to retired or disabled employees. In most cases, the recipients of pension funds have to pay taxes on the money only as they receive it.

PENSION RESERVE. An accounting of the amount of money a company must pay in the future to its pension or retirement account.

PENSION TRUST. A pension fund that a company establishes to provide retired and disabled employees with an income, even if the employees have not made any contributions to the fund.

PENTAPHILIA THEORY. A theory that the stock market will go up in calendar years that are divisible by five, such as 1990, 1995, and 2000.

PER CAPITA DEBT. A general obligation bond's total bonded debt divided by the issuing municipality's population.

PER CAPITA TAX. A tax determined by dividing the amount of money needed by the number of people who will pay the tax. As such, each person pays the same amount, despite the person's income or use of the resulting services.

PERCENTAGE LEASE. A lease stipulating that a company will pay rent in an amount equal to a percentage of its gross sales or profits.

PERCENTAGE ORDER. A customer's order to his or her broker to buy or sell a specific number of shares after a particular number of the same shares have been traded in one trading day.

PERCENT RETURN ON INVESTMENT. The amount of money a company receives compared to the amount of money invested in the company.

PERFECT COMPETITION. Occurs in the market when buyers and sellers have no power to influence a good's or a service's market price because everyone has an equal knowledge of the market and discrimination is nonexistent. Perfect competition is a goal, but not a truly realistic one.

PERFECT LIEN. A legal, documented security interest in an asset, with the creditor's claim protected.

PERFECT TITLE. A complete, legal, and total title.

PERFORMANCE APPOINTMENT MARKET MAKER. An exchange member who has to maintain two-sided markets in specific classes of options traded on the Chicago Board Options Exchange. In return for providing market depth and for supplementing the activities of competitive market makers, the CBOE provides performance appointment market makers with a number of economic advantages.

PERFORMANCE BOND. A surety debt security that protects the buyer in case the seller does not fulfill the contract terms. For example, if a person added a garage onto his or her house, he or she could request a performance bond from the contractor so that if the construction work was not satisfactory, he or she would be reimbursed or financially compensated.

PERFORMANCE FEE. An incentive fee that a customer pays his or her mutual fund manager when the manager's investment strategies help the fund outperform the general market averages during a specific time period.

PERFORMANCE FUND. A mutual fund with investments concentrated in speculative common stock for short-term profits.

PERFORMANCE INDEX. An index of an investment's performance, including dividends and other distributions.

PERFORMANCE STOCK. A growth stock, which is a security that is expected to increase in price either in a short time or over a long period.

PERFORMANCE UNIT PLANS. An incentive plan that provides executives with cash bonuses or stock shares when the company reaches its profit goals.

PERIODICALLY ADJUSTABLE RATE TRUST SECURITIES. A pass-through mortgage trust made up of municipal loans, so interest is exempt from federal taxes.

PERIODICITY. The market condition as it is affected by different cycle shifts.

PERIODIC PAYMENT PLAN. A mutual fund in which the investor makes payments at regular intervals in exchange for fund benefits.

PERIODIC PURCHASE DEFERRED CONTRACT. A fixed or variable annuity contract in which the investor makes regular, fixed payments, and payouts are deferred until the investor determines which payout method he or she wants.

PERIOD OF DIGESTION. The time period after a new security issue is released in which the security's market price is established and during which the price could go through considerable volatility.

PERIOD OF REDEMPTION. The time during which a mortgagor can call in the title and property by paying off the debt.

PERMANENT ASSET. A fixed asset.

PERMANENT CAPITAL. Any stock or retained earnings that do not have to be repaid.

PERMANENT FINANCING. Any long-term debt or equity financing.

PERMANENT INCOME. The average amount of income expected over a specific time period.

PERMANENT MORTGAGE REAL ESTATE INVESTMENT TRUST. A trust that makes long-term loans for developing commercial and residential construction projects.

PERMANENT PORTFOLIO. A group of investments with the character of those investments remaining unchanged from year to year.

PERPENDICULAR SPREAD. An investment strategy that includes using options with the same expiration dates, but with different strike prices. This spread can be bullish or bearish.

PERPETUAL BOND. A bond with either no maturity date or a maturity date that is so far in the future that the bond will pay interest indefinitely.

PERPETUAL INVENTORY. A company's accounting system in which the on-hand inventory continuously is reflected in the book inventory through a daily record of physical inventory and the dollar amounts, each of which is periodically reconciled.

PERPETUAL WARRANT. A warrant to buy a specific amount of a company's common shares at a particular price, with the warrant carrying no expiration date.

PERPETUITY. An annuity or bond with payments lasting indefinitely.

PER SHARE NET. The number of outstanding shares divided into the company's earnings after it has paid taxes.

PERSONAL FINANCE COMPANY. A company that loans people small amounts of money at high interest rates to fill personal needs.

PERSONAL FINANCIAL STATEMENT. An individual's account of obligations and income sources.

PERSONAL HOLDING COMPANY. A company with no more than five people owning more than 50 percent of the stock which receives at least 60 percent of its income through investments instead of through business activities.

PERSONAL PROPERTY. A person's rights and ownership in chattels, which is all property other than real estate.

PERSONAL SAVINGS. The difference between a person's disposable personal income and his or her expenses.

PERSONAL SECURITY. An unsecured loan backed by the borrower's net worth and business stature instead of by collateral.

PERSONAL SERVICE INCOME. A company's or an individual's earned income.

PERSONAL SURETY. Surety that is provided by an individual instead of an insurance company.

PERSONALTY. Describes an individual's personal property.

PESO. The primary monetary unit of Spain and other colonized Spanish countries such as Argentina, Mexico, and the Philippines.

PETITION IN BANKRUPTCY. A document used to voluntarily declare bankruptcy.

PETROBOND. A Mexican financial instrument backed by a specific number of Mexican barrels of oil.

PETRODOLLARS. The large dollar balances that oil-producing countries, earned through oil sales, have deposited in financial institutions worldwide.

PETTY CASH. Money set aside, in cash or a bank deposit, to be used as change for small transactions.

PHANTOM STOCK PLAN. A corporate incentive plan in which corporate officers will receive bonuses if the company's common stock increases in value.

PHILADELPHIA EXCHANGE. An exchange that has a futures contract on its own over-the-counter index. The Philadelphia Exchange is affiliated with the Philadelphia Stock Exchange.

PHILADELPHIA PLAN. A method of transferring equipment ownership through equipment trust certificates, with a trustee holding the equipment title until the entire debt is paid.

PHILADELPHIA STOCK EXCHANGE. A Pennsylvania stock exchange that serves as an alternate exchange for many others, including the exchanges in New York, by actively trading the other exchange's listed securities.

PHILADELPHIA STOCK EXCHANGE AUTOMATED COMMUNICATION AND EXECUTION SYSTEM. A computer system that connects Philadelphia Stock Exchange specialists with the Computer Assisted Execution System and the Intermarket Trading System so the specialists can check prices and execute orders.

PHONY DIVIDENDS. An illegal act in which a company pays dividends from the money it receives from people buying shares instead of from stock earnings.

PHYSICAL ACCESS MEMBER. A person who pays an annual fee for the right to use the New York Stock Exchange trading floor for buying and selling securities. A physical access member cannot vote on any exchange matters and is not entitled to any compensation if the exchange liquidates.

PHYSICAL COMMODITY. The actual, tangible commodity, such as corn or soybeans, that a seller delivers to the buyer of a commodities contract.

PHYSICAL VERIFICATION. Occurs when an auditor physically inspects a company's inventory to verify its existence and value.

PICKUP. Bonds with similar coupon rates and maturities are swapped at a basis price that is beneficial to the swapper.

PICKUP BOND. A bond with a high coupon and a short callable date. If interest rates drop, the issuer probably will call the bonds, therefore, the investor will get higher-than-expected returns because of the premium the issuer will pay.

PICTURE. The prices at which a dealer will trade.

PIECE-OF-THE-ACTION FINANCING. A loan agreement in which the lender receives interest plus a percentage of an income property's gross profits or the borrowing company's net profits.

PIGGYBACK EXCEPTION. A Securities and Exchange Commission rule that a company can substitute frequent and regular stock quotes in an actively traded market for other factual information the company must submit. The SEC allows the substitution because the market will not trade if the company hesitates at all in providing both positive and negative information.

PIGGYBACK REGISTRATION. Occurs when an issuer making a primary distribution allows those who privately bought stock earlier to include their shares in the offering. Such primary-secondary distributions are so described in the issue's prospectus.

PINCH. A quick rise in prices.

PINK SHEETS. A quotation service that provides bid and ask prices and the market maker's name for over-the-counter stocks that are not listed by the National Association of Securities Dealers Automated Quotations. The quotes, printed on pink paper, are distributed to brokerage firms daily, but do not include stocks listed in newspapers.

PIP. A foreign exchange figure equaling 0.00001 of a unit.

PIPELINE. All of the underwriting procedures that precede the public offering.

PIT. The trading area in a futures exchange.

PIT BOSS. A Chicago Board Options Exchange member who assists floor officials in several areas of concern, such as settling disputes over rule violations and overseeing quotation accuracy.

PITI. The abbreviation for principal, interest, taxes, and insurance.

PIVOTAL STOCK. A stock that does or can influence the market activity of other stocks.

PLACEMENT. Securities distribution, either public or private.

PLACEMENT MEMORANDUM. A document that a syndicate manager prepares in the Eurocredit market to provide pertinent information to other potential syndicate managers that will help them decide whether to join in the credit.

PLACEMENT RATIO. The percentage of new municipal issues involving at least $1 million that has been syndicated and sold in the last week.

PLACING POWER. The success of a broker in selling securities.

PLAINTIFF. The person or company that initiates a court action against the defendant.

PLAIN VANILLA. A traditional, routine security offering with no special features.

PLAN COMPANY. A company registered with the Securities and Exchange Commission that sells contractual funds on behalf of the fund's underwriter. The company is certified as a participating unit investment trust.

PLAN COMPLETION INSURANCE. A group term life insurance policy for investors in a mutual fund contract plan. If the investor dies before the contract is completed, the difference between his or her contributions and the total plan amount is paid to the custodian financial institution, which completes the plan with the insurance money and holds the shares for the investor's estate.

PLAN HOLDER. A person who owns shares in a pension plan.

PLANT. All of a company's fixed assets, including real estate and equipment.

PLATEAU. A horizontal price movement after a period of increasing prices. Plateaus often indicate uncertainty, and usually are followed by a price drop.

PLATO. A computer teaching and testing system, designed by the Control Data Corporation, for investment industry examinations, such as those involved in blue sky qualifying.

PLAY. A speculative investment.

PLEDGE. To transfer property to a lender as security for a loan or other obligation.

PLEDGED-ACCOUNT MORTGAGE. A mortgage in which part of the borrower's down payment pays for a pledged savings account, which helps pay the first year's monthly mortgage payments.

PLEDGED ASSETS. Bank-owned securities used as collateral for government deposits.

PLEDGED LOAN. A mortgage that is used to secure a loan.

PLEDGED SECURITIES. Securities used as collateral for a long- or short-term debt.

PLOWBACK. Instead of distributing dividends to stockholders, a company holds on to its earnings so the money can be reinvested in the business.

PLUM. Additional or unexpected profits or dividends.

PLUNGE. A quick, sudden drop in the market or a security's price.

PLUNGER. A person who invests in speculative securities.

PLUNK DOWN. To pay for in cash.

PLUS. Follows a security's price quote to indicate a point fraction in 64ths.

PLUS TICK. A transaction completed at a higher price than the previous transaction.

PLUS-TICK RULE. A Securities and Exchange Commission regulation that round-lot short sales of listed securities must be at a price that reflects an increase over the last different transaction price, unless the last price already reflects an increase.

PO. A principal only bond. *See* Stripped Bond.

POINT. Used to quote securities prices. One point for a stock equals $1; for a bond, one point equals $10 assuming a $1,000 par value.

POINT AND FIGURE CHART. A measure of price changes and the direction of the changes without any consideration for volume or time.

POISON PEN. A corporate warrant transferring a stockholder's right to consider tender offers for his or her shares to the board of directors.

POISON PILL. A method used by a board of directors to discourage a takeover bid by making the company less attractive to the potential raider. A poison pill normally indicates the company has distributed convertible preferred stock shares as dividends to the existing stockholders, with the stock convertible to a number at least equal to the number of outstanding shares. The stockholders have no desire to convert the stock because of the dividend adjustments, unless the company is to be taken over. The raider's takeover, in turn, would increase the price of the stock many times over again, so the price the raider would have to pay for the company also would increase many times over.

POLICY HOLDER. A person covered by insurance.

POLICY LOAN. A low-interest insurance company loan with the policy's surrender value used as collateral.

POLICY VALUE. The amount of money an insurance policy is worth at maturity.

POLYOPSONY. Occurs when the market has so few buyers that their actions materially affect stock prices, but the number is great enough that the buyers cannot significantly judge the effect of their actions on the other buyers.

POLYPOLY. Occurs when the market has so few sellers that their actions materially affect stock prices, but the number is great enough that the sellers cannot significantly judge the effect of their actions on the other sellers.

PONZI SCHEME. Named after Charles Ponzi, who cost investors millions of dollars in the 1920s. This is a scheme in which people are promised high returns on an investment, with the money taken from new investors used to pay off earlier investors. Such a scheme theoretically could go on indefinitely, except that the amount owed to investors continues to balloon.

POOL. A group of debt instruments, with another security representing an undivided interest.

POOLED INCOME FUND. A fund to which contributors transfer property and retain income interest, then transfer the rest to a charity.

POOL FINANCING. When a municipal financing sponsor floats an issue with several municipalities underwriting the expenses and, in turn, receives lower interest rates.

POOLING OF INTEREST. When one company merges with another company, all assets and liabilities also are merged, and the difference between the acquired company's purchase price and its net tangible value is entered on the balance sheet as goodwill.

POOLING OPERATION. A company that solicits and accepts money from other funds for the purpose of trading commodity futures contract deliveries.

POPULARIZING. An exchange specialist's advertisements, marketing activities, or sales literature that promotes his or her activities.

PORK BELLY. A speculative commodity involving frozen pork.

PORTFOLIO. Either a combination of assets, or all of a person's investments.

PORTFOLIO BETA SCORE. A portfolio's volatility, determined by the beta coefficients of its securities, with a beta 1 reflecting the same volatility as the general market. A higher beta would reflect securities that are more volatile, and a beta of less than 1 would be less volatile than the general market.

PORTFOLIO MANAGER. Any broker, dealer, or other person who makes daily investment decisions on behalf of another person.

PORTFOLIO OPTIMIZATION. After considering all of the securities available, an investor selects those securities that will minimize risk and maximize returns.

PORTFOLIO THEORY. An investment strategy in which an investor controls the amount of risks and returns by determining the relationship among all of the securities in a portfolio instead of their individual characteristics.

POSITION. The nature of investment account holdings. For example, an investor who owns securities has a long position in those securities, and an investor who sells short, which is selling securities he or she doesn't own in anticipation of buying them back at a lower price, holds a short position.

POSITION BID. A broker's bid when that broker wants to buy a large block of securities for his or her own account to accommodate an institutional client.

POSITION BUILDING. The establishment of net long or net short positions for a portfolio, which cuts down on the number of securities the account executive must follow while increasing the risks.

POSITION LIMITS. An options exchange regulation that prohibits investors from holding 2,000 or more put or call contracts against the same underlying security on the same side of the market.

POSITION OFFER. A broker's offer when that broker wants to sell a large block of securities for his or her own account to accommodate an institutional client.

POSITION TRADER. A commodities broker who tries to achieve long-term profits by taking only calculated risks and by dealing in contracts that have durations of six months or longer.

POSITIVE CARRY. Occurs when money is borrowed to buy interest-bearing securities and the income received from the securities exceeds the loan's interest rate. For example, if an investor borrows money at 11 percent interest to buy a security that will produce 12.5 percent interest, the investor will have a positive carry.

POSITIVE YIELD CURVE. A graph that displays the relationship between the maturities and yields of securities with the same issuer or with similar credit ratings. When the graph has a positive yield curve, the longer-term securities have higher yields than the shorter-term securities.

POST. The area of an exchange floor where specific securities are traded and where the exchange specialist accepts bids and offers and provides price quotes.

POSTAL SERVICE. A federal agency that issues debt securities to pay for capital improvements, using its own assets as collateral.

POSTDATED. Any instrument or document that carries a date that is later than the date it was signed.

POST EXECUTION REPORTING. A computer network for routing market, limit and odd-lot orders, and executing those orders, for members of the American Stock Exchange.

POST 30. A special New York Stock Exchange trading post for transactions involving inactive stocks and round lots of fewer than 100 shares.

POT. Shares of a newly issued security that are held to fill institutional orders.

POTENTIAL STOCK. The difference between the amount of capital stock a company has authorized to be issued and the total number of stock that actually has been issued. For example, if a company has authorized the issuing of 30,000 shares of stock and 20,000 actually have been issued, the potential stock would total 10,000.

POT IS CLEAN. An underwriting syndicate manager's announcement to account members that all shares reserved for institutional sales have, indeed, been sold.

POT LIABILITY. An underwriter's financial liability for those securities in the pot that remain unsold after the manager removes price restrictions.

POT PROTECTION. An issuer's promise to an institution that the institution definitely will receive a specific number of securities from a pot.

POUND. The primary monetary unit of Great Britain.

POWER OF ATTORNEY. One person's authorization for another person to sign the first person's name on a legal document, or for that other person to vote on behalf of the first person.

PRAECIPIUM. A borrower must pay a Euromarket credit manager a fee, of which the manager will deduct and keep a portion, and the rest of which is divided among the other management group members. The praecipium is the portion that the manager keeps.

PRECAUTIONARY LIQUIDITY BALANCE. The cash, securities, or other assets that an investor holds onto and uses only in case of an emergency.

PRECEDENCE. A broker's right to buy a security before other brokers, even though the other brokers could complete the transaction. A broker is given precedence based on the time of his bid and the size of that bid.

PRECEDENCE OF ORDER. One security's priority over another security when buy or sell orders are received.

PRECOMPUTE. When the interest on an installment loan is determined by deducting the amount of annual interest from the loan's face value as the loan's proceeds are disbursed, or by adding the amount of annual interest to the total amount that will be repaid in equal installments.

PRE-EMPTIVE RIGHT. A shareholder's privilege to maintain his or her proportionate share of company ownership when the company offers additional stock shares for sale publicly. The company usually will let the existing stockholders have the first crack at the new shares before offering the stock to the general public.

PREFERENCE. The broker who receives priority after reaching an impasse with another broker who has offered the same amount for the same number of shares. Because neither broker holds precedence, the broker who entered the crowd first receives preference.

PREFERENCE AS TO ASSETS. After a company liquidates and before declared dividends are distributed, the holders of preferred stock can make a claim for payments before the holders of common stock are entitled to their claims.

PREFERENCE INCOME. Income a person does not list in his or her adjusted taxable income. If the amount exceeds a specific limit, the person must compute an alternative minimum tax.

PREFERENCE STOCK. Preferred stock that has priority over ensuing preferred and common stock issues when dividends are paid, and when proceeds are distributed following liquidation.

PREFERRED DIVIDEND COVERAGE. The ratio of the annual preferred stock dividends to the company's aftertax income.

PREFERRED DIVIDENDS PAYABLE. A record of how much in dividends a company owes to preferred stockholders.

PREFERRED PREFERRED. A preferred stock that has priority over other preferred stock of the same company in dividends and claims.

PREFERRED STOCK. Stock shares that represent a portion of ownership in a company, with the shares normally carrying fixed dividends and voting rights.

PREFERRED STOCK FUND. A mutual fund with investments concentrated in preferred stocks to preserve capital and achieve higher income.

PREFERRED STOCK RATIO. A company's total capitalization divided into the par value of its outstanding preferred stock.

PREGNANCY NOTES. A debt instrument that postpones payments for 10 months.

PRELIMINARY AGREEMENT. A contract between a company and the underwriter of the company's securities that serves as a temporary commitment until the final registration statement is issued. The registration statement replaces the preliminary agreement after the underwriter and company agree on the offering's potential for success, and the securities' terms and conditions.

PRELIMINARY OFFICIAL STATEMENT. A detailed, preliminary report, similar to a prospectus, that covers a new municipal securities offering.

PRELIMINARY PROSPECTUS. An early, detailed registration report that covers a new securities issue. The preliminary prospectus does not offer the security for sale and does not list the security's expected price.

PRELIMINARY TITLE REPORT. A title company's statement after conducting a title search and before it issues an insurance commitment binder.

PREMIUM. The amount for which a security is selling above its par value.

PREMIUM BOND. A bond that is selling at a price that is higher than its face value. The amount the price exceeds the bond's face value is the premium.

PREMIUM FOR RISK. An investment's yield after subtracting its basic, prevailing yield at the time.

PREMIUM INCOME. An investor's income from selling either a put or a call option.

PREMIUM ON BOND. The percentage over a bond's face value for which it can be bought, sold, or redeemed.

PREMIUM ON CAPITAL STOCK. The amount over a stock's cash value for which it can be bought or sold.

PREMIUM ON FUNDED DEBT. The amount over a funded debt security's cash value for which it can be issued or assumed.

PREMIUM ON SECURITIES. The amount over a security's value for which it can be bought or sold.

PREMIUM OVER BOND VALUE. The difference between a convertible bond's market value and the general market price of a regular bond from the same issuer.

PREMIUM OVER CONVERSION VALUE. The difference between the market price of a convertible stock or bond and the price at which it can be converted.

PREMIUM RAID. Occurs in Great Britain when an investor quickly buys a sizeable percentage of a company's securities at a price higher than the current market price. The purchases are made so quickly that few of the company's stockholders can take advantage of the chance to sell their stock at the premium price.

PREMIUM RECAPTURE. The length of time needed for a convertible security's yield advantage to recoup its conversion value premium.

PREMIUM STOCK. A stock that generates profits at a greater rate than that displayed by the general market.

PREPAID CHARGE PLAN. A contractual mutual fund with a sales charge that is paid in the fund's early years.

PREPAID EXPENSES. A balance sheet entry that includes items that normally must be paid in advance.

PREPAYMENT. When a brokerage firm pays a selling client for a security before the transaction's predetermined settlement date.

PREPAYMENT PENALTY. A bank charge that a borrower must pay for a loan without a prepayment clause when the borrower repays the loan before it reaches maturity.

PREPAYMENT PRIVILEGE. A mortgage clause that gives the mortgagor the right to pay off the debt before it matures.

PREREFUNDING. When a bond issuer uses a second bond issue to pay for the future refunding of an outstanding bond which is not yet callable.

PREROGATIVES. A person's rights or privileges that no one else possesses.

PRESALE ESTIMATES. The price range within which an auction house believes an item will sell.

PRESALE ORDER. A buy order that a municipal syndicate manager has accepted for part of the issue, even though all of the offering's details have not been released.

PRESCRIBED RIGHT TO INCOME AND MAXIMUM EQUITY (PRIME). One of two component parts of a unit trust, sponsored by the Americus Shareowner Service Corporation, which separates the income portion of a stock from its potential appreciation. The prime is the income producing portion and the score (special claim on residual equity) is the potential appreciation. This unit trust, which trades on the NYSE, allows investors who want to enhance their income or appreciation a conservative, leveraged approach.

PRESENT VALUE. The discounted value of an amount that will be payable at a specific future date.

PRESENT VALUE OF EXPECTED CASH FLOW. The amount of money a company expects to make from holding an asset with the interest rate discount subtracted.

PRESERVATION OF CAPITAL. An investment with the goal of securing the value of the principle by avoiding speculative situations.

PRESIDENT. A company's second-highest officer, falling in rank just below the company's board chairperson. The president is elected to the position by the company's board of directors and usually reports directly to the board.

PRESIDENTIAL ELECTION CYCLE THEORY. A theory that stocks will drop in price immediately after a new president is elected, after which the president will raise taxes or take other unpopular steps to correct the economic problem. After two years, the stocks will go up because the president, as an incumbent, is looking for a strong economy at election time. After the election, the cycle starts over again.

PRESOLD ISSUE. An issue of government or municipal securities that has been sold even before the coupon rate or price has been announced.

PRESUMPTIVE UNDERWRITER. An investor who buys 10 percent of a company's stock in a public offering and resells the stock for a profit within two years.

PRETAX EARNINGS. A company's net income before federal taxes have been subtracted.

PRETAX RATE OF RETURN. A security's yield before taxes have been subtracted.

PRICE ALERT. Occurs when a security's price pushes above or below a previous resistance level and exceeds its previous high or low point during a specific time period. A strength or weakness in the market can be measured by totaling all the stocks that have upside or downside breakouts.

PRICE AVERAGING. Buying several equal amounts of a security at different prices to achieve a better overall price per share. For example, if an investor bought 100 shares of a stock at $10 a share, then bought 100 shares at $16 a share, and then bought 100 shares at $20 a share, the overall price per share would be $15.33, while the stock's price continued to climb.

PRICE CHANGE. The net rise or drop in a security's market price.

PRICE/DIVIDEND RATIO. A company divides its stock's annual dividend per share into the current market value per share.

PRICED OUT OF THE MARKET. Occurs when an item is priced so high that no one will buy it, which ultimately leads to a drop in sales.

PRICE/EARNINGS RATIO (P/E). The relationship between the price of a stock and its earnings per share. This figure is determined by dividing the stock's market price by the company's earnings per share figure. The higher the P/E, the more earnings growth investors are expecting. A growth stock will have a higher price/earnings ratio than a stock that is expected to grow at a slower rate. Stocks with a higher P/E, usually over 20, are considered riskier than stocks with lower growth and proven earnings with a lower P/E.

PRICE GAP. Occurs when a security's price range in one day does not overlap its price range from the day before.

PRICE INDEX. A gauge that measures price changes for different goods and services compared to an earlier period.

PRICE INFLATION. Occurs when general price levels increase.

PRICE-LEVEL-ADJUSTED ADJUSTING MORTGAGE. A mortgage plan with the outstanding loan balance indexed and with the interest rate net of any inflation premium. Because the payments are based on the interest rate, the outstanding balance at the end of the year is adjusted for inflation. The initial payments are lower than most other types of mortgages.

PRICE LIMIT. The highest amount a futures contract is allowed to fluctuate from the previous record's settlement price.

PRICE LOCO. An item's purchase price.

PRICE POTENTIAL. A technical, analytical estimate of a security's future market value.

PRICE RANGE. The prices that fall between a security's highest and lowest prices during a specific time period.

PRICE SPREAD. The difference between a security's bid and ask prices.

PRICE SUPPORT. A government-set minimum price for farm products designed to protect farmers against low prices for their goods. If prices drop below the minimum level, the government pays the difference.

PRICE TAKER. An investor whose securities transactions are so small that they have no impact on the market.

PRICE TALK. Underwriters' preliminary discussion of a negotiated issue's offering price or a competitive issue's bid price.

PRICE-VOLUME ALERT. A price breakout combined with a volume breakout. A breakout occurs when a security's price pushes above or below a previous resistance level.

PRICE-WEIGHTED INDEX. An index in which component stocks are weighted by their individual prices, with lower-priced stocks having a smaller impact than those with higher prices.

PRICEY. An underpriced bid or an overpriced offer.

PRIMARY DEALER. A group of dealers and banks that can buy and sell government securities while working directly with the Federal Reserve Bank of New York.

PRIMARY DISTRIBUTION. The first time a new securities issue is offered publicly for sale. The primary distribution usually involves an investment banker selling the issue as an over-the-counter security.

PRIMARY EARNINGS. A company's net income after taxes and preferred dividends, divided by the number of common shares the company has outstanding.

PRIMARY MARKET. The market in which investment bankers first sell newly issued securities to investors.

PRIMARY OFFERING. The first time a company publicly sells its stock.

PRIMARY POINTS. The main agricultural commodities exchanges.

PRIMARY TREND. A market trend or price movement that lasts for a long period of time, sometimes as long as several years.

PRIME. *See* Prescribed Right to Income and Maximum Equity.

PRIME INVESTMENT. A high-quality, low-risk investment expected to bring in high profits.

PRIME PAPER. Commercial paper that Moody's Investors Services has given a rating of P, with the rating broken into three categories: P-3 is high quality, P-2 is higher quality, and P-1 is the highest quality.

PRIME RATE. The interest rate on loans that commercial banks quote as an indication of the rate being charged on loans to its best commercial customers. Interest rates on other loans often are based on the prime rate which is frequently more, but can be less, is based on past and potential future trends.

PRINCIPAL. The client for whom a broker makes an investment. Also the basic amount of money invested, or the balance of an obligation.

PRINCIPAL AMOUNT. A debt security's par value, or a loan's face amount.

PRINCIPAL BALANCE. Any debt's, or obligation's, outstanding and unpaid balance less interest.

PRINCIPALS. A company's stockholders.

PRINCIPAL STOCKHOLDER. Any shareholder who owns 10 percent or more of a company's voting stock.

PRINCIPAL SUM. The same as "principal," or the total amount of a financial obligation, such as a loan, less interest.

PRINT. The exchange-tape record of securities transactions.

PRIOR DEDUCTIONS METHOD. An improper interest or dividend calculation in which senior obligations are subtracted from the earnings first, then the junior issues are subtracted from the balance.

PRIORITY. The first broker to make the highest bid or the lowest offer. Because the broker has priority, he or she always receives at least partial execution of the order.

PRIOR LIEN. A mortgage that has priority over other mortgages.

PRIOR LIEN BOND. A debt instrument that has priority over the issuing company's other issues.

PRIOR PREFERRED STOCK. Preference stock, which is a security that has priority over ensuing preferred and common stock issues when dividends are paid, and when proceeds are distributed following liquidation.

PRIOR REDEMPTION. A debt paid before maturity.

PRIOR REDEMPTION PRIVILEGE. Occurs when the holder of called bonds is allowed to redeem the bonds before maturity or before the bonds' call dates.

PRIOR SALE. When demand for an item exceeds supply and an investor offers it for sale at a specific price that is based on that short supply, the investor will sell the item to the first bidder. Potential bidders will be told beforehand that the supply is limited and the first bidder will receive the item, so subsequent bidders will be out of luck because of the prior sale.

PRIOR STOCK. Preferred stock.

PRIVATE DISTRIBUTION. A company distributing its securities to a small, select group of investors.

PRIVATE EXPORT FUNDING CORPORATION. A private company that loans money to foreign importers of American goods and services, with the Export-Import Bank guaranteeing the loan's principal and interest, which also is guaranteed by the United States government's full faith and credit.

PRIVATE LIMITED PARTNERSHIP. With memberships sold through an investment advisor, this type of partnership has no more than 35 limited partners and is not registered with the Securities and Exchange Commission. It is designed to create tax benefits, income, or capital gains for its members. Such partnerships often will invest in research, real estate, or oil and gas drilling.

PRIVATELY HELD. Either a company owned by a few people, or the shares of a company that have never been offered publicly for sale.

PRIVATELY OWNED CORPORATION. A company owned by only a few people, with those people chiefly responsible for the company's operations and holding the majority of stock.

PRIVATE OFFERING. A company offering a new stock issue to a small, select group of no more than 25 investors.

PRIVATE PLACEMENT. A large block of securities offered for sale to an institutional investor or a financial institution through private negotiations.

PRIVATE SECTOR. The section of the economy that is controlled by corporations and individuals, as opposed to the public sector, which is controlled by the government.

PRIVATE SECTOR PASS-THROUGH. A bank-issued, nongovernment, mortgage-backed security that sometimes is privately guaranteed.

PRIVATE TRUST. As opposed to a charitable trust fund, this is a trust fund with limited, designated beneficiaries, such as family members.

PRIVATE WIRE FIRM. A large brokerage house that uses telegraphs to communicate between branches.

PRIVILEGE DEALER. A trader who sells options contracts.

PRIVILEGE ISSUE. A convertible or participating security, or a stock that carries a purchase warrant.

PROCEEDS. The profit a seller receives for selling assets. The amount of the proceeds is calculated by subtracting all fees and commissions from the total sale price.

PROCEEDS SALE. Securities sold in the secondary market, with proceeds from the sale used to buy securities in the secondary market.

PROCESS EFFECTS. An increase in consumer spending and private investments that follows a public works project.

PROCESSING. A lender's preparation and consideration of a mortgage application.

PRODUCE EXCHANGE. An agricultural commodities exchange for trading futures contracts.

PRODUCER. A broker who brings in a large amount of profits and commissions for his or her firm.

PRODUCERS' PRICE INDEX. Used to gauge inflation trends, this is a market index that measures price changes for goods sold to their final users.

PRODUCTION RATE. The coupon rate for issuing Government National Mortgage Association pass-through securities, with the interest rate set at 0.5 percent below the prevailing Federal Housing Administration mortgage rate.

PROFESSIONAL. A person who buys and sells securities for a living.

PROFESSIONAL CORPORATION. A company that provides professional services such as medical care, legal services, or psychiatric counseling.

PROFIT. The amount an investment earns or the amount a company earns through its business activities.

PROFITABILITY. The ability of a company to generate profits.

PROFITABILITY INDEX. A company's predicted future cash flow divided by its initial investment.

PROFITABILITY RATIO. The degree and ratio through which a company can determine its profitability.

PROFIT AND LOSS ACCOUNT. An account transferred from the accounts receivable to a different account and subtracted from the accounts receivable balance because it is considered uncollectable.

PROFIT AND LOSS RESERVE. An amount of money a company sets aside to take care of uncollectable accounts.

PROFIT AND LOSS STATEMENT. A company's accounting statement that shows net profits, losses, income sources, and expenses.

PROFIT AND LOSS SUMMARY ACCOUNT. A company's account of all income and expenses, transferred to this summary ledger at the end of the company's fiscal year.

PROFIT CENTER. A company's department, branch or subsidiary that is directly responsible for generating its own profits. For example, a newspaper's advertising and circulation departments would be considered the newspaper's profit centers, while the news department would not be.

PROFIT MARGIN. A company divides its net sales into its net income to measure, through a percentage figure, its profitability.

PROFIT ON FIXED ASSETS. The profit from a fixed asset sold for a price above its book value.

PROFIT ON NET WORTH RATIO. By dividing a company's net worth into its net profit after taxes, the resultant number can determine how well the company is investing its funds.

PROFIT-SHARING PLAN. A fund that a company sets up and through which employees can share in the company's success, often through the distribution of stock shares.

PROFIT-SHARING SECURITIES. Stocks or bonds purchased for employees through a profit-sharing plan.

PROFIT-TAKING. Describes when stock is being sold for capital gains.

PRO FORMA. A financial statement reflecting the company's financial condition using hypothetical data to determine the effects of an idea that has been proposed, but not yet consummated.

PROGRAM BUYING. The initial stock purchase as determined by a large spread, or premium, between the stock's price and the futures' contract prices.

PROGRAM EXECUTION PROCESSING. A system in which orders for multiple issues can be issued easily and simultaneously through an institutional investor's portfolio.

PROGRAM SELLING. A stock sale as determined by a small spread, or premium.

PROGRAM TRADING. Institutional buying and selling of huge amounts of stocks based on the spread, or premium between an index future and the market prices of the stocks involved.

PROGRESSIVE PAYMENTS. Money that a contractor or supplier periodically receives while properly and satisfactorily completing his or her work. The regular payments reduce the initial total amount of working capital the contractor or supplier actually needs to complete the job.

PROGRESSIVE TAX. An income tax system in which people who have higher incomes pay a higher rate of income tax than those with lower incomes so that the people who make lesser amounts do not end up paying a disproportionate share. People who have higher incomes, for example, have more tax breaks and shelters available to them than the poorer segment of society, so they end up paying a lower percentage of taxes on a straight percentage tax system.

PROJECTION. The forecast of expected future price movements based on historical performances.

PROJECT LINK. A Nobel Prize-winning economic model that connects all of the world's economies and predicts the effects that changes in one country's economy will have on another country's economy.

PROJECT NOTE. A government-issued, guaranteed, short-term debt security that finances public housing construction.

PROMISSORY NOTE. A written commitment to pay another party a specific amount of money by a specific date. A note, for example, is a promissory note.

PROMOTER. The intermediary between those proposing a business venture and the people with money to invest in business ventures.

PROMPT DATE. The date a metal must be delivered to fill purchase contract terms on the London Metal Exchange.

PROPERTY ASSESSMENT. A determination of a property's value, with taxes based on that assessed value.

PROPERTY CAPITAL. Ownership of debts or securities.

PROPERTY DIVIDENDS. Dividends that a company pays in the stock shares of another company. The company may have received the stock shares through selling property.

PROPORTIONAL REPRESENTATION. An equalizing method of electing a company's board of directors in which each stockholder gets as many votes as he or she has shares of stock, multiplied by the number of board vacancies. Such methods give smaller shareholders the ability to obtain representation on the board.

PROPORTIONAL TAX. A tax based on a percentage rate that remains the same as the tax base increases.

PROPORTIONATE SHARE OF ASSETS. After a company liquidates or dissolves, and after its debts have been satisfied and the holders of preferred stock have been paid, the holders of the company's common stock divide the remaining assets among themselves.

PROPRIETARY ACCOUNT. An account that reflects the company's actual financial condition by providing such numbers as the exact inventory count, the dollar amount of earnings, and the dollar amount of the company's reserves.

PROPRIETOR. A person who has an exclusive interest in a company or other business venture and who is personally responsible for all liabilities.

PROPRIETORSHIP. A company that is owned by only one person, with that person holding all financial liabilities and receiving all profits.

PRO RATA. A method of equally and proportionately allocating money, profits or liabilities by percentage. For example, if a gas company is found to have overcharged consumers and is subsequently forced to pay rebates, each consumer would get an amount proportionate to the amount he or she overpaid in the first place.

PRO RATE CANCELLATION. Occurs when a bond or other contract is canceled and the premium is charged according to the actual length of ownership.

PROSPECT. Any potential business customer or potential investor.

PROSPECTUS. A document the Securities and Exchange Commission requires a company that is newly issuing securities to provide to prospective investors. The prospectus includes such information as the financial background of the company or the company's officers, and the company's investment potential.

PROTECTIVE COMMITTEE. A panel organized to protect and represent stockholders in negotiating defaulted securities.

PROTECTIVE COVENANT. A municipality's agreement to protect the buyers of its municipal issues and promise to service, insure, and cover interest on the issue.

PROVISIONAL ALLOTMENT LETTER. As the British equivalent to an American rights offering, the provisional allotment letter gives a company's current stockholders the right to buy additional shares from the company before the stock is offered publicly.

PROXIMO. Next month.

PROXY. One person grants another person the right to vote on behalf of the first person in corporate matters.

PROXY CONTEST. A person or group of people try to gather a sufficient number of stockholders' proxies to swing a corporate vote.

PROXY DEPARTMENT. The area of a brokerage firm that distributes financial statements, voting information, and other corporate publications to beneficial owners. The department acts as an intermediary between the issuing company and the beneficial owners, and votes on behalf of those owners.

PROXY STATEMENT. A report a company submits to stockholders that explains issues on which they will be asked to vote on at an upcoming meeting.

PRUDENT INVESTMENT-COST STANDARD. A company's value is determined by subtracting the costs incurred through bad investments from the original cost of the company's assets.

PRUDENT MAN RULE. An investment system in which the investor will invest conservatively to receive a stable income with little risk.

PUBLIC CORPORATION. A company that has publicly issued and sold ownership shares of stock.

PUBLIC CREDIT. A government's ability to obtain money, through bonds or notes, by promising to repay.

PUBLIC DEBT. Any government debt.

PUBLIC FINANCING. Any funding received from a government or a government agency.

PUBLIC HOUSING AUTHORITY BOND. A long-term municipal debt security that finances low- and middle-income housing projects.

PUBLIC LIMITED PARTNERSHIP. A partnership with shares sold publicly through a broker and registered with the Securities and Exchange Commission.

PUBLICLY HELD. A company with stock shares owned by a large number of people.

PUBLICLY TRADED INVESTMENT FUND. Any closed-end investment firm.

PUBLIC MARKET. A securities market with relevant information publicly available.

PUBLIC OFFERING. A company offers a large number of its shares to the general public for sale.

PUBLIC OFFERING PRICE. A company's asking price for its securities during the first public sale.

PUBLIC ORDER EXPOSURE SYSTEM. A system through which customers are ensured that their orders are not crossed in-house before they have a chance to hit a better price in the public market.

PUBLIC OWNERSHIP. The publicly owned portion of a company's stock that is actively traded.

PUBLIC SECTOR. The section of the economy that is controlled by the government, as opposed to the private sector which is controlled by corporations and individuals.

PUBLIC SECURITIES ASSOCIATION. An organization of banks, brokers, and dealers who deal in government securities.

PUBLIC UTILITIES. A publicly or privately owned company that sells electricity, natural gas, telephone service, water, or other utilities. Most utilities operate as monopolies in their respective geographical areas.

PUBLIC UTILITY BOND. A high-quality, utility-issued debt instrument backed by building or equipment mortgages.

PUBLIC UTILITY HOLDING COMPANY ACT. A law that requires publicly held trading companies involved in either the electrical or the natural gas business to register with the Securities and Exchange Commission.

PUBLIC UTILITY STOCK. A stable, high-yield, utility-issued equity stock.

PULL. To cancel a securities order, to increase the offering price, or to lower the bid price.

PULL THE PLUG ON THE MARKET. To cancel supporting bids that were entered just below a leading security's prevailing market price.

PUNT. A stock that probably will not bring the holder any profit.

PUP. An inactive, low-priced security.

PURCHASE ACQUISITION. One company pays cash for another company or pays in Treasury stock, with the cost higher than the acquired company's net tangible assets.

PURCHASE FUND. A clause in a preferred stock or bond contract that requires the issuer to buy a specific number of shares or bonds each year at a par value price or below. While the issuer is not actually required to make the purchases, the issuer is required to exert the best possible effort to do so.

PURCHASE GROUP. An underwriting syndicate consisting of an organization of investment bankers that buys new securities issues from the issuer and resells the issues publicly.

PURCHASE-MONEY MORTGAGE. A mortgage that a buyer provides a property seller instead of paying cash for a piece of property. A buyer may provide such a mortgage when he or she is unable to obtain mortgage money, and another buyer cannot be found.

PURCHASE OPTION. A rent-to-buy option that gives the renter the option to buy the property or equipment when the lease expires, with some of the rent or lease money going toward the purchase price.

PURCHASE ORDER. A buyer's written permission to a seller to deliver goods or services at a predetermined price.

PURCHASE OUTRIGHT. To pay the entire purchase price for an item in cash.

PURCHASING POWER. The amount of goods or services that one unit of money or one unit of an asset can buy.

PURCHASING POWER OF THE DOLLAR. The amount of goods or services available for $1.00 during a specific time period compared to the amount of goods and services available for $1.00 during another time period, with an inflation or deflation factor taken into consideration for each period.

PURCHASING POWER PARITY. The exchange rate at which one nation's price level equals another nation's price level.

PURE PLAY. A company involved strictly in only one line of business, such as a restaurant chain, as opposed to a conglomerate which may be involved in a number of different businesses.

PURE PREMIUM. A premium that equals a company's losses divided by exposure and that contains no commissions, taxes, or other fees.

PURPOSE LOAN. Money borrowed to buy, carry, or trade securities which uses other securities as collateral.

PURPOSE STATEMENT. A document a borrower must provide the lender when margin securities are used as collateral for a loan. The document describes the purpose of the loan.

PUT. *See* Put Option.

PUT A LINE THROUGH IT. A British transaction wherein the buyer and seller mutually agree to cancel, so named because years ago transactions were written on a piece of paper, and putting a line through the deal would cancel it out.

PUT AND CALL BROKER. A broker who trades options contracts and who is not permitted on the stock exchange floor.

PUT BOND. A bond stipulation that allows the holder to redeem the bond at face value at a specific, predetermined time so that if interest rates go up, the holder can avoid losing money as long as the stipulation is operative.

PUT INTO PLAY. Rumors are spread and blocks of less than 5 percent of stock are purchased from a company that potentially could be a takeover target, but is not yet such a target. By doing so, the instigator or purchaser can woo others into buying blocks of the company's stock.

PUT OPTION. An agreement that gives the buyer the right to sell a specific quantity of a particular security by a specific date. The option is not obligatory and is traded during its life. The holder hopes the stock will drop in price.

PUT OUT A LINE. Occurs when an investor sells a large quantity of stock short over an extended period of time because he or she believes that prices will fall.

PUT SPREAD. When an investor writes a put option contract and buys a put option on the same underlying security, but with different expiration dates or different exercise prices.

PUT TO. A put option buyer's right to sell a round-lot share of a specific stock at a particular price to the option writer who sold an option on the stock.

PYRAMIDING. An investor increases his or her holdings by using the highest level of available buying power in his or her margin account with both paper and real profits.

Q

Q. Represents a company that will be liquidated or reorganized under federal bankruptcy laws.

Q-RATIO. Economist James Tobin developed this theory to explain how stock prices affect capital spending and the general economy. The ratio is determined by comparing the market value of a company's physical assets to the amount of money it would take to replace those assets. If the ratio is greater than one, the stock market believes that one dollar of the company's assets is actually worth more than one dollar.

Q-TIP TRUST. Represents a Qualified Terminable Interest Property Trust through which one spouse transfers specific asset income to the other spouse until that spouse's death, after which the first spouse designates a third person to receive the assets and asset income.

QUALIFIED ACCEPTANCE. A counter offer.

QUALIFIED EMPLOYEE STOCK OPTIONS. A company program through which its employees can buy stock shares from the company at a specific price within a predetermined time period, after which the offer expires.

QUALIFIED ENDORSEMENT. A signature that limits the endorser's liability. For example, if Sam cashes Joe's check at the bank with a qualified endorsement and Joe's check bounces, Sam's account will not be debited.

QUALIFIED OPINION. An auditor's opinion that is given with restrictions and limitations because of information that was not available during the audit. For example, if the company has a lawsuit pending against it, the results of that suit could dramatically change the auditing opinion.

QUALIFIED RETIREMENT PLAN. A private, tax-sheltered retirement plan approved by the Internal Revenue Service.

QUALIFIED TRUST. A tax-deferred plan through which employees can build up a retirement or termination savings chest.

QUALIFYING ANNUITY. A tax-sheltered annuity that can be included in a profit-sharing or retirement plan approved by the Internal Revenue Service.

QUALIFYING COUPON RATE. A Government National Mortgage Association coupon rate that is below the current production rate and therefore is deliverable against the contract.

QUALIFYING DIVIDEND. A dividend in which $100 can be deducted from the investor's income.

QUALIFYING SHARE. A common stock share that gives the holder the right to be one of the issuing company's directors.

QUALIFYING UTILITY. A utility with stockholders who can defer taxes by reinvesting a maximum of $750 in dividends back into stock shares. The investors have to pay taxes on the deferred amount only after selling the stock.

QUALITATIVE ANALYSIS. A subjective analysis of a security, with the judgment not based on financial information such as that found on a balance sheet or on an account statement. Instead, the judgment may be based on such issues as labor relations.

QUALITY CONTROL. An inspection method of making sure a good or service lives up to high quality standards.

QUALITY OF EARNINGS. A company's additional earnings that come from higher sales instead of from inflation or some other source. During periods of inflation, most companies have low-quality earnings because sales actually drop while the company's asset values increase.

QUALITY RATING. An evaluation, such as the Standard and Poor's and Moody's rating, given to a security, with the grading based on such factors as the issuing company's financial condition, strength, and proven management ability.

QUALITY STOCK. A highly graded stock.

QUANTITATIVE ANALYSIS. An analysis of a security, with the judgment based on financial information such as that found on a balance sheet or on an income statement.

QUARTERLY. A three-month period that acts as a basis for the reporting of earnings or the paying of dividends.

QUARTER STOCK. Any stock with a $25-a-share par value.

QUARTILE. Statistics, such as performance gauges or ratios, that are grouped into four equal parts.

QUASI-CORPORATION. Any organization's political subdivision, such as an unincorporated village.

QUASI-MONEY. A bank note, deposit, or other asset that has the properties and characteristics of money.

QUASI-PUBLIC CORPORATION. A privately owned company such as a non-public utility that provides the public with goods or services in such a way as to hold a high degree of public responsibility; it is therefore government-regulated.

QUASI-RENT. The total returns from an investment in capital goods if they have no alternative use, or the returns over the alternative use if such a use exists.

QUASI-REORGANIZATION. A restructuring or reorganization that is undertaken to eliminate a deficit or to avoid bankruptcy, but that does not result in the formation of a new company.

QUICK ASSET. A current asset that can be readily converted into cash.

QUICK ASSET RATIO. *See* Quick Ratio.

QUICK BUCK. Money made on a short-term investment or from a highly speculative venture.

QUICK RATIO. Also called the acid ratio, this figure gauges a company's short-term liquidity by dividing its current liabilities into its cash, cash equivalents, and account receivables.

QUICK TURN. Occurs when a security is sold immediately after it is purchased, with the investor seeking short-term profits.

QUID PRO QUO. Occurs when one item of value is traded for another item of the same value, even if that item is intangible, such as research information concerning a specific security.

QUIET PERIOD. The 90 days, as required by the Securities and Exchange Commission, between an issuer's first public offering and the first time underwriters distribute research information about the issuing company. The purpose of the quiet period is to make sure that traders do not try to influence investors because the trader has a beneficial interest in the offering's secondary market.

QUIET TITLE SUIT. A lawsuit or legal maneuver designed to remove a questionable claim filed against a property's title.

QUOTATION. A figure that reflects a security's current transaction, bid, or ask price.

QUOTATION BOARD. A security's exchange board that displays a security's daily market prices, ticker symbol, transaction price, and the number of shares traded.

QUOTATION TICKER. An exchange's ticker tape that displays transaction prices.

QUOTED PRICE. The last transaction price of any stock, bond, or commodity.

QUOTE MACHINE. An electronic system that provides securities' transaction prices.

QUOTE WIRE. An electronic connection between a brokerage house and the New York Stock Exchange that carries a listed security's highest bid and lowest offer prices.

QUO WARRANTO. A lawsuit designed to determine who actually is in power or in charge of a corporation, or to test the authority of that person.

═ R ═

R. Appears in newspaper stock listings to describe an option that has not been traded.

RACKETEER INFLUENCED AND CORRUPT ORGANIZATION ACT. A federal law outlawing participation in organized crime, racketeering activities, and securities fraud.

RADAR ALERT. When a specific security is closely monitored to see if large chunks are being accumulated in a takeover attempt. If so, company officials are notified immediately so they can take defensive steps.

RAG STOCK. A security with a low price.

RAID. A manipulative move to drive stock prices down.

RAIDER. A person or company that is trying to buy a controlling interest in another company in an effort to take that other company over.

RALLY. A short, sharp rise in the general level of the market, commodity futures, or a security's price after a period of a downward or sideways movement.

RANDOM WALK. The path of stock prices, in that past prices cannot always be used to determine future prices because of the many and varied influences that can affect the prices.

RANGE. All of the prices that fall between a highest and lowest price during a specific time period.

RANGE FORWARD CONTRACTS. A forward exchange agreement designed to limit the downside currency risk and protect the upside profit potential. It allows the customer to choose either end of a currency range as well as the contract's expiration date, with the issuer choosing the other end of the currency range.

RANKING. The rating of a security's performance during a specific time period compared to the performance of other securities rated during that same period.

RAPID AMORTIZATION. A method for the owner of an asset to write off its cost for short-term tax savings.

RATABLE DISTRIBUTION. Occurs when the assets of an estate are distributed proportionally to all heirs.

RATE BASE. The base value that a regulatory panel establishes for a utility to determine the utility's allowed rate of return. The panel bases the value on the utility's operating costs.

RATE COVENANT. A municipal revenue bond with the provision that rates will be adjusted for the facility's use so that revenues can provide maintenance, repairs, and bond debt service.

RATE OF RETURN. A measure of a company's profitability, the rate of return is determined by dividing stockholders' equity into net income. This produces a security's yearly aftertax profit, expressed as a percentage of the original capital investment.

RATE REOPENER. Long-term financing with an interest rate that is adjusted every three to five years. In addition, the issuer allowed to terminate the loan for a premium each time.

RATING OF SECURITIES. The determination of an issuing company's financial strength and stability, based on the company's management ability, debts, and payment history.

RATIO. The comparison of different financial variables and their relationship to one another.

RATIO ANALYSIS. Studying, interpreting, and comparing different financial ratios.

RATIO BULL SPREAD. A call option spread with one long call option and two short call options all on the same underlying stock and with the same expiration date, but with the long call having a lower striking price.

RATIO OF ACCOUNTS PAYABLE TO PURCHASES. Determines whether obligations are paid on time during one period compared to another period.

RATIO OF CAPITAL TO FIXED ASSETS. Determines how long it probably will take to convert the owners' investments into fixed assets.

RATIO OF COLLATERAL TO DEBT. Determines how effectively a stock margin can be achieved.

RATIO OF FINISHED GOODS INVENTORY TO THE COST OF GOODS SOLD. Determines sales stability to gauge inventory turnover. This is measured by dividing the cost of goods sold by the average finished goods' inventory.

RATIO SCALE. A graph with the percentage difference between two prices that cover the same vertical distance.

RATIO SPREADING. Simultaneously buying one number of option contracts and selling a different number of option contracts on the same underlying security.

RATIO WRITER. An individual who owns an underlying security writes more call option contracts than he or she actually could cover if they all were called.

REACH BACK. An improper benefit through which a tax shelter, such as a limited partnership, can offer year-end deductions that cover the entire year-to-date, thus reaching back over the year. For example, an investor who entered a partnership in November could claim the partnership expense deductions for the entire year.

REACH THROUGH. A broker carelessly enters a price quotation into the Intermarket Trading System that falls below the best quote for that security. The ITS will reject the broker's quote.

REACQUIRED STOCK. Stock shares that a company has issued to stockholders, and then bought back.

REACTION. Occurs when a security's price changes directions then stabilizes, usually following a lengthy and strong up or down price movement.

READING THE TAPE. An investor can determine a stock's price performance by reading the stock exchange's ticker tape, which regularly displays prices. The investor can then judge whether the stock's price will go up or down.

READY TRANSFERABILITY. The holder of a publicly traded security can sell or give away the security without the issuer's permission.

REAL ACCOUNTS. Accounts with balances that are carried over to the next fiscal period instead of being canceled. Liabilities, for example, would be included in a real account.

REAL CAPITAL. Equipment or machinery that is used in a company's production.

REAL EARNINGS. Income that has been adjusted to eliminate any effects from price changes.

REAL ESTATE. Any piece of land and all buildings and physical characteristics that are attached to it.

REAL ESTATE APPRECIATION NOTE. The loan a company takes out using real estate as collateral, with the loan carrying a fixed interest rate as well as the underlying property's accrued appreciation.

REAL ESTATE INVESTMENT TRUST (REIT). A closed-end investment firm that deals in real estate investing.

REAL ESTATE LIMITED PARTNERSHIP. A public investment program that must be registered with the Securities and Exchange Commission.

REAL ESTATE LOAN. A loan with real estate used as collateral.

REAL ESTATE OWNED. All bank-owned property except that taken in consideration of a defaulted loan.

REAL ESTATE SETTLEMENT PROCEDURES ACT. A federal law that covers the costs involved with loan closings as well as property settlement activities. For example, the law requires lenders to disclose the actual closing costs and the land's previous selling price.

REAL ESTATE SETTLEMENT PROCEDURES ACT AMENDMENTS. A federal amendment that slightly altered the previous procedures act. For example, the amendment says a lender can give the borrower a good faith estimate of the closing costs instead of the actual charges, and the lender does not have to disclose the land's previous selling price.

REAL ESTATE SOLD ON CONTRACT. Occurs when the property buyer does not have enough of a down payment to take title to the property. The contract stipulates that when the loan balance is reduced to a certain level, the buyer can refinance the property and take title to it.

REAL INCOME. One person's purchasing power, or his or her income as adjusted for the rate of inflation.

REAL INTEREST RATE. An interest rate from which the inflation rate has been subtracted.

REAL INVESTMENT. An expense that creates a new capital asset.

REALIZATION ACCOUNT. A consolidated account summarizing all of the accounts of a company that is going out of business. The account reflects assets that are reduced to cash or applied to reduce the company's liabilities.

REALIZE. An investor's actual cash profit or loss, as opposed to a paper profit or loss.

REALIZED YIELD. The bond's return based on its original purchase price.

REALIZING. The repurchasing of a short sale, or any profiting from a liquidation sale.

REALLOWANCE. Occurs when an underwriting syndicate allows members of the National Association of Securities Dealers to receive a sales commission for shares sold to the members' clients.

REAL MONEY. Coins, as opposed to paper currency, that contain intrinsic value.

REAL PROPERTY TRANSACTION. When credit is extended because an interest in a piece of property will be used as collateral.

REAL RETURN. A return that has been adjusted for inflation.

REAL STOCK. A long stock position versus a short position.

REAL TERMS. A measure of the degree to which inflation has affected purchasing power.

REALTOR. A real estate broker who belongs to a National Association of Realtors board.

REAPPRAISAL. The second appraisal of a piece of property.

REASSESSMENT. The changing of a property's base value, usually as the result of a reappraisal.

REBATE. The return of a portion of money that has been paid. For example, a return of unearned interest to a borrower if the loan is paid off before maturity.

RECAPITALIZATION. When a company changes its financial structure (e.g., an exchange of bonds for stock, or bonds for another type of bond). Companies often perform a recapitalization in the event of a bankruptcy or when a healthy company is seeking to improve its tax situation.

RECAPITALIZATION SURPLUS. Occurs when a stock's par value is reduced and bonds are exchanged for securities that have a lower value.

RECAPTURE. A contract stipulation that permits one person to at least partially retrieve asset ownership. For example, a contractor may be able to take a percentage of a development's profits.

RECASTING A MORTGAGE. Changing a mortgage by altering its principal amount, interest rate, or maturity.

RECEDING MARKET. A period when the market's prices are dropping.

RECEIVABLES. Accounts receivable.

RECEIVABLES TURNOVER. A company can gauge the quality of its account receivables by comparing its net sales to the receivables' current value, which provides a ratio that helps the company determine the length of time that the receivables may remain outstanding.

RECEIVER. A court-appointed person who oversees a company that is going through bankruptcy.

RECEIVERS' AND TRUSTEES' SECURITIES. The debt securities a court-appointed trustee issues.

RECEIVER'S CERTIFICATE. A document that represents the securities of a company that has gone through a receivership, which is similar to bankruptcy. Holders can publicly trade their receiver's certificates on the open market.

RECEIVERSHIP. A form of bankruptcy in which a company can avoid liquidation. The company reorganizes with the help of a court-appointed trustee, who helps to resolve the company's financial troubles.

RECEIVE VERSUS PAYMENT. A buyer pays the seller in cash for a security when that security is delivered.

RECESSION. Occurs when a nation's living standards drop and prices increase. This downturn in economic activity is widely defined as a decline in a country's gross national product for at least two quarters.

RECIPROCAL BUSINESS. One investor wants to buy or sell securities in a deal with a person who later will enter another deal with the investor.

RECLAIM. A security certificate is recovered after a flaw was found and corrected.

RECLASSIFICATION OF STOCK. Occurs when a company changes its capital structure.

RECOGNIZANCE. The recording of a former debt.

RECONVEYANCE. Occurs when a property title is transferred back to its original owner.

RECORDATION. A written acknowledgment that a lien exists against a piece of property.

RECORD DATE. The date an investor must be registered with the issuing company as a security's owner of record to receive dividends or other ownership privileges.

RECORDS OF ORIGINAL ENTRY. A record of all cash receipts and expenses, with entries recorded before they are made in the general ledger.

RECOURSE. The right of a person who owns a negotiable instrument to insist that the former endorser make good on the instrument if the acceptor has refused to honor it. For example, if one person wrote a check to another person and the bank refused to honor the check, the first person, through recourse, can force the second person to honor the check.

RECOURSE LOAN. A loan taken out by a partnership or other concern carrying the provision that if the borrower defaults, the lender can not only take the collateral, but also some of the partners' personal assets.

RECOVERY. A period in which securities prices are climbing steadily after a period in which they dropped or were inactive.

RECURRING CHARGES. Fees that continue regularly.

REDEEM. The issuing company repurchases a bond at maturity by paying the holder its face value.

REDEEMABLE BOND. A bond that the issuing company can buy back before maturity, usually by paying the holder a premium.

REDEEMABLE STOCK. Any preferred stock that the issuing company can call in for redemption.

REDEMPTION. When a security's issuer repurchases the security.

REDEMPTION FUND. A fund used to retire a debt.

REDEMPTION NOTICE. A document that tells stockholders whose securities are being called in with the time and terms through which their securities will be redeemed.

REDEMPTION PERIOD. The time period that a debtor can buy back a piece of property by paying the total amount due on a foreclosed mortgage.

REDEMPTION PRICE. The price at which a bond can be redeemed before maturity or the price at which the shares from a mutual fund can be redeemed.

REDEMPTION RIGHT. The right of a person who has defaulted on a mortgage to buy his or her property back after the court judgment.

REDEMPTION VALUE. The amount for which a security can be redeemed.

RED HERRING. A preliminary prospectus, so named because of the red print on the front page of some copies which explains that the prospectus is incomplete.

REDISCOUNT. When a bank that is a member of the Federal Reserve System uses a customer's pledged collateral as collateral for a loan the bank takes out from the Federal Reserve.

REDLINING. The improper practice of some financial institutions to refuse to make home improvement loans or mortgages in a financially depressed area. The practice is called redlining because the institution will use a red marker to outline the area on a map.

REDUCIBLE RATE BOND. A bond on which the issuer can reduce the interest rate and call premium.

REFERENCE CURRENCY. Any cash that is used to pay bondholders.

REFINANCING. An issuer sells new bonds at lower interest rates to raise money to pay off an older debt that had a higher interest rate.

REFLEX RALLY. A price correction from an oversold condition. The security's price moves up, but does not change the price's established trend.

REFLEX REACTION. A price correction from an overbought condition. The security's price drops, but does not change the price's established trend.

REFUNDING. When the proceeds of a security's sale are used to pay off the issuing company's existing debt securities.

REFUNDING MORTGAGE. A mortgage loan that is refinanced with another loan.

REGIONAL BANK. A bank that operates in a specific area of the country, as opposed to a money center bank which operates at least nationally.

REGIONAL FUND. A mutual fund with investments concentrated in companies located in a specific area of the country, such as Texas oil or Idaho potato products.

REGIONAL STOCK EXCHANGE. A national stock exchange located outside of New York City, such as the Philadelphia Stock Exchange, that lists securities that often are not listed elsewhere.

REGISTER. To formally record.

REGISTERED AS TO INTEREST ONLY. Bonds with interest that is sent directly to the registered holder and with the face value payable only to the bearer.

REGISTERED AS TO PRINCIPAL ONLY. A coupon bond with its face value payable only to the registered holder at maturity.

REGISTERED BOND. A bond registered in the owner's name and payable only to that owner, as opposed to a bearer bond.

REGISTERED CHECK. A check that a bank issues on behalf of a customer who sets aside special funds for the check. A bank-issued cashier's check or a money order, for example, would be considered a registered check.

REGISTERED COMPANY. A company registered with and, therefore, regulated by, the Securities and Exchange Commission.

REGISTERED COMPETITIVE MARKET MAKER. A New York Stock Exchange floor broker who can make transactions with his or her own firm as well as for other brokerage firms, and who, upon request, must make a bid or offer on a security to maintain a fair market.

REGISTERED COMPETITIVE TRADER. A New York Stock Exchange member who can trade for his or her own account, but 75 percent of his or her transactions must be stabilizing, which means they cannot be higher or lower than the last transaction's price.

REGISTERED COUPON BOND. A bond registered in the owner's name, but with interest coupons paid only by delivering the coupon to a disbursing agent.

REGISTERED EQUITY MARKET MAKER. A competitive market maker on the American Stock Exchange.

REGISTERED EXCHANGE. A securities exchange governed by the Securities and Exchange Commission, or a commodities exchange governed by the Commodities Exchange Commission.

REGISTERED FORM. A document issued in the owner's name and payable only to that owner.

REGISTERED HOME OWNERSHIP SAVINGS PLAN. A Canadian savings account in which a person can deposit up to $1,000 a year, to a total of $10,000, in tax-deductible income as long as the money eventually is used to buy a home.

REGISTERED INVESTMENT COMPANY. An investment company that is certified by the Securities and Exchange Commission.

REGISTERED OPTIONS PRINCIPAL. An employee of an exchange-member firm who handles the options transactions of the member firm's customers.

REGISTERED OPTIONS TRADER. An American Stock Exchange specialist who deals in several of the exchange's options contracts and who must maintain a fair market in those options.

REGISTERED OVER-THE-COUNTER STOCK. An unlisted security that can be traded in a margin account.

REGISTERED REPRESENTATIVE. An employee of a stock exchange broker-dealer who advises and trades customers' accounts while generating commissions.

REGISTERED REPRESENTATIVE RAPID RESPONSE PROGRAM. A New York Stock Exchange communications computer through which member firms can quote execution prices to their customers without having to wait for the exchange floor to confirm the trade.

REGISTERED RETIREMENT SAVINGS PLAN. A Canadian retirement plan in which a person can deduct either $5,500 or 20 percent of his or her annual taxable income each year and deposit the amount in a bank account or mutual fund.

REGISTERED SECONDARY. A security sold by its owner, who is registered with the Securities and Exchange Commission, with a prospectus issued. The sale may perhaps be part of a primary secondary offering.

REGISTERED SECURITY. A security that has been recorded with its issuer.

REGISTERED TRADER. An exchange member who can trade on the exchange floor for his or her own account and whose transactions must meet certain requirements.

REGISTRAR. A person who keeps a bank's or a company's financial books and who oversees stock certificates.

REGISTRATION. A procedure through which the Securities and Exchange Commission must review and approve publicly traded securities before they can be publicly sold.

REGISTRATION FEE. A Securities and Exchange Commission fee charged on a public securities offering.

REGISTRATION STATEMENT. A document that spells out a company's public securities sales. The document must be filed with the Securities and Exchange Commission.

REGRESSION ANALYSIS. A method of comparing two investment variables to determine an independent variable's impact on a dependent variable, with the end result providing a prediction on future performance. For example, a computer manufacturer may determine what effect a population burst will have on the manufacturer's business.

REGRESSIVE TAX. A tax system in which a community's taxes will drop as the community's tax base increases.

REGULAR DIVIDEND. The dividend rate that the issuing company's board of directors sets.

REGULARITY OF DIVIDENDS. A company's pattern of paying dividends may be used as a gauge for investors to determine a wise investment.

REGULAR LOT. A normal security or commodity trading unit.

REGULAR SPECIALIST. A stock exchange member who must maintain a fair and orderly market in a group of specific stocks by accepting orders from other members and by buying and selling for his or her own account.

REGULAR-WAY DELIVERY (SETTLEMENT). A securities transaction in which the selling broker delivers the security to the buying broker, who in turn pays the selling broker within five business days after the transaction transpired. Other securities such as governments, options, and money market funds settle on the next business day.

REGULAR-WAY SALE. Any sale that is not a short sale.

REGULATED COMMODITIES. Commodities that the Commodities Futures Trading Commission governs and regulates. The CFTC, which covers all commodities traded in contract markets, handles fair trading practices, ethical conduct, and commodities information disclosure.

REGULATED INVESTMENT COMPANY. A company that invests money for other people. The company issues and publicly sells stock shares, then invests the proceeds.

REGULATION A. Securities offerings between $50,000 and $300,000 must file a prospectus, though a less-detailed one than is required from an offering of more than $300,000.

REGULATION G. Regulates the amount of credit that can be extended for buying securities in some situations that otherwise are unregulated.

REGULATION Q. A Federal Reserve System ceiling on the interest rates that banks pay.

REGULATION T. Regulates the amount of credit that brokers or dealers can extend to customers who want to buy securities.

REGULATION T CALL. A brokerage firm's margin call.

REGULATION T EXCESS. The amount of credit a broker-dealer can extend to a margin account customer above the amount of credit the customer already is using.

REGULATION U. Regulates the amount of credit a bank can extend to customers who want to buy securities.

REGULATION W. Regulates commercial credit concerning loan maturities and down payments for consumer products such as cars and large appliances.

REGULATION X. Regulates the type and amount of credit extended to people for buying, carrying, or trading securities.

REGULATION Z. Regulates, oversees, and enforces the Truth in Lending Act, which covers disclosure requirements.

REHYPOTHECATION. When a stockbroker uses the securities from a client's margin account as collateral for a bank loan to finance the debit balance in the client's account.

REINVESTMENT. When dividends and capital gains are put back into buying more shares.

REINVESTMENT PRIVILEGE. The right of mutual fund investors to have their dividend payments automatically put back into additional mutual fund shares.

REINVESTMENT RATE. The rate of return achieved through reinvesting the proceeds from the sale of a fixed-income investment.

REIT. *See* Real Estate Investment Trust.

REJECTION. A buyer's refusal to accept delivery of a security.

RELATIONSHIP TRADING. Basis trading in which an investor hedges by taking advantage of unusual price movements. The investor will buy or sell securities while simultaneously taking the opposite position with options contracts.

RELATIVE PRIORITY. Occurs in a reorganization when creditors take losses in inverse proportion to their seniority.

RELATIVE STRENGTH. A security's market performance compared to other securities in its industry.

RELATIVE VALUE. The value comparison of one security or commodity to another.

RELEASE CLAUSE. A stipulation in a mortgage contract that frees a portion of the covered property after a percentage of the mortgage has been paid.

RELEASE LETTER. A document that a syndicate manager sends to other syndicate members with details of the offering.

RELEASE OF PREMIUMS ON FUNDED DEBTS. Occurs when a portion of the sale premium is credited to income each fiscal period, based on a comparison of the fiscal period to the securities' maturities.

RELIEF SPECIALIST. An exchange member who can takeover for a regular specialist if such a need should arise.

RELOADER. A person who can sell additional securities to an investor who wanted to buy only a smaller, more limited number.

REMAINDER BENEFICIARY. A trust beneficiary who immediately can receive the principal after the earlier beneficiary has ended his or her interest.

REMAINDER ESTATE. Occurs when one grant simultaneously creates two or more estates. The interest on each estate depends on and remains after the other estates have ended.

REMAINDERMEN. The final trust or estate beneficiaries.

REMARGINING. When an investor puts up additional securities or money because the equity in his or her margin account has fallen below accepted levels.

REMIT. To pay for goods or services.

RENEGOTIABLE RATE MORTGAGE. A 20- to 30-year real estate loan with interest rates fixed for three to five years, after which the interest rate is changed according to the average national mortgage rate.

RENTES. Austrian, Italian, or French bonds and the annual interest payment on those bonds.

RENTIER. A person who lives on fixed-investment income.

REOPEN AN ISSUE. Occurs when the Treasury sells more outstanding shares of an old government security at prevailing prices with the same conditions.

REORGANIZATION. A form of involuntary bankruptcy in which the company can avoid liquidation. The company's financial structure changes and its management is replaced by a court-appointed trustee, who tries to solve the company's financial troubles.

REORGANIZATION BOND. A bond that a company issues to raise needed capital while it is going through bankruptcy reorganization.

REORGANIZATION DEPARTMENT. The cashiering area where one security can be exchanged for another, rights can be executed and tender offers can be transacted.

REPATRIATION. Occurs when a person's or a company's assets are returned from a foreign country to that person's or company's home country.

REPEAT PRICES OMITTED. A consolidated tape designation that appears when the tape is late and therefore only a security's first transaction price is printed instead of all of the security's transaction prices.

REPLACEMENT COST ACCOUNTING. An accounting method in which the difference between an asset's original cost and the current replacement cost can be further depreciated.

REPORTING LIMIT. The number of futures contracts in which an investor can hold a position before he or she must report that position to the commodities exchange.

REPRESENTATIONS AND WARRANTIES. Legal opinions and performance guarantees in a contract, with the signing attorney responsible for backing the contract.

REPRESENTATIVE BID AND ASK PRICES. An old system used by the National Association of Securities Dealers Automated Quotation in which the median bid and median offer prices were quoted.

REPRESENTATIVE MONEY. Money that is fully backed by a commodity or by a monetary metal, such as gold or silver.

REPURCHASE. A security's issuer buys back shares.

REPURCHASE AGREEMENT. An agreement in which an investor sells an investment to another investor with the provision that the first investor can buy it back for a specific price by a specific date.

REQUEST FOR A REPORT. An investor's inquiry to a brokerage house on the status of a securities order.

REQUIRED RATE OF RETURN. The rate of return an investor must reach on an investment to keep the systematic risk from pushing the investment's value down.

REQUIRED RETURN. The lowest return an investment needs to become profitable.

REQUISITIONIST. A person or group of people who want to takeover a company's management.

RESCIND. To cancel an offer or a contract.

RESEARCH AND DEVELOPMENT. A company's department or branch that seeks new, more efficient ways to conduct its business or improve its goods or services. Normally, the more money a company invests in research and development, the faster the company grows.

RESEARCH AND DEVELOPMENT LIMITED PARTNERSHIP. An investment through which investors can finance a research and development venture and, in turn, receive a percentage of any new development's profits.

RESEARCH DEPARTMENT. The department in a financial institution or brokerage house that analyzes securities and commodities and makes predictions on future movements.

RESERVE. Capital that is set aside to take care of future losses or demands.

RESERVE BANK. A bank that is a member of the Federal Reserve System.

RESERVE CITY BANK. A Federal Reserve member bank in a city that has a Federal Reserve District bank or branch.

RESERVE FOR RETIREMENT OF SINKING FUND BONDS. A fund set aside so the issuer will have enough money by a certain date to redeem outstanding bonds.

RESERVE FUND. Cash or a liquid asset created to meet an upcoming expense.

RESERVE REQUIREMENT. The percentage amount of a bank's deposits that a bank must keep in its vault or in a noninterest-bearing reserve bank account.

RESERVE SPLIT. Occurs when the number of capital shares are reduced, but the total dollar amount stays the same because each share's par value increases. A company can achieve a reverse split by substituting one new share for a number of outstanding shares, thus increasing the par value of each while decreasing the actual number of outstanding shares.

RESIDENTIAL ENERGY CREDIT. A tax credit homeowners can claim on their federal income tax forms when they improve the energy efficiency of their homes through insulation, storm window installation, or other home additions and improvements.

RESIDUAL SECURITY. A convertible security, or a security with rights or warrants, that possesses traits which could result in a reduced amount of earnings per share. Such dilution would increase the number of common shares that compete for the same earnings, thus reducing the earnings per share.

RESIDUAL VALUE. *See* Salvage Value.

RESIDUARY CLAUSE. The contract or will clause that distributes all of the decedent's property after all taxes and debts have been satisfied.

RESIDUARY ESTATE. All of the assets and property left in an estate after all taxes and debts have been satisfied.

RESIDUARY LEGATEE. The person who receives all of the assets and property left in an estate after all taxes and debts have been satisfied.

RESIDUARY TRUST. A trust into which all of an estate's assets and property are deposited after all taxes and debts have been satisfied.

RESISTANCE LEVEL. A security's price level at which persistent selling occurs at a certain price to stop a price increase. Technicians believe that a breakout above a resistance level will lead to new highs.

RESOLUTION. An individual's intention, or a security's clause that expresses an intention.

RESOURCE. Anything of value or that can be used in exchange for something else.

RESPONDEAT SUPERIOR. When a complaint is made against a company's employee because of the employee's error or oversight, the complaint actually is made against that employee's superior because the superior is responsible for supervising the employee.

RESTING ORDER. Any securities order that remains in effect until the order cannot be filled because of high market prices if it is a buy order or because of low market prices if it is a sell order.

RESTORATION PREMIUM. The extra charge a person must pay to restore an instrument that has dropped in value to its original value.

RESTRICTED ACCOUNT. A margin account that has fallen below margin requirements.

RESTRICTED ASSET. Any resource that has a limited legal use, such as an asset from a revenue bond indenture.

RESTRICTED LIST. A list of securities issuers and specific issues that cannot be traded, but can be sold only for a customer who does not solicit the sale. A broker-dealer usually gives the restricted list to the firm's selling employees.

RESTRICTED SHARES. A common stock that will not pay dividends until a specific event has occurred, such as the company achieving a certain earnings level.

RESTRICTED STOCK OPTION. An employee's privilege to buy a specific amount of his or her company's capital stock during a specific time period for the current market price.

RESTRICTED SURPLUS. The part of a company's retained earnings that it cannot use to pay dividends.

RESTRICTIVE COVENANTS. A bond indenture that limits the debtor from taking certain actions to protect the creditor.

RESTRICTIVE ENDORSEMENT. The endorsement on a securities certificate that names one person or one company name.

RESTRIKE. A coin that was stamped at the U.S. Mint after the date marked on the coin.

RESYNDICATION LIMITED PARTNERSHIP. A partnership that buys property which previously was owned by another partnership, thus enabling the new partners to take new tax credits and depreciation after the previous partners exhausted their credits and depreciation benefits.

RETAIL AUTOMATIC EXECUTION SYSTEM. A computer system for the quick execution of five or fewer option orders on the Chicago Board Options Exchange.

RETAIL HOUSE. A brokerage firm with retail investors, not institutional investors, as customers.

RETAIL INVESTOR. An individual investor as opposed to an institutional investor.

RETAIL REPO. A collateralized loan with the bank borrowing from the lender. Basically, the depositor buys the collateral, then sells it back to the bank, which pays the initial price plus interest for a flexible amount of time, usually less than 90 days. This money is not insured since it is considered an investment, not a deposit.

RETAINED EARNINGS. The portion of a company's earnings that it does not pay out to stockholders.

RETAINED EARNINGS STATEMENT. A detailed financial record of annual and past dividend payments, which accompanies the company's annual report.

RETENTION. That part of an underwriting member's takedown that can be sold after enough shares are held back to ease institutional and selling group sales. For example, if the member has a takedown of 20,000 shares and holds on to 5,000 shares for institutional and selling group sales, the member's retention is 15,000.

RETENTION RATE. As the opposite of a dividend payout ratio, this is a percentage of a company's profits after taxes have been paid that can be credited to its retained earnings.

RETENTION REQUIREMENT. A broker must retain 50 percent of the customer's margin account proceeds to lower the customer's debt. The customer can withdraw the other 50 percent.

RETIRE. To cancel or redeem a securities issue.

RETIRED SECURITIES. A company's outstanding shares that the company calls back in or cancels and thus can no longer be sold.

RETIREMENT OF DEBT. When principal is paid off.

RETRACTABLE LOAN. A debt security on which the issuer can regularly change the interest rate. The investor can redeem the security for its par value if the new interest rate is not profitable.

RETREAT. Describes a drop in prices.

RETROACTIVE RESTORATION. A bond stipulation which states that its original coverage will be restored after a loss is paid to take care of potential future losses.

RETURN. An investment's profits, whether through interest or dividends.

RETURN OF CAPITAL. Nontaxable cash payments to shareholders that represent a return of invested capital instead of a dividend distribution. The investor decreases the investment's cost by the payment amount.

RETURN ON ASSETS. One can determine a company's profitability by dividing its total assets into its net income.

RETURN ON EQUITY. A stockholder's equity divided into the net income.

RETURN ON INVESTED CAPITAL. A company's total capitalization divided into its net income and interest expense.

RETURN ON INVESTMENT. Divide an investment into the pretax income to obtain a figure that represents the relationship of investment and profit.

RETURN ON NET WORTH. A stockholder can determine his or her rate of return by comparing the issuing company's aftertax net profit to its net worth.

RETURN ON SALES. To determine a company's operating efficiency, one can compare the percentage of its net sales that represent before-tax profits to that same figure from prior time periods. The percentage that represents that the company is operating efficiently will vary from industry to industry.

REVALUATION. The changing of the value of a country's currency not by market fluctuations but on decisions made by authorities.

REVENUE ANTICIPATION NOTE. A short-term municipal note that the government has backed with expected revenues.

REVENUE APPLICATION NOTES. A short-term note that a company or bank distributes to raise money because it is expecting to receive an amount of revenue with which it can pay off the notes.

REVENUE BOND. A revenue bond that is backed by a tax placed on a special project, such as the construction of a toll road.

REVENUE INDEXED MORTGAGE BOND. A real estate-backed security with interest payments supplemented by a predetermined percentage of the issuer's earnings.

REVENUE SHARING. When the federal government, or any larger governmental entity, returns some tax money to a local government, or any smaller governmental entity.

REVERSAL. Occurs when a security's price movement changes, with the new direction continuing at least for several days. A down reversal occurs when the price drops, and an up reversal occurs when the price starts going up.

REVERSE ANNUITY MORTGAGE. Enables an elderly property owner to borrow against the collateral value of his or her property, but the annual payments will not decrease the property value during the person's life. The borrower therefore has a continuous income for the rest of his or her life.

REVERSE A SWAP. A second transaction in bonds that re-establishes a client's original portfolio position, thereby eliminating any effects from the market changes that have transpired. For example, if a yield spread expanded, making it profitable to sell one bond and buy another, then returned to its original condition, the investor would make a reverse swap by selling the bond that was purchased and buying back the bond that was sold.

REVERSE CONVERSION. A technique, usually implemented by brokerage firms, which involves simultaneously selling an underlying security short, buying a call and selling a put, all with the same striking price. The options will hedge against a sharp rise while the brokerage firm collects the interest received by investing the money in short-term money market installments.

REVERSE DOLLAR ROLL. An investor who owns a high-coupon Government National Mortgage Association bond sells it after interest rates drop, but agrees to buy it back in a month, thus obtaining higher returns in a short time.

REVERSE HEDGE. The owner of common stock sells a convertible security short because he or she believes the premium over conversion parity will drop so he or she can close the position at a profit.

REVERSE REPURCHASE AGREEMENT. A customer sells a group of securities to a broker-dealer under the provision that the customer will buy them back by a predetermined date for a specific price. The difference between the amount the customer received for the securities and the amount he or she will pay the broker-dealer when buying them back represents the interest.

REVERSE SPLIT. Used to reduce the number of outstanding shares. For example, an investor with two shares will have only one share after a 1 for 2 reverse split.

REVERSE YIELD GAP. Occurs when a fixed-interest security earns more than an industrial security.

REVOCABLE TRUST. A contract that deeds a piece of income-producing property to a person's beneficiaries, with the holder able to change the contract or cancel it any time he or she wants. Because the property automatically goes to the owner's beneficiaries according to the contract's terms, it does not go through probate.

REVOLVING LINE OF CREDIT. A line of credit a bank extends to a customer, with the amount available to the customer whenever he or she needs it.

REVOLVING UNDERWRITING FACILITIES. A long-term debt contract between a group of investment bankers and the issuer of Eurodollar securities in which the underwriter offers three- to six-month obligations at more profitable short-term rates, then continues to reoffer the notes as previously issued ones mature.

RIALTO. Any commodities or securities exchange.

RICH. A price that is too high.

RIGGED MARKET. A market with securities prices that have been manipulated to attract unsuspecting buyers.

RIGGING. Any illegal stock price manipulation.

RIGHT. A stipulation in a securities contract that allows the holder to subscribe to other securities at a specific ratio.

RIGHT OF ACCUMULATION. The right of a mutual fund investor to reinvest if the value of the fund's holdings exceeds a certain price level.

RIGHT OF REDEMPTION. The right to take back a piece of property by paying off the mortgage.

RIGHT OF RESCISSION. The right to cancel a contract within three business days with full refund and no penalty. This right, granted by the Federal Consumer Credit Protection Act of 1968, protects consumers from high pressure sales and other sales tactics.

RIGHT OF SURVIVORSHIP. When two people own a piece of property and one dies, the deed automatically is transferred to the other person.

RIGHT OF WAY. The right of the public to allow utilities or transportation companies to use land that will benefit the general public.

RIGHTS. The option a company gives to shareholders in which the shareholders can buy a pro rata share of a new common stock issue at a specific price. Because the rights carry a market value, they can be actively traded.

RIGHTS OFFERING. A company gives the holders of common stock the right to buy a proportionate number of new issue shares at a lower price before the new issue is offered publicly.

RIGHTS OF SHAREHOLDERS. Stockholders' rights to vote on some company matters such as board election, charter changes, reorganization, and merger proposals.

RIGHTS ON. A security that carries the right for the investor to buy a pro rata amount of any new offerings.

RING. A commodity exchange's trading area, or the area in the New York Stock Exchange where commodities are traded.

RINGING UP. Occurs when two commodities brokers settle a deal before the contracts mature and before the contracts are deliverable. Such practices enable the brokers to take care of their commitments before the last minute so they will have time to take care of other deals that may become more pressing.

RISING BOTTOMS. The chart pattern that occurs when a security's or a commodity's low prices are moving up, which indicates that the basic price support levels also are moving up.

RISK. The probability that an investment will earn the amount of profit that it is supposed to earn. The chance an investment will drop in value.

RISK-ADJUSTED DISCOUNT RATE. The risk-free rate plus a risk premium that investment advisors use to determine the present value of a speculative income source, with the figure based on the investment's characteristics.

RISK ARBITRAGE. Occurs when an arbitrageur buys stock shares of a target company and then sells the shares to the raider.

RISK AVERSE. A wise investor given two investment alternatives with equal returns and different risks will take the investment with the lesser risk.

RISK CAPITAL. Investment capital.

RISK-FREE ASSET. A noncallable bond such as a government security with inflation as the only risk.

RISK-FREE RATE OF RETURN. The return on a default-free Treasury security.

RISKLESS TRANSACTION. Occurs when a broker-dealer takes a position in a security only after receiving a firm buy order, thereby eliminating any risk involved in taking a position.

RISK OF CAPITAL. The possibility that part of an investment will be lost.

RISK OF INFLATION. The possibility that an investment will have a lower buying power after awhile because of the effects of inflation.

RISK OF SELECTION. The possibility that an investor, given several investment alternatives, will choose the wrong or least profitable one.

RISK OF TIMING. The possibility that an investor will put money into a security at an unwise time, such as right before the price is about to drop.

RISK PREMIUM. The amount above the risk-free rate that investors seek before they will put money into a risky asset.

RISK RATING. A method of determining the relative, estimated risk of a mortgage investment.

RISK REWARD. The most an investment can lose compared to the most the investment can gain.

ROBINSON-PATMAN ACT. A 1936 law prohibiting price discrimination, false brokerage deals, and excessive quantity discounts.

ROLL DOWN. An options position is closed and a new position with a lower exercise price is established immediately.

ROLL FORWARD. An options position is closed and a new position with a later expiration date is established.

ROLLING OVER. Exchanging a near option for a far option on the same underlying security, with both options carrying the same striking price.

ROLLING STOCK. A transportation company's movable equipment, including cars, trucks, and trains.

ROLLOVER. An investor takes money from a maturing security, such as a futures or options contract, and invests it in longer-term securities.

ROLLOVER CERTIFICATE OF DEPOSIT. Also called a roly-poly certificate of deposit, this is a package of 12 six-month CDs, each of which matures in three years.

ROLLOVER MORTGAGE. A short-term mortgage in which the unpaid balance is refinanced every two or three years and thus the interest rate is adjusted each time it is refinanced.

ROLL UP. An options position is closed and a new position with a higher exercise price is established immediately.

ROLL-UP FUND. An investment fund that pays no dividends, with money concentrated in world currencies. Returns are considered capital gains and not income.

ROLY POLY CERTIFICATE OF DEPOSIT. A group of six-month certificates of deposit with expiration dates that stretch over at least two years. As one matures, the investor is required to buy another for the same amount to replace it.

ROOK. To cheat.

ROUND DOWN. Buying a specific amount of securities through the fixed dollar amount system of investing while leaving a surplus in the account. The investor buys as much as he or she can with the amount in the account.

ROUND LOT. The smallest transaction that will not involve a service fee for being small, usually 100 shares.

ROUND LOT CASH BUY-SELL RATIO. The cash account selling of round lots divided into the cash account buying of round lots.

ROUND LOT MARGIN BUY-SELL RATIO. Margin account selling divided into margin account buying.

ROUND LOT SHORT-COVER RATIO. The total round lot shares covered divided into the round lot shares shorted.

ROUND LOTTER. A person who trades in packages of 100 shares of actively traded securities or 10 shares of inactive securities.

ROUND TRIP. As the basis upon which a commodities commission is charged, this refers to the opening and closing prices of a futures position.

ROUND TRIP TRADE. A security or commodity bought and sold within a short time period.

ROUND UP. Buying a specific amount of securities through the fixed dollar amount system of investing while leaving a debit in the account. The investor pays the additional amount.

ROYALTY. Payment to the owner of a patent or copyrighted materials such as books, movies, properties, or products.

ROYALTY TRUST. An oil or gas company spins off property to its shareholders, which means it will not be taxed at the corporate level and will offer high returns to stockholders.

R-SQUARED. The way in which a percentage of a portfolio's total returns represents the portfolio's beta measure.

RULE 144. A Securities and Exchange Commission regulation that covers the selling of restricted securities.

RULE 405. A New York Stock Exchange regulation that members must know specific information about their customers, their customers' accounts, and their customers' transactions. This know your customer rule deals with the suitability of certain investments for individuals with different conditions.

RULE OF 20. A theory that says the annual inflation rate added to the price/earnings ratio of the Dow Jones Industrial stocks should add up to 20 because as inflation rises, the P/E ratios drop.

RULE OF 72. To determine how long it would take for an investor to double his or her money, divide the fixed rate of compound interest into 72.

RULE OF 78. A system of calculating interest refunds when a debt is paid off early. The sum of the numbers one through 12 equals 78, thus assuming equal monthly payments, the interest for the first month would be 12/78, the second would be 11/78, and so on.

RULES OF FAIR PRACTICE. National Association of Securities Dealers' regulations that govern ethical practices, such as fair pricing and proper disclosure.

RUN. A market maker's list of offerings, including bid and offer prices and par values. Also, when a securities price rapidly increases.

RUNAWAY INFLATION. A swift rise in prices that special controls will not be able to reign.

RUNDOWN. The dollar amounts available in a municipal bond issue series.

RUNNING AHEAD. Illegal practice occurring when a registered representative enters a personal order to buy or sell a security before entering a similar order for a client.

RUNNING BOOK. The activities of a person who specializes in trading a specific stock on the exchange floor.

RUNNING IN THE SHORTS. An investor buys a number of varied securities that are sold short in an effort to push the price up because doing so encourages the sellers to buy the securities back, which will push the prices up even further.

RUNNING THROUGH THE POT. Occurs when a syndicate manager calls back some shares that the syndicate has taken down and puts them into the pot for institutional investors.

RUNOFF. The ticker tape that shows an exchange's closing prices.

RUN ON A BANK. Occurs when a large number of a bank's depositors want to withdraw their money at the same time. Because a bank does not keep all of the money on hand, it could be in danger of closing its doors.

S

S. Indicates a stock split or stock dividend when it appears in newspaper stock listings.

S & P INDEXES. *See* Standard and Poor's Indexes.

SADDLED. A situation in which an investor pays more than the market price for a security, then is forced to hold onto it because its value has failed to increase up to that price paid.

SAFE HARBOR. An action to avoid legal and tax consequences.

SAFEKEEPING. A brokerage action to store and protect an investor's securities by segregating and identifying the securities.

SAFETY. A minimal risk that creates the investor belief that an investment will not lose money.

SAFETY OF INCOME. The probability that a company will continue making timely interest and dividend payments.

SAFETY OF PRINCIPAL. The probability that money invested with a particular company will remain stable.

SAFETY STOCK. A group of securities held to prevent stockouts.

SAG. Occurs when a security's price drops slightly after demand for the security has been depleted.

SAIF. *See* Savings Association Insurance Fund.

SALARY REDUCTION PLAN. A program in which an employee can have a percentage of his or her gross salary withheld and invested in his or her choice of securities or money markets. The employer, in turn, matches the contributions up to a predetermined limit. The employee does not have to pay taxes on the amount contributed or on any profits until the he or she leaves the company.

SALE. Occurs when a buyer and a seller agree on a price in a securities transaction.

SALE AND LEASE BACK. An agreement in which a company sells an item to another company or to an investor, then agrees to lease the item back for a specific length of time. Such agreements can be profitable because of the tax advantages they provide.

SALE AND SERVICING AGREEMENT. A secondary market transaction in which the seller-servicer supplies, and the buyer purchases loans every so often, as prescribed in the agreement.

SALE ON APPROVAL. A contract with the seller retaining the risk and the buyer not taking title until he or she indicates approval.

SALE OR RETURN. A contract with the buyer taking immediate title unless he or she returns the goods to the seller.

SALES AGREEMENT. A contract in which a seller agrees to transfer goods or services to the buyer for a predetermined price.

SALES CHARGE. A fee that an open-end investment company charges for buying fund shares.

SALES LITERATURE. Any written material that promotes a specific investment by detailing its advantages. The material is distributed to potential investors.

SALES LOAD. *See* Sales Charge.

SALES TAX. A state or city tax placed on a purchase based on the dollar amount of that purchase.

SALLIE MAE. Nickname for the United States' Student Loan Marketing Association.

SALT-DOWN STOCK. Occurs when an investor buys securities and keeps them for a long time, even if the securities show large paper profits.

SALVAGE VALUE. The realized value of an asset at the end of its useful life. Also called residual value and scrap value.

SAME-DAY SUBSTITUTION. Occurs when an investor sells one security and buys another of equal value in the same day.

SAMMIE BEE. Nickname for a Small Business Administration Loan.

SAMURAI BOND. A debt instrument denominated in Japanese yen, but not issued by a Japanese agency or company.

SATISFACTION OF MORTGAGE. The document issued by the lender verifying that a mortgage has been paid in full.

SATISFACTION PIECE. The document verifying that a debt has been paid in full.

SATURATION. Occurs when supply exceeds demand to such a degree that the prices must drop to absorb any further supply.

SATURATION POINT. The point at which supply begins to exceed demand.

SATURDAY NIGHT SPECIAL. One company's sudden attempt to takeover another company by tendering a public offer, so named because of a series of such attempts in the 1960s, most of which were announced during the weekends.

SAUCER PATTERN. A price chart that displays little activity after a steady price decline followed by a slight upturn.

SAVER'S SURPLUS. The difference between the interest a saver received and the higher amount of interest at which he or she would have agreed to loan money, if a demand for loans had existed. For example, if a person earned 8 percent interest on his or her savings, but would have earned 8.5 percent interest if he or she had loaned the money instead of saving it, 0.5 percent would be the saver's surplus.

SAVINGS ACCOUNT. Money deposited in a bank, with the account paying interest and the funds payable on demand of the depositor. Such accounts normally carry no penalties for early withdrawal.

SAVINGS AND INVESTMENT THEORY. A theory that says business cycles occur when people save more or less than the amount invested in new capital.

SAVINGS AND LOAN ASSOCIATION. A government-chartered financial institution that carries customer deposits and makes real estate mortgage loans.

SAVINGS ASSOCIATION INSURANCE FUND (SAIF). Formerly the Federal Savings and Loan Insurance Corporation, this fund insures deposits of up to $100,000 per account.

SAVINGS BANK. A government-chartered bank that invests customers' deposits in real estate, mortgages, government bonds, and other permissible securities.

SAVINGS BANK LIFE INSURANCE. An over-the-counter method of buying limited amounts of life insurance coverage from a bank without using an agent.

SAVINGS BOND. A U.S. Treasury bond that cannot be traded on the public market.

SAVINGS DEPOSIT. A bank account deposit that bears interest; the contents of which normally can be withdrawn upon demand without prior notice.

SBA. *See* Small Business Administration.

SCALE. Represents the number of bonds, their maturity dates, interest rates, and offering prices in the initial offering of a serial bond issue.

SCALING. Occurs when an investor places a series of buy and sell orders at different prices or at different times instead of placing only one order for all of the securities.

SCALPER. A market maker who excessively marks up or marks down securities that carry little risk to the market maker.

SCALPING. An unethical and sometimes illegal practice when a trader buys securities for his or her firm's account, then improperly tries to influence investors to buy the securities in an effort to drive the price up.

SCHEDULE C. A National Association of Securities Dealers regulation requiring principals, financial principals, and representatives to be registered.

SCHEDULE 13-D. A form the Securities and Exchange Commission requires the buyer of 5 percent of a registered equity security to file within 10 days of the purchase.

SCHEDULE 13-G. A short form the Securities and Exchange Commission requires the owner of 5 percent of a registered equity security to file at the end of the year.

SCHULDSCHEIN. Collateralized ownership in a German loan, with the lending bank participating in an underwriting syndicate. After the first 90 days, ownership of the security cannot be transferred more than three times before it matures.

SCIENTER. To knowingly transact a fraudulent securities deal.

SCORCHED EARTH TACTIC. A takeover target tries to discourage the takeover either by selling its most valuable and attractive assets or by entering a long-term contract.

SCORE. *See* Special Claim on Residential Equity.

SCOREX SYSTEM. *See* Securities Communication, Order Routing and Execution.

SCOTTISH DIVIDEND. A reverse split in which, for example, a company trades two shares for one.

SCRAP VALUE. *See* Salvage Value.

SCREEN. To search for securities that meet certain investment goals and criteria, such as a certain price/earnings ratio.

SCRIP. A document that a company issues to indicate ownership of a share fraction, usually following a stock split. Some companies pay dividends in scrip instead of in cash when they are short of money.

SCRIPOPHILY. The hobby of collecting old securities certificates.

SEALING. Concealed bids, usually enclosed in sealed envelopes, that all are opened at the same time, with the best bid accepted immediately.

SEASONAL TREND. A consistent, short-lived rise or drop in business or economic activity that regularly occurs as a result of changes in climate, holidays, vacations, and so on.

SEASONED SECURITY. A publicly held security, so any future transaction would involve a deal between two investors and not between the issuer and an investor.

SEAT. A securities or commodities exchange membership.

SEC. *See* Securities and Exchange Commission.

SECONDARIES. Small, speculative companies that investors are attracted to because of their potential for major advances.

SECONDARY BANK RESERVE. High-grade securities that easily can be converted into cash.

SECONDARY DISTRIBUTION. Occurs when an issuing company publicly offers a large block of stock for sale after the stock's primary distribution.

SECONDARY FINANCING. A second loan using the same collateral as the first loan, with the first loan having priority over the second.

SECONDARY MARKET. A securities transaction that takes place after the initial distribution.

SECONDARY MORTGAGE MARKET. The trading of existing mortgage loans and mortgage-backed securities.

SECONDARY MOVEMENT. A sharp price rally in a bear market, or a sharp drop in a bull market.

SECONDARY REACTION. A price change that moves against the general market trend.

SECOND MARKET. The over-the-counter securities market with the exchanges being the first.

SECOND MORTGAGE BOND. A bond backed by a mortgage, with the first mortgage bonds taking priority over the second.

SECOND MORTGAGE LENDING. A mortgage secured by a piece of property that already has been pledged on another mortgage. The first mortgage always has priority over the second.

SECOND PARTNER. Also called a secret partner, this is an active partner whose association with the company is not public knowledge.

SECOND PREFERRED STOCK. One preferred stock issue that ranks below another preferred stock issue in priority in dividend payments and on assets in the case of a liquidation.

SECOND ROUND. The venture capital stage between startup and the mezzanine level, when the company has matured either to where it may consider accepting management's leveraged buyout or an initial public offering.

SECTION 403 PLAN. A section of the Internal Revenue Code that allows the employees of some charitable groups or of some public schools to create tax-sheltered retirement plans, with the programs normally invested in mutual funds or annuities.

SECTOR. Bonds in the same class with similar ratings, close maturity dates, and similar coupons that are expected to have parallel movements.

SECULAR TREND. An up or down long-term market trend, with no regard to seasonal variations, in the price or levels of commodities, inflation, the stock market, and so on.

SECURED ACCOUNT. Any collateralized account.

SECURED BOND. A bond for which the issuer has set aside assets as collateral to ensure timely interest and principal payments.

SECURED DEBT. Any collateralized debt.

SECURED LOAN. A loan with collateral pledged in exchange for the funds.

SECURITIES. Usually describes stocks and bonds, but can be expanded to describe any financial instrument.

SECURITIES ACT OF 1933. A law that regulates securities markets by requiring, among other things, registration before any sale and by requiring disclosure of all pertinent information about the issuing company.

SECURITIES ACT OF 1934. A law that created the Securities and Exchange Commission to govern securities markets, which outlawed price manipulation, the misrepresentation of facts, and other possible abuses.

SECURITIES ACTS AMENDMENTS OF 1975. A law that calls for a national market system and a national process through which securities transactions can be cleared and executed.

SECURITIES ANALYST. A brokerage employee who reviews and judges securities investments and the financial condition of publicly held companies.

SECURITIES AND COMMODITIES EXCHANGES. National exchanges which trade securities, options, and futures contracts by members for their customers and personal accounts.

SECURITIES AND EXCHANGE COMMISSION (SEC). The government agency that regulates and supervises the securities industry. The commission administers federal laws and formulates and enforces rules to protect against malpractice and provide investors the fullest possible disclosure.

SECURITIES AND EXCHANGE COMMISSION FEE. The SEC imposes a one-cent charge on every $300 involved in a securities transaction. The seller normally pays the fee, which applies only to exchange-registered equity securities.

SECURITIES AND EXCHANGE COMMISSION ORGANIZATION MEMBER. A broker-dealer who is registered with the SEC and is not a member of the National Association of Securities Dealers or of a national exchange.

SECURITIES COMMUNICATION, ORDER ROUTING AND EXECUTION. Commonly referred to as the SCOREX System, this is a Pacific Stock Exchange computer network through which members can automatically send and execute market orders of less than 600 shares at the best available Intermarket Trading System price.

SECURITIES DEPOSITORY. The place where a security's certificate is physically filed before a bookkeeping transfer.

SECURITIES INDUSTRY ASSOCIATION. An organization of broker-dealers that is aimed at training members' employees and lobbying for members' interests.

SECURITIES INDUSTRY AUTOMATION CORPORATION. A company that handles a trading communications system for the American and New York stock exchanges.

SECURITIES INVESTOR PROTECTION CORPORATION (SIPC). A private, government-sponsored company that insures brokerage accounts for up to $500,000 in securities with $100,000 for cash in case the brokerage firm goes bankrupt.

SECURITIES LOAN. When one broker-dealer loans securities to another broker-dealer to complete a short sale.

SECURITIZATION. Pooling loans into packages of securities in Great Britain.

SECURITY ELEMENT. Any type of collateral.

SECURITY INSTRUMENT. Either the mortgage or the deed to property that has been pledged as collateral.

SECURITY MARKET LINE. The ratio of an asset's expected rate of return and its systemic risk.

SECURITY PURCHASE CONTRACT. A debt instrument that converts to an equity security of the same issuer after a specific date.

SECURITY RATINGS. Evaluations of the credit and investment risk of securities which are rated by independent agencies.

SECURITY VALUATION MODEL. A theory that says a common stock's value can be reached by adding the discounted present value to the total expected dividends.

SEED MONEY. The first money put into a business venture, usually a loan, that allows those opening the business to move closer to a startup.

SEEK A MARKET. To try to find orders for the appropriate security to complete a transaction.

SEGREGATE. To separate clients' securities from the broker's securities.

SEGREGATED SECURITIES. Clients' securities kept separate from a broker-dealer's securities and that a broker-dealer cannot use to transact the firm's business.

SELECTED DEALER AGREEMENT. An underwriting syndicate's contract for distributing new securities, with the agreement stipulating the syndicate members' rights and responsibilities, such as the obligation to sell the securities at the agreed upon price.

SELF-DEALING. A transaction between company officers, family members, or business associates, with no concern for interest payments.

SELF-DIRECTED INDIVIDUAL RETIREMENT ACCOUNT. An IRA in which the holder governs the account and the account's investment direction.

SELF-LIQUIDATING. An asset that easily can be converted to cash, or with a value that ultimately can be recovered in full.

SELF-LIQUIDATING ASSET PURCHASE (SLAP). This is a method in which a newly issued debt is used to buy a company that has a high level of cash flow. The large cash flow is used to pay off the debt issue.

SELF-REGULATORY ORGANIZATION. A stock exchange, securities, or commodities organization that is registered with the Securities and Exchange Commission and that is responsible for making sure members obey rules and regulations.

SELF-SUPPORTING. Occurs when project revenues will amount to enough alone, without help, to pay off the bonds that funded the project. For example, if the taxes assessed against people who get a new sewer line will be sufficient to pay off the bond issued to fund the project, the project is considered self-supporting.

SELF TENDER. Often used to fend off a takeover attempt, a company will buy back a specific number of its outstanding stock shares.

SELL AT BEST. This is said when an over-the-counter broker-dealer asks another broker-dealer to help sell part of a market order at the best available price.

SELL-DOWN. The security shares an underwriting syndicate offers to those who are not syndicate members.

SELLER FINANCING. Occurs when a buyer cannot get a loan to buy an asset or a piece of property, so the seller—instead of a bank—provides a secondary trust or a mortgage through which the buyer pays the money back in monthly installments.

SELLER'S CALL. Buying a commodity that is the same quality as described in a contract establishing its future price.

SELLER'S MARKET. Occurs when demand exceeds supply, which benefits anyone trying to sell a security or other asset.

SELLER'S OPTION TRADE. A transaction in which the seller can, after notifying the buyer in writing, deliver the security's certificate on or before the day the option expires in 60 days, instead of settling the transaction in a regular-way delivery.

SELLER'S SEVEN SALE. Occurs when the seller agrees not to deliver the security certificate to the buyer for at least seven days.

SELLER'S 30. A contract that gives the seller the option of delivering the security certificate within 30 days.

SELLING AWAY. Occurs when a broker sells a security that his or her firm has not authorized the broker to sell.

SELLING BELOW THE MARKET. Occurs when one security is selling for less than other similar securities.

SELLING CLIMAX. Describes a downward price trend that suddenly creates a volume increase, which plunges the price dramatically.

SELLING CONCESSION. Brokers who receive a commission to help distribute a securities offering.

SELLING DIVIDENDS. An improper activity in which a trader influences his or her client to buy investment company securities only so he or she can receive an approaching dividend. In essence, the customer is actually paying for the dividend with his or her own money because the dividend already is included in the fund's net asset value.

SELLING FLAT. Occurs when an investor buying a bond does not have to pay any additional amount, such as accrued interest, other than the bond's actual purchase price.

SELLING, GENERAL, AND ADMINISTRATIVE EXPENSES (SG&A). An expense section of a company's profit and loss statement that includes items such as advertising, salaries, commissions, travel, entertainment, and promotion.

SELLING GROUP. A group of dealers that helps an underwriting syndicate distribute a new or secondary issue by distributing the securities to the public. The group, in turn, receives a commission from the sales.

SELLING ON BALANCE. Occurs when supply exceeds demand and thus prices are falling and securities are being sold in high volume.

SELLING ON THE GOOD NEWS. Occurs when an investor sells his or her holdings in a security after the release of positive information about that security. They believe the stock has reached its top price and that profit taking will occur.

SELLING SHORT. *See* Short Sale.

SELLING THE CROWN JEWELS. Often used to fend off a takeover attempt, a company will sell some of its more valuable assets to make the company less attractive to the raider.

SELLING THE INTERMARKET SPREAD. Occurs when an investor simultaneously sells short a Treasury bill future and buys a certificate of deposit futures contract.

SELL OFF. Occurs when prices are dropping because of heavy selling pressure.

SELL ORDER. An investor's directions to his or her broker to liquidate a specific number of shares.

SELL OUT. Occurs when a buyer refuses to accept delivery or pay the agreed upon price. A sell out also occurs when a broker liquidates a margin account because the investor has failed to bring the account up to the minimum level following a margin call.

SELL-OUT NOTICE. A notice from a broker to a client telling the client he or she must pay an amount due immediately or the broker will begin selling the client's securities to satisfy the debt.

SELL-OUT PROCEDURE. When a buying broker fails to honor a contract by refusing to pay for securities he or she agreed to buy, the selling broker can turn around and sell the securities to someone else without notifying the defaulting buyer, or the seller can hold the buyer liable for any losses incurred because of the default.

SELL PLUS. A market order to sell a security at a price higher than that security's last transaction price.

SELL SIGNAL. A market gauge that indicates a security could soon drop in price.

SELL THE BOOK. A seller's request to sell as many shares as possible at the best bid price.

SENIOR BOND. A bond that has priority over other bonds in claiming assets and dividends.

SENIOR DEBT. Any debt security that takes priority over other debts from the same issuer.

SENIOR REFUNDING. Occurs when securities that mature in five to 12 years are replaced with securities that have original maturities of 15 years or longer. Senior refunding often is done to reduce interest costs, to extend a maturity date or to consolidate several different issues.

SENIOR REGISTERED OPTION PRINCIPAL. A company's officer who is responsible for customer accounts and for customer options transactions.

SENIOR SECURITIES. Debt and equity securities that have priority over other securities when claiming assets and dividends.

SENSITIVE MARKET. Also describes an insecure market in which the release of either positive or negative information will cause major price shifts.

SENTIMENT INDICATOR. A market gauge that indicates changes in investors' moods, psychology, and strategies.

SEP. *See* Simplified Employee Pension Plan.

SEPARATE ACCOUNT. Describes a variable annuity in which the issuer cannot commingle the investor's funds with the issuer's funds because the investor holds all of the risk. The investment, therefore, is kept in a separate account.

SEPARATE CUSTOMER. Describes the highest level of customer protection that the Securities Investor Protection Corporation provides. The SIPC keeps one investor's cash, margin, and special bond accounts separate from another customer's by listing each individual ownership under the investor's name.

SEPARATE PROPERTY. Property that is not jointly owned.

SEPARATE TRADING OF REGISTERED INTEREST AND PRINCIPAL OF SECURITIES (STRIPS). This is a U.S. Treasury method of selling interest and principal payments separately on certain qualified government-issued securities (*See also* Stripped Bond).

SEQUENTIAL TRANSACTIONS. When a security is heavily traded on an exchange, the exchange's ticker tape lists the transactions in consecutive order by volume and by price, but without constantly repeating the identifying stock symbol.

SERIAL BONDS. A group of bonds from the same issue that have different maturity dates.

SERIAL BONDS PAYABLE. A liability account of outstanding serial bonds' face values.

SERIES BOND. One bond that is offered publicly on a number of different dates instead of on one particular issue date.

SERIES E BOND. A former government savings bond series, issued from World War II to 1979, that will pay the owner interest for up to 40 years of ownership. The Series E Bond was replaced by the Series EE Bond, for which it can be exchanged.

SERIES EE BOND. A discounted, nontransferable U.S. government savings bond. These bonds are sold in denominations of at least $25 and mature in seven to 10 years.

SERIES HH BOND. A nontransferable U.S. government current income bond that sells at face value. These bonds are sold in denominations of at least $500 and mature in 10 years.

SERIES OF OPTIONS. A group of call or put option contracts, with each based on the same underlying security, having the same striking price, and expiring on the same date.

SERIES 7 EXAM. A test of the basic understanding of the securities industry required and administered by the NASD of all registered representative candidates. The multiple choice test is developed by the New York Stock Exchange.

SERVICE. To make regular interest and sinking fund payments on a long-term obligation.

SERVICING A MORTGAGE. The financial preparation, bookkeeping, analysis, and follow-up care of a mortgage pool, with such service carrying a fee, which is subtracted from the borrower's mortgage payments.

SESSION. One trading day.

SETTLE. To finalize a securities transaction, usually with the physical delivery of the security and the payment of the purchase price.

SETTLEMENT DATE. The day that securities must be delivered and paid to complete a transaction.

SETTLEMENT PRICE. A commodity's closing price.

SETTLOR. A person who created a trust between two living people as opposed to a person who creates a trust through a will.

SEVERALLY AND JOINTLY. An Eastern account, with the underwriting syndicate agreeing to buy a municipal issue in which the syndicate members, individually and as a group, will be responsible for any unsold securities.

SEVERALLY BUT NOT JOINTLY. A Western account, with the underwriting syndicate agreeing to buy part of a corporate issue in which the syndicate members individually, but not as a group, will be responsible for any unsold securities. For example, if one member sells all of his or her shares but another member does not, the first will not be liable for the securities that the second member did not sell.

SG&A. *See* Selling, General, and Administrative Expenses.

SHADOW CALENDAR. An issue that, because of a Securities and Exchange Commission backlog or because of a volatile market, has no effective registration date yet available.

SHADOW MARKET. Occurs when options and futures are manipulated because of their high level of leverage.

SHADOW PRICE. The price at which a security would sell under equilibrium conditions.

SHADOW WARRANT. Occurs when additional loan interest payments are tied to a common stock's market performance.

SHAKEOUT. Occurs when market conditions change and create an atmosphere in which marginally financed participants in an industry are eliminated.

SHARE. A single stock unit that represents a portion of company ownership.

SHARE BROKER. A discount broker who bases his or her commissions on the number of shares that are involved in the deal. The more shares involved, the lower the commission per share.

SHAREBUILDER INVESTMENT PLAN. A plan in which a bank depositor's account is regularly debited for an amount that will be invested in the securities market the next day.

SHARE CAPITAL. Capital that stockholders provide.

SHARED APPRECIATION NOTE. A fixed-rate mortgage with the borrower and lender sharing in the value appreciation's equity interest during the mortgage's life.

SHARED EQUITY MORTGAGE. Occurs when an investor makes the down payment for a home buyer, then pays a portion of the monthly mortgage payments, in exchange for a percentage of the home's appreciation.

SHAREHOLDER. Any person who owns units of a company's stock.

SHARE OF BENEFICIAL INTEREST. A security that represents an undivided interest in a debt security pool.

SHARE REGISTER. A company's record of who owns the publicly held shares.

SHARE REPURCHASE PLAN. A plan that allows a company to buy back its outstanding shares, usually because the shares are undervalued. Thus, the plan helps the company increase its stock's market value because the reduction of outstanding shares pushes up the earnings per share, which pushes up the market price.

SHARES AUTHORIZED. The maximum number of stock shares a company can sell as prescribed in its articles of incorporation. The company can sell more shares only if the board passes a charter amendment increasing the maximum number of shares authorized.

SHARK. A company that tries to takeover another company when it is vulnerable to such an act.

SHARK REPELLENT. Used to describe a company's actions when it changes its charter to make the company less attractive to a corporate raider.

SHARK WATCHER. A company that watches for early indications of a takeover attempt, identifies the raider, then solicits proxies of any client company that probably will become a target.

SHAVE. An extra charge added to a security purchase when the buyer wants to extend the delivery time.

SHEARED. An unsuccessful broker or dealer.

SHELF DISTRIBUTION. A company officer's right to sell a large number of shares from his or her portfolio within nine months after their effective date.

SHELF REGISTRATION. A Securities and Exchange Commission registration that carries the right for a security to be sold at some unspecified future date.

SHELL COMPANY. An issuing company that has no assets and no operations. While the company is not necessarily a cover for fraud, its securities are high risk.

SHERMAN ANTI-TRUST ACT. Passed in 1890, this law was designed to curtail monopolies and cartels and their growing influence on the nation's economy by limiting and restricting those businesses that dominate a specific industry. Such domination allows the companies to manipulate prices.

SHIBOSAI. A private, Japanese placement market.

SHINGLE THEORY. A broker's responsibility to treat clients fairly and equally when he or she advertises, or "hangs out a shingle," to do business publicly.

SHOGUN SECURITY. A U.S. corporation-issued, dollar-denominated security distributed in Japan.

SHOP. A broker-dealer's office, or the production area of a company.

SHORT AGAINST THE BOX. Occurs when an investor sells the same number of securities short that he or she owns.

SHORT BOND. Either a bond that once had a long maturity but that now is nearing that maturity date, or any bond that has been sold short.

SHORT CALL. A call option sold on an opening sale transaction.

SHORT COUPON. A newly issued bond with a first coupon due in less than six months.

SHORT COVERING. Occurs when an investor buys securities or commodities to close a short position or to return a security that previously was borrowed.

SHORTCUT FORECLOSURE. A mortgage clause that allows the lender to sell the property if the borrower defaults.

SHORT DATES. Any date falling within the next month.

SHORT EXEMPT. A short-sale order that does not require the sale to be made on an uptick, such as one that is part of an arbitrage transaction.

SHORT FUNDED. Occurs when an investor buys short-term money at a high interest rate because he or she believes interest rates will soon fall, making it cheaper to obtain lendable funds.

SHORT HEDGE. A method of reducing the risk of a security's falling value without requiring ownership of that security, such as buying a put option or selling short against the box.

SHORT INTEREST. The total number of shares investors have sold short but have not yet bought back.

SHORT INTEREST RATIO. The average daily trading volume for a specific time period divided into the total number of shares an investor has sold short.

SHORT INTEREST THEORY. Predicts an upward price movement when short interest is 1.5 to 2 times higher than the security's average daily volume.

SHORT LEG. A short option that is part of a spread position.

SHORT MARKET VALUE. The current market value of securities sold short.

SHORT OF THE MARKET. Occurs when an investor holds a short position in a security because he or she believes the security's price will drop.

SHORT POSITION. An investor's situation after shorting a security, option, or futures contract.

SHORT PURCHASE. Occurs when an investor buys stock to cover a previous short sale in the same security.

SHORT PUT. A put option sold on an opening sale transaction.

SHORTS. A British, gilt-edged security that matures in less than five years.

SHORT SALE. The sale of a security that the seller does not own, based on the belief that the seller will be able to buy it back at a lower price, thus profiting from the difference. Short sales can be executed only through a brokerage margin account, with the brokerage firm loaning the seller the security so he or she can deliver it to the buyer.

SHORT SALE RULE. A Securities and Exchange Commission regulation that all short sales must be on a zero-plus tick or on an uptick.

SHORT SQUEEZE. A situation in which the price of a security or futures contract moves up sharply, forcing traders with short positions to buy back the position in order to cover and prevent losses.

SHORT SWING. Occurs when a company's directors, officers, stockholders, or others with access to inside information transact a profitable deal by buying and then selling back the company's securities within six months, or selling the securities and then buying them back within six months. Such transactions normally are prohibited, and the company often can recover any profits, because U.S. securities laws assume the directors, officers, or stockholders acted on inside information, which is illegal.

SHORT TENDER. An illegal practice in which a person accepts a tender offer by delivering borrowed securities. According to the Securities and Exchange Commission, only long securities can be included in a tender offer.

SHORT TERM. For purposes of capital gains tax, an investment of one year or less.

SHORT-TERM AUCTION RATE (STAR). This is a money market, cumulative preferred stock with a dividend rate that a Dutch auction adjusts every 49 days. If a holder is unhappy with the new dividend, he or she can redeem the stock at any of the seven yearly auctions.

SHORT-TERM CAPITAL GAIN. The profit from an investment held for one year or less.

SHORT-TERM CAPITAL LOSS. The loss from an investment held for one year or less.

SHORT-TERM DEBT. A bond or other debt instrument that will mature within the next five years.

SHORT-TERM INDEXED LIABILITY TRANSACTIONS (STILTS). This is a debt that the issuer can convert into commercial paper at a specific interest spread for a series of short-term rollover periods.

SHORT-TERM INVESTMENT FUND (STIF). This is a pool of money invested in money markets that matures in less than 90 days.

SHORT-TERM NOTE ISSUANCE FACILITY. Since replaced by the revolving underwriting facilities, this once represented the placing of one- to five-year Eurodebt securities.

SHORT-TERM SAVINGS ACCOUNT. An account the depositor closes within two years of the date he or she opened it.

SHORT-TERM SECURITY. A security that is payable on demand and that matures in a year or less.

SHORT-TERM TRADING. Holding an investment for a brief period of time with the hopes of making a quick profit.

SHORT-TERM TRADING INDEX (TRIN). To determine a stock exchange's intraday market movements, divide the advance-decline volume ratio into the advance-decline ratio. The New York and American stock exchanges calculate the short-term trading once every minute. The TRIN measuring less than 1.0 is bullish while a higher number is bearish.

SHOW STOPPER. A legal maneuver a company takes to fend off a takeover attempt. A company will convince government officials to pass certain laws that would make a takeover impossible.

SHRINKS. Common stock purchases.

SHUT-OFF RATE. A high mortgage rate established to discourage potential home buyers.

SICK MARKET. A weak market.

SIDE-BY-SIDE TRADING. Occurs when an investor simultaneously trades a security and an option on that security on the same exchange.

SIDE COLLATERAL. Collateral that is too small to cover the total loan amount.

SIDELINER. An investor who closes out his or her positions, then waits for a better time to get in the market.

SIDEWAYS MARKET. Occurs when market prices remain relatively stable, not moving up or down to any great degree.

SIGHT DRAFT. A negotiable instrument similar to a check used to immediately transfer money from a buyer to a seller. Aside from the buyer's signature, the draft includes the paying agent's name.

SIGNAL. A gauge that indicates when a price is expected to rise or fall, thus giving an investor a way of knowing when to buy or sell a particular security.

SIGNATURE AUTHORITY. Occurs when one person gives another person permission to trade for the first person's account.

SILENT PARTNER. A limited partner who does not vote on management aspects.

SILENT SALES. An illegal procedure through which a homeowner secretly sells his or her home without notifying the local government or the original mortgagor of the ownership transfer. This type of sale sometimes occurs because the buyer refuses to pay a new mortgage rate or is unable to obtain a mortgage.

SILVER THURSDAY. Occurred on March 27, 1980, when the Hunt brothers failed to meet a margin call for $100 million in silver futures contracts, which had disastrous effects on the commodities and financial markets. The brokers' brokerage firm later covered the call, but the damage had already been done.

SIMPLE ARBITRAGE. Arbitrage that an investor can achieve by using three markets.

SIMPLE INTEREST. Interest that is based on the original principal amount instead of compounding.

SIMPLE MAJORITY. Occurs when the owners of at least 50 percent of a company's outstanding shares agree to vote together on a corporate matter.

SIMPLIFIED EMPLOYEE PENSION PLAN (SEP). A plan in which a company contributes vested, tax-sheltered funds on behalf of employees who are at least 25 years or older and who have worked for the company for at least three years. The contribution amounts usually are based on company profits, so the plan becomes a pension-profit-sharing plan combination.

SINGLE CAPITAL STRUCTURE COMPANY. A company that has issued only one class of securities.

SINGLE DEBT. An accounting method in which the lender records installment payments as a lump sum.

SINGLE LIABILITY. When a person is responsible for a company's liabilities, but only for the percentage he or she originally invested.

SINGLE OPTION. Used to differentiate between a put and a call option, or between a spread and a straddle.

SINGLE PREMIUM DEFERRED ANNUITY (SPDA). A tax-deferred investment in which a person makes a lump-sum payment to an insurance company or to a mutual fund selling the annuity, with the annuity depreciating over the years. Such annuities have no ceiling on the amount a person can contribute.

SINGLE-PURCHASE CONTRACT. An annuity in which the investor can make lump-sum purchases and can receive immediate or future payments.

SINGLE-STATE MUNICIPAL BOND FUND. A mutual fund with investments concentrated in obligations from governments within one state.

SINKER. A bond that carries a sinking fund stipulation.

SINKING FUND. A fund that a company sets aside each year to retire outstanding bonds or preferred stock.

SINKING FUND BOND. A bond issued with the stipulation that the issuer has, indeed, set up a fund through which the bond can be redeemed.

SINKING FUND REQUIREMENTS. The amount that a sinking fund must regularly increase so the fund will have enough money to redeem the bonds at maturity.

SIPC. *See* Securities Investor Protection Corporation.

SITES. A British purchase in which the item is in a sealed container, so the buyer will not know what he or she is getting until after buying the item.

SIZE. The number of stock shares available at the bid and ask prices.

SIZED OUT. Occurs when a broker cannot cross stock at a block trader's price because another broker is offering a larger number of shares at the trader's price, which makes the other broker's offer more attractive.

SIZE OF THE MARKET. The number of round lots that are bid on at the specialist's highest book price, and the number that simultaneously is being offered at the specialist's lowest book price.

SKIMMING PRICES. A high initial price followed by several price drops. Skimming allows the seller to attract as many buyers as possible at the highest price before dropping the price some more, which attracts more buyers at that next level.

SKIP-DAY SETTLEMENT. Occurs when a security is to be paid for and delivered on the second day after the transaction date.

SKIP-PAYMENT PRIVILEGE. An installment mortgage stipulation in which a borrower can skip a payment if previous payments have been made ahead of schedule.

SLAP. *See* Self-Liquidating Asset Purchase.

SLD LAST SALE. Appears on an exchange's consolidated tape to indicate "sold last sale" when a great change has occurred between transactions in a securities issue, with the change usually consisting of one or two points, depending on the issue's price.

SLEEPER. An underpriced stock that unexpectedly rose sharply in price.

SLEEPING BEAUTY. A takeover target that the raider has not yet approached.

SLIDE. Occurs when a bookkeeper mistakenly moves the decimal point on a figure when recording the figure on the company's books.

SLMA. *See* Student Loan Marketing Association.

SLOW MARKET. A market with little trading activity.

SLUGS. Nonmarketable U.S. Treasury securities sold to states and municipalities, which deposit the securities into escrow accounts until they need them to pay off their own bonds upon maturity.

SLUMP. A temporary, but steady, decline in market prices.

SMA. *See* Special Miscellaneous Account.

SMALL BUSINESS ADMINISTRATION (SBA). A government agency that provides management advice and government-guaranteed loans to small businesses. SBA securities are exempt from state and local taxes, but not from federal taxes.

SMALL BUSINESS ADMINISTRATION LOAN. Commonly referred to as a Sammie Bee, this is an SBA loan with a unit trust certificate as collateral. A commercial bank will combine these loans into $1 million to $25 million, SBA-backed pools and then will sell the pools to institutional investors.

SMALL BUSINESS INVESTMENT COMPANY. A federal agency that, under the auspices of the Small Business Administration, loans money to small businesses.

SMALL CAP. A company with a small amount of capitalization.

SMALL INVESTOR. As opposed to an institutional investor, this individual usually buys stock shares in small, odd-lot quantities.

SMALL ORDER EXECUTION SYSTEM. A National Association of Securities Dealers program through which over-the-counter deals involving not more than 1,000 shares of a qualified issue can be matched immediately to the best available price.

SMALL SAVER CERTIFICATE. A savings account in which the money must remain deposited for at least 30 months, but deposits need not be any larger than $100, with interest rates tied to U.S. Treasury security yields.

SMART MONEY. A wise investor who has more knowledge and experience in the market than the average investor.

SMASH. A dramatic drop in market prices.

SNAKE. A European agreement to let a nation's currencies flow freely in the open market, with a charting of the configuration resembling a snake, unless certain conditions or measures are exceeded.

SNOWBALLING. Occurs when a stop order is executed and causes the market to drop or increase even more, depending on whether the market had been going up or down. When the market reacts, even more stop orders are executed.

SOCIAL CONSCIOUSNESS MUTUAL FUND. A mutual fund with investments directed to bring capital appreciation and with the investments made in companies that meet certain social criteria. For example, such a fund would not have investments in South Africa because of apartheid.

SOCIALISM. A system of government in which the government controls all production, utilities, manufacturing, etc., and in turn pays for its citizens' medical care and equally provides income to workers.

SOCIALLY RESPONSIBLE INVESTMENT. An investment that carries a lower rate of return, but that provides society with many benefits. For example, a socially responsible investment would describe an investment made in a company that provided many jobs for the area.

SOCIETY FOR WORLDWIDE INTERBANK FINANCIAL TELECOMMUNI-CATIONS (SWIFT). A computer network for transferring financial data and foreign currencies.

SOFT ARBITRAGE. An arbitrage achieved between the public sector and private paper.

SOFT CURRENCY. A nation's currency that cannot be exchanged for another country's hard currencies because the first is fixed at an unrealistic exchange rate and is not backed by gold. The Soviet Union's ruble, for example, is soft currency.

SOFT DOLLARS. Research and brokerage services, instead of hard dollars, are used to pay for underwriting credits and portfolio transaction commissions.

SOFT LANDING. Occurs when inflation ends without resulting in a depression.

SOFT MARKET. A relatively inactive market with little demand and in which a small amount of selling pressure will drive prices down.

SOFT SPOT. Securities that are weak when the rest of the market is strong and on the upswing.

SOLD-OUT MARKET. A commodity futures contract that is not available because offerings are limited or because of contract liquidations.

SOLD TO YOU. One trader's reconfirmation to another that an offer was accepted.

SOLE PROPRIETORSHIP. A business owned by one person, who carries all liabilities and receives all profits.

SOLVENCY. A company's ability to meet its financial obligations.

SOLVENT DEBTOR SECTION. A federal law that requires a company to buy back its own bonds at a discount to pay income tax on the difference between the bond's original sale price or its face value and the discount repurchase price.

SOPHISTICATED INVESTOR. A wealthy investor who studies market movements and, based on experience and knowledge, invests large sums of money.

SOURCE AND APPLICATIONS OF FUNDS STATEMENT. The comparison of a company's financial situations in two or more different accounting periods.

SOVEREIGN RISK. A person's risk involved in foreign investments because of currency value changes or because of government instability.

SPACE ARBITRAGE. Simultaneously selling and buying the same security on two different exchanges to take advantage of price differences.

SPDA. *See* Single Premium Deferred Annuity.

SPECIAL ARBITRAGE ACCOUNT. A margin account in which a customer receives advantageous credit terms when he or she simultaneously buys a security and sells it in a different market, or simultaneously buys one security and sells an equal one in the same market to profit from any price differences.

SPECIAL ASSESSMENT BOND. A municipal bond issued to pay for a civic project, such as a sewer or a road improvement, with those who benefit from the project assessed a special tax.

SPECIAL BID. A fixed bid for a block of stock in which the buyer pays for all transaction costs.

SPECIAL BOND ACCOUNT. A brokerage account used to show the firm's purchasing power from bonds that were bought on margin.

SPECIAL CASH ACCOUNT. A margin account in which a customer can buy or sell any security long, with all securities delivered within seven days.

SPECIAL CLAIM ON RESIDUAL EQUITY (SCORE). One of two component parts of an Americus Trust for which holders receive no dividends, but do receive the trust's asset value up to an agreed upon per-share dollar value. The other component is the Prescribed Right To Income and Maximum Equity, better known as PRIME.

SPECIAL COMMODITY ACCOUNT. A brokerage account through which a customer can buy and sell commodities and commodity futures contracts.

SPECIAL CONVERTIBLE DEBT SECURITY ACCOUNT. A margin account in which the customer can finance a short sale of a bond that can be converted into margin stock or that carries a subscription warrant to margin stock.

SPECIAL DEAL. Occurs when the underwriter of investment company securities pays another dealer's employee in connection with the sale. The National Association of Securities Dealers prohibits this practice.

SPECIAL DEPOSITORY. Any bank that the U.S. Treasury allows to receive deposits from the sale of government bonds.

SPECIAL DEVISE. A gift of property.

SPECIAL DRAWING RIGHTS. An International Monetary Fund credit against which specific nations can draw to pay off their payment deficits.

SPECIAL INSURANCE PREMIUM FUNDING ACCOUNT. A brokerage account through which the customer can buy a life insurance policy, with the equity placed in shares of a registered investment company or trust bought along with the policy.

SPECIAL ISSUES. U.S. Treasury securities for investing in government trust fund reserves.

SPECIALIST. An exchange member whose job is to maintain an orderly market in a specific group of securities by buying and selling for his or her own account and for clients.

SPECIALIST BLOCK PURCHASE. Occurs when a specialist buys a large block of stock for his or her own account.

SPECIALIST BLOCK SALE. Occurs when a specialist sells a large block of stock for his or her own account.

SPECIALIST MANAGER. An investment manager who researches and handles only one class of investments.

SPECIALIST MARKET. A market where investment information can be obtained only through a dealer.

SPECIALIST PERFORMANCE EVALUATION QUESTIONNAIRE. A series of questions the New York Stock Exchange has floor brokers answer concerning specialists and their performances. The questionnaire is used to screen specialists.

SPECIALIST'S ACCOUNT. A brokerage account through which exchange specialists and market makers who deal in listed options can take advantage of credit to pay for their dealer inventories.

SPECIALIST'S BOOK. The book a specialist uses to keep track of all limit, stop, and market orders for which he or she is responsible.

SPECIALIST'S SHORT-SALE RATIO. A comparison of the amount of stock a

New York Stock Exchange specialist sold short to the total number of short sales. The ratio provides a gauge of how the specialists perceive the market and whether they believe the market will be moving up or down.

SPECIALIST UNIT. A group of at least three specialists responsible for maintaining an orderly market in specific stocks.

SPECIALIZED MUTUAL FUND. A mutual fund with investments concentrated in a specific industry.

SPECIAL LOAN. A loan with unusual collateral and normally carrying a higher interest rate.

SPECIAL MISCELLANEOUS ACCOUNT (SMA). A special brokerage account that shows how much unpledged money a customer has available in his or her margin account.

SPECIAL OFFERING. An issuing company's secondary distribution that has been registered in detail with the Securities and Exchange Commission.

SPECIAL OMNIBUS ACCOUNT. A broker-dealer account in which a second broker-dealer who is registered with the Securities and Exchange Commission can transact for the customers without giving those customers' names.

SPECIAL OPTION. An over-the-counter option that still is effective and that a broker-dealer or a customer in the secondary market offers to resell.

SPECIAL PARTNER. A business partner who does not actively participate in the company's management, and who is responsible for the company's liabilities only up to the percentage of investment that he or she originally made.

SPECIAL SECURITY. A Federal National Mortgage Association security that a bank has purchased with deposits from a tax-exempt savings certificate.

SPECIAL SITUATION. Occurs when a security will earn higher-than-average profits because of a unique and unexpected event involving the security itself or the issuing company.

SPECIAL SUBSCRIPTION ACCOUNT. A margin account through which a client can receive credits to buy a margin security by exercising a right or warrant.

SPECIAL TAX BOND. A municipal revenue bond with a luxury tax, such as one on liquor, which pays for the debt service.

SPECIFIC RISK. A risk that involves the issuing company *only*—not other securities from other issuers and not securities from other companies in the same industry.

SPECTAIL DEALER. A broker-dealer who spends more time taking speculative positions in his or her own account than he or she does on retail customers.

SPECULATION. The risk that an investment will, indeed, bring higher profits.

SPECULATION INDICATOR. A gauge to determine how much risk investors are willing to take by putting money into a speculative security.

SPECULATIVE. An unproven, high-risk investment.

SPECULATIVE POSITION. An open, unhedged position.

SPECULATOR. A person who will invest in high-risk securities because he or she believes they will bring higher returns.

SPIKE. A quick, dramatic price increase.

SPIN OFF. A dividend made up of assets, such as another company's stock, that is distributed to stockholders. Also, a company divestiture resulting in the transfer of assets or an entire subsidiary.

SPLIT. Occurs when stock shares are divided into a larger or smaller number of stock shares. For example, the issuing company will issue two stocks for every one turned in, which would cut the stock's par value in half.

SPLIT CLOSE. Occurs when one closing index average is higher, while another closing index average is lower on the same day.

SPLIT COMMISSION. A transaction commission that is divided between the executing broker and the person who brought the deal to the broker's attention.

SPLIT DOWN. A company charter amendment that diminishes the number of issued shares while proportionately pushing up the issue's par value.

SPLIT FUNDS. A British mutual fund with two classes of security shares: capital shares and income shares.

SPLIT INVESTMENT COMPANY. A closed-end investment company that issues two different capital stock issues, one paying investment dividends and the other paying dividends from investment appreciation.

SPLIT OFF. Occurs when a stockholder trades in shares of a controlling company for shares of a subsidiary.

SPLIT OFFERING. Occurs when a bond issue consists of both serial maturities and term maturities.

SPLIT OPENING. Occurs when a security opens at two different prices, usually because traders simultaneously but separately entered their first quotes on the same security.

SPLIT ORDER. A large securities transaction that is broken into several smaller transactions to avoid causing market fluctuations in the security's price.

SPLIT RATING. Occurs when two bond rating services give the same issue two different ratings.

SPLIT-SCHEDULE LOAN. A mortgage with an interest rate that lasts only a few years, after which it is amortized according to a schedule.

SPLIT UP. *See* Split.

SPONSOR. A person who acts as an officer or board director of an unincorporated company.

SPONSORSHIP. Occurs when several professional investors, such as broker-dealers, actively support a particular security.

SPOT. Available for immediate delivery.

SPOT COMMODITY. A commodity that will be delivered upon settlement, as opposed to the delivery of a futures contract.

SPOT DELIVERY MONTH. The nearest month a commodity can be delivered.

SPOT EXCHANGE RATE. The amount of one country's currency needed to buy a unit of another country's currency, with the purchase requiring immediate delivery.

SPOT LOAN. As opposed to a housing development mortgage, this is a single mortgage made on a single-family home.

SPOT MARKET. Either a commodity transaction in which the commodity will be delivered immediately or in which a futures contract will expire in one month or less.

SPOT MONTH. The month in which a formerly traded commodity is to be delivered.

SPOT NEWS. A sudden news report that could temporarily affect market prices.

SPOT PRICE. The price quoted for a cash commodity.

SPOT SALE. The purchase of an item to be delivered immediately.

SPOT SECONDARY. A secondary offering made without a registration statement.

SPOTTED MARKET. A market with small up and down price movements, but showing no major trends.

SPOUSAL INDIVIDUAL RETIREMENT ACCOUNT. An IRA opened in the name of a spouse who is not employed outside of the home, with the employed spouse making the contributions. The maximum annual amount that can be contributed for both spouses is $2,250. If both spouses worked, $2,000 could be contributed for each for a total of $4,000.

SPOUSAL REMAINDER TRUST. A method in which income-earning assets are transferred to a person who is taxed at a lower rate, such as a child. Income from the trust is distributed to the beneficiary for costs such as paying for his or her college education.

SPREAD. The difference between the bid price and the ask price.

SPREAD BANKER. A commercial banker who matches the maturities of the loans he or she has taken out to the maturities of loans he or she has extended in an effort to profit from the interest rate differences.

SPREADING. Buying and selling option contracts of the same class on the same underlying security to profit from price differences.

SPREAD LOAD. A mutual fund in which the sales charge principal is paid during the contract's first four years, with the rest paid in equal payments throughout the contract's life.

SPREAD LOAN. A mutual fund with the principal part of the sales charge paid in the first four years, with the rest paid in equal installments for the life of the contract.

SPREAD OPTION. Occurs when an investor buys and sells option contracts of the same class on the same underlying security with one or more of the terms in each being different.

SPREAD ORDER. An order for a listed option that the investor plans to use in a spread strategy.

SPREAD POSITION. A client account with long and short options on the same underlying security and of the same class.

SPREAD SHEET. The ledger sheet of a company's financial statement, with all income and expenses laid out in columns and rows.

SPREAD SWAP. An illegal practice in which an underwriter agrees to buy an investor's securities in exchange for the investor buying the new issue, with the price set before the registration statement is effective.

SQUAWK BOX. A telephone system broker-dealers use to communicate with the firm's different branches, departments, and offices.

SQUEEZE. Occurs when securities or commodities futures begin increasing in price and investors who sold them short must cover their short positions to avoid major losses, thus driving up the prices even more.

STABILIZATION. A lateral price movement usually preceding a change in price direction.

STABILIZING BID. The bid price that an underwriter will offer immediately after a new security is issued to maintain the security's market level.

STAG. A person in Great Britain who buys a new securities issue with the intention of selling it immediately at a premium.

STAGFLATION. A period of inflation and stagnation.

STAGGERED BOARD. A company's board of directors with terms that are offset so stockholders do not vote for all board members at the same time. For example, if terms run three years and the board has 12 members, four new members are elected each year. A staggered board often will discourage a corporate raider because the raider could not takeover the entire board all at once.

STAGGERING MATURITIES. A method that bond investors use to reduce risk through buying short-, medium- and long-term bonds. If interest rates go up, the short-term bonds will hold their value better, and if interest rates drop, the long-term bonds will increase faster in value.

STAGNATION. Occurs when a country's economy slows substantially.

STAGS. *See* Sterling Transferable Accruing Government Securities.

STAKE-OUT INVESTMENT. Occurs when one holding company buys another holding company's nonvoting, convertible preferred stock with the hope that banking laws will change to allow some interstate banking, after which the first company will have a claim on the second company.

STAMPED SECURITY. A security certificate that has been stamped to indicate it has been altered since it was originally issued.

STANDARD AND POOR'S. An investment service that rates securities.

STANDARD AND POOR'S INDEX. As a market performance gauge, this index checks the movement of 500 of the most commonly held stocks and generalizes the findings to predict the potential movements of other securities and market volatility.

STANDARD AND POOR'S INDEXES. An average of securities traded on the New York Stock Exchange as determined by multiplying the price of each issue by the number of outstanding shares.

STANDARD AND POOR'S RATING. A rating of stocks and bonds of risk with AAA, AA, A, and BBB considered investment grade, indicating minimal risk.

STANDARD COST. Normal production costs that include no unforeseen conditions. A company can determine its cost efficiency by calculating the difference between standard costs and actual costs.

STANDARD DEDUCTION. The amount of money a taxpayer can deduct from his or her annual income on their tax forms without itemizing.

STANDARD DEVIATION. A measure of the degree to which an individual probability value varies from the distribution mean. The higher the number, the greater the risk.

STANDARD INDUSTRIAL CLASSIFICATION SYSTEM. A numbering system used to identify companies and to provide information about that company. The numbers indicate the business's industry and is used by analysts and researchers.

STANDARDIZED EXPIRATION DATES. The Options Clearing Corporation has three fixed expiration dates for its options; each period runs for three months.

STANDARD STOCKS. Stock from an established, well-run companies.

STANDBY COMMITMENT. A contract between a company and a banking group in which the banking group agrees to buy a portion of a securities issue offered in a rights offering after the current shareholders fail to buy all that was offered during the prescribed period.

STANDBY FEE. The commission an underwriter receives when he or she agrees to buy any stock shares left after current stockholders have exercised their rights offering.

STANDBY UNDERWRITING. Occurs when a company that is issuing rights hires an investment banker to stand by to buy the remaining shares and to take over the rights that investors do not exercise.

STANDSTILL. A contract between a securities issuer and the owner of a large block of the securities in which the holder agrees not to buy any more shares or sell the shares he or she owns without the issuer's permission.

STAR. *See* Short-Term Auction Rate.

STARTUP. The point of a new business venture when an investor will provide the beginning company with venture capital.

STATE BANK. A bank that falls under a state's regulations, as opposed to a national bank, which falls under the auspices of the federal government.

STATED CAPITAL. The amount of money that stockholders contribute to the company.

STATED PERCENTAGE ORDER. An order to buy a block of stock large enough to represent a specific percentage of the security's market volume.

STATED VALUE. As opposed to a market value or par value, this is a per-share value a security carries only for accounting purposes.

STATEMENT. A summary of charges, expenses, and purchases, as well as a description of financial condition.

STATEMENT ANALYSIS. An analyst studies a company's accounting statements and analyzes such ratios as turnover and current, then determines the company's future financial potential.

STATEMENT OF CHANGES IN FINANCIAL POSITION. The part in a company's annual report that shows changes in the company's working capital.

STATEMENT OF CONDITION. A summary of the status of a company's assets, liabilities, and equity.

STATEMENT OF POLICY. Securities and Exchange Commission standards governing investment companies and covering such issues as disclosure, commissions, and management approaches.

STATEMENT SAVINGS ACCOUNT. A savings account in which the depositor keeps his or her own records, tracking deposits and withdrawals. The financial institution, in turn, sends the depositor regular statements summarizing the account, against which the depositor can check his or her own records. Also called a No Passbook Account.

STATION. The stock exchange area where a specialist completes transactions.

STATUTE OF LIMITATIONS. U.S. securities laws prohibit civil actions on most securities matters after three years.

STATUTORY INVESTMENT. A state-approved investment through which a trustee can administer a trust.

STATUTORY MERGER. Occurs when two companies merge into one, with one of the companies maintaining its identity.

STATUTORY UNDERWRITER. A person who inadvertently performs underwriting functions and therefore subjects himself or herself to Securities and Exchange Commission regulations regarding the sale of unregistered securities.

STATUTORY VOTING. Occurs when each stockholder gets one vote for each share he or she owns for each board director to be elected.

STAYING POWER. An investor's financial ability to hold on to an investment that has dropped in value.

STEADY. A market that is not moving up or down much.

STEENTH. Designates a bid that is quoted in 16ths.

STEPPED COSTS. Costs that incrementally climb as volume increases.

STEPPED COUPON SECURITIES. A bond series with all issues paying the same interest rate each year, but with that rate increasing periodically.

STERILE INVESTMENT. An investment in a precious metal (e.g., silver or gold) that does not pay any dividends.

STERLING SECURITY. Either a bond denominated in British sterling pounds, or a corporate bond issued in Great Britain.

STERLING TRANSFERABLE ACCRUING GOVERNMENT SECURITIES (STAGS). This is a British, zero-coupon bond based on British Treasury bonds.

STICKY DEAL. An underwriting issue that probably will be hard to market.

STICKY PRICES. Prices that are not subject to major price fluctuations either up or down.

STIF. *See* Short-Term Investment Fund.

STILTS. *See* Short-Term Indexed Liability Transactions.

STOCK. A unit of company ownership.

STOCK AHEAD. Occurs when one investor's orders were put in before another investor's orders on the exchange floor, so the price could change before the later investor's order comes up for execution.

STOCK ALLOTMENT. The number of shares an underwriting manager sets aside for each syndicate member to distribute.

STOCK APPRECIATION RIGHTS. A security provision granting special financial benefits to the officers of a publicly owned company based on the number of shares that are granted to his or her company account, with the profit coming from the difference between price changes between the day the right was granted and the day it was exercised.

STOCK ASSESSMENT. The amount of money a stockholder must pay to make up for negative developments in the issuing company's activities.

STOCK ASSOCIATION. A capital stock corporation in which investors sink operating capital by buying ownership interest in stock.

STOCK-BONUS TRUST. A program through which a company gives employees stock shares to reward them for high productivity.

STOCKBROKER. A person registered to trade securities for customers.

STOCK BUSINESS. Describes a dealer who buys a portion of a new municipal bond issue for his or her own account in hopes of making a quick profit by reselling the bonds.

STOCK CERTIFICATE. A document that verifies stock ownership and details such information as the security's par value, the number of shares involved, the issuing company's name and the owner's name.

STOCK CLEARING CORPORATION. A company that handles the delivery of securities and payments between exchange members.

STOCK COMPANY. A company with stockholders providing all of the operating capital, paying all losses, and sharing all profits.

STOCK DISCOUNT. The amount a stock's par value exceeds its paid-in capital.

STOCK DIVIDEND. A portion of a company's retained earnings that are distributed to stockholders, with the amount dependent on the number of shares the stockholder owns.

STOCK EXCHANGE. An institution wherein members can trade stocks, bonds, and other financial instruments.

STOCK EXCHANGE AUTOMATED QUOTATIONS. Similar to the National Association of Securities Dealers Automated Quotations, this British system allows market makers to quote prices on 3,500 actively and inactively traded British and international securities.

STOCKHOLDER. A person who has ownership units in a publicly held company.

STOCKHOLDER OF RECORD. The stockholder whose name is registered with the issuing company or with the transfer agent and who is entitled to dividend payments.

STOCKHOLDER'S EQUITY. A company's net worth, which is its liabilities subtracted from the value of its assets.

STOCK INDEX. A measure in value changes among a group of similar securities, with the gauge used to predict possible future movements. A group of similar securities are measured to determine differences and trends.

STOCK INDEX FUTURE. A futures contract that uses a stock index as its base.

STOCK INDEX OPTION. A put or call option with any profit or loss settled in cash.

STOCK JOBBER. A British commission broker.

STOCK JOBBING. Price manipulation.

STOCK LIST. A registered exchange's investigation into a company that wants to list its securities on that exchange or wants its securities approved for unlisted trading.

STOCK LOAN BUSINESS. A brokerage firm branch designated for earning profits from lending securities.

STOCK MARKET. The organized trading of securities on one of the many exchanges.

STOCK OPTION. The privilege an issuing company gives to people to buy a specific number of shares within a particular time period and for a price below the market value.

STOCK POWER. A document that gives one party permission to transfer stock ownership into another person's name.

STOCK PURCHASE PLAN. A company program that allows employees to regularly buy company stock, often at a reduced price or with reduced commission fees.

STOCK PURCHASE TRUST. A program through which the surviving stockholder of a closed company can buy a deceased stockholder's shares.

STOCK RATINGS. A judgment of the issuing company's financial strength and management ability, with high ratings given to stocks that probably will increase in value.

STOCK RECORD. A brokerage firm department responsible for handling and following all of the firm's securities, identifying their owners, and keeping track of the securities' locations daily.

STOCK REGISTRAR. A fiduciary who certifies that a company has not issued more shares than are allowed in the company's charter.

STOCK RIGHTS. A stockholder's right to buy shares of the company's new issue at a predetermined price. The number of shares the stockholder can buy is set according to his or her current holdings.

STOCK TABLES. A newspaper listing of market information, such as stock opening and closing prices, trading volumes and price/earnings ratios.

STOCK TICKER. An old device that printed trading information on a narrow ticker tape.

STOCK WATCHER. A New York Stock Exchange computer network used to follow the movements and transactions of NYSE-listed securities.

STOCK YIELD. A security's rate of return, as determined by its market value and dividend payments.

STOP. The lowest rate the central bank will charge dealers who trade their government securities in for cash.

STOP-LIMIT ORDER. A request to buy or sell a security, directing the broker to make the order a limit order as soon as the security's price hits a predetermined stop level.

STOP-LOSS ORDER. An investor's order to his or her broker to sell a security if its price drops to a specified level.

STOP ORDER. A request to buy or sell a security as soon as the security's price hits a specific level.

STOP-OUT PRICE. The lowest price that will be accepted at a Treasury auction.

STOP-OUT RATE. The lowest interest rate the Federal Reserve will allow a nonbank dealer to pay on a repurchase agreement.

STOP PAYMENT. Occurs when a check issuer asks the bank to refuse to honor the check. The issuer is usually charged a fee for this request.

STOPPED OUT. Occurs if an order is executed at the specialist's guaranteed price.

STOPPED STOCK. An order with a price that a specialist has guaranteed to the exchange member. The member then can seek a better price; if one is unavailable, he or she still can take advantage of the guaranteed price.

STORY. A scenario for buying a specific stock as described by an analyst. For example, the analyst may tell the potential investor about positive factors that are influencing the issuing company's management.

STRADDLE. Occurs when an investor buys a put option and a call option on the same underlying security with the same expiration price and maturity date.

STRAIGHT BOND. A bond that cannot be converted.

STRAIGHT INVESTMENT. An investment made because of its current value and income and not because of any expected increase.

STRAIGHT-LINE DEPRECIATION. A method in which the company's cost of a qualified asset can be apportioned in equal amounts over the length of the asset's life. To obtain the amount that can be depreciated, subtract the asset's salvage value at the end of its useful life from the asset's original cost.

STRAIGHT-LINE INTEREST. Annually computed interest payments based on a percentage of the unpaid balance.

STRAIGHT MORTGAGE. A mortgage on which the borrower must pay interest, with the full mortgage amount falling due at the end of the mortgage period.

STRANGLE. Selling an out of the money call and a put option with the same expiration date on the same underlying security. To profit, the investor would have to see minor volatility in the security's market.

STRAP OPTIONS. Occurs when an investor buys one put and two calls with the same series on the same underlying security.

STRATEGICS. A precious metal investment.

STREET. Nickname for Wall Street and any other area's major financial center.

STREET BROKER. Any over-the-counter broker who is not an exchange member.

STREET CERTIFICATE. A securities certificate with a blank endorsement by an owner with a guaranteed signature, which allows the security to be transferred without the transfer having to be recorded on the company's books.

STREET NAME. Describes securities that are being held in the name of a broker for a customer.

STREET PRICE. The price of a security that is involved in a transaction not connected to one of the exchanges.

STREET SIDE. The brokerage side of a broker-customer relationship.

STRETCHING THE PAYABLES. Occurs when accounts payable are deferred past the due date.

STRIKE FROM THE LIST. An exchange order to stop all transactions in a specific security.

STRIKESUIT. A minority stockholder's lawsuit designed to convince management to buy out his or her shares.

STRIKING PRICE. The exercise price, or the price at which an option holder can buy an asset.

STRINGENCY. Occurs when interest rates are rising and finding credit is difficult.

STRIP. An option strategy in which the investor buys one call and two puts on the same underlying security with the same exercise price and expiration date.

STRIPPED BOND. A bond which can be bought in either a principal only (PO) or interest only (IO) package.

STRIPPED TREASURY OBLIGATIONS. Zero-coupon Treasury bonds that mature in three months to 29 years and are backed by the full faith and credit of the U.S. government.

STRONG HANDS. A person who holds on to an investment for a long period of time, as opposed to a person who buys and sells quickly to make a fast profit.

STRONG MARKET. Occurs when demand exceeds supply.

STUDENT LOAN MARKETING ASSOCIATION (SLMA). A "Sallie Mae" security based on a pool of student loans, which financial institutions make to college students; guaranteed by the U.S. government's full faith and credit.

SUBCHAPTER M. An Internal Revenue Service regulation that gives investment companies special tax allowances when they distribute at least 90 percent of their income to stockholders.

SUBCHAPTER S CORPORATION. A small company taxed as a partnership and, as such, has some taxable income and liabilities falling on the shoulders of the individual officers' tax reports.

SUBJECT MARKET. A trader's quote that has yet to be confirmed and authorized by the trader's customer.

SUBJECT PRICE. A negotiated, estimated price that is subject to confirmation.

SUBJECT TO OPINION. An auditor's statement in an audit report stipulating that the results fairly represent the publicly owned company's financial status subject to some specific adjustments.

SUBJECT TO PRIOR SALE. When the market is strong, the supply of a security limited, and buy orders exceed the security's supply, bid orders often will be filed early so the investor will be able to obtain whatever amount of the limited security is available. Those investors filing their bids later will not be able to buy the security because none will be left.

SUBJECT TO REDEMPTION. Stocks that a company can call in without notifying the shareholders ahead of time.

SUBMISSION. A mortgage banker's offer to sell mortgage shares to an investor.

SUBMITTAL NOTICE. The notice a broker sends to a property owner when that property has been offered for sale. It includes the property's offering price and the potential buyer's name and address.

SUBMORTGAGE. Occurs when a mortgage lender pledges that mortgage as collateral for his or her own loan.

SUBORDINATED. A security with a lower priority than other securities when dividends and assets are distributed in liquidations or bankruptcies.

SUBORDINATED DEBENTURE. A high-risk debenture, the holder of which may receive lower payments than other creditors of the same issuer.

SUBORDINATED DEBT INSTRUMENT. A bond over which another bond has priority in case of liquidation or asset distribution.

SUBORDINATED EXCHANGEABLE VARIABLE-RATE NOTE. A note that allows a company to borrow at low, short-term interest rates and that guarantees the company access to capital for a longer time. The interest rate floats for five years, then is fixed for another five years, after which the company can exchange the notes for others with fixed interest rates.

SUBORDINATED INTEREST. A financial property interest that is inferior in claims to another financial interest in that same property.

SUBSCRIBER. An investor who promises to buy a specific number of shares of a newly issued security.

SUBSCRIPTION. An agreement to buy a certain number of shares of a newly issued security.

SUBSCRIPTION CAPITAL. The money an issuer receives from the public in a new securities offering.

SUBSCRIPTION CASH RECORD. A cash record of all a capital stock subscriber's payments, including the down payment.

SUBSCRIPTION LIST. A document a subscriber signs verifying the number of shares he or she has agreed to buy.

SUBSCRIPTION PRICE. The set, established price at which a new security is offered publicly for sale.

SUBSCRIPTION PRIVILEGE. The right that a stockholder has to buy a portion of the company's new offering in proportion to the number of shares he or she already holds.

SUBSCRIPTION RATIO. The number of subscription rights a stockholder needs to subscribe to one share or to a convertible bond.

SUBSCRIPTION RIGHT. A security that provides the number of rights a stockholder has when subscribing to either new shares or new convertibles. For example, a stockholder would receive one right for each share he or she owned.

SUBSCRIPTIONS RECEIVABLE. A company's account that indicates how much each capital-stock subscriber owes to the company for his or her shares.

SUBSCRIPTION WARRANT. A subscription right that is valid longer and therefore carries the probability it will be more profitable when exercised.

SUBSIDIARY. One company owned by and controlled by another company.

SUBSIDIARY COIN. A coin denominated in an amount less than a dollar, such as a U.S. quarter or dime.

SUBSTANTIVE. Describes the situation in which corporate activities will affect stockholders directly.

SUBSTITUTION. One security is sold and another purchased to replace it in order to take advantage of price differences while maintaining the same volume of ownership.

SUBSTITUTION OF COLLATERAL. Occurs when a borrower substitutes one collateral, such as property, for another collateral, such as securities.

SUITABILITY. Guidelines that brokers who deal in speculative securities must follow to make sure the investors actually can afford to assume such risks.

SUMMARY COMPLAINT PROCEEDINGS. A National Association of Securities Dealers code that says a person charged with NASD code violations may, in some cases, plead guilty to a minor infraction as long as the person pays a fine and promises not to appeal.

SUM-OF-THE-YEARS' DIGITS METHOD. An accelerated depreciation method that creates higher depreciation charges and higher tax savings in a fixed asset's earlier years. The method is based on an inverted scale for the total number of years in the asset's useful life.

SUNDRY ASSET. An asset that the company does not use in day-to-day production, but that it plans to hold on to for a long period of time. Undeveloped land, for example, would be considered a sundry asset.

SUNRISE INDUSTRIES. Growth industries that will be vital to the future economy, such as the electronics industry.

SUNSET PROVISION. A legal provision that indicates the law or provision will expire on a certain future date.

SUNSHINE LAW. A law that opens government meetings, including those of the Securities and Exchange Commission and the Commodities Futures Trading Commission, to the public.

SUPERBOWL THEORY. An investment strategy theory that predicts that when a member of the National Football League wins the Superbowl, the stock market will go up, and when a member of the American Football League wins, the stock market will drop.

SUPER DOT. An automated order processing and trade reporting system through which New York Stock Exchange members can quickly execute price orders.

SUPER MAJORITY. Occurs when at least 80 percent of a company's outstanding shares are voted for or against a company issue or a board member.

SUPER NOW ACCOUNT. A Negotiable Order of Withdrawal Account that pays money market rates and through which depositors who have at least a $2,500 balance are given unlimited checking account privileges.

SUPERPRIME INSTRUMENT. A nonrenewable, 10-day note that costs only slightly more than the amount a bank pays itself for funds.

SUPER RESTRICTED ACCOUNT. A defunct description of a brokerage account margined at less than 30 percent of the account securities' market value.

SUPERSEDED SURETY RIDER. A continuing coverage clause in a new fidelity bond that takes the place of another bond. The holder is protected against any losses from the preceding bond as long as the chain of riders remains unbroken.

SUPER SINKER BOND. A bond with a long-term coupon and a short-term maturity.

SUPER STOCK. A security that will multiply several times in value.

SUPER TRUST. A fund created to refunnel the union employee's benefit money to financing for construction projects.

SUPERVISORY ANALYST. An exchange member employee who, after passing a written examination, can authorize publicly distributed research reports.

SUPPLEMENTAL AGREEMENT. A contract that supersedes a previous contract, with the newer contract including additional provisions and elaborating clauses.

SUPPLY. The number of shares available publicly for sale.

SUPPLY AND DEMAND INDICATORS. A gauge that measures how much money is coming in and out of the market.

SUPPLY AREA. The place on a price chart that indicates the price's resistance level.

SUPPLY-SIDE ECONOMICS. An economic theory that says tax cuts will stimulate large private investments from wealthy business people, which, in turn, will benefit the economy as a whole.

SUPPORT. The price level that buyer demand is expected to keep a security's price from dropping below.

SUPPORTING. Occurs when an investor buys securities at prices that will keep the securities' values from dropping in an effort to discourage people from exercising their put options.

SUPPORTING ORDERS. Buy orders entered to support a security's price.

SUPPORTING SCHEDULES. A supplementary report of information added either to a company's balance sheet or to its profit and loss statement.

SUPPORTING THE MARKET. Occurs when a bid falls at or slightly below a security's prevailing market price. The bid is usually designed to balance the price and to encourage it to go up.

SUPPORT LEVEL. The price at which buyers have tended to purchase a security, thus overcoming the downward pressure from sellers.

SURCHARGE. One charge that is added on top of another charge.

SURETY. A security that protects the holder in case a party owing money to the issuer defaults or, for example, if a company officer embezzles money from the company.

SURPLUS EQUITY. The amount by which a margin account security's market value exceeds the amount needed to satisfy a margin requirement.

SURPLUS RESERVES. A company's financial reserve that is not available for paying dividends.

SURROGATE COURT CERTIFICATE. A probate court document that lists a trustee who is authorized to settle an estate.

SURTAX. The tax a company or individual must pay after attaining a certain income level.

SURVEILLANCE DEPARTMENT OF EXCHANGES. An exchange department that watches for unusual securities transactions that could indicate illegal activity is under way.

SUSHI BOND. A Japanese bond denominated in Eurodollars.

SUSPENSE ACCOUNT. A broker-dealer's account of security balance discrepancies.

SUSPENSION. Occurs when a brokerage employee is either permanently or temporarily stopped from working because he or she has violated securities regulations.

SUSPENSION OF TRADING. Occurs when an exchange temporarily halts trading in a particular security to stabilize the market.

SWAP. Occurs when a government agrees to borrow a foreign currency from the issuing country to pay for an intervention in the foreign exchange market. Also, the sale of one security to purchase another security with similar features.

SWAP FUND. A pooled investment portfolio fund with several investors, each sharing in a proportionate percentage of the earnings. The fund was designed to diversify the investors' holdings without them having to pay capital gains tax on stock sales.

SWAP RATE. The difference between the spot price of one nation's currency and the current futures trading prices.

SWEEP ACCOUNT. A central assets account that allows an investor to transfer cash into an interest-bearing account such as a money-market mutual fund.

SWEETENER. An additional value included with a proposal to make the deal more attractive.

SWEETENING A LOAN. Occurs when an investor deposits additional securities to margin a loan after the existing securities have dropped in value. Sweetening a loan is done either to maintain the margin level or to improve its condition.

SWIFT. *See* Society for Worldwide Interbank Financial Telecommunications.

SWIMMING MARKET. A strong, active securities market.

SWING. A price movement, usually in the opposite direction of the previous movement.

SWINGER. A financial manager who handles a heavy volume of business.

SWING LINE. A bank line of credit through which a customer can borrow a predetermined amount of money each day.

SWISS FRANC. Switzerland's primary monetary unit.

SWISS FRANC NOTE. A Eurodebt denominated in Swiss francs with a maturity of five to 10 years.

SWITCHING. Selling some securities from a portfolio and replacing them with different securities.

SWITCH ORDER. An investor's request to simultaneously buy one stock and sell another because of beneficial price differences.

SYMBOL. An acronym used to identify securities that are traded on a ticker tape or exchange, or are listed in newspapers.

SYNCHROVEST. An investment in which the investor buys varying amounts of a stock or a mutual fund, depending on how the investment performs. For example, if the price of the shares drop, the investor puts more money into the investment, and if the price goes up, he or she buys fewer shares.

SYNDICATE. A group of investment bankers that underwrites and distributes a new securities issue.

SYNDICATE ACCOUNT. An underwriting syndicate's financial condition.

SYNDICATE AGREEMENT. A contract that creates an underwriting group.

SYNDICATE MANAGER. The lead underwriter who, among other things, is in charge of organizing the syndicate, distributing member participation shares, and making stabilizing transactions.

SYNDICATE RESTRICTIONS. The binding requirements to which an underwriting syndicate must adhere. The restrictions govern such things as distribution and price limits.

SYNDICATE TERMINATION. After a security has been issued and distributed, the underwriting syndicate is released from its restrictions.

SYNERGY. Occurs when, after two companies merge, the new company has higher earnings than the two previous companies combined.

SYNTHETIC PUT. An unregistered over-the-counter put option a broker-dealer issues to accommodate a client's request for a put option.

SYSTEMATIC RISK. A risk that all assets possess, or that all securities of the same class have in common.

T

T. Appears in newspaper stock listings to indicate the security's main trading place is the Toronto Stock Exchange.

TACKING. Occurs when a third mortgage holder tacks the first mortgage onto the third so he or she will have a superior claim over the second mortgage.

TAFT-HARTLEY ACT. A 1947 federal law that restricts unions from, among other things, refusing to bargain in good faith, coercing employees to join, and participating in sympathy strikes.

TAG ENDS. Indicates that only a small number of debt securities are available from the underwriting syndicate because the rest have been sold.

TAIL. The difference between the lowest bid accepted and the average bid in a U.S. Treasury auction.

TAILGATING. Occurs when a registered representative buys a security for a customer, then buys more shares of the same security for his or her own account.

TAKE. Indicates that buyers are accepting another broker's offering price to complete a transaction.

TAKE A FLIER. Occurs when an investor knowingly makes a risky investment.

TAKE A POSITION. Occurs when an investor creates a long or short position.

TAKE BACK. Occurs when a syndicate regains those securities it had allotted for the selling group.

TAKEDOWN. The number of securities for which an underwriting syndicate member is financially responsible.

TAKE IT. A broker's indication that he or she will buy a specific security at a specific price.

TAKE ON A LINE. Occurs when an investor buys a large block of stock over a period of time because he or she expects the stock's price to climb.

TAKE-OR-PAY CONTRACT. A contract that binds the buyer to pay the seller a minimum amount of money, even if the seller does not provide the buyer with the promised goods or services. Such contracts protect bondholders.

TAKEOUT. The amount of money an investor withdraws to sell one security and buy another at a lower price.

TAKEOVER. The attempt of one company to buy another company, either in a hostile or friendly manner.

TAKEOVER ARBITRAGE. Occurs when an investor buys and/or sells securities issued by a company targeted for a takeover, or the acquiring company, because the investor believes such a transaction will bring him or her a profit.

TAKEOVER CANDIDATE. Any company that is vulnerable to a takeover, or is looking to be taken over by another company.

TAKE PROFITS. Occurs when an investor earns money from selling a security.

TAKER. A person who borrows money or securities.

TAKE UP. Occurs when an investor pays all that is due on a margined security so he or she can take full ownership of that security.

TAKING A BATH. Occurs when an investor is losing a lot of money on an investment.

TAKING A VIEW. Indicates a British prediction of interest rates, security prices, and yields.

TAKING DELIVERY. Accepting the delivery of securities to complete a transaction.

TALON. Any special coupon that carries extra income or rights.

TANDEM OPTION. A stock option that carries qualified as well as nonqualified plans.

TANDEM PLAN. A plan in which the Government National Mortgage Association pays above-the-market value for some mortgages and simultaneously sells them through the Federal National Mortgage Association in the secondary market. By doing this, the GNMA pays for some housing projects without having to put out much money.

TANDEM SPREAD. A strategy in which an investor buys one security and sells another short to take advantage of price differences between the two.

TANGIBLE ASSET. An asset with physical substance, such as a machine. An intangible asset would be an asset without physical substance, such as one's reputation.

TANGIBLE COST. The amount of money it costs to buy oil and gas drilling equipment that can be used over a period of time.

TANGIBLE NET WORTH. Achieved by subtracting a company's intangible assets from its tangible assets.

TANGIBLE VALUE. The difference between a stock option contract's exercise price and the underlying security's market price.

TAP CERTIFICATE OF DEPOSIT. A one-month, as-required certificate of deposit in denominations of at least $25,000.

TAPE. Short for a ticker tape, which is an exchange's system for physically recording and reporting securities transactions and volume information.

TAPE DANCING. Occurs when a trader pays an institutional investor 1/8 to 1/4 over the last transaction price for a block of equity securities, then imposes a heavier commission in an effort to cushion trading losses and to make it appear on the ticker tape as if buyers are anxious to buy the stock, a notion that attracts speculators.

TAPE PRICE. The last price shown on the ticker tape for a specific security.

TAPE RACING. Occurs when a broker improperly buys or sells a security using the knowledge that a client plans to execute a large order in the same security shortly thereafter.

TAPE READING. A method of analyzing and predicting price movements by studying only the information appearing on an exchange's ticker tape, such as the price and trading volume.

TAP ISSUE. A securities offering with the same terms and conditions as a previous issue, even though the prices may be different. The tap issue is so named because the issuer is tapping the same market.

TARGET. A company that another company wants to buy out.

TARGET PRICE. The price to which an investor expects his or her newly purchased securities to rise.

TARIFF. An import and export tax imposed usually to balance competition.

TAW. The amount of money necessary to completely finance a new business venture.

TAX ABATEMENT. A cut or refund in taxes because the amount paid was too high or was improperly imposed.

TAXABLE DISTRIBUTION. An amount of money distributed on which the receiver must pay taxes.

TAXABLE EQUIVALENT YIELD. A bond that yields taxable income compared to a tax-exempt bond's yield.

TAXABLE ESTATE. The amount of a deceased person's estate after all administrative, funeral, transfer, and other exempted costs have been subtracted.

TAXABLE EVENT. An occasion that can be taxed. For example, the issuing of dividend payments would be considered a taxable event.

TAXABLE GIFT. An asset transferred to another person, with the asset worth more than the government-allowed exemption.

TAXABLE INCOME. The amount of a company's or an individual's yearly income that is subject to tax after all legal and appropriate credits, adjustments, and deductions have been applied.

TAXABLE VALUE. An assessed value of assets, income or property, with the government using the value to determine the amount of tax due on the assets, income or property.

TAX ADJUSTMENT ACT. A 1966 federal law that, among other things, reinstated the excise taxes on transportation equipment and on telephone service rates.

TAX-ADVANTAGED INVESTMENT. A tax-free investment or an investment that lowers the holder's tax liabilities.

TAX AND LOAN ACCOUNT. A government-owned demand deposit account in a commercial bank, with companies and people who owe Social Security payments or employee withholding taxes as depositors.

TAX ANTICIPATION BILL. A Treasury-issued, short-term debt instrument issued to meet short-term financial needs.

TAX ANTICIPATION NOTE. A short-term, municipal note issued to meet short-term financial needs, and which is repaid upon maturity with tax receipts.

TAX ANTICIPATION OBLIGATION. A government-issued debt instrument that will be repaid with tax receipts.

TAX AVOIDANCE. Legal methods a taxpayer can use to reduce his or her tax liabilities.

TAX BASE. The taxable portion of any asset or property.

TAX-BASED INCOME POLICY. An extra corporate income tax imposed if the company raises its employees' salaries above a certain level. If the company keeps salaries below the government-set limit, it receives a corporate income tax break.

TAX BASIS. The total price an investor paid for a security, including the brokerage commission.

TAX BRACKET. The tax schedule level in which a taxpayer's income falls, with each level carrying a different percentage level of tax liability. For example, a person earning more money would fall in a higher tax bracket and therefore would be responsible for paying a higher percentage of tax.

TAX CAPITALIZATION. To capitalize a tax at an assumed interest rate, divide the interest rate into the tax change, then subtract that amount from the asset's value before the tax change.

TAX CERTIFICATE. A government-issued document that verifies the title transfer of a tax-delinquent property. If the owner does not pay the delinquent amount, the certificate holder can foreclose.

TAX COST. The base figure representing the difference between the amount of money paid for a property and the amount of money for which the property is sold. The difference determines a taxable gain or loss.

TAX COURT OF THE UNITED STATES. A federal court that has jurisdiction over Internal Revenue Service tax disputes.

TAX CREDIT. A reduction in tax liabilities, expressed as a percentage of the individual's tax bracket.

TAX DEED. The deed that is given to a person who buys property that was sold because of tax delinquency.

TAX DEFERRED. An investment that allows a person to put off paying income taxes on money deposited into the investment until he or she actually takes possession of the money. Many retirement accounts, for example, are tax deferred.

TAX EQUITY AND FISCAL RESPONSIBILITY ACT. A federal law that imposed levies and improved taxpayer compliance to increase revenues.

TAX EQUIVALENT. The payment a government-owned utility makes to other government units instead of paying taxes for which it is exempt.

TAX EVASION. Occurs when a taxpayer illegally falsifies his or her financial records in an effort to avoid paying taxes.

TAX-EXEMPT BOND. A municipal debt security that pays the holder interest that is free from federal and state and local taxes if the investor resides in the state offering the bond.

TAX-EXEMPT DEFERRED INTEREST SECURITY. A tax-exempt security issued at a discount. The security pays no interest for a specific number of years, after which it becomes a bond with a fixed par value and pays interest twice a year.

TAX EXEMPTION. A right attached to some assets and activities that frees them from paying taxes.

TAX-EXEMPT SECURITY. Any municipal security, so named because the interest usually is at least partially tax-exempt.

TAX-FREE INSTRUMENT. A government-issued debt security that pays the holder tax-free interest or dividends, or interest or dividends with reduced tax liabilities.

TAX-FREE ROLLOVER. A person who receives a lump-sum pension distribution can avoid paying taxes on the amount by depositing it into an Individual Retirement Account or into some other tax-deferred program.

TAX LEASE. A long-term lease on a tax-delinquent property that is given when the law prevents the property from actually being sold.

TAX LIEN. A government lien on property that has been imposed because the property-owner is delinquent in paying taxes.

TAX LIENS RECEIVABLE. An account of delinquent taxes and all legal claims against those delinquent properties.

TAX LIMIT. A law that limits all government-imposed tax ceilings.

TAX LOOPHOLE. Any tax exemption.

TAX-LOSS CARRY FORWARD. The dollar amount of a net capital loss that taxpayers can carry over to subsequent years on their tax forms to reduce tax liability.

TAX-MANAGED FUND. A fund in which investment earnings constantly are reinvested. Because the fund brings the investor no profits without selling all shares, the investor does not have to pay taxes on the fund's increased value.

TAX MANAGED UTILITY MUTUAL FUND. A reinvesting mutual fund that concentrates investments in utility securities. Because interest and dividends are reinvested in the fund, investors profit only by selling shares.

TAX OFFSET. Occurs when one tax is eliminated because another tax has been paid.

TAX ON NET INVESTMENT INCOME. A 4 percent excise tax imposed on a tax-exempt, private foundation's net investment income.

TAXPAYER IDENTIFICATION NUMBER. A nine-digit number, usually an individual's social security number, used to identify every taxpayer in the United States.

TAX PREFERENCE ITEM. An asset the Internal Revenue Service requires a taxpayer to count when adding together the alternative minimum tax liability. A tax-shelter deduction, for example, would be a tax preference item.

TAX REDUCTION ACT. A 1975 law that provided, among other things, increased standard deductions, low-income credits, and increased investment tax credits.

TAX REDUCTION ACT STOCK OWNERSHIP PLAN. A program, running from 1975 to 1981, that allowed a company to take a 1 percent tax credit on its capital investments if the company contributed 1 percent to its Employee Stock Ownership Plan.

TAX REDUCTION AND SIMPLIFICATION ACT. A 1977 law that cut taxes by $34 billion and simplified tax forms.

TAX REFORM ACT OF 1969. A federal law that limited corporate tax benefits such as accumulated earnings credits and multiple surtax exemptions.

TAX REFORM ACT OF 1976. A federal law that restricted tax benefits. Among other things, the law set a capital gains tax on home sales, extended the holding period for long-term capital gains, and limited home-office use deductions.

TAX REFORM ACT OF 1984. A federal law aimed at reducing the national deficit. Among other things, the law raised the liquor tax, extended a telephone excise tax, and tightened tax-shelter partnership rules.

TAX SEARCH. A records search conducted to find out if a piece of property has any history of tax delinquency.

TAX SELLING. Occurs when an investor sells a security in an effort to achieve a capital loss, which provides tax breaks.

TAX SHIELD. The tax-exempt depreciation charged against a person's income.

TAX SHIFTING. Occurs when a manufacturer or service-provider passes its tax liabilities on to the consumer. For example, a service station must pay gasoline tax, so the station owner adds that tax onto the price of gasoline.

TAX STRADDLE. Occurs when an investor takes off-setting positions in the commodities market to achieve short-term capital gains. By taking a short-term loss in the same year as he or she received the capital gains, the net position is not taxed, and the investor receives long-term gains the next year on the remaining position.

TAX SWAPPING. Occurs when an investor sells a security for a loss at the end of the tax year to take advantage of tax breaks on capital losses, then invests the tax savings in another security because he or she believes that security offers a better chance for profit.

TAX TITLE. A property title issued on property that was sold because of tax delinquency.

TAX UMBRELLA. A company's current and past losses that it can carry over to a subsequent year to shield future earnings.

TAX WAIVER. A document that accompanies a will and states either that estate taxes have been paid, or do not need to be paid immediately.

TEAR SHEET. Standard and Poor's individual stock comments, which the firm lists in a loose-leaf binder from which it tears out the appropriate individual sheets to send to interested customers.

TECHNICAL ADJUSTMENT. A short-term reversal of the current market trend, usually the reaction to investor overbuying or overselling.

TECHNICAL ANALYSIS. Studying and interpreting the supply of, and demand for, certain securities, with the end result a prediction of future trends.

TECHNICAL CORRECTION. A short-term, temporary reversal of the current market trend.

TECHNICAL DIVERGENCE. Occurs when one market average does not conform to the pattern or movement of another market average.

TECHNICAL DROP. The drop in a security's or commodity's price caused by market conditions and not by any changes in supply and demand.

TECHNICAL INDICATORS. Charts, ratios, graphs, or other methods of evaluating market trends and defining possible future trends.

TECHNICALLY STRONG MARKET. A market with high trading volume and increasing prices.

TECHNICALLY WEAK MARKET. A market with high trading volume and decreasing prices.

TECHNICAL MARKET ACTION. The market activity caused by volume, odd-lot transactions, and other technical factors.

TECHNICAL MOVE. A fluctuation in a stock's price interpreted as a self-adjusted movement.

TECHNICAL POSITION. The position of the market when it is affected only by internal conditions such as short-term interest or steady price declines.

TECHNICAL RALLY. A short-term price increase in a declining market, indicating a surge of bargain buying, but not a permanent change in the overall market condition.

TECHNICAL SIGN. A security's price movement that represents the onset of a short-term price trend.

TECHNICIAN. An analyst, also called a chartist, that uses indicators such as ratios and graphs to predict future market trends instead of studying the issuing companies' management and fundamentals.

TECHNILIST. A newsletter a financial institution sends to subscribers with recommendations on what securities to buy or sell and at what prices.

TELEGRAPHIC TRANSFER. The electronic transfer of money wherein the receiving firm actually remits the funds, and the sender then owes the receiving firm the money.

TELEPHONE BOOTHS. A communications booth on an exchange floor that members use to obtain buy and sell orders and to provide transaction information.

TELEPHONE SWITCHING. Occurs when a telephone is used to shift assets from one mutual fund to another.

TEMPORARY AGENT TRANSFER PROGRAM. Using the National Association of Securities Dealers' Central Registration Depository, the North American Securities Administrators Association designed a program through which salespeople can obtain temporary registration before they file their permanent registration forms.

TEMPORARY RECEIPT. A document acknowledging security ownership until the engraved certificate is ready.

TEMPORARY SPECIALIST. An exchange member who temporarily takes over for a specialist in all capacities if that specialist cannot, for some reason, perform his or her duties.

TENANCY. Any property ownership.

TENANCY AT SUFFERANCE. A person who takes title to a property and then retains that property even after the title or interest has ended.

TENANCY AT WILL. An estate that the lessor or lessee can end at any time.

TENANCY FOR YEARS. A tenancy that lasts a predetermined number of years, and in which no party has any right to terminate the tenancy before the end of that period.

TENANCY IN COMMON ACCOUNT. A savings account owned by at least two people.

TENANT. A person who is part owner of a security or a joint account.

TENANTS BY THE ENTIRETY. When a husband and wife jointly own an asset, piece of property, or margin account.

TENANTS IN COMMON. A form of joint ownership by two or more people whereby the portion owned by one who dies is passed to his or her heirs rather than to another party in the agreement.

TENDENCY. The probability or likelihood of a security's price to shift up, down, or sideways.

TENDER. To formally bid on a security.

TENDERABLE. A commodity that meets the commodity exchange's quality standards and delivery requirements.

TENDER OFFER. One company's public announcement that it plans to buy as many shares of another company's securities as possible, usually in an effort to take that company over.

TENDER OPTION PUT SECURITY. A long-term municipal security with a short-term put option that gives the owner the right to redeem the security at par, which, in essence, makes the long-term security a short-term trading instrument.

TEN-FORTY. A government bond that can be redeemed in 10 years and is due after 40 years.

TEN-K REPORT. The annual report that any company issuing listed securities must file with the Securities and Exchange Commission.

TENNESSEE VALLEY AUTHORITY (TVA). A government agency established in 1933 to develop the Tennessee River area using money raised through the issuing of debt securities.

1099. An Internal Revenue Service form on which a taxpayer lists interest, dividend, and fee payments.

TENOR. A bond's maturity.

TEN PERCENT GUIDELINE. A city's bonded debt never should exceed 10 percent of the city-owned real estate's market value.

TERM. The time between the issuing date and the date of maturity.

TERM BOND. An issue with all of the bonds in the series maturing on the same date.

TERM BONDS PAYABLE. A liability record of outstanding bonds and their face values.

TERM CERTIFICATE. A certificate of deposit that matures in two to five years and pays interest twice a year.

TERM FEDERAL FUNDS. A commercial bank's excess reserves that it loans at negotiated interest rates for longer-than-normal periods of time.

TERMINAL MARKET. A futures market.

TERMINATION CLAIM. The predetermined, allowable level of the appreciation in stockholders' shares.

TERM ISSUE. A bond issue with each bond in the issue maturing in the same future year.

TERM LOAN. A loan that lasts a specific time period.

TERM MORTGAGE. A mortgage with all interest to be paid within a predetermined time, after which the principal is due.

TERM REPURCHASE AGREEMENT. A repurchase agreement that lasts a longer-than-normal period of time.

TERTIARY MOVEMENT. Small, unimportant, daily price shifts.

TEST. Occurs when a price is challenging a resistance level. If the price does not break through the level, the resistance level is said to have passed the test.

TESTAMENTARY ACCOUNT. A savings account with funds invested in some sort of trust, with a beneficiary to receive all of the money upon the account holder's death.

TESTAMENTARY DISTRIBUTION. The distribution of a person's estate after the person's death.

TESTAMENTARY GUARDIAN. A person named in a will to takeover the guardianship of a child.

TESTAMENTARY TRUST. A contract that allows one person to administer another person's assets after the second person's death.

TESTATE. Describes a person who died without leaving a will.

TESTING. A market price that challenges the resistance level, but will not break through that level.

THEORETICAL VALUE. Any evaluation that considers only mathematical variables, but no other market situations.

THEORY OF CONTRARY OPINION. A theory that says that when no great difference of opinion exists, the majority will be wrong.

THIN CORPORATION. A company with debts that greatly outweigh its equity.

THINLY HELD STOCK. Shares owned by a small number of people, which results in wide price fluctuations even when the trading volume is low.

THIN MARKET. A market with little interest in buying or selling a particular security, which prompts large price fluctuations in the few shares that are traded.

THIRD MARKET. Occurs when a trader who is not a member of an exchange trades exchange-listed securities either over the counter or off the board.

THIRD MORTGAGE. A mortgage that falls beneath the first and second mortgage in claims priority.

THIRD-PARTY ACCOUNT. An illegal brokerage account that one person carries in his or her name, even though another person actually owns the account.

THIRD-PARTY BROKER. A broker who routinely executes institutional trades, then returns a portion of his or her fee to a fund such as a pension program.

THIRD-PARTY CHECK. A check that is payable to someone other than the bearer.

THIRD-PARTY REPURCHASE AGREEMENT. A broker's deal with a bank customer in which the bank guarantees the loan and the broker uses government securities as collateral.

THIRTY-DAY VISIBLE SUPPLY. A list of securities that will be offered publicly within 30 days.

THIRTY-DAY WASH RULE. With this regulation, the Internal Revenue Service prohibits an investor who suffered a loss on a stock sale from using that loss for tax benefits if the investor bought the stock back 30 days after the sale date, or owned the stock for only 30 days before the sale.

THREADNEEDLE STREET. London's financial district.

THREE-AGAINST-ONE RATIO WRITING. Occurs when an investor sells three call options for every 100 shares of the underlying security he or she owns.

THREE-HANDED DEAL. A securities issue that puts together serial maturity bonds with two-term maturity bonds.

THRESHOLD COMPANY. A company run by entrepreneurs and not by seasoned professionals, but that still is on the brink of becoming a mature company.

THRIFT INSTITUTION. A savings and loan, credit union, or savings bank.

THROUGH THE MARKET. Occurs when a new bond offering has a lower yield-to-maturity than comparable outstanding bonds.

THROWAWAY OFFER. An approximate bid or offer price that is not binding and is not a definite transaction quote.

TICK. A security's successive transaction prices.

TICKER TAPE. An exchange's system for physically recording and reporting securities transactions and volume information. The ticker tape also is referred to as a ticker or a tape.

TICK INDEX. Subtract an exchange's downtick volume from its uptick volume to determine the net tick volume.

TICKLER. A financial institution's list of bonds and their maturity dates, with such an index reminding the institution of which bonds will fall due and when.

TICK VOLUME. The downtick volume compared to the uptick volume of a certain security in one trading day.

TIDAL WAVE PURCHASE. A cash-rich corporate raider quickly and openly buys up all of the target company's outstanding stock, catching the target off guard.

TIE GAUGE THEORY. A market indicator that says when men's ties are wider, stock prices decline, and when men's ties are narrower, stock prices rise.

TIER. Differentiates one class of securities from another.

TIFFANY LIST. The nickname for a group of companies that issue high-grade commercial paper.

TIGHT MARKET. An active, competitive market with little difference between bid and offer prices.

TIGHT MONEY. Occurs when there is not enough money to lend, often because of the government's attempts to ebb inflation by manipulating the money reserves.

TIGR. *See* Treasury Investment Growth Receipt.

TIME. *See* Trusts for Investments in Mortgages.

TIME BARGAIN. An agreement between a buyer and seller to trade a specific security at a particular price at a specific future date.

TIME BILL. A bill of exchange with a fixed payment date.

TIME CERTIFICATE OF DEPOSIT. A financial instrument with a specific amount and maturity date.

TIME DEPOSIT. A deposit in an interest-paying account that requires the money to remain on account for a specific length of time. If the depositor withdraws the money before the end of that period, he or she must pay a heavy interest penalty.

TIME DRAFT. A post-dated financial instrument that transfers money from one person to another.

TIME ORDER. A market order that becomes a limit order on a specific date or at a specific time.

TIMES FIXED CHARGES. The bond interest and preferred stock dividend coverage that a company's income provides.

TIMES INTEREST AND PREFERRED DIVIDEND EARNED. A preferred stock's earnings protection, achieved by dividing the interest and preferred dividend requirements into the net earnings per year.

TIMES INTEREST EARNED. A bond's earnings protection, achieved by dividing its interest requirements for the year into its net earnings per year.

TIME SPREAD. An option strategy in which the investor buys and sells option contracts with the same exercise prices, but different expiration dates.

TIME VALUE. A part of a stock option contract's premium that shows how much time is left before the contract expires, thereby indicating how much the premium exceeds the contract's intrinsic value.

TIME WARRANT. A negotiable, government obligation with a term that is shorter than bonds. Time warrants often are used to pay people and companies for goods provided or for services rendered.

TIME WEIGHTED RATE OF RETURN. The investment performance of assets held for a specific time period.

TIMING. The proper time to buy or sell securities according to impending trends.

TIN PARACHUTE. A plan that offers benefits to all employees who lose their jobs following a corporate takeover. This employee protection plan attempts to guarantee employees health and life insurance benefits, severance pay, and out placement assistance.

TIP. An inducement to buy or sell securities, with the tip carrying the assumption that it is based on inside information.

TIPPEE. A person who accepts inside information.

TIPSTER. A person who claims he or she has inside information on an investment.

TIPSTER SHEET. A list of recommended securities.

TITLE DEED. A document verifying property ownership.

TITLE DEFECT. A situation that challenges property ownership.

TITLE GUARANTY COMPANY. A company paid by a property buyer to research real estate files in order to determine the property's legal status, delinquencies, or defects.

TO COME. The number of shares that will be sold, but that have not yet been transferred.

TOEHOLD PURCHASE. Buying less than 5 percent of a company's outstanding stock before the company notifies the Securities and Exchange Commission about the purchase.

TO GO. The number of shares that will be purchased, but that have not yet been transferred.

TOLL REVENUE BOND. A municipal bond that will be repaid from toll revenue generated by the project the bond was issued to finance.

TOMBSTONE. A public announcement that a new security will be offered for sale. A tombstone is not, however, an advertisement to buy the security, but merely an announcement that it will be available.

TOM-NEXT. Tomorrow's business day to the next business day. A next business day settlement.

TON. Nickname for $100 million.

TOP. A security's highest price during a particular time period.

TOP-DOWN APPROACH TO INVESTING. An investment strategy in which an investor studies economic trends, then picks an industry and a company within that industry that will probably benefit the most from the trends.

TOPHEAVY. Occurs when a security, commodity, or the general market is priced so that it is expected to fall.

TOPIC. A British information system that provides timely transaction information to subscribing investors.

TOP MANAGEMENT. A company's highest ranking officers.

TOPPING A BID. Occurs when an investor bids a higher amount than the prevailing market price.

TOPPING OUT. Occurs when a security's steadily increasing price stabilizes and then begins to decline.

TOPPY. Occurs when the general market or an individual security hits its resistance level and subsequently drops.

TORONTO STOCK EXCHANGE. A major Canadian securities exchange governed by the Ontario Securities Commission. The TSE lists both Canadian and American securities.

TORRENS CERTIFICATE. A document that shows the name of the person who owns a title.

TOTAL ASSET TURNOVER. Obtained by dividing a company's total operating assets into its sales.

TOTAL CAPITALIZATION. A company's complete capital structure.

TOTAL COST. The amount of money it costs to buy a security, including the purchase price, fees, and commissions.

TOTAL DEBT TO TANGIBLE NET WORTH. To determine whether a company's creditors own more equity in the company than the company owners, divide the company's tangible net worth into its total current and long-term debts. If the figure is higher than 100 percent, the creditors own more.

TOTAL OF PAYMENTS. All of the amount financed plus all finance charges involved with the loan.

TOTAL RETURN. An investment's current cash flow combined with its ultimate gains or losses.

TOTAL RETURN INVESTMENT. A low-risk investment which provides income with growth.

TOTAL VOLUME. The number of shares or contracts traded on all exchanges and in all marketplaces.

TO THE BUCK. An offer when the bid and offer amounts are close, and the offer is a round point.

TOTTEN TRUST. A trust in which the initiator deposits money in his or her name, but which is designed to benefit another person. The initiator can cancel the trust at any time, but after his or her death, the fund is transferred to the beneficiary.

TOUCH OFF THE STOPS. Occurs when stop orders become market orders because the price indicated in the order was hit.

TOUT. A subjective endorsement of an investment.

TRADE ACCEPTANCE AND RECONCILIATION SERVICE. Sponsored by the National Association of Securities Dealers, this is a computer network through which over-the-counter contracts can be compared and problems can be resolved.

TRADE CREDIT. An account that a supplier keeps for the company buying its goods or services. The account outlines all of the purchases as well as the buying company's payment record. The supplier's trade liabilities are included in its accounts payable.

TRADE DATE. The day a securities transaction is negotiated and executed.

TRADE DEFICIT. The amount by which a country's imports exceed its exports, creating a negative balance of trade.

TRADE HOUSE. A brokerage firm that buys and sells futures and actuals for its own account and for the accounts of customers.

TRADEMARK. A slogan, emblem, or identifying mark registered to one company, to which it has exclusive rights. The company can obtain an exclusive trademark by registering its request with the government.

TRADE PROCESSING AND OPERATIONS DEPARTMENT. A broker-dealer's area responsible for processing all securities transactions.

TRADER. A person who buys and sells securities for short-term profits.

TRADER'S MARKET. Occurs when market conditions are positive for profiting from short-term investments.

TRADES ON TOP OF. The relationship between two debt instruments with little or no yield differentials.

TRADE SUPPORT SYSTEM. Used at the Chicago Board Options Exchange to transmit price information.

TRADE SURPLUS. The amount by which a country's exports exceeds its imports, creating a positive balance of trade.

TRADE THROUGH. A normally unethical practice in which an exchange member transacts a deal on the exchange floor even though a better price is available through the Intermarket Trading System.

TRADING AUTHORIZATION. An agreement in which an account owner allows another person to buy and sell securities for the owner's account.

TRADING CROWD. A group of exchange members who gather to trade securities.

TRADING DAY. Any day a securities exchange is open, normally Monday through Friday except for holidays.

TRADING DIFFERENCE. The point-fraction difference between the price in an odd-lot transaction and the price of those securities if they had been purchased in a round lot.

TRADING DIVIDENDS. Occurs when a company buys and sells securities to increase the number of annual dividends subject to a tax exclusion.

TRADING DOWN. Occurs when an investor buys and sells high-risk or low-rated securities in an attempt to increase his or her capital gains.

TRADING FLOOR. The exchange area where securities are bought and sold.

TRADING HOURS. The times a securities exchange is open, normally 9:30 a.m. to 4 p.m.

TRADING INDEX. A ratio that compares advances and declines to up and down volumes.

TRADING INSTRUCTIONS. An investor's orders to his or her broker that limits a transaction through a stop order or other restriction.

TRADING LIMIT. The price range within which a commodity can be bought or sold within a given day, with high and low limits marking the edges of that range. A commodity cannot be sold below the low limit or above the high limit.

TRADING MARKET. A low-volume market with few price fluctuations, in which professional traders, not the general public, make up most of the trading business for the day.

TRADING ON THE EQUITY. A high-risk practice in which a company issues a funded debt so it can leverage its investments.

TRADING ON THE PERIMETER. Occurs when the trading at an exchange's trading post is so active that many transactions are executed on the edge of the trading crowd. Because they are on the edge, the specialist is not always immediately aware of the deals.

TRADING PAPER. A negotiable, short-term certificate of deposit.

TRADING PATTERN. The long-term direction of a security's price movements.

TRADING POST. The area of an exchange where one particular security is traded.

TRADING RANGE. The price difference between a security's highest and lowest transaction price in a specific time period.

TRADING RING. The New York Stock Exchange area where listed bonds are traded.

TRADING ROTATION. One method of opening the trading of option series, securities, and commodities futures contracts, after which individual trading can continue.

TRADING THROUGH THE FUND'S RATE. A debt security with a yield to maturity that is lower than the federal fund's rate, which is vulnerable to interest rate changes. When this occurs often, the Federal Reserve probably is preparing to change its monetary policies.

TRADING UNIT. A round lot.

TRADING UP. Occurs when an investor trades securities from his or her portfolio for securities with higher ratings, which thereby reduces the investor's portfolio risks.

TRADING VARIATION. The fractions to which a security's price is rounded. For example, stocks are rounded up and down and traded in eighths.

TRADING VOLUME. The number of shares a security has traded on a particular exchange during a specific time period.

TRANCHE. One class of a bond or securities issue. This is done to meet the needs of the issuer and to meet different objectives of investors.

TRANSACTION. The execution of a securities deal.

TRANS-CANADA OPTION. A Canadian put or call option with the underlying security issued by a Canadian company.

TRANS-CANADA OPTIONS INC. A Canadian company that issues options with the underlying securities issued by Canadian companies. The options are traded in both the U.S. and Canada.

TRANSFER. To change ownership from one party to another.

TRANSFERABLE NOTICE. A document a seller issues to announce his or her plans to deliver a commodity in order to fill a futures contract. The recipient is allowed to transfer the document to another party who will then receive the commodity.

TRANSFER AGENT. A person who physically records the transfer of a securities-ownership.

TRANSFER AND SHIP. A security owner's order to his or her broker to have the security registered in his or her name and shipped to the address on the account.

TRANSFER INITIATION REQUEST. A contract issued by the National Securities Clearing Corporation that approves the transfer of securities from one member's account to another's.

TRANSFER JOURNAL. A company's book that shows all securities issued, transferred, and canceled.

TRANSFER PRICE. The price one entity of a corporation charges another entity of the same corporation for completing a transaction with the corporation.

TRANSFER TAX. A modest tax on securities transactions, normally paid by the seller.

TRANS-LUX. An electrically run screen in a brokerage firm's board room that projects commodity and security price quotes from the various exchanges.

TRANSMITTAL LETTER. The letter a seller attaches to the document or securities he or she is sending to the buyer describing the shipment's purpose and contents.

TRAPPER. Nickname for a registered representative, so named because the business used to be so slow that representatives would have to try to "trap" their customers.

TREASURER. A company's officer who receives, manages, and invests the company's funds. If the company is publicly held, the treasurer also must maintain the market.

TREASURIES. Nickname for any Treasury security.

TREASURY BILL. A short-term discounted, government debt instrument of one year or less, issued in $10,000 denominations that pays its face value at maturity. The government issues Treasury bills weekly.

TREASURY BILL AUCTION. A weekly Treasury Department auction in which short-term government obligations are sold.

TREASURY BOND. A long-term, Treasury-issued debt instrument issued at par and maturing in at least 10 years in minimum denominations of $1,000. Treasury bonds pay interest, which is exempt from state and local taxes, twice a year.

TREASURY CERTIFICATE. A short-term government security with a maturity of six months to a year that has been issued to ease Federal Reserve transfers to banks.

TREASURY INVESTMENT GROWTH RECEIPT (TIGR). A Treasury bond that has been stripped of its coupons, with ownership of individual coupons, or of bond principal sold at a discount as a zero coupon. All interest is paid at maturity.

TREASURY NOTE. A medium-term, government debt instrument that is issued at par in $5,000 to $10,000 denominations, and matures in one to 10 years. Treasury notes pay interest that is exempt from state and local taxes biannually.

TREASURY RECEIPTS. Stripped Treasury bonds.

TREASURY STOCK. Stock a company issues then buys back, at which time it is placed in the company's treasury, where it earns no dividends and carries no voting privileges.

TREND. A prevailing price movement.

TRENDLESS. A price movement that fluctuates up and down to the extent that no specific trend can be identified.

TRENDLINE. A chart slope representing price movements, connecting the highest and lowest prices of a security. Technical analysts use this line to indicate an uptrend or downtrend.

TRIANGLE. A charted price pattern that forms a triangle because the security's price has gone down, then up, then back down again.

TRIANGULAR ARBITRAGE. Arbitrage achieved through the exchange rates of three foreign currencies.

TRICK. A long-term, municipal bond issue's special low coupon with a high yield, which allows a bidder to lower the issuer's net interest cost in an attempt to win the bid.

TRICKLE-DOWN THEORY. An economic theory stating that giving money to businesses is more important than giving money to consumers because if businesses are promoted and expanded, the individuals ultimately will benefit.

TRIN. *See* Short-Term Trading Index.

TRIPLE BOTTOM. A chart that shows a security's price has hit three bottom prices within a short time, but will not drop below the most recent low price.

TRIPLE EXEMPTION. A municipal bond that provides tax-exempt interest income to the holder. The triple exemption is so named because it is exempt from local, state, and federal taxes.

TRIPLE NET LEASE. A rental contract in which the renter pays the property owner a fixed amount, then is responsible for maintenance and all other costs involved.

TRIPLE OPTION PREFERRED STOCK. A preferred stock that gives the owner the right to sell the stock back to the issuing company quarterly for an equal amount of common stock, an equal amount of a debt security, or cash.

TRIPLE TOP. A chart that shows a security's price has hit three top prices within a short time, but will not rise above the most recent high price.

TRIPLE WITCHING HOUR. The final hour of trading before equity, index options, and index futures contracts expire. Because of contract schedules, a triple witching hour will occur four times a year, each of which marks heavy trading.

TROUGH. An activity's economic bottom.

TRUNCATION. The elimination, reduction, or consolidation of paper work to reduce operating expenses. Feeding information from paper documents into a computer system and then throwing the paper documents away would be an example of truncation.

TRUST. A contract in which a person deposits and holds money, securities, or other assets for the ultimate benefit of another person.

TRUST COMPANY. A financial institution that handles trust funds.

TRUSTEE. One person who is legally responsible for another person's investments, property, or other assets.

TRUSTEED FUND. Any accumulation of money held for a future use such as a retirement or an education.

TRUSTEED PENSION PLAN. A pension plan in which the company puts its contributions into a trust fund for investing.

TRUSTEE SHARES. The certificates of beneficial interest in an investment company.

TRUST INDENTURE ACT. A federal law that requires issuing companies to fully disclose information about their securities as well as pertinent information concerning their own management. The law covers securities that were not included in the Securities Act of 1933.

TRUST INSTITUTION. Any company with at least one department handling trust business, even if the company's general business is in another field.

TRUST INSTRUMENT COMMITTEE. A trust institution panel of officers that oversees and decides how to invest the institution's trust funds.

TRUSTS FOR INVESTMENTS IN MORTGAGES (TIME). This gives mortgage-backed securities bond characteristics, such as twice-a-year payments and repayment protection.

TRUTH IN LENDING ACT. A federal law that requires lenders to provide the true cost of loans and all terms involved to the borrower.

TRUTH IN SECURITIES ACT. A law that requires full disclosure of information concerning publicly issued securities.

TSE. *See* Toronto Stock Exchange.

TURKEY. A security that has lost money for its investors.

TURN. Occurs when a price movement or trend changes directions.

TURNAROUND. A security with a price that has rebounded.

TURNAROUND SITUATION. Occurs when an unprofitable company becomes profitable by changing its internal management, marketing, or other corporate structure situation.

TURNKEY. A product manufactured to completion, then turned over to the user, who needs no expert knowledge to make the product work. A computer that needs no installation other than plugging it in would be an example of a turnkey.

TURNOVER. The number of securities in an investor's portfolio that were bought and sold within a specific time period.

TURTLE-BLOOD. A stable security with low volatility and a price that is not expected to increase quickly.

TVA. *See* Tennessee Valley Authority.

12B-1 MUTUAL FUND. A no-load mutual fund which is registered with the Securities and Exchange Commission, in which investors must pay usually 1 percent or less toward promotion expenses. Such promotion is necessary because no brokers are involved in the sale of such funds, so the fund manager must pay for advertising.

TWENTY-DAY PERIOD. Also called the cooling-off period, this is the time between the day a company files its registration statement with the Securities and Exchange Commission and the day the security can be publicly sold.

TWENTY-FIVE PERCENT RULE. A city's bonded debt never should exceed 25 percent of its yearly budget.

TWENTY PERCENT CUSHION RULE. A project funded by a municipal bond should produce revenue that exceeds 20 percent of the cost of maintaining and servicing the bond.

TWISTING. An unethical practice of persuading a person to switch from one mutual fund to another because the other carries an additional sales charge.

TWO-AGAINST-ONE RATIO WRITING. Occurs when an investor sells two call options for every 100 shares of the underlying security he or she owns.

TWO-DOLLAR BROKER. An exchange member who executes transactions for other brokers who are too busy to handle their own high-volume businesses. Two-dollar brokers are so named because they used to charge $2 for every 100-share deal.

TWOFER. A long call at a lower striking price and two short calls at higher striking prices, with all expiring on the same date.

TWO-HANDED DEAL. Occurs when two broker-dealers co-manage a new securities distribution.

TWO HUNDRED-DAY MOVING AVERAGE. A daily chart that looks at price averages over the past 200 days, which often provides a better indicator of trends. The averages include the reporting day's averages and the averages of the past 199 days.

TWO-SIDED MARKET. Also called a two-way market, this occurs when a market maker is willing to provide firm bid and offer prices for a round lot of a security.

TWO-TIER PRICING. Occurs in a takeover attempt when the raider pays the person who owns the controlling stock a higher price than the other stockholders.

TWO-WAY TRADE. Occurs when an investor simultaneously buys one security and sells another.

TYPE OF OPTIONS. Indicates either a call option or a put option.

U

U. Appears in newspaper stock listings to indicate a security has reached a new high for the past year.

U-4. An application used to register agents and representatives with an exchange and with the National Association of Securities Dealers. The registration will provide the personal, legal, and business background of the applicant.

U-5. A document used to notify an exchange and the National Association of Securities Dealers that an agent's registration has been terminated.

ULTIMATE BENEFICIARY. A principal beneficiary that will receive the trust's principal amount in the final distribution.

ULTIMO. The previous month.

ULTRA VIRES. An action a company takes when a prior event exceeds the boundaries of what is allowed according to the company's charter. Ultra vires often lead to shareholder or third-party suits.

UNACCRUED. Income from payments made before their due date.

UNAMORTIZED BOND DISCOUNT. The difference between a bond's face value and the amount of money the issuing company received from selling the bond, minus any amortized portion.

UNAMORTIZED DISCOUNTS ON INVESTMENTS. The difference between a security's face value and the amount the issuing company received for selling the security, minus any amortized portion.

UNAMORTIZED PREMIUMS ON INVESTMENTS. The unexpensed part of the amount that a security's purchase price exceeded its par or market value.

UNAPPROPRIATED PROFITS. The portion of a company's profits that the company has not paid out in dividends or used to retire existing debts.

UNASSENTED SECURITIES. Securities that the issuing company wants to change, but which have yet to receive stockholder approval.

UNAUTHORIZED GROWTH. A capital investment with different growth rates in different economic areas.

UNAUTHORIZED INVESTMENT. A trust investment that the trust instrument has not approved.

UNCALLED CAPITAL. The part of a company's issued share capital that the company has not called.

UNCERTIFIED SHARES. Fund shares an investor owns in his or her account, even though no stock certificates have been issued for the shares.

UNCOLLECTED FUNDS. Describes a check the bank returns to a customer when that customer wrote a check without having sufficient funds in his or her account to cover the check.

UNCOVERED. A short option position for which the seller does not own the underlying security and is therefore not in a hedged position.

UNCOVERED WRITER. A person who sells an option contract without owning any shares of the underlying security.

UNCOVER THE STOPS. Depressing a security's price to the extent that investors begin creating stop orders.

UNDERBANKED. A proposed underwriting in which the syndicate manager is having trouble recruiting other syndicate members to share in the underwriting risk.

UNDERBOOKED. A proposed underwriting in which the investing public's interest is extremely limited, so the supply of the security may outweigh the demand.

UNDERCAPITALIZED. A company that does not have enough money to conduct its day-to-day business.

UNDERCUTTING AN OFFER. An attempt to sell securities below the prevailing offer price.

UNDERLYING DEBT. A lower municipality's debt for which residents of a higher municipality have some responsibilities. A county, for example, would have an underlying debt if its residents had a partial liability for the debts of a city within that county.

UNDERLYING FUTURES CONTRACT. A futures contract upon which a futures option is written.

UNDERLYING MORTGAGE. A mortgage that takes priority over another mortgage, even though the senior mortgage is for a smaller amount.

UNDERLYING SECURITY. The security on which an options contract is written. Underlying security is also the common stock which can be issued by a corporation to an investor who exercises a stock option, right offering, warrant, or convertible security.

UNDERLYING SYNDICATE. The original syndicate members who underwrote a new securities issue.

UNDERMARGINED ACCOUNT. A margin account that has dropped below the margin requirement.

UNDERPRICED. Used to describe a stock price that is low compared to its potential future value.

UNDER REVIEW (UR). Indicates a bond that a rating service has yet to rank.

UNDER THE RULE. Occurs when exchange officers buy or sell securities to complete a transaction that a delinquent exchange member entered but failed to settle. The delinquent member is charged with any price discrepancies.

UNDERTONE. The market's strong or weak base.

UNDERVALUED. Occurs when a security's price is lower than its liquidation price or the market value placed on it by analysts. An undervalued stock justifies a higher market price and price/earnings ratio.

UNDERWRITING. The business of investment bankers to assume the risk of buying new issues of securities from a corporation or government entity and distributing them to the public. The underwriters will profit from the difference in the purchase and selling price.

UNDERWRITING AGREEMENT. The contract between an underwriting syndicate and the security's issuer, with the agreement spelling out the terms, price, and account settlement details.

UNDERWRITING FEE. The spread that accrues to syndicate members in proportion to the number of shares for which each member was responsible.

UNDERWRITING RECAPTURE. A syndicate member who also is a broker-dealer sells part of the underwriting to an institutional portfolio.

UNDERWRITING SPREAD. The difference between the amount of money an issuer receives per security in a public offering, and the actual public offering price.

UNDERWRITING SYNDICATE. A group of people who contract with the securities issuer and, upon agreement, guarantee a new securities issue by buying the entire issue, then reselling it publicly.

UNDIGESTED SECURITIES. A securities issue in which more shares are issued than the market can absorb.

UNDILUTED STOCK. A security with an earnings per share that has not been reduced for any reason.

UNDISTRIBUTED PROFIT. A company's earnings before those earnings have been divided among the company's owners or stockholders.

UNDISTRIBUTED PROFITS TAX. A tax placed on a company's undistributed profits that is designed to discourage a company from holding on to the profits without having a sound business reason for doing so. Without the tax, a company could hold on to the profits so stockholders could avoid paying income taxes on the distribution amounts.

UNDIVIDED ACCOUNT. A municipal securities underwriting with each syndicate member holding an undivided selling liability. Also known as an Eastern Account.

UNDIVIDED PROFITS. A bank account showing profits that have not been paid out as dividends or transferred to the surplus account.

UNDIVIDED RIGHT. The portion of ownership that cannot be separated from other ownership parts, such as those found in joint tenancy.

UNEARNED DISCOUNT. A lending institution's account of interest that will be taken as income earned over the life of the loan.

UNEARNED INCOME. Income such as dividends, interest payments, or other income that is not earned through salaries or wages.

UNEARNED INCREMENT. A property value increase caused by changing conditions that are beyond the property owner's control, as opposed to increases because of home improvements or other conditions over which the property owner has influence.

UNEARNED INTEREST. Interest that a lending institution has not yet collected, but that is part of its earnings.

UNENCUMBERED. An asset that has no liens and that is not pledged as collateral against a loan.

UNEVEN MARKET. A market with fluctuating prices.

UNFUNDED DEBT. Any short-term debt or a debt that is not protected by a bond.

UNIFIED CREDIT. A credit that can be applied only once in a person's life against that person's gift or estate taxes.

UNIFORM COMMERCIAL CODE. A statute that standardizes commercial customs and practices, with many local modifications.

UNIFORM GIFTS TO MINORS ACT. A state law which designates the distribution and administration of assets in the name of a child by a custodian who is of legal age.

UNIFORM PRACTICE CODE. A National Association of Securities Dealers regulation governing the execution, settling, and clearing of over-the-counter transactions.

UNIFORM SECURITIES AGENT STATE LAW EXAMINATION. A state test, administered by the National Association of Securities Dealers, given to people who want to become registered representatives.

UNISSUED COMMON STOCK. Common stock shares that a company has authorized to be issued publicly, but that have not yet been issued. Unissued common stock shares do not include those shares the company has reacquired.

UNIT. The group of exchange specialists who maintain an orderly market in a particular group of securities.

UNITARY INVESTMENT FUND. A mutual fund with no directors and no stockholder voting rights.

UNITARY TAX. A state calculation in which a company's tax liabilities within that state are figured as a percentage of its total, worldwide profits, not only on the profits of the company's subsidiary or branch within that state.

UNITED STATES GOVERNMENT SECURITIES. Any debt issued by the U.S. government such as Treasuries and Series EE and HH savings bonds.

UNIT INVESTMENT TRUST. A portfolio made up of a variety of different income securities that are pooled together and sold to investors as units. Each unit represents a fractional, undivided interest in the portfolio's principal and income.

UNIT PRICE DEMAND ADJUSTABLE TAX-EXEMPT SECURITIES (UPDATES). This is a variable-rate municipal security with a put feature attached. The variable rate is reset each day, and interest is paid monthly. The investor can redeem the security once a month or once a week (depending on the security type) for its face value.

UNIT STOCK INVESTMENT TRUST. An Americus Trust involving the Prescribed Right to Income and Maximum Equity (PRIME), in which investors receive dividend distributions and a partial asset value when the trust is dissolved, and the Special Claim On Residual Equity (SCORE), in which investors do not receive dividends, but do receive a partial asset value when the trust is dissolved.

UNLEVERAGED PROGRAM. A limited partnership that invests in real estate or other property or equipment and that borrows less than 50 percent of a property's purchase price to buy the property.

UNLIMITED MORTGAGE. An open-ended mortgage.

UNLIMITED TAX BOND. A municipal securities issue to be repaid with general, unrestricted tax collections.

UNLISTED OPTION. An option contract that is traded directly from the buyer to the seller and not traded on an organized exchange. An unlisted option is not issued by the Options Clearing Corporation.

UNLISTED STOCK. A security such as an over-the-counter stock that is not listed with a registered exchange.

UNLISTED TRADING. An exchange transaction involving an unlisted security. Such a transaction is allowed only with the special permission of the Securities and Exchange Commission.

UNLOADING. When an investor sells securities or commodities that have dropped in price to prevent any further losses.

UNMARGINABLE. A security that cannot be used as margin for buying stock shares.

UNPAID DIVIDEND. A dividend a company has declared, but not yet paid to stockholders.

UNPARTED BULLION. A bullion that carries other metals besides the primary precious metal.

UNREALIZED APPRECIATION. Occurs when a security's market value increases above its purchase price, but the owner does not sell it. The appreciation will remain unrealized, or a paper profit, until the investor sells the security.

UNREALIZED LOSS. Occurs when a security's market value drops below its purchase price, but the owner does not sell it. The loss will remain unrealized, or a paper loss, until the investor sells the security.

UNRECOVERED COST. The part of an investment that has not been amortized.

UNREGISTERED STOCK. Limited-issue stock that is not registered with the Securities and Exchange Commission. The issues are either confined to certain buyers or issued by a small company to raise money for a limited, specific purpose.

UNSEASONED SECURITY. A newly issued security with no prior exposure to the effects of supply and demand.

UNSECURED DEBT. A debt obligation with no collateral, and backed only by the debtor's creditworthiness.

UNSTEADY MARKET. A market in which securities prices fluctuate to the point that specialists cannot identify any trends.

UNSUBSCRIBED SHARES. Shares in a securities offering that the underwriting syndicate has not yet sold to the public.

UNSYSTEMATIC RISK. A risk that is limited or unique to one asset or investment. A company can eliminate its unsystematic risk by diversifying its holdings.

UNVALUED STOCK. Stock for which the issuing company has recorded on its books as having no par or stated value.

UNWIND A TRADE. A transaction that voids a previous transaction. For example, to unwind the purchase of a security, an investor would sell that security.

UP. Follows a number to indicate the dollar amount that a security's price has increased.

UP-AND-OUT OPTION. An over-the-counter put option that will be canceled if the price goes up.

UPDATE. An upward trend in a security's price.

UPDATES. *See* Unit Price Demand Adjustable Tax-Exempt Securities.

UPGRADE. Occurs when an investor sells the low-quality securities from his or her portfolio, and replaces them by buying higher quality securities.

UP REVERSAL. A sudden, short-term price increase in a security that has been dropping in value.

UPSET PRICE. The lowest price a seller will consider before selling an item, security, or property.

UPSIDE. A security's price increase.

UPSIDE BREAK-EVEN. The most a security's price will have to rise before the investor starts to make a profit.

UPSIDE-DOWNSIDE VOLUME RATIO. The total number of traded shares that dropped in value divided into the total number of traded shares that rose in value during a specific time period.

UPSIDE GAP. A gap that appears on a chart when a security's highest price on one day is lower than its lowest price on the next day.

UPSIDE POTENTIAL. The price to which an investor expects a security to rise based on all fundamental and technical predictions. The upside potential of a stock may also be a buy-out price.

UPSIDE TREND. A period of at least several months during which prices steadily climb, even if it is a market with a few temporary down reversals.

UPSTAIRS MARKET. A brokerage firm area where a transaction involving a listed security is completed without sending that transaction to the exchange floor. The deal, for example, would be negotiated between one broker-dealer and another broker-dealer.

UPTICK. A security transaction made at a higher price than the previous transaction in the security.

UPTICK-DOWNTICK BLOCK RATIO. The number of security blocks traded on downticks divided into the number traded on upticks. A ratio below 0.4 indicates the market is oversold, and a ratio above one indicates the market is overbought.

UP TREND. Occurs when a security's price continues to climb steadily over a period of time.

UPVALUATION. Revaluation or restoring an inflated currency's purchasing power.

UR. *Se* Under Review.

USABLE BOND. A debenture with a detachable warrant, which allows the investor to use the bond's face value to subscribe to common stock.

U.S. RULE. A method in which a first mortgage's payments are applied first to the interest due, and then to reducing the principal due.

U.S. TERMS. The number of American dollars needed to buy one unit of a foreign country's currency.

USURY. The loaning of money with interest.

UTILITY REVENUE BOND. A municipal bond issued to pay for a utility service project such as a generating plant or sewer system. The bond is repaid through the revenues produced from the project.

V

VALEUR. A French security.

VALUATION. An appraisal.

VALUATION RESERVE. To provide for any changes in a company's asset value, the company creates a reserve through a charge to expenses.

VALUE-ADDED TAX. A value-based excise tax added to a product at each production stage.

VALUE ASSET. To determine the value asset for each share of common stock, divide the number of common shares outstanding into the issuing company's net resources. To determine the value asset for each share of preferred stock, divide the number of preferred shares outstanding into the issuing company's net resources.

VALUE BROKER. A discount broker who bases his or her rates on a percentage of each transaction's dollar value. Smaller orders, therefore, are less expensive when settled through a value broker.

VALUE CHANGE. The net change of all individual securities weighted to represent the number of shares outstanding.

VALUE COMPENSATED. Buying or selling a foreign currency, with the transaction executed by cable, after which the buyer pays back the seller for the earlier value.

VALUE DATE. A foreign currency settlement date.

VALUE FUND. A mutual fund with investments concentrated in securities issued by companies with low price/earnings ratios.

VALUE LINE INVESTMENT SURVEY. A service that rates securities for risk potential and timely investing using a computer model based on the issuing company's earnings momentum. The highest ranking is one, and the lowest is five.

VANILLA TRANSACTION. Occurs when a company sells shares of its own stock or takes out long-term loans, lasting up to 30 years, at a fixed interest rate.

VARIABILITY. Rate of return fluctuations.

VARIABLE ANNUITY. An annuity contract investing in a certain portfolio with lifetime retirement payments varying according to the results of the investments.

VARIABLE COST. A cost that will change as production costs (such as labor and equipment) change.

VARIABLE INCOME SECURITY. A security with its dividend payments dependent on the company's ability to make a profit.

VARIABLE INTEREST PLUS. A defunct certificate of deposit with the interest rate tied to the Treasury rate, and against which the investor could borrow at an interest rate of 1 percent above the weekly rate that the CD was earning.

VARIABLE LIFE INSURANCE. A whole life insurance policy giving policy holders benefits based on the performance of the securities in the portfolio.

VARIABLE PORTFOLIO. A group of investments that changes with the securities' market value.

VARIABLE RATE CERTIFICATE. A savings certificate with the government-set interest rate varying according to the length of time for which the money was pledged.

VARIABLE RATE CERTIFICATE OF DEPOSIT. A 360-day certificate of deposit with an interest rate tied to the issuing bank's rate on 90-day CDs and changed every 90 days accordingly.

VARIABLE RATE DEMAND NOTE. A note that is payable on demand and bears interest rates tied to money market rates.

VARIABLE RATE MORTGAGE. An amortized real estate loan with an interest rate that is adjusted twice a year. Payments vary according to the different interest rates on the loan, which usually will run 20 to 30 years.

VARIABLE RATIO PLAN. A formula investing plan in which part of the investment capital is in common stock and part is in bonds or preferred stock.

VARIABLE SPREAD. A strategy in which an investor simultaneously buys and sells options, with the number of options sold different from the number bought. Both are based on the same underlying security and have the same expiration dates, but varying exercise prices.

VARIANCE. A statistical difference in a distribution dispersion, calculated by adding together the squares of the mean deviations.

VAULT CASH. Cash that a bank keeps on reserve in its vault to take care of demand deposits and drafts.

VELOCITY. The number of times a dollar is spent within a given time period; the turnover of money.

VELOCITY OF MONEY. The turnover of money used to buy goods or services. To obtain the velocity of money, divide the country's money supply into its gross national product.

VELOCITY SHOP. A mortgage lender who creates secondary lending markets to make money so it can increase the number of mortgages it sells, which allows it to make even more mortgages.

VENDOR. A person or company that supplies goods or services.

VENTURE CAPITAL. An investment in a new business.

VENTURE CAPITAL FUND. A mutual fund invested in securities of new companies and in the securities of companies that are not registered with the Securities and Exchange Commission.

VENTURE CAPITAL LIMITED PARTNERSHIP. An investment aimed at providing startup costs for beginning businesses, with investors receiving private stock shares.

VERTICAL LINE CHARTING. A chart that uses a vertical line to represent a security's high and low prices, and a horizontal line to represent the security's closing prices.

VERTICAL MERGER. Occurs when two companies, who control different ends of producing the same item, combine. For example, if a petroleum producer merges with a painting company, it would be considered a vertical merger.

VERTICAL SPREAD. An investment strategy in which an investor holds long and short options of the same class that have the same expiration month, but different exercise prices.

VESTED ESTATE. A property interest carrying current as well as future rights, but which has transferrable current interest rights.

VESTED INTEREST. A person's personal or financial right to an asset.

VESTED REMAINDER. A fixed property interest that does not allow the owner to take possession of the property until the previous estate is terminated.

VESTING. Rights an employee receives for working at the same company a specified length of time. The rights normally include such things as pension payments, participation in a stock plan, and profit-sharing benefits.

VETERANS ADMINISTRATION MORTGAGE. A Veterans Administration-guaranteed mortgage loaned to veterans or to their surviving spouses. The loan requires a smaller down payment and carries a lower interest rate.

V FORMATION. On a vertical line chart, a V-shaped pattern indicates a bottoming out, thus a bullish movement, followed by a current uptrend. An inverted-V pattern indicates a bearish movement.

VI. Appears in newspaper stock listings to indicate a company that is going through a bankruptcy reorganization.

VOID. A document that has been canceled or that has no legal standing or worth.

VOIDABLE. A transaction that can be voided because it originally was not properly or legally executed.

VOLATILE. The condition of fluctuating prices in a security without any marked trends.

VOLATILITY. The extent to which a security's price fluctuates back and forth within a short time.

VOLATILITY RATIO. To reach a company's volatility percentage for the year, subtract a security's lowest price for the year from its highest price, then divide the lowest price for the year into the remainder. For example, a stock's year high and low is 80 and 40, respectively. Divide the difference, 40 by 40 to get a volatility ratio of 100%.

VOLUME. The total number of shares traded for a market or for a particular stock, bond, option, or futures contract.

VOLUME ALERT. Occurs when a security's volume surpasses its moving average during a specific time period.

VOLUME DELETED. Usually appears on an exchange's consolidated tape when the tape is running at least two minutes late. This announcement indicates that only stock symbols and transaction prices will be reported on the tape unless a transaction involves more than 5,000 shares.

VOLUME DISCOUNT. A discount often given to institutional investors when an order exceeds a certain level.

VOLUME OF TRADING. The sum of successive futures contract sales or successive futures contract purchases.

VOLUNTARY ACCUMULATION PLAN. A mutual fund in which the investor accumulates shares regularly over a prescribed time period, with the stockholder determining the spending intervals and the amount to be invested each time.

VOLUNTARY ASSOCIATION. An unincorporated membership organization, with each member carrying an unlimited financial responsibility.

VOLUNTARY BANKRUPTCY. Occurs when the debtor, not the creditor, petitions the U.S. District Court to reorganize and payoff any debts because of insolvency.

VOLUNTARY CONVEYANCE. The transfer of title from one person to another without the transfer being court-imposed.

VOLUNTARY PLAN. A mutual fund program in which an investor can buy an unlimited additional number of shares whenever he or she wants.

VOLUNTARY TRUST. A voluntary deed transfer made to benefit a specific person or trustee for a specific purpose.

VOLUNTARY UNDERWRITER. The opposite of a statutory underwriter in that this person intentionally and voluntarily buys a securities issue from the issuer and resells the issue publicly.

VOTING RIGHTS. The rights of stockholders to elect the issuing company's board of directors and to vote on other corporate matters because the stockholders are, in essence, the company's owners.

VOTING STOCK. A security that gives the owner the right to vote on corporate matters.

VOTING TRUST. Occurs when a stockholder temporarily turns over his or her voting rights to a trustee, whose decisions during that time are binding.

VULTURE FUND. Nickname for a pool of money aimed at buying commercial property at distressed prices.

W

WACHOVIA ADJUSTABLE MORTGAGE. A 30-year loan in which the original mortgage rate is tied to money market and local market rates with interest rate adjustments every quarter according to Treasury bill rates. Monthly mortgage payments remain constant for five years, after which the payment amounts are adjusted up to 25 percent to compensate for the changing rates. The payments continue to be adjusted every five years.

WAITER. A British floor broker who assists brokers in obtaining market information and execution reports.

WAITING PERIOD. The 20 days between a company's filing of its registration statement, and the date the Securities and Exchange Commission has approved for the company's securities to be publicly sold.

WALK-AWAY MORTGAGE. A mortgage in which the lender cannot force the defaulting borrower to pay the difference between the loan balance and the price at which the property is sold at foreclosure.

WALLFLOWER. A stock that no longer is popular with the investing public.

WALLPAPER. A worthless securities certificate.

WALL STREET. A street in Manhattan that represents the primary financial district in the United States.

WALL STREET JOURNAL. A highly respected newspaper that concentrates on financial and corporate news.

WANTED FOR CASH. Indicates on an exchange's tape that a buyer will pay cash the same day for a block of securities.

WAR BABIES. Securities issued from companies involved in the defense industry.

WAREHOUSE RECEIPT. A document that lists the commodities an investor is holding in a warehouse for safekeeping. The investor can use the document to transfer ownership of the commodities without worrying about physically transferring the actual commodities.

WARRANT. A company-issued certificate that represents an option to buy a certain number of stock shares at a specific price before a predetermined date. A warrant, because it has a value of its own, can be traded on the open market.

WARRANTS INTO NEGOTIABLE GOVERNMENT SECURITIES (WINGS). These are options to buy a specific number of Treasury notes at a predetermined price to be delivered at a stated future date.

WARRANTS TO BUY TREASURY SECURITIES (WARTS). These represent rights to buy a specific amount of government issues at specific prices within six months to one year.

WARRANT VALUE. An investor can determine a warrant's theoretical value by subtracting the common stock's exercise price from its market price, then multiplying the sum by the number of shares the warrant can buy.

WARTS. *See* Warrants to Buy Treasury Securities.

WASHINGTON METROPOLITAN AREA TRANSIT AUTHORITY. A municipal agency that issues federally guaranteed bonds to pay for a mass transit system in Washington D.C.'s metropolitan area.

WASH SALE. A transaction in which an investor simultaneously buys and sells a security through two different brokers. Such a transaction is considered a manipulation and is illegal if it artificially increases the security's trading volume or changes the price.

WASTING ASSET. An investment with a value that continually drops or delays, as it gets closer to its expiration date.

WASTING TRUST. A trust fund with assets that are gradually dropping in value or are being consumed.

WATCH FILING. A procedure by which an investor who incurs a loss from a low-risk investment brings that loss to the underwriter's attention.

WATCH LIST. A list of securities the exchange is monitoring for potential illegal practices. An exchange will, for example, watch a security that a broker-dealer is about to underwrite, or a security that is heavily traded by the issuing company's officers.

WATCH MY NUMBER. Each broker is assigned an identification number, which is flashed on an annunciator board if the broker is being summoned to his or her firm's booth on the edge of the exchange floor. When a broker leaves the exchange floor for a few minutes, he or she asks another broker to "watch my number" so the broker knows if he or she was summoned while away from the floor.

WATERED STOCK. A security issue that adds no extra value to the issuing company's position.

WEAK HOLDINGS. Securities a speculator will keep on margin only long enough to sell them.

WEAL MARKET. A short-term drop in general market prices.

WEALTH. Any item or resource that can be used, exchanged, or sold.

WEDGE. A chart pattern in which two converging lines moving in the same direction to connect a group of price peaks and troughs to form a wedge. Upward wedges indicate an interruption in a declining trend, and downward wedges indicate an interruption in a rising trend.

WEEKLY SHEET. A list the National Quotation Bureau publishes each week for market makers, which provides prices for over-the-counter securities.

WEEK ORDER. A buy or sell order that expires automatically if it cannot be executed on the exchange floor within a week.

WEIGHTED AVERAGE COST OF CAPITAL. The required rate of return a company must pay to raise long-term capital.

WEIGHTING. Comparing the importance of one investment to another investment.

WELLHEAD PRICE. The price paid for gas drawn from leased property.

WELLS SUBMISSION. A procedure through which a person that the Securities and Exchange Commission is investigating can respond to the allegations in an attempt to get the SEC to drop its investigation.

WENT TO THE WALL. A person or company who went through bankruptcy.

WE OFFER RETAIL (WOR). This indicates the seller will assume all transaction costs.

WESTERN ACCOUNT. A plan in which each underwriting syndicate member is responsible for distributing only his or her agreed upon shares and not the shares of any other syndicate member. Also known as a Divided Account.

W FORMATION. A chart that shows a security's price fluctuations form a pattern.

WHEN DISTRIBUTED. A security traded before the final certificate has been printed. The investor will receive the certificate as soon as it is complete.

WHEN ISSUED. A security traded before it receives final trading authorization with the investor receiving the certificate only after the final approval is granted. The transaction would be canceled automatically if the security failed to receive the approval.

WHIPSAWED. Describes an investor who lost money on both sides of a price swing, such as an investor who bought a security just before the price dropped, then sold it right before the price rose again.

WHITE ELEPHANT. An asset or property that costs more to maintain than it is worth, or an asset or investment that will definitely lose money.

WHITE KNIGHT. A party a company chooses to merge with in order to fend off an unwanted corporate raider.

WHITE SHEET. A list the National Quotation Bureau publishes daily for market makers, which provides prices for over-the-counter securities traded in Chicago, Los Angeles, and San Francisco.

WHITE SQUIRE. A risky management antitakeover maneuver in which the company places a large block of its shares into the hands of a friendly party whose financial interests are similar to the target company.

WHITE'S RATING. White's Tax Exempt Bond Rating Service ranks municipal bonds according to the municipal trading markets instead of the issuer's credit rating. The ranking gives investors an indication of a bond's expected yield.

WHOLE LIFE INSURANCE. An insurance policy which offers protection in the event the policy holder dies. The holder will pay a set annual premium during his or her lifetime while building up a cash value. Earnings on the cash are tax deferred and can be used as collateral.

WHOLE LOAN. An individual mortgage that is not part of any investment pool.

WHOLESALE PRICE INDEX. A Bureau of Labor Statistics gauge that measures price changes in goods sold wholesale.

WHOLESALER. A mutual fund underwriter.

WHOOPS BOND. Nickname for a bond issued by the Washington Public Power Supply System to pay for a nuclear power plant.

WIDE MARKET. A market with many investors.

WIDE OPEN. An underwriting with additional securities available for sale because the syndicate members did not subscribe to all that was available, either because some members withdrew from the syndicate or because the syndicate had too few members to begin with.

WIDE OPENING. A large price difference between the opening bid and ask prices.

WIDGET. A plastic tube that carries exchange information through the exchange's pneumatic tube system. Also, a hypothetical product used to illustrate an economical concept.

WIDOW-AND-ORPHAN STOCK. A low-risk security paying high dividends that is issued by a noncyclical business or a business that is not seasonal.

WILD CARD. An investment that carries either the highest interest rate allowed by law or an unlimited yield.

WILDCAT DRILLING. A speculative oil or gas drilling venture in an area where no oil or gas previously has been found.

WILDCAT SCHEME. A speculative investment that is not expected to succeed.

WILL. A document in which a person assigns the distribution of all of his or her assets to take place after his or her death.

WILLIAMS ACT. A 1968 federal law requiring those planning to tender offers to file their intentions with the target company as well as with the Securities and Exchange Commission. The filing must include such information as cash sources and plans for the company once it has been taken over.

WILSHIRE INDEX. A gauge of 5,000 securities, including a number of securities from smaller companies as well as some over-the-counter securities. Some say the gauge is more accurate than other indexes because of the wide cross section of securities used.

WINDFALL. An unexpected, unspent profit or investment appreciation.

WINDFALL PROFITS TAX. Tax on the profits a particular company or industry must pay after receiving some sort of windfall.

WINDING UP. Liquidating a company.

WINDOW. The specific, limited time a person has to take advantage of a price situation or other favorable condition.

WINDOW DRESSING. Temporary or superficial means of making a portfolio or security look more profitable.

WINDOW SETTLEMENT. The physical place where the selling broker delivers securities to the buying broker. Most deals, however, are settled through a depository instead of the window.

WINGS. *See* Warrants Into Negotiable Government Securities.

WINNING A BID. The bid that is attractive and profitable enough to a seller to lead to a completed transaction.

WIPED OUT. An investor who has lost all of his or her money in the market.

WIRE HOUSE. An exchange-member firm connected to other offices by a communications system.

WIRE ROOM. A brokerage firm area that changes customer orders into floor tickets so the orders can be executed in the market with the best available prices.

WITHDRAWAL PLAN. A mutual fund program in which the investor, at his or her option, receives monthly or quarterly fund distributions.

WITHHOLDING. Occurs when a broker-dealer keeps part of the securities from an offering and sells the remaining portion to employees.

WITHHOLDING TAX AT THE SOURCE. A domestic issuer's obligation to withhold part of a foreign corporation's dividends and interest, usually 30 percent, to pay for the U.S. tax on those distributions.

WITH INTEREST. Used to indicate that a bond buyer must pay the bond seller all interest that accrued on the bond between the bond's last payment date and the transaction's settlement date.

WITH OR WITHOUT. Instructions an investor gives his or her broker to sell an odd-lot limit order either for the stock quote or in the round-lot market, whichever comes first.

WITHOUT AN OFFER. A one-sided quote in which a dealer is willing to bid a certain price for a security, but is unwilling to sell it at that price, either because the dealer does not want to sell the security short or because the dealer does not actually have possession of the security.

WITHOUT INTEREST. When a security that is in default is sold without interest, and the buyer does not make any additional accrued interest payments to the seller.

WITH PREJUDICE. Accompanies the dismissal of a legal action to indicate that the case cannot be reopened. If a case is closed without prejudice, it can be reopened.

WITH RIGHT OF SURVIVORSHIP (WROS, JTWROS). This is a joint account with the ownership of all assets automatically passing to the surviving tenant if the other tenant dies.

WOLF. An experienced speculator.

WOLF PACK. Describes a situation in which one investor buys a block of a company's stock, then signals a group of others to do the same on the premise that the issuing company is vulnerable to a takeover.

WOODEN TICKET. Occurs when a broker-dealer indicates he or she is executing an order to a customer when, in fact, the broker has not confirmed the order. A broker-dealer will improperly try this maneuver on the belief that market conditions will change before the actual execution. In this way, the broker-dealer hopes to earn larger profits.

WOR. *See* We Offer Retail.

WORKED OFF. A slight drop in a security's or commodity's price.

WORKING ASSET. An asset, invested in securities, with a price that fluctuates along with common stock prices.

WORKING CAPITAL. A company's current liabilities subtracted from its current assets, which gives the company the amount of money it probably will need to maintain operations for a year.

WORKING CONTROL. The ability of those who own less than 50 percent of a corporation's stock to dictate corporate policy because of the wide dispersion of shares.

WORKING INTEREST. An investor's financial interest in an oil or gas drilling partnership, often with that interest representing borrowed capital and not equity.

WORKING ORDER. An investor's order to his or her broker to buy or sell a large block of stock gradually so that the transaction does not affect the stock's market price.

WORKOUT MARKET. An estimated price quoted for a security.

WORLD BANK. The International Bank for Reconstruction and Development, established to provide loans for promoting the economic redevelopment of member countries.

WORLD RESERVE. In an antiques auction, a consignor sets this minimum price for the sale of an entire collection, which gives the auctioneer a range within to sell individual items from the collection.

WORTH. An asset's or investment's total value.

WRAP-AROUND ANNUITY. An annuity that shelters dividends, interest, and capital appreciation from taxes, and with the investor choosing the securities in which the annuity should be invested. The insurance company does not assume principal risk until the contract earns an annuity.

WRAP-AROUND MORTGAGE. A low-interest mortgage made up of both an assumable mortgage from the previous seller and a new loan from the carrying bank.

WRINKLE. A security feature that could potentially be profitable to the investor.

WRITE. To sell a put or call option in an opening transaction.

WRITEOFF. Charging an asset amount to a loss, which subtracts the asset's value from the company's profits and therefore lessens the company's tax liabilities.

WRITE OUT. Occurs when a specialist trades an order that is on his or her books by having the broker who entered the order write the order, after which the specialist becomes the contra broker. The broker who wrote the order receives all fees and commissions.

WRITE UP. An asset's book value increase that is not due to added costs or asset account adjustments reflected from an updated appraisal.

WRITING CASH-SECURED PUTS. A put option seller who does not want to use a margin account can instead deposit cash equal to the option's exercise price with the broker. By doing this, the seller is not responsible for any further margin requirements, even if the underlying security's price changes.

WRITING PUTS TO ACQUIRE STOCK. An option seller who believes a stock's price will drop will write a put that can be exercised at that expected price. If the stock does go up, the option will not be exercised, and the seller still has earned a premium. If the price does, indeed, drop, the seller has obtained the security at a low price and, in addition, has earned a premium.

WRITTEN-DOWN VALUE. An asset's net book value after depreciation or amortization.

WROS. *See* With Right Of Survivorship.

X

XCH. Used to indicate that a securities transaction will be completed outside of the normal clearing procedures.

XD. Appears in newspaper stock listings to indicate a security is trading ex-dividend.

X-DIS. Used to indicate that a securities buyer is not entitled to a dividend distribution.

XENOCURRENCY. A currency that is traded in money markets outside of its own country.

XR. Appears in newspaper stock listings to indicate a security is trading ex-rights.

XW. Appears in newspaper stock listings to indicate a security is trading ex-warrants.

XX. Used to indicate without securities or warrants.

═ Y ═

YANKEE BOND. A foreign bond denominated in U.S. dollars and registered with the Securities and Exchange Commission for sale in the United States.

YANKEES. American securities traded in Great Britain.

YEAR-END DIVIDEND. An additional dividend that a board of directors approves for distribution to stockholders at the end of the company's fiscal year.

YELLOW BOOK. A listing of requirements for British market quotations.

YELLOW COLOR THEORY. A market theory that says that when yellow clothes, yellow furnishings, and yellow packaging are popular, the market will rise.

YELLOW KNIGHT. One company that tries to takeover another company, after which the two companies discuss a merger.

YELLOW SHEETS. A list the National Quotation Bureau publishes daily for market makers which provides over-the-counter corporate bond prices.

YEN. Japan's primary currency unit.

YEN BOND. A bond denominated in Japanese yen. While not registered for sale in the U.S., it can be traded in America after it has been traded for a reasonable length of time outside of the U.S.

YIELD. The dividends or interest a security will earn, with the yield expressed as a percentage of the amount paid for the security or of the security's par value.

YIELD ADVANTAGE. The difference between a convertible security's current yield and its underlying common stock's current yield.

YIELD CURVE. A chart consisting of the yields of bonds of the same quality but different maturities. This can be used as a gauge to evaluate the future of the interest rates. An upward trend with short-term rates lower than long-term rates is called a positive yield curve while a down trend is a negative or inverted yield curve.

YIELD EQUIVALENCE. A measurement used to compare the yield on a taxable investment versus a nontaxable investment.

YIELD MAINTENANCE CONTRACT. Provides a price adjustment on mortgage securities (such as a Government National Mortgage Association security) upon delivery to give the buyer the same yield as that which was originally agreed upon.

YIELD SPREAD. A comparison between the yields of different quality issues.

YIELD TEST. The relationship of the yield of individual bonds in an insurance company's portfolio to the yield of taxable government bonds with the same maturity.

YIELD TO ADJUSTED MINIMUM MATURITY. Provides the yield for a bond's shortest possible life.

YIELD TO AVERAGE LIFE. The yield achieved by substituting a bond's average maturity for the issue's final maturity date.

YIELD TO CALL. The amount of money an investor would receive from a bond investment which is expressed as an average annual return from the purchase date to the call date.

YIELD TO LESSOR. A lease transaction's internal rate of return.

YIELD TO MATURITY. A debt security's average return based on its interest income, capital gains, or capital losses incurred until the security matures.

YIELD TO PUT. A bond's return if it is held until a specific date and is then sold back to the issuer for a particular price.

YO-YO OPTION. An executive option program in which a company officer's option price is lowered by a dollar every time the company's stock price goes up by a dollar.

YO-YO STOCK. A volatile stock with a price that continually rises and falls quickly.

≡Z≡

Z. Appears in newspaper stock listings preceding a number to indicate that the number represents a total volume, so it should not be multiplied by 100.

Z CERTIFICATE. A Bank of England certificate issued to discount houses instead of stock certificates so the houses can deal in gilt-edged securities with short maturities.

ZERIAL BOND. A stripped Treasury bond or other zero-coupon debt instrument issued in serial form.

ZERO-BASE BUDGETING. A budgeting method in which all spending must be justified, instead of only those expenses that exceeded the previous year's allocations. Budget lines, therefore, begin with a zero base with no consideration given to the previous year's levels.

ZERO BASIS. Occurs when a convertible bond is selling at such a high premium that the interest is equal to or less than the premium.

ZERO-BRACKET AMOUNT. The portion of a person's income that is not subject to federal income tax. This standard deduction is already figured into the Internal Revenue Service tax tables, so the taxpayer does not have to subtract the amount from his or her income before calculating tax liabilities.

ZERO COUPON BOND. A bond sold at deep discount that pays no interest until maturity, at which time the holder receives the bond's face value plus all accrued interest. While holders receive no interest on the bond until maturity, they are responsible for paying taxes each year on the unpaid interest.

ZERO-COUPON EUROBONDS. A deep-discount American corporate issue that pays no interest.

ZERO DOWNTICK. *See* Zero Minus Tick.

ZEROES. Nickname for zero coupon bonds.

ZERO MINUS TICK. Also called a zero downtick, this is a security transaction that occurs at the same price as the previous similar transaction in that same security, but less than the last different transaction in that security.

ZERO PLUS TICK. Also called a zero uptick, this is a security transaction that occurs at the same price as the previous similar transaction in that same security, but higher than the last different transaction in that security.

ZERO RATE MORTGAGE. A mortgage that requires a hefty down payment with a one-time finance charge, after which the mortgage is repaid in monthly installments. Because the term of the loan is so short, it appears to be nearly interest free.

ZERO UPTICK. *See* Zero Plus Tick.

ZETA. An index model that weighs the importance of seven financial variables for more than 1,600 industrial companies, then adds together the weighted values to develop a zeta score index.